ASIAN DEVELOPMENT OUTLOOK 2001

Special Chapter
Asia's Globalization Challenge

Published for the Asian Development Bank
by Oxford University Press

OXFORD
UNIVERSITY PRESS

Oxford University Press is a department of the University of Oxford.
It furthers the University's objective of excellence in research, scholarship,
and education by publishing worldwide in

Oxford New York

Athens Auckland Bangkok Bogotá Buenos Aires Cape Town
Chennai Dar es Salaam Delhi Florence Hong Kong Istanbul Karachi
Kolkata Kuala Lumpur Madrid Melbourne Mexico City Mumbai Nairobi
Paris São Paulo Shanghai Singapore Taipei Tokyo Toronto Warsaw

with associated companies in Berlin Ibadan

Oxford is a registered trade mark of Oxford University Press

Published in the United States by Oxford University Press Inc., New York

First published in 2001
This impression (lowest digit)
1 3 5 7 9 10 8 6 4 2

This book was prepared by the staff of the Asian Development Bank,
and the analyses and assessments contained herein do not
necessarily reflect the views of the Board of Directors
or the governments that they represent. The Asian Development Bank
does not guarantee the accuracy of the data included in this publication
and accepts no responsibility whatsoever for any consequence for their use.
The term "country" does not imply any judgment by the Asian Development Bank
as to the legal or other status of any territorial entity.

Published for the Asian Development Bank by
Oxford University Press

British Library Cataloguing in Publication Data
available

Library of Congress Cataloging-in-Publication-Data
available

ISBN 0-19-592976-4
ISSN 0117-0481

Printed in Hong Kong
Published by Oxford University Press (China) Ltd
18th Floor, Warwick House East, Taikoo Place, 979 King's Road, Quarry Bay
Hong Kong

Asian Development Outlook 2001

FOREWORD

The *Asian Development Outlook 2001* is the 13th in a series of annual economic reports on the developing member countries (DMCs) of the Asian Development Bank (ADB). *ADO,* as it is popularly known, provides a comprehensive analysis of macroeconomic and development issues in 39 DMCs of ADB and this year includes a theme chapter on the challenges of globalization.

In the first half of the year 2000, the world economy continued to build on the momentum created in 1999. Growth increased in many industrial economies, including the euro area and Japan. There was further consolidation of gains in the developing regions of Asia, Latin America, Africa, and the Middle East. However, the United States (US) economy, which had served as the primary locomotive for economic growth for several years, began to show strains of prolonged rapid growth in late 1999. Interest rates in the US began to rise in early 2000, reflecting a policy stance of slowing the economy. These increases spread gradually to the rest of the world. The economy of the US and that of the world generally began to slow in the second half of 2000.

Nevertheless, the Organisation for Economic Co-operation and Development countries as a whole grew faster in 2000 than in 1999 as rates of growth increased in both the euro area and Japan. The overall economic performance among DMCs was more than satisfactory in 2000. Economic growth picked up in several countries and export growth accelerated, while inflation was held in check and domestic demand increased. In 2001, growth in the euro area and Japan is expected to slow marginally though still keeping its momentum. The US economic slowdown is expected to be brief.

The five countries most affected by the Asian financial crisis continued to recover. Growth accelerated rapidly in Indonesia and Malaysia, and more moderately in the Philippines and Thailand. In the Republic of Korea, growth decelerated slightly but remained strong.

The People's Republic of China and the countries of South Asia, which had not been affected by the financial crisis to a significant extent, were generally able to maintain strong growth momentum. Growth in Central Asia was buoyant, fueled by higher mineral and petroleum prices, while poor weather conditions and soft raw materials prices adversely affected several of the Pacific DMCs.

In 2000, many of the DMCs made significant progress in addressing the various policy issues facing them. As the outlook for the world economy has recently become less upbeat, it is necessary for DMCs to reinvigorate their efforts to carry out the outstanding reforms required in financial and corporate restructuring, capital market development, good governance, and improved social equity.

ADB has taken a keen interest in the five countries most affected by the financial crisis, and it continues to provide assistance to them and to the rest of the Asian and Pacific region. The agenda for reform is daunting but with renewed efforts from governments these economies should emerge and will be able to deal effectively with the challenges that they face.

Part I of the *ADO* provides an overview of economic developments and prospects for DMCs, set in a global context, and discusses in detail the risks and uncertainties.

Part II examines economic developments and presents a forecast for the coming two years for 39 DMCs. Newly independent East Timor, with which ADB is actively involved within a framework of concerted international cooperation, is also reviewed. Part II also discusses economic management and policy issues.

Part III analyzes trends in globalization and the challenges that arise for DMCs, and reviews their participation in this process. DMCs have been generally successful in integrating themselves into the global economic system. Indeed, they have attracted significant amounts of foreign investment, while trade is a strong and integral driver of economic growth. They have also had to develop the necessary policies and institutions to deal with volatility stemming from large capital movements.

DMCs face a number of policy issues and challenges. In the context of globalization, the first challenge for DMCs is to continue to move into areas where global demand is rising and where the opportunities for those countries with comparative advantage are manifest. The second challenge is to assess and manage the risks presented by the evolving global economic system. The commitment among governments to addressing this challenge is healthy and encouraging, particularly in light of the difficulties experienced during the Asian financial crisis.

Powerful economic and technological forces are at work that are likely to render the world economy even more globalized in the future than it is today. The challenge for DMCs and emerging economies elsewhere is, therefore, how to capitalize on the opportunities for growth and development afforded by globalization, while at the same time minimizing the risks. In an obvious sense, this means taking appropriate policies to maintain a stable macroeconomy, maintaining prudent financial policies, and adopting sound regulatory practices. The fundamental challenge is how governments, in cooperation with the private sector, can develop capabilities and capacities to determine appropriate policies and implement them.

Governments should also be able to facilitate the development of a social consensus on goals and instruments, and an equitable means for sharing the benefits of implementing appropriate policies and programs. Governments should also maintain flexibility to modify their policy stance as circumstances change.

The *Asian Development Outlook 2001* makes an important and useful contribution to ADB's overarching goal of poverty reduction. Through its analysis of, among others, the impact and challenges of globalization, it aims to provide useful insights into how DMCs can effectively respond to the challenges of poverty reduction, taking advantage of the benefits while minimizing the risks of participating in a globalizing world.

Tadao Chino
President

ACKNOWLEDGMENTS

The *Asian Development Outlook 2001* was made possible through the efforts of many individuals, both inside and outside the Asian Development Bank. The following people provided guidance and advice on various matters relating to the preparation of the *ADO*: Charles Adams, Basudev Dahal, Gunter Hecker, Yoshihiro Iwasaki, Ayumi Konishi, Jeoung-Keun Lee, G.H.P.B. van der Linden, Rajat Nag, Shoji Nishimoto, Filologo Pante, Jr., Brahm Prakash, Kazu Sakai, Cedric D. Saldanha, Kunio Senga, Marshuk Ali Shah, Robert Y. Siy, Jr., Toru Tatara, Xianbin Yao, and Yuejiao Zhang. Special thanks are due to James P. Lynch and Hisashi Ono for comments on various parts of the *ADO*. John Cole, Ian Gill, Tsukasa Maekawa, Lynette Mallery, Carola Molitor, Ann Quon and Robert H. Salamon of the Office of External Relations provided advice and assistance in disseminating the *ADO*. The prepress work was done by the Printing Unit under the supervision of Raveendranath Rajan. The support of the Resident Missions, Office of Administrative Services, and Office of Information Systems and Technology in the preparation of the *ADO* is also gratefully acknowledged.

A group of economists and scholars from the region, as well as other international organizations, participated in the *Thirteenth Workshop on Asian Economic Outlook,* which discussed a set of background materials. Those who prepared papers or acted as designated commentators for the workshop include Charles Adams, Vladimir Bohun, Basudev Dahal, Rino A. Effendi, Donald Hanna, Francis Harrigan, Fred Hu, A. V. Hughes, Ponciano Intal, Sailesh Jha, Nanak Kakwani, Hun Kim, Yak Yeow Kueh, Jang-Yung Lee, Chi Lo, Linda Low, Takashi Omori, David J. Robinson, Cedric D. Saldanha, Veerathai Santiprabhob, Robert Y. Siy, Jr., Dong Tao, Hans Timmer, Epa Tuioti, Peter Tulloch, An-chi Tung, Shujiro Urata, Xianbin Yao, Harrison Young, Yuejiao Zhang and Yunling Zhang. Additional background papers were prepared by Ismail Alowi, Nguyen Dinh Cung, Tarun Das, Teresa K. B. Fung, Ki-Seok Hong, Yushi Mao, Eshya Mujahid-Mukhtar, Kobsak Pootrakool, Yusuf Riza, P. A. Nimal Siripala, Myat Thein, and Chung Shu Wu.

The *ADO* has benefited from the contribution of Barry Eichengreen who prepared the background paper for Part III.

Several international institutions shared their research and data with the *ADO* team. In particular, the contribution of the International Monetary Fund and the World Bank is gratefully acknowledged. Staff from both these organizations also participated in the *Thirteenth Workshop on Asian Economic Outlook.*

I also take the opportunity to express special thanks to Yoshihiro Iwasaki and Charles Adams who have, respectively, acted as the officer-in-charge of the Economics and Development Resource Center during the time *ADO* has been under preparation.

Arvind Panagariya
Chief Economist

19 April 2001

Asian Development Outlook 2001

THE TEAM

The *Asian Development Outlook 2001* was prepared by the Economic Analysis and Research Division, in collaboration with the Programs Departments and Office of Pacific Operations of the Asian Development Bank. The team that prepared the *ADO* was led by Brahm Prakash, Assistant Chief Economist and assisted by Cindy Houser, Purnima Rajapakse, along with Charissa N. Castillo, who was responsible for coordination. The other members of the team included Emma Banaria, Marichu Duka, Ben Endriga, Archimedes Gatchalian, Maritess Manalo, Ma. Erlinda Mutuc, Olive Nuestro, Aludia Pardo, Jennifer Simon, James Villafuerte, and Cherry Lynn Zafaralla.

The team was assisted by the following staff of the Economic Analysis and Research Division, Programs Departments, and Office of Pacific Operations: Johanna Boestel, Shiladitya Chatterjee, Brett Coleman, Dilip Das, Amado De Andres, Padmini Desikachar, Brian Fawcett, Yushu Feng, David Green, Sophia Ho, Sailesh Jha, Rezaul Khan, Hun Kim, Yun-Hwan Kim, Seung Beom Koh, Rajiv Kumar, Christine Kuo, Eunkyung Kwon, Yeo Lin, Srinivasa Madhur, Soo-Nam Oh, Valerie Repellin-Hill, Diwesh Sharan, Yumiko Tamura, Min Tang, Hong Wang, and Tao Zhang. Veronica Bayangos, Alely Bernardo, Franklin De Guzman, Carmela Espina, Annie Ignacio, Lilibeth Poot, Pilar Sahilan, and Marcus Ynalvez provided additional support in the preparation of country reports.

The work was carried out under the overall direction of Myoung-Ho Shin, Vice-President (Region West), and the supervision of Yoshihiro Iwasaki and Charles Adams. Part I of *ADO* especially benefited from contributions and guidance of Charles Adams.

John Malcolm Dowling as the principal economic editor made important substantive as well as advisory contributions. Jonathan Aspin did the copy editing.

The statistical database and country tables were prepared by staff from the Economic Analysis and Research Division with some assistance from the Statistics and Data Systems Division. James Villafuerte was responsible for data management and preparation of the Statistical Appendix. Ma. Teresa Cabellon and Corrito N. Fajardo provided the main secretarial and administrative support, with additional assistance from Zenaida Acacio and Nilo Sandoval. Imagesetters designed the cover and overall book topography. Ma. Lourdes Maestro was responsible for typesetting, assisted by Mercedita Cabaneros. Computer graphics were done by Anna Maria N. Juico and Edmond Sid M. Pantilo.

Asian Development Outlook
2001

Contents

Part

III

TEXT TABLES

STATISTICAL APPENDIX TABLES

Asian Development Outlook 2001

ACRONYMS AND ABBREVIATIONS

ADO	Asian Development Outlook
ADB	Asian Development Bank
AMC	Asset management company
APEC	Asia-Pacific Economic Cooperation
ASEAN	Association of Southeast Asian Nations
B2B	Business to business
B2C	Business to consumer
DMC	Developing member country
EU	European Union
FDI	Foreign direct investment
GDP	Gross domestic product
GNP	Gross national product
ICT	Information and communications technology
IMF	International Monetary Fund
Lao PDR	Lao People's Democratic Republic
NIE	Newly industrialized economy
NGO	Nongovernment organization
NPL	Nonperforming loan
OECD	Organisation for Economic Co-operation and Development
OPEC	Organization of Petroleum Exporting Countries
PRC	People's Republic of China
R&D	Research and development
SAARC	South Asian Association for Regional Cooperation
SME	Small and medium-sized enterprise
SOCB	State-owned commercial bank
SOE	State-owned enterprise
TFP	Total factor productivity
UK	United Kingdom
UN	United Nations
US	United States
WTO	World Trade Organization

Asian Development Outlook 2001

DEFINITIONS

The classification of economies in the *Asian Development Outlook 2001*, by major analytic or geographic groupings such as industrial countries, developing countries, Africa, Latin America, Middle East, Europe, and transition economies generally follows the classification adopted by the International Monetary Fund (IMF). However, the IMF classification refers to Latin America as developing countries in the western hemisphere.

For purposes of *ADO 2001*, the following apply:

- **Developing Asia** refers to 39 developing member countries (DMCs) of the Asian Development Bank discussed in this *ADO*.
- **Newly industrialized economies** (NIEs) comprise Hong Kong, China; Republic of Korea; Singapore; and Taipei,China.
- **South Asia** comprises Bangladesh, Bhutan, India, Maldives, Nepal, Pakistan, and Sri Lanka.
- **Southeast Asia** comprises Cambodia, Indonesia, Lao People's Democratic Republic, Malaysia, Myanmar, Philippines, Thailand, and Viet Nam.
- **Central Asian republics** comprise Kazakhstan, Kyrgyz Republic, Tajikistan, Turkmenistan, and Uzbekistan.
- **The Pacific** comprises Cook Islands, Fiji Islands, Kiribati, Marshall Islands, Federated States of Micronesia, Nauru, Papua New Guinea, Samoa, Solomon Islands, Tonga, Tuvalu, and Vanuatu.
- **G7** comprises Canada, France, Germany, Italy, Japan, United Kingdom, and United States.
- Unless otherwise specified, the symbol "$" and the word "dollar" refer to US dollars. Currency abbreviations are given in Statistical Appendix Table A20.

ADO 2001 is based on data available up to 1 March 2001.

PART I

Developing Asia and the World

Economic Developments and Prospects

INTRODUCTION AND OVERVIEW

Growth in the world economy accelerated to an impressive 4.8 percent in 2000, more than a percentage point higher than in 1999 and the fastest in over a decade. The very strong performance for the year as a whole, however, masks a significant downshift in the second half as the United States (US), in particular, reached a cyclical peak and began to slow. As a result, the world economy entered the current year with considerably less growth momentum. Notwithstanding considerable uncertainty about near-term prospects, the *Asian Development Outlook (ADO) 2001* is cautiously optimistic that the world economy will experience only a relatively shallow and short-term slowdown in 2001 before returning to trend growth in 2002. On the other hand, there are some significant downside risks in the near-term outlook. Should these materialize, a much less favorable outcome may be possible.

The rebound in global growth from the slowdown that occurred in 1997/98—induced by the Asian financial crisis that began in 1997 and the Russian crisis of 1998—picked up momentum in the first half of 2000 (see Figure 1.1). The main driver continued to be the US, where the growth of domestic demand accelerated further, but the expansion also started to become more broad based. Growth in both the euro area and Japan picked up while activity remained strong, or strengthened, in many other industrial countries, including Australia, Canada, and United Kingdom (UK).

In addition, a number of developing countries in Latin America, Africa, and Europe began to share in the favorable global conditions. Following its sharp slowdown in 1999, the Russian Federation experienced a bounce back in 2000 with favorable implications for the transition economies of Europe and Central Asia. Those Asian countries affected by the 1997/98 crisis also continued their strong recoveries in early 2000, growing, in some cases, at high single-digit rates or faster. Growth also remained strong in the People's Republic of China (PRC) and India. World trade expanded very rapidly during the first half of the year, as exports, especially of technology products from Asia, grew in line with "new economy" fervor.

During the second half of the year, the world economy began a cyclical slowdown. This was particularly pronounced in the US, where domestic demand growth began to shift to a much more moderate pace following several years of high growth. Japan's economy grew more rapidly than in 1999 but showed some signs of weakness after midyear. Growth also began moderating in several of the developing member countries (DMCs) of the Asian Development Bank (ADB) with close trading links to the US. Growth, however, held up or accelerated in much of western and eastern Europe, as seen in

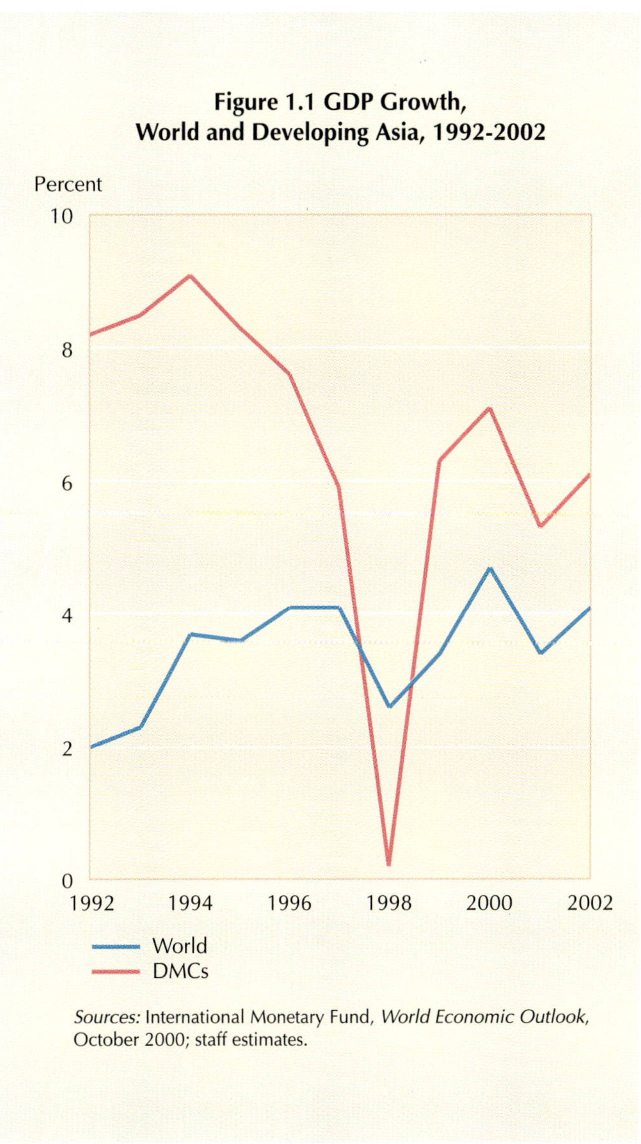

Sources: International Monetary Fund, *World Economic Outlook*, October 2000; staff estimates.

continued strength in the more buoyant euro area and robust growth in the Russian Federation.

A contributing factor to the slowdown in the global economy was the steep rise in world oil prices. After extreme weakness early in 2000, oil prices rebounded and reached a peak of over $35 a barrel in September, before falling somewhat. While the effects on inflation were generally small, the implied terms-of-trade losses for net oil importing countries may have shaved 0.2–0.5 percent off global growth in 2000 and early 2001. Among DMCs, significant net oil importers such as India and the Republic of Korea (Korea) were particularly hit, while net oil exporters such as Indonesia and the Central Asian republics benefited.

Despite resource use rising to high levels in several major industrial countries, inflation generally remained subdued in 2000. Average inflation in the major industrial countries continued at its lowest rate for several decades before rising modestly in the second half of the year in response to a run-up in world oil prices. Among developing countries, inflation was also generally moderate.

Through most of the year, the dollar strengthened further in foreign exchange markets as the large and growing US current account deficit continued to be more than adequately financed by large capital inflows. In addition to strengthening against many developing country currencies—including those in Asia—the dollar continued to strengthen against the euro during much of the year. This prompted the major central banks to undertake a coordinated intervention in September to slow the decline of the euro. In the fourth quarter, the dollar began to weaken, especially against the euro, as clear evidence appeared that the US economy was slowing.

Concerned about possible overheating, the authorities in the major industrial countries gradually tightened monetary policy during the early part of 2000. The Federal Reserve nudged up short-term interest rates in several steps in the US through midyear; the European Central Bank also raised policy interest rates in the euro area, as did the authorities in several other industrial economies. In the second half of the year, the Bank of Japan abandoned its long-standing zero interest rate policy and raised short-term rates slightly. Long-term interest rates remained generally low or declining in many industrial countries. To varying degrees, this reflected relatively strong actual and prospective budgetary positions and benign inflationary expectations.

Major equity markets remained at high levels in early 2000 with technology stocks, in particular, beginning the year with significant further advances. However, volatility in international financial markets began to increase later in the year as equity valuations, especially in the technology sector, collapsed and spreads on risky assets—including emerging market debt—increased. Within Asia, those DMCs that had benefited from the technology boom saw sharp further downward movements in their equity markets, in some cases reversing much of the gains made in 1999. The sizes of the corrections were also influenced in some countries by domestic political problems and uncertainties, and by concerns about the pace of domestic economic reform and financial restructuring. Worldwide, as the appetite for risk taking diminished, several developing countries experienced a weakening of their external capital account and downward pressure on exchange rates (see Figure 1.2). Although Argentina and Turkey had severe financial problems late in the year, the spillover to other countries was relatively limited, in part because of the prompt response of the international financial community.

Looking forward, the outlook is for more moderate growth in 2001 and 2002 compared with the first half of 2000 as the world economy moves to a more sustainable growth trajectory. *ADO* projections are that, following a cyclical slowing to around 3.5 percent in 2001, world growth will pick up to almost 4 percent in 2002, broadly in line with longer-term trends. As regards the major industrial countries, this strongly reflects a temporary sharp slowing of the US economy to a shade below 2 percent in 2001 followed by a recovery to around 3 percent in 2002. Although *ADO* forecasts are that growth in the euro area should be relatively well sustained, some moderation to 2.5–3.0 percent is expected in both 2001 and 2002, from 3.4 percent in 2000. After some weakness in early 2001, growth in Japan is expected to pick up modestly to 1–2 percent in 2002.

The near-term outlook for developing countries is mixed. The DMCs as a group are expected to experience one of the sharpest slowdowns as aggregate growth declines from over 7 percent in 2000 to 5.3 percent in 2001, before rebounding somewhat in 2002. This would, for the most part, reflect the effects of the slowing US economy and the moderation of the technology boom on many DMCs' recent dynamic export performance. Even then, the DMCs would still constitute one of the fastest-growing regions in the world. Parts of Latin America are also expected to slow quite sharply in 2001, given close trade linkages with the US, but the region as a whole is expected to hold up quite well. Eastern Europe and Africa are expected to be less affected by the US slowdown, provided that growth is reasonably well maintained in the euro area.

The projected slowdown for the DMCs as a whole in 2001 masks variations across subregions. Among DMCs, those expected to see fairly sharp slowdowns are the newly industrialized economies (NIEs)—namely Hong Kong, China; Korea; Singapore; and Taipei,China—and the countries of Southeast Asia depending heavily on technology exports and on the US market. Some of these economies began to slow in 2000 as their recoveries matured and the technology boom cooled. Conversely, growth in the PRC and India is expected to hold up quite well, if domestic demand can be maintained. Growth in Cambodia, Lao People's Democratic Republic (Lao PDR), and Viet Nam, as well as the Pacific DMCs is likely to be sustained or to strengthen in 2001–2002, on the assumption that the authorities persevere with crucial domestic reforms. Growth is

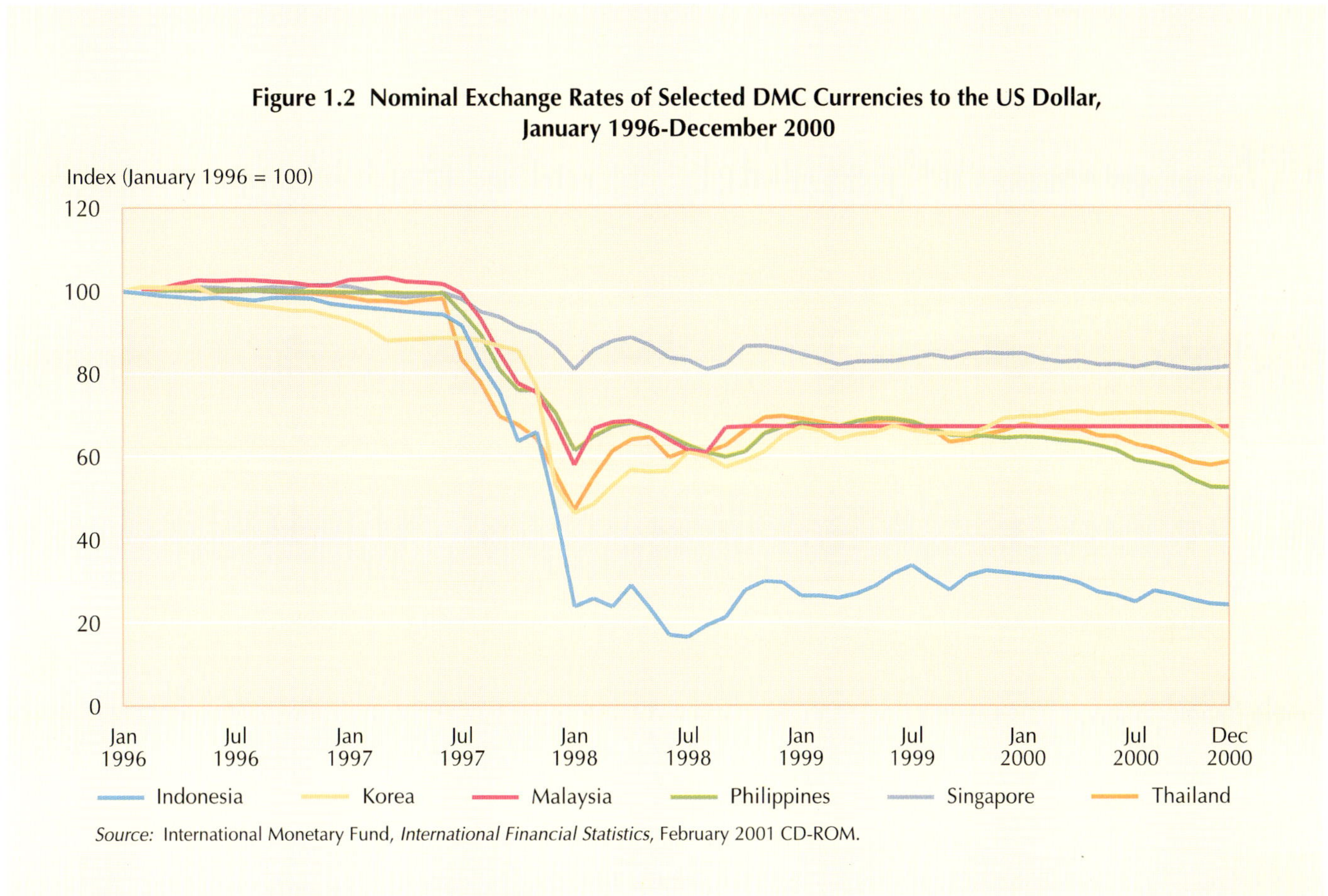

Figure 1.2 Nominal Exchange Rates of Selected DMC Currencies to the US Dollar, January 1996-December 2000

Source: International Monetary Fund, *International Financial Statistics*, February 2001 CD-ROM.

expected to slow sharply in the Central Asian republics, reflecting pressures of a projected slowdown in the Russian Federation. Nevertheless, in many of these countries, the foundations are gradually being laid for sustained medium-term growth.

This relatively sanguine outlook for the global economy is subject to a number of near-term risks and uncertainties. Foremost among these is the risk of a deeper and more long-lived slowdown in the US and the uncertain outlook for Japan. In an environment of slowing global growth, the risks on the oil price front have receded as oil prices have fallen from their peak in 2000. In the absence of major supply disruptions, oil prices should not present a major risk.

Key short-term risks for DMC economies relate to the expected continued weakness of the US economy in the first part of 2001, development in the technology sector, and the prospects for the Japanese economy. The risks are especially significant for those DMCs where recoveries depend heavily on exports, where financial and corporate restructuring is incomplete, and where political uncertainties remain. The less favorable external environment will present challenges for these DMCs as they continue to implement structural reforms and seek to reestablish the conditions for strong and sustained medium-term growth.

THE WORLD ECONOMY

Growth in world gross domestic product (GDP) accelerated to 4.8 percent in 2000—one of the most impressive performances of the last two decades—but began to lose momentum in the latter part of the year as the US economy slowed. Sluggish US growth is expected to continue to at least the middle of 2001 before activity begins to pick up. In 2002, the world economy is forecast to strengthen and record a growth rate of around 4 percent. With the rapid economic growth in 2000 came an acceleration in the volume of international trade, rising by over 12 percent in that year, one of the strongest performances for many years. This rate will likely moderate to about 7 percent in 2001 as the pace of economic growth slows. Notwithstanding strong economic growth, world inflation remained low in 2000, maintaining a record for price stability set in 1999, when it declined to its lowest level in several decades. Inflation is expected to remain moderate over 2001 and 2002.

Industrial Countries

GDP growth in the industrial countries accelerated to 3.8 percent in 2000, led by US growth of 5.0 percent. The euro area picked up to 3.4 percent as buoyant domestic demand was reinforced by export strength, particularly in the early part of the year. Japan recorded growth of 1.7 percent, up from the 1999 rate, led by private nonresidential investment and exports. In the UK, growth accelerated by nearly one percentage point to 3.0 percent in 2000, while in Australia growth fell slightly but still remained strong at around 4.3 percent. In Canada, growth was similar to that in the US.

Inflation in industrial countries picked up somewhat to a little over 2 percent in 2000, from 1.5 percent in 1999, primarily because of higher oil prices and slightly higher inflation in the US. Inflation was 2.4 percent in the euro area, a shade higher than in the previous year but generally subdued. Prices fell at a faster rate in Japan even as its economy recovered early in the year.

Stock markets were volatile in 2000. In the US, technology stocks weakened after reaching a peak in March as investors began to reevaluate earnings prospects and the outlook for further interest rate increases. Europe's bourses also showed some weakness but this was less severe, due to the emerging strength of domestic demand and robust export performance. In Japan, stock prices were under downward pressure for most of the year, in part due to weakness in the technology sector.

In foreign exchange markets, the euro depreciated against the dollar up until late October before strengthening somewhat through the end of the year. During the year, both the yen and the dollar experienced slight real effective appreciation.

Unemployment rates either fell or remained stable in 2000 in most industrial countries. In the euro area, unemployment fell by nearly a full percentage point to 9.0 percent against the background of increased labor market flexibility and the pickup in growth. In the US, where unemployment was lower, the decline was more modest; but the rate fell to 4.0 percent, a rate not seen in over 30 years, reflecting the growth improvement early in the year. The unemployment rate remained steady in Japan as restructuring continued.

Short-term interest rates rose slightly in most industrial countries over the year. The US Federal Reserve raised short-term rates in the first half of 2000, as did the European Central Bank. Long-term interest rates remained relatively low, reflecting a benign view of long-run inflation and, in some countries, strong budgetary positions.

Helped by continued strong revenue performance in the last few years, fiscal positions in most industrial countries improved further in 2000. The US federal surplus grew to around 2 percent of GDP in 2000 from about 1 percent in 1999, while the euro area also had a small surplus compared with a deficit of more than 1 percent of GDP in 1999. For the Organisation for Economic Co-operation and Development (OECD) as a whole, the central government budget switched from a deficit of about 1 percent of GDP in 1999 to a surplus of 0.5 percent of GDP in 2000. Conversely, the central government deficit widened further in Japan.

International imbalances increased further in 2000 as the US continued to grow more rapidly than other major industrial countries. In particular, the US current account deficit widened to almost 4.4 percent of GDP but was easily financed by strong capital inflows from the rest of the world. Interest rate differentials between the relatively high rates in the US and the lower rates in other industrial countries persisted and even widened slightly over the year. The US continued to serve as a safe haven for some capital flows from developing countries.

The near-term outlook for industrial countries is dominated by the anticipated slowdown in US growth to less than 2 percent in 2001, followed by an upturn in 2002. In the euro area, growth is expected to moderate slightly in 2001 and 2002 but to remain relatively strong. In Japan, the outlook is for continued growth of 1–2 percent, with the momentum sustained by restructuring—intended to increase efficiency and improve resource allocation—and by fiscal and monetary support. The unemployment rate should continue to fall in the euro area but may level off or increase slightly in Japan and the US. Reflecting the global slowdown, industrial countries' inflation is expected to generally remain subdued or soften.

Transition Economies

The transition economies of central and eastern Europe in 2000 continued the economic recovery that began in the preceding year. Output growth was strong, accelerating to 5–6 percent, thanks partly to faster growth in the euro area and the revival in domestic demand in some of the transition economies. Supportive macroeconomic policies, including lower interest rates, some fiscal stimulus, and strong export performance, fueled growth of over 7 percent in the Russian Federation, 4–6 percent in Hungary and Poland, and 2.8 percent in the Czech Republic. Inflation was moderate in the Czech Republic but reached double-digit rates in Hungary, Poland, and particularly the Russian Federation, where it was just over 20 percent.

Aside from the Russian Federation, where the current account surplus improved to almost 20 percent of GDP as a result of higher prices for petroleum and metals, the external balance of these economies deteriorated somewhat in 2000. The current account deficit in Poland was around 6 percent of GDP and about 3.5 percent of GDP in both the Czech Republic and Hungary.

Growth in the transition economies is expected to remain relatively strong in 2001–2002 but more muted than in 2000. Much will depend on the progress in domestic economic reform and the external environment. Somewhat slower growth in the euro area, the major trading partner for these economies, will have a mild negative effect as will expected slower growth in the Russian Federation and a leveling off or slight decline in oil prices. The current account surplus is expected to narrow in the Russian Federation and the current account deficits in the other countries widen somewhat. Throughout this region, inflation should generally moderate as growth slows.

DEVELOPING ECONOMIES

Growth in the developing regions of the world improved to 5–6 percent in 2000 from less than 4 percent in 1999 and 3.5 percent in 1998. The DMCs as a group continued to be among the strongest performers. The strengthening of Southeast Asia was particularly significant. Growth picked up from 3 percent in 1999 to 5.1 percent in 2000. Economic performance also improved elsewhere. After many countries in Latin America experienced weak or negative economic growth in 1999, the region revived to over 4 percent in 2000, led by strong performance in Mexico, Chile, and Brazil. In Africa, growth also accelerated as economic performance in South Africa strengthened, as did that of the oil exporters in the region—Algeria and Nigeria. In the Middle East, income rose more rapidly in 2000 than in 1999 on the back of higher oil prices in the second half of the year.

Notwithstanding the strong global economy, commodity price trends diverged in 2000. Agricultural prices increased by about 5 percent as did prices for some metals and minerals, led by strong markets for nickel, aluminum, and copper. Other metal prices remained unchanged or softened because of weak demand or high stock levels. Oil prices increased sharply in the second half of the year, reaching a peak of $35 a barrel before easing somewhat.

The Institute of International Finance estimates that net capital inflows to developing countries increased to just over $150 billion in 2000, only modestly higher than in 1999 and less than half the precrisis inflows of about $315 billion in 1997. Official flows to developing countries were negative in 2000, because official flows from international financial institutions remained low at $1 billion–$2 billion while net flows from bilateral creditors were negative as debt repayments from developing countries were greater than new lending to them. Recent official debt relief measures for heavily indebted poor countries are expected to influence finances, mainly official, in 2001 and beyond.

Growth in developing countries in 2001 is likely to depend on several factors that will vary from country to country. In a globalizing world, the external environment plays a key role. Commodity prices continue to be a critical external factor for many countries in Africa and the Middle East and to a lesser extent for Latin American countries and DMCs. Petroleum is probably the most critical of these commodities, and if oil prices remain firm, oil exporters will continue to benefit (see Box 1.1). The likelihood of stable non-oil commodity prices will depend on the general strength of the world economy, weaker performance being generally associated with softer commodity prices. The pace of growth in industrial countries will also be a critical factor that will impact on developing countries, and exporters of manufactured goods will be among the first to suffer. Domestic macroeconomic and structural policies will be equally or, in some cases, more important, particularly where countries have

deep-seated weaknesses. Policies and reforms are needed in some countries to address issues of governance, law and order, and civil society.

Africa and the Middle East

In the past few years, Africa and the Middle East have been exposed to a number of external factors—primarily developments in commodity markets—that have had a significant impact on their economic performance. In 2000, buoyant oil markets gave a strong boost to oil producing countries in these two regions. The effect of higher prices and greater export volume had a widespread salutary effect on economic growth, domestic demand, fiscal health, and current account balances in these countries. Conversely, many of the non-oil producing countries suffered from adverse terms of trade as the price of their exports failed to keep up with the cost of imported oil and manufactured goods. Nevertheless, those non-oil producing countries that had adopted prudent macroeconomic and structural policies managed to overcome this adverse effect and experienced accelerated growth. Those countries where government policies have been weaker and/or where the adverse terms-of-trade effect has been compounded by civil disturbance or drought performed poorly.

Economic growth resumed in Saudi Arabia and other Gulf and Middle East oil exporting countries in 2000. These countries have also begun to benefit from structural reforms undertaken, when petroleum prices were much lower, to stimulate the non-oil private sector. Measures have included the privatization of some utilities (including telecommunications) and the adoption of regulations designed to attract foreign direct investment (FDI) and the private sector generally. In Egypt, growth slowed a little in 2000 from the 1999 level. Fiscal and monetary policies were tightened in response to a deteriorating external payments position, as seen in a loss of foreign reserves and pressure on the exchange rate.

Within Africa, output growth accelerated to about 3 percent, from around 2 percent in 1999, as a result both of more buoyant markets for some commodities, particularly petroleum, and the effects of implementation of better macroeconomic policies and structural reforms. The two largest economies in the region—Nigeria and South Africa—recorded growth of about 3 percent, the former aided by higher oil prices and the latter by greater external demand and growing international competitiveness.

Several other African countries also grew more rapidly as they effectively implemented macroeconomic and restructuring policies. However, some countries suffered from a range of constraints including weak commodity prices, drought, and civil conflict. Capital inflows to the region remained small in 2000. Official inflows were negative for the fourth year in a row at $1.7 billion (due to loan repayments) while private flows fell from $10 billion to around $7 billion.

Box 1.1 Oil and Energy Issues in Developing Member Countries

Oil prices have recently exhibited considerable volatility. Having increased from a little over $10 a barrel in February 1999 to $30–$35 a barrel in November 2000, they have come down to a range of $24–$30 a barrel in January–February 2001. The rapid increase in oil prices initially reflected production cutbacks among major oil producing countries in 1999. This was accompanied by high and persistent world demand for oil, due to the strong rebound in economic activity in Asia and continued robust growth in the US economy through mid-2000. As a result, commercial inventories of oil were drawn down to their lowest levels since the 1970s.

In April 2000, the Organization of Petroleum Exporting Countries (OPEC) reversed its production cuts of the previous year and adopted a target price range of $22–$28 per barrel. Despite subsequent increases in oil production, prices remained above the upper limits of OPEC's price band until the end of the year. The decline in prices in early 2001, however, coincided with a drastic cut in Iraqi oil production because of a dispute with the United Nations over its oil-for-food program. In an attempt to maintain prices, OPEC announced another production cutback in January 2001.

Prospects for world oil prices remain subject to considerable uncertainty arising from both supply and demand factors. On the supply side, immediate prospects depend on the extent to which OPEC members adhere to their reduced production quotas and the extent to which higher prices reactivate oil wells capped during the oil price slump of 1998. The forecasts for non-OPEC production indicate that output will grow slowly. At present, nearly all oil producing countries, except Saudi Arabia, are producing at or near full capacity. Moreover, in March 2001 OPEC agreed to restrict production to maintain prices within its target band. On the demand side, while the onset of warmer weather in the northern hemisphere will inevitably lead to a downturn in demand, prospects for the year are highly dependent on how much the global economy in general—and the US economy in particular—slows. Any such slowdown will, to some extent, be offset by the oil companies' need to replenish depleted stocks of oil. Barring supply disruptions caused by ongoing tensions in the Middle East, a moderate decline in oil prices is assumed, in line with oil futures prices. However, if oil prices remain higher than they are expected to, then this would have several adverse implications for global economic prospects, as follows.

Higher oil prices can affect the global economy through various channels. The initial impact is likely to be felt on the trade balance of both oil exporting and oil importing countries. The resulting income transfer from oil importers to oil exporters is likely to lead to a fall in global demand because oil importing countries have a higher propensity to spend than oil exporting countries. Higher oil prices can also have an impact on price inflation and economic growth. Inflationary pressures arising from higher costs of production can feed into a wage-price spiral and lead to higher interest rates. This could reinforce the negative effects of terms-of-trade shocks on output for oil importing countries and lead to lower GDP growth. Moreover, if governments derive revenue from imported oil and/or subsidize the domestic use of oil, this could complicate fiscal management, especially if higher prices persist.

Many analysts, however, feel that the world economy today can better cope with the adverse consequences of an oil price shock than it did during the previous oil price surges of 1973/74, 1979/80, and 1990, when sharp rises in oil prices led to higher inflation and global recession. In real terms, prices today are one third below their levels in the 1990s and one half of their levels in the 1970s. Oil also now accounts for a smaller proportion of world production and consumption. This is especially true for the industrial countries.

Since the 1970s, due to energy conservation, a switch to other fuels, and technology developments, industrial countries have greatly reduced their dependence on imported oil. At the same time, their services and information, communications, and technology sectors (which have a lower oil intensity of production) have increased their share of GDP at the expense of manufacturing (with a higher oil intensity). This has been facilitated by the relocation of manufacturing activities to lower-cost developing countries. As a result, industrial countries now use only about half as much oil for every dollar of GDP compared with the early 1970s. In developing member countries (DMCs), although the growth in consumption of natural gas has outpaced that of oil in recent years, their share of global oil consumption, nevertheless, increased from 17 percent in 1980 to 26 percent in 1998, due in part to rapid growth in manufacturing activity. As a result, the oil intensity of production in DMCs has remained broadly constant since the early 1970s. As DMCs have relatively few oil producers, they are likely to suffer more from an increase in oil prices than industrial countries.

According to IMF's *World Economic Outlook* of September 2000, a sustained $5 a barrel increase in the price of oil over a baseline figure of $26.53 a barrel in December 2000 would, after one year, lead to a fall in GDP of 0.2 percent for the major industrial countries while inflation would rise by 0.2–0.4 percent. For developing countries in Asia, GDP would decline by 0.4 percent, inflation would rise by 0.7 percent, and the current account balance would deteriorate by around 0.5 percent of GDP. These aggregate figures, however, conceal large differences between individual countries within Asia. While slower growth will undoubtedly be a setback for a recovering Asia, for a number of the newly industrialized economies and Southeast Asian net oil importers currently enjoying large current account surpluses and subdued inflation, the impact of higher oil prices is unlikely to be a cause of concern. However, for some of the South Asian countries running large current account deficits, further deterioration of their external accounts and output losses due to higher oil prices could have potentially serious effects.

Latin America

Growth in Latin America rebounded strongly to around 4 percent in 2000, from negligible growth in 1999. The region benefited from a combination of strong growth in the US, higher prices for some commodities, and generally sounder macroeconomic policies and performance, particularly with respect to inflation. The two largest economies in the region—Mexico and Brazil—performed well in 2000, growing at about 7 percent and 4 percent, respectively. Export growth was very strong in both countries. Mexico's buoyant economy was led by soaring exports, primarily of oil, to the US and by strong investment growth. Brazil benefited from greater export competitiveness following its currency depreciation in early 1999. The Brazilian Government improved its fiscal situation as stronger consumer and investment spending resulted in higher tax receipts. Argentina, the third largest economy in the region, began to recover from a severe recession in 2000 but growth was slower than expected leading to continued pressure on the budget and to less favorable terms in international capital markets. This resulted in severe financial pressures toward the end of the year. Venezuela benefited from higher oil prices, while the economies of Chile and Peru continued to perform well. Inflation in the region abated somewhat in 2000 as many countries have adopted either inflation targeting or policies with a strong inflation containment component. The current account deficit decreased slightly for the region as a whole.

Asian and Pacific Developing Member Countries

The DMCs' recovery from the financial crisis of 1997/98 strengthened in 2000 (see Table 1.1). The strong performance reflected the favorable external environment through most of 2000; expansive macroeconomic policies; competitive exchange rates; and, in varying degrees, progress in financial and corporate restructuring, and in economic reforms. Higher oil prices toward the end of the year had different effects on oil exporters and importers, but on balance were a negative factor for growth, and in some countries pushed up inflation slightly. In several countries, the impact of oil prices on inflation was offset by the influence of moderate food prices.

Many DMCs were well positioned in 1999 and 2000 to take advantage of the rapid growth in import demand from industrial countries, especially the US. GDP growth for the region was over 7 percent for the whole of 2000, up from just over 6 percent in 1999, though the pace slowed during the second half of the year. Domestic demand began to strengthen in a number of economies relative to the preceding two years. Hong Kong, China and Singapore led the continued strong performance of the region, with economic growth in 2000 of 10 percent or more. In Indonesia, Philippines, and Thailand, recovery continued but remained somewhat fragile due to incomplete structural reforms, political uncertainty, and gener-

ally weak private investment. Growth in the PRC and India, where the impact of the Asian crisis was more limited, continued at a rapid pace, primarily due to strong domestic demand and buoyant export performance. Strong agricultural performance took GDP growth to its highest rate in four years in Pakistan, while in Bangladesh, Nepal, and Sri Lanka economic growth was also higher. Agriculture also played a major role in boosting growth in Bangladesh and Nepal, while industry was an important source of growth in Sri Lanka. Most of the economies in the Central Asian republics, Azerbaijan, and Mongolia grouping benefited from improved economic performance in the Russian Federation as well as from higher prices for oil and natural gas, which are the leading exports for several of them. The Pacific DMCs showed weaker performance due to political problems in some countries and continued softness in world nonenergy commodity prices. In the second half of 2000, many of the larger DMCs started slowing as GDP growth in industrial countries, particularly the US, slowed.

Inflation was benign in 2000 for most DMCs. In the NIEs, except Hong Kong, China, prices rose slightly faster than in 1999 as a result of higher oil prices but, even so, inflation remained at less than 2.5 percent in Korea; Singapore; and Taipei,China as macroeconomic policies remained prudent and money supply growth was held in check. In Hong Kong, China, the consumer price index continued its deflationary trend due to weakness in property rental prices, but the rate of decline showed signs of moderating. In the PRC, a strengthening of private consumption reversed the 1998–99 deflationary trend; the consumer price index rose by 0.4 percent. In Southeast Asia (except the Lao PDR and Myanmar), despite a small pickup in inflation in the last quarter of 2000, overall inflation remained low and relatively stable. In the Central Asian republics, Azerbaijan, and Mongolia; Lao PDR; and Myanmar, inflation remained high, primarily due to the effect of currency depreciation on import prices and accommodative monetary policies. In South Asia, India experienced somewhat higher inflation due to deregulation of fuel prices and the depreciation of the rupee. More prudent fiscal and monetary management was generally important in holding down inflation elsewhere in this subregion.

Several DMCs recorded double-digit export growth in 2000. The continuing global demand for goods related to information and communications technology (ICT) led to a surge in exports from India; Korea; Malaysia; Singapore; Taipei,China; and Thailand. Rising international oil prices stimulated exports from Indonesia and many of the Central Asian republics and Azerbaijan, while the PRC benefited from higher demand for its labor-intensive manufactured goods. Notwithstanding strong exports, more rapid growth of imports in 2000 led to a narrowing of current account surpluses in many DMCs. These surpluses were in some cases used to finance both external debt repayments and a further buildup in reserves, albeit generally at a much slower pace than in 1999.

Table 1.1 Selected Economic Indicators, Developing Member Countries, 1998–2002

	1998	1999	2000	2001	2002
Gross domestic product (annual percent change)					
DMCs	0.2	6.3	7.1	5.3	6.1
Newly industrialized economies	-2.9	7.9	8.4	4.3	5.6
PRC	7.8	7.1	8.0	7.3	7.5
Central Asian republics, Azerbaijan, and Mongolia	1.5	4.7	7.8	3.3	4.8
Southeast Asia	-9.0	3.1	5.1	4.0	4.8
South Asia	6.1	5.8	5.8	5.8	6.5
India	6.6	6.4	6.0	6.2	7.0
Pacific DMCs	-2.0	4.1	-1.8	3.4	5.0
Crisis-affected economies	-8.3	6.8	6.8	3.9	5.1
Inflation (percent change in consumer price index)					
DMCs	8.0	2.3	2.1	3.4	3.3
Newly industrialized economies	4.6	-0.1	1.1	2.2	2.5
PRC	-0.8	-1.4	0.4	2.0	2.5
Central Asian republics, Azerbaijan, and Mongolia	9.7	20.2	15.2	10.6	10.0
Southeast Asia	26.5	9.4	2.7	5.4	4.4
South Asia	6.3	4.2	6.2	5.4	4.8
India	5.9	3.3	7.0	5.5	4.8
Pacific DMCs	10.1	10.0	11.5	8.3	5.0
Crisis-affected economies	17.8	5.4	2.6	4.3	3.5
Current account balance (percent of GDP)					
DMCs	4.1	3.7	2.8	2.5	2.4
Newly industrialized economies	7.4	6.3	4.7	4.6	5.0
PRC	3.1	1.6	1.5	1.2	1.0
Central Asian republics, Azerbaijan, and Mongolia	-5.5	-1.3	2.5	2.6	3.6
Southeast Asia	4.7	6.6	5.2	3.6	3.0
South Asia	-1.4	-1.6	-1.9	-1.7	-1.5
India	-1.0	-0.9	-1.3	-1.2	-1.0
Pacific DMCs	1.2	3.0	6.4	—	—
Crisis-affected economies	6.5	5.9	3.8	2.8	2.3

— Not available.
Source: Staff estimates; and see Statistical Notes.

Equity and currency markets declined significantly in 2000 in many DMCs. Externally, rising interest rates, slower growth in the US in the second half of the year, and the popping of the technology bubble triggered downward adjustments in equity markets. The response of Asian equity markets to the worldwide correction in prices of ICT stocks, particularly the fall in the NASDAQ index, was especially strong (see Figures 1.3 and 1.4). Domestic considerations also, in some cases, dampened investor enthusiasm and confidence in the region. These included incomplete restructuring of banks and corporations, limited progress in structural reforms, and perceived heightening of political risks in some countries. Domestic currencies weakened in the region due to concerns over an international growth slowdown and any resultant impact on regional growth through the export sector.

NIEs and ASEAN-4 Countries

The NIEs recorded the strongest growth performance as a group in the region in 2000, with GDP growth picking up to 8.4 percent. Growth also picked up in three of the ASEAN-4 countries (Indonesia, Malaysia, and Philippines).

In terms of GDP growth, Hong Kong, China; Singapore; and Taipei,China performed well in 2000. GDP growth acceler-

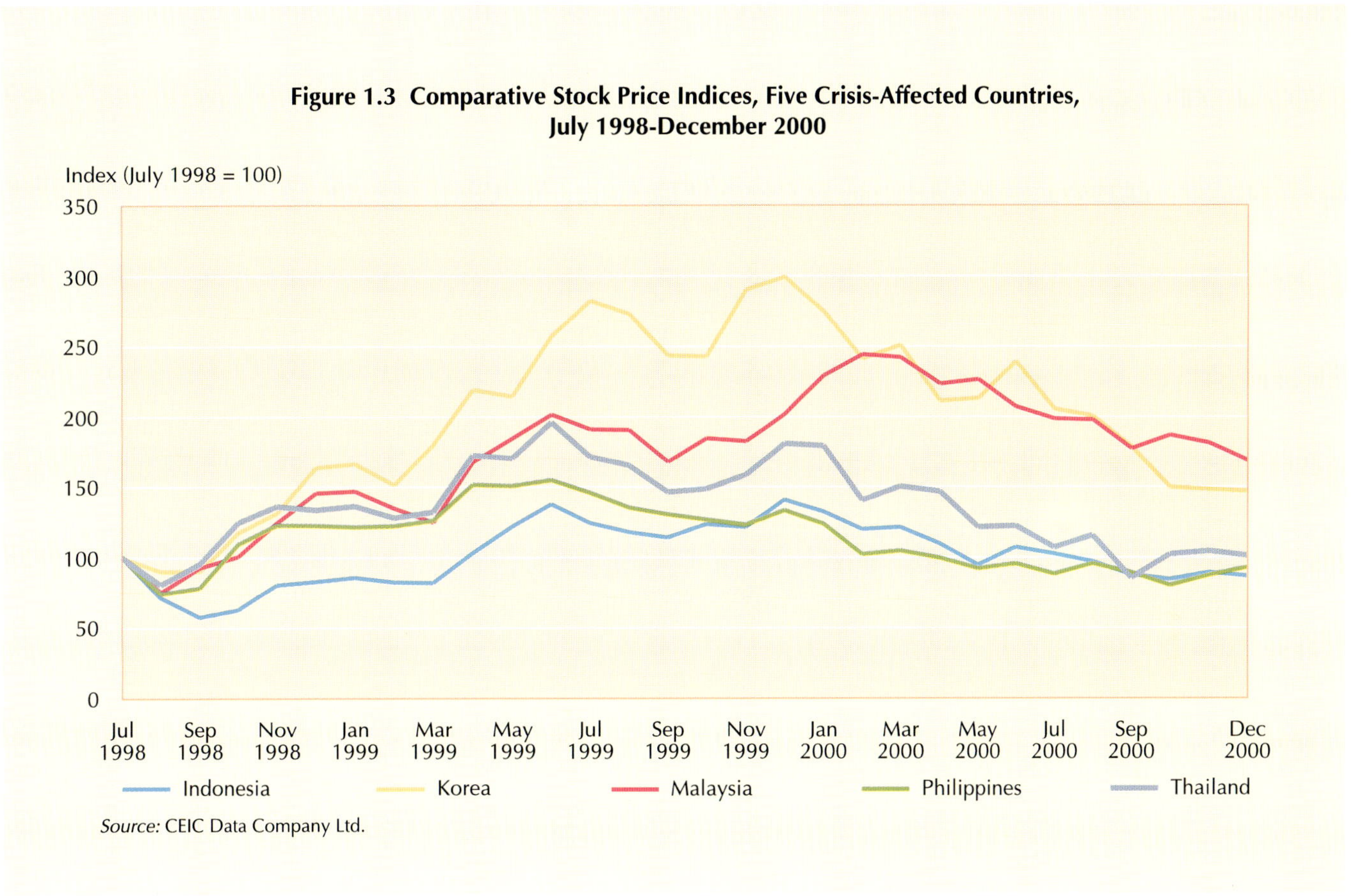

Figure 1.3 Comparative Stock Price Indices, Five Crisis-Affected Countries, July 1998–December 2000

Source: CEIC Data Company Ltd.

ated from 4.8 percent in 1999 to an exceptionally strong 7.9 percent in 2000. At the same time, the variation in economic performance was smaller relative to that observed in 1999. Hong Kong, China and Singapore recorded similar growth rates in 2000, with that of Taipei,China somewhat lower. Buoyant exports, led by electrical and electronics products, were the primary growth engine as the rate of export increase more than doubled to around 20 percent in these three economies. Domestic demand also accelerated as consumer and investor confidence rose. Labor market conditions improved and property prices saw some recovery, while spending on new plant and equipment in the technology sectors increased. Imports also picked up, reflecting a combination of restocking of intermediate inputs and rising demand for consumer goods.

Inflation rose a little in Singapore and Taipei,China as a result of higher oil prices in the latter part of the year, combined with faster growth and falling unemployment, but remained relatively low. In Hong Kong, China prices continued to fall as a result of flat or declining prices for retained imports and consumer goods as well as continued slack in the economy. Strong growth generally helped Singapore increase its fiscal surplus, and Taipei,China reduce its fiscal deficit, though the budget

balance in Hong Kong, China deteriorated slightly from a modest surplus to a small deficit. As exports of goods and services were generally larger than imports, the current accounts were in surplus in 2000, though at slightly lower levels than in 1999, ranging from 23.6 percent of GDP in Singapore and to 2.4 percent in Taipei,China.

The economic recovery in the five countries most affected by the Asian financial crisis (Indonesia, Korea, Malaysia, Philippines, and Thailand) remained relatively strong in 2000 and has taken the form of a "V" shape. Growth accelerated in Indonesia, Malaysia, and Philippines but fell slightly in Korea and remained virtually unchanged in Thailand. Economic performance was the result of a combination of domestic and external factors. Domestically, accommodative monetary policy, as reflected in low interest rates and more competitive exchange rates, as well as government budget deficits, generally provided a stimulus. The recovery was also supported by the implementation of measures to address corporate and financial sector problems. These measures have generally helped reduce the level of nonperforming loans (NPLs). Additional supportive external factors included the strength of the US economy. Korea remained the fastest-growing economy of the group, mainly due to a surge in fixed investment spending and rapid growth in

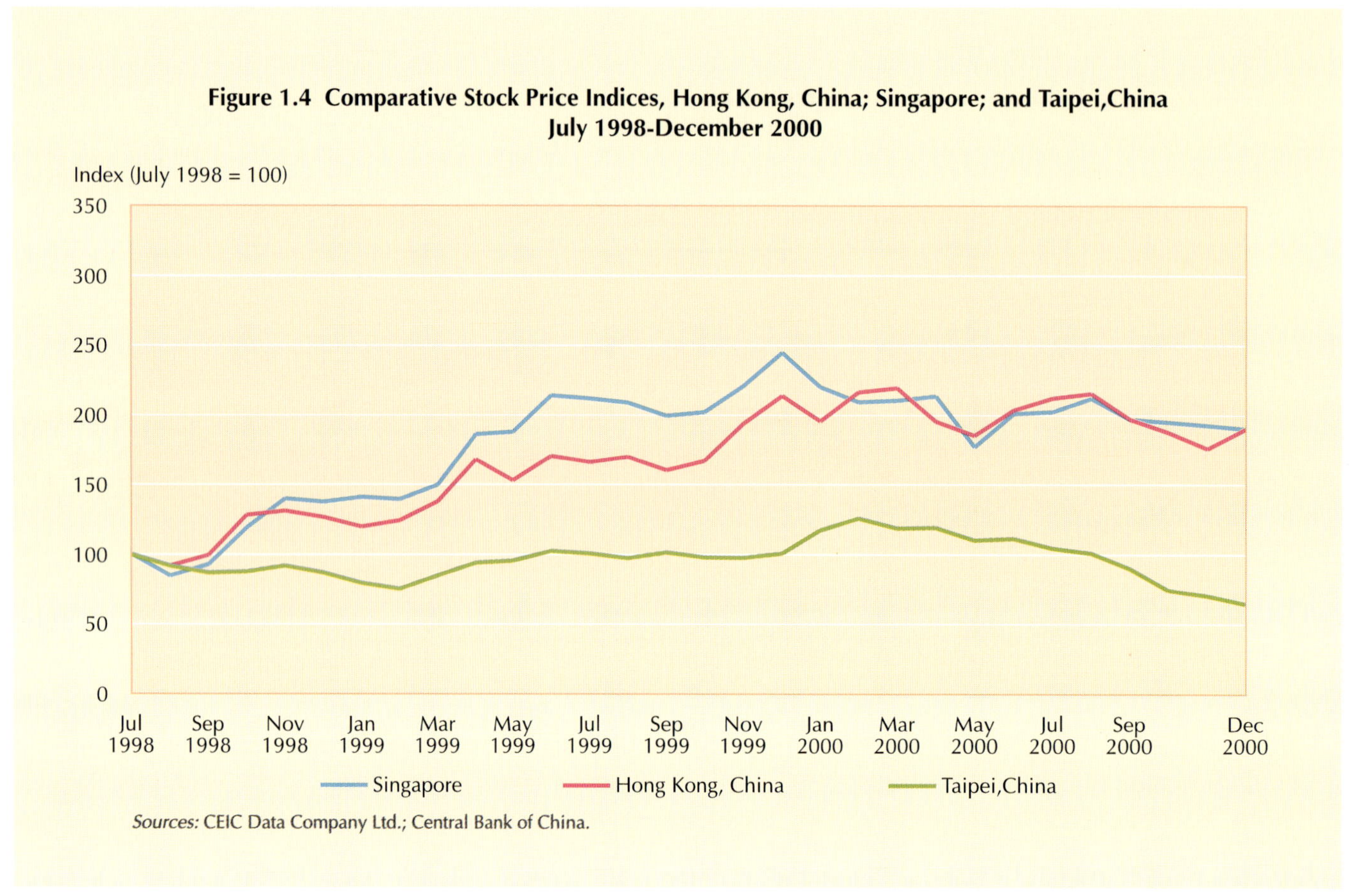

Sources: CEIC Data Company Ltd.; Central Bank of China.

manufacturing. In the other four countries, the recoveries varied in strength; in Malaysia growth picked up to over 8 percent, while in Indonesia, Philippines, and Thailand it was around 4–5 percent.

Despite relatively strong growth, considerable weakness in domestic demand was still in evidence in Indonesia, Philippines, and Thailand. Conversely, domestic demand was somewhat stronger in Korea and Malaysia, where both consumption and gross fixed capital formation increased and the recovery has been reinforced by greater consumer confidence. Private investment, particularly FDI, was somewhat weak due to a combination of factors that included excess capacity in nonexport industries and weak corporate sector profitability related to incomplete corporate and financial restructuring (see Box 1.2). Domestic equity markets moved down with equity markets in the US in 2000, alongside some net capital outflows or slowing of inflows.

Despite firmer prices during the last quarter of 2000, inflation generally remained low and stable during the year in the five countries due to moderation of food prices and continued excess capacity in certain sectors. Toward the end of the year, weakness in the currencies of several of these countries added somewhat to price pressure.

Continued strong global demand for electronic goods led to a surge in exports from Korea, Malaysia, and Thailand in 2000, while rising international oil prices stimulated exports from Indonesia. Export growth ranged from about 9 percent in the Philippines to 28 percent in Indonesia. Exports of electronic products softened toward year-end, as the US economy slowed and global demand for electronics weakened. While the current account surplus of Indonesia and the Philippines increased, those of the other economies narrowed.

Cambodia, Lao PDR, and Viet Nam

Against a background of improved domestic macroeconomic management and economic reforms, economic growth in these three countries was affected to some degree by developments in the global economy in 2000. Higher world oil prices and a robust industry sector helped Viet Nam achieve a stronger rate of growth in 2000 than in 1999 while seasonal floods hampered otherwise good performance in Cambodia. Strong agricultural performance made an important contribution to growth in the Lao PDR. Greater price stability among the three countries was generally achieved through prudent monetary and fiscal policies, a fall in world food prices, particularly of rice, and

Box 1.2 Financial Sector and Corporate Restructuring in Five Crisis-Affected Countries

Since the onset of the Asian financial crisis in July 1997, all of the five most seriously affected countries (Indonesia, Korea, Malaysia, Philippines, and Thailand) have made significant progress in the immense task of financial and corporate sector restructuring. The focus of their efforts has been on resolving the problem of insolvent financial institutions by closure, merger, or recapitalization; addressing the corporate debt overhang; and improving corporate governance. The broad principles of financial and corporate restructuring have been similar, but the actual patterns of implementation have varied. Indonesia, Korea, and Malaysia have adopted restructuring programs that have stressed coordination by the central government. They have established central agencies to manage nonperforming loans (NPLs) and to carry forward the recapitalization process. The Thai Government has followed a more market-oriented approach, though it has restructured public banks and finance companies and absorbed some of their losses. The Philippines adopted no explicit set of restructuring measures since it was, to some degree, less affected by the crisis.

The first objective in all the countries was to resolve the problems of financial institutions in trouble. Banks were mandated to meet international standards of capital adequacy, loan classification, loan-loss provisioning, accounting, and disclosure. Also, many nonviable institutions were closed, but the viable ones were merged or recapitalized through the injection of public money.

Financial restructuring moved forward on several fronts in 2000. The Financial Supervisory Service of Korea introduced new and more stringent criteria for classifying NPLs in December 1999, leading to an increase in the NPL ratio from the one based on the old criteria. Reflecting restructuring, however, the NPL ratio for Korea is now the lowest among the five countries. Together with Malaysia, Korea now has an NPL ratio for commercial banks of less than 10 percent. During 2000, debt restructuring through asset management companies (AMCs) made further progress in Korea and Malaysia. The Korea Asset Management Corporation had purchased more than 50 percent of the banking system's NPLs by July 2000 and disposed of 40 percent of those it had acquired. In Malaysia, Danaharta—the agency set up to purchase and rehabilitate the financial sector's bad debt—had acquired a little more than 40 percent of NPLs by August 2000, amounting to about 15 percent of the country's GDP. It is estimated that, as of June 2000, it had disposed of 61 percent of the NPLs under its jurisdiction.

In Indonesia, the NPL ratio has also fallen. As of June 2000, it was reported to be about 30 percent for the country's banking system as a whole, down from a peak of 70 percent. More than 75 percent of the total NPLs in the banking system, amounting to 60 percent of GDP, are now under the control of the Indonesian Bank Restructuring Agency. However, uncooperative debtors, and an inadequate legislative and regulatory environment have hampered the recovery of asset values in the country. As of June 2000, the Agency had disposed of only 0.35 percent of acquired NPLs.

In Thailand, progress has been made in reducing NPLs, which had declined from a peak of about 48 percent in May 1999 to 18 percent by December 2000. However, for two reasons, the resolution of the NPL problem is incomplete and remains a significant challenge to the Government. First, the sharp decline in NPLs was largely due to the transfer of some NPLs to AMCs, which were created to remove bad loans from bank balance sheets. If these NPLs were included in the calculation of the NPL ratio, together with new NPLs and reentry NPLs, the NPL ratio would be around 30 percent rather than 18 percent. Moreover, as of December 2000, state-owned commercial banks and finance companies had significantly higher NPLs than private commercial banks, averaging around 22 percent and 25 percent, respectively. Second, as economic growth has slowed, some restructured loans have resurfaced as reentry NPLs. Some commercial banks were reluctant to accept losses and tended to simply reschedule the payments. New NPLs have continued to emerge, particularly in those industries that continue to struggle, such as real estate and construction. So, though Thai banks have made significant progress in meeting capital adequacy standards, additional capital may be required.

Corporate restructuring in these five countries also progressed through government-sponsored voluntary workout arrangements and outside this framework. But, in many countries, much more needs to be done. In Korea, the restructuring of the top four *chaebol* is moving ahead. They have all met the overall requirements of the Capital Structure Improvement Plans for 1999. Some progress has also been made in the restructuring of smaller *chaebol* and firms. In Thailand, by end-September 2000, the participant debtors in the Corporate Debt Restructuring Advisory Committee owed about B2.6 trillion in loans. About 43 percent of the loans referred to the Committee had been resolved. Although many large loans have been voluntarily resolved, some have not. Indonesia has seen some progress in government-supervised debt restructuring. In August 2000, the Jakarta Initiative Task Force reported the completion of 24 (out of 67 active) debt-restructuring cases. The completed cases involved $5.2 billion in debt, accounting for almost 40 percent of the total value of active cases. This is a substantial improvement on the less than $1 billion debt restructured as of February 2000. Particularly helpful was the adoption of time limits for mediation procedures and the improvement in regulatory incentives for corporate restructuring.

In the case of formal insolvency, recent data are not available. But earlier reports suggest that few bankruptcy cases have been filed in these countries and even fewer cases completed. Gaps in bankruptcy legislation and weak institutional capacity in some countries suggest that formal resolution of debts may continue to be a slow process.

Source: Adapted from Regional Economic Monitoring Unit, Asian Development Bank.

generally good agricultural performance. Fiscal deficits worsened in all three countries, but only slightly in Cambodia and Viet Nam. Export growth was robust, led by crude oil in Viet Nam and by garments in Cambodia and the Lao PDR. However, import growth was also strong and the current account balance weakened to a smaller surplus in Viet Nam and deteriorated to a substantially larger deficit in Cambodia.

PRC and India

During and following the Asian crisis, the PRC and India maintained generally robust growth, despite a slowdown in exports. This was mainly because both economies have relatively low export-to-GDP ratios while capital account restrictions cushioned them somewhat against sharp currency and asset market fluctuations in the region.

The PRC continued to show strength in 2000. Real GDP growth was 8 percent, up from 7 percent in 1999, driven by an acceleration in industrial growth. However, agriculture suffered from a severe drought and grain output fell by 8 percent. The deflationary trend experienced in the previous two years was largely arrested and the consumer price index experienced virtually no change. The fiscal deficit rose to about 2.8 percent of GDP compared with 2.1 percent in 1999. Money supply growth provided sufficient funds for continued rapid expansion, with M2 rising by 12.3 percent, slightly lower than the rate in 1999. Further steps toward liberalizing the financial sector in preparation for entry into the World Trade Organization were taken, e.g., liberalizing interest rates on foreign currency loans and large deposits. With strong growth in the US economy during the first half of the year and the recovery of the crisis-affected countries in Asia, export growth surged to 27.8 percent. The rapid increase in input needs of exporting industries and the industry sector boosted import growth to 36.8 percent in 2000. The current account surplus continued moving downward, falling to 1.5 percent of GDP. This decline was due to the chronic deficit in the services balance and a narrowing of the trade surplus. FDI fell moderately during 2000 as a result of the lagged effects of the Asian financial crisis, resulting in a substantial drop in contracted FDI in 1998–1999. However, approved foreign investment rose by 25 percent. With foreign exchange reserves of about $160 billion, external debt of $156 billion, which is mostly of medium- and long-term maturity, and a debt-service ratio of about 8 percent, the external situation continues to be very strong.

In India, GDP growth was around 6 percent in 2000, led by a strong services sector. The agriculture sector grew more slowly, by 0.9 percent, as production was adversely affected by poor weather. The inflation rate rose temporarily to 7 percent from 3.3 percent in the previous year, largely as a result of higher fuel prices following deregulation and the effect of higher world oil prices. Measures to bring spending under control were generally successful and the tax base broadened. The central

Government deficit is likely to be contained within the budget estimate of 5.1 percent of GDP. Rising interest rates in the US in the first part of the year resulted in an outflow of funds and a consequent decline in the rupee against the dollar. In response, the Reserve Bank of India raised interest rates moderately in July and tightened monetary conditions. Nevertheless, commercial sector demand for credit continued to grow, mainly as a result of oil companies' greater financing needs to pay for higher import costs. Exports maintained their strong performance, growing by 17 percent in 2000. Robust economic growth in the US and the rest of Asia continued to increase demand for Indian manufactured goods. Software exports, while accounting for only 10 percent of total exports, have been growing at 50 percent year on year. Imports also grew strongly as a result of higher oil import costs and a more rapid pace of capital imports. The overall current account deficit was 1.3 percent of GDP in 2000 compared with 0.9 percent of GDP in 1999.

Bangladesh, Nepal, Pakistan, and Sri Lanka

In these four countries, GDP growth generally accelerated in 2000. Growth in Bangladesh and Nepal was higher than at anytime since the mid-1990s, and was higher than in the previous year in Pakistan and Sri Lanka. Stronger agriculture was largely responsible for the enhanced performance. Bangladesh achieved food self-sufficiency for the first time in many years, and Pakistan and Nepal turned in bumper harvests. Except for Sri Lanka, inflation generally moderated on the back of stable food prices and prudent monetary management. Large fiscal deficits, however, remained a major concern in several of these countries. The budget deficit, excluding transfers, stayed stable in Nepal but rose in the other three countries to at least 6 percent of GDP—in Sri Lanka reaching as much as 10 percent of GDP. External trade played an important role in the stronger economic performance of this region, with rapid growth in exports of garments and textiles. Buoyant exports resulted in a general improvement in the countries' balance of payments, and the current account deficits fell in some of them.

Central Asian Republics, Azerbaijan, and Mongolia

The economic turnaround in the Russian Federation from 1999 and the rise in international energy prices helped generate strong aggregate GDP growth of below 5 percent for this group in 1999 (excluding Mongolia) that improved further to 8 percent in 2000. Growth performance would have been even more impressive if the agriculture sector had not suffered a severe drought that affected both the cotton crop, a major export item, and food grain production in some of these countries. In Mongolia, not an oil exporter, circumstances were somewhat different as economic performance fell far below potential due to the impact on agriculture of a severe drought. GDP growth was close to zero compared with average growth of 3.6 percent between 1997 and 1999.

Aside from Mongolia, in 2000 the average level of inflation in these countries fell to 15.2 percent though this level is still high. Generally, this reflected the positive effects of exchange rate stability and appropriately restrained monetary policies. In Mongolia, on the other hand, inflation accelerated to double-digit levels as an expansionary fiscal and monetary stance was adopted to offset the poor performance of the economy.

Higher revenues from the oil sector and efforts at improving public expenditure management and tax administration have helped the countries improve their fiscal performance. Fiscal deficits on average declined from 5.6 percent of GDP in 1999 to 2.8 percent in 2000. Taking advantage of high international oil and gas prices and greater access to pipelines and other supply outlets, this group's export earnings increased by 0.4 percent and 25 percent in 1999 and 2000, respectively. This enabled many of the countries to improve their external positions, as reflected in a decline in current account deficits, a buildup of international reserves, and a significant improvement in external debt-servicing ability. However, in Mongolia the current account deficit deteriorated.

Pacific DMCs

The economic recovery in the Pacific that began in 1999 was not sustained in 2000 due to political instability and social unrest in the Fiji Islands and Solomon Islands. In addition, growth in the largest economy in the subregion—Papua New Guinea—slowed significantly in 2000 with weak performance in agriculture and industry. As a result, the growth performance of the Pacific DMCs as a group declined by about 2 percentage points in 2000. Growth was generally led by tourism or construction activity. Inflation in several countries rose as a result of weakening currencies and increased world oil prices.

Government deficits widened in five of the Pacific DMCs for various reasons, including a fall in revenue, political instability, and social unrest, or the launch of large development projects. In contrast, budget outcomes improved in the other countries. In all but three Pacific DMCs, the overall balance-of-payments position deteriorated, due mainly to higher oil costs.

Prospects for 2001 and 2002

Compared with GDP growth of just over 7 percent in 2000, growth in the DMCs is expected to slow to 5.3 percent in 2001 before picking up to just over 6 percent in 2002. The anticipated slowdown reflects primarily a sharp deceleration of export growth to single-digit levels in 2001 and spillover effects to domestic economic activities. Private consumption is expected to moderate in 2001 as the income effects from the export sector spread during the year. Monetary policy is generally expected to be accommodative. Fiscal policy will be constrained by the need to reduce fiscal deficits in some countries, but it can provide support for domestic demand in others.

The projections for 2001 have been revised from the *ADO 2000 Update* to incorporate the effects of the sharper than expected slowdown in the global economy that is under way, as well as the stronger outturn for 2000. On balance, the *ADO 2001* projections imply that the level of GDP in the DMCs at the end of 2001 will be around 0.8 percent lower than implied by the *ADO 2000 Update* and that growth in 2001 will be half a percentage point lower than the *ADO 2000 Update*.

The *ADO 2001* projections are based on a number of assumptions about the external environment. First, the US economic slowdown will only be brief with the US recovering to close to its long-term trend growth in 2002. Growth in the euro area and Japan is expected to slow marginally, though still maintain momentum in 2001 and 2002. (The risks to this baseline set of assumptions are discussed in detail in the next section.) Second, growth in world trade volume is expected to drop quite sharply in 2001 and then level off in 2002, while oil prices are assumed to remain in the $23–$28 per barrel range in 2001 and 2002. Third, macroeconomic policies in industrial countries are assumed to be supportive of the recovery to stronger growth in 2002 through an accommodative monetary and fiscal stance.

In Hong Kong, China; Singapore; and Taipei,China export growth is expected to slow sharply in 2001, with a negative impact on aggregate supply. Domestic demand growth will be weaker than in 2000, particularly in electronics-related private investment. Monetary policy is expected to remain accommodative. Strong trading relationships with the PRC will help offset the impact of slower exports to the rest of the world. GDP growth in these economies is forecast to decelerate to about 4.8 percent in 2001 before rising to around 5.7 percent in 2002.

In the five crisis-affected countries, export performance is likely to lose much momentum in 2001 as the global environment becomes less favorable and the boom in electronics moderates. As export growth slows, manufacturing and services will be adversely affected. The extent of the impact on domestic demand will depend both on the extent of the slowdown and on export dependence (see Box 1.3). While the use of fiscal policy is generally constrained by public debt burdens, monetary policy is expected to be accommodative to cushion the slowdown. GDP growth is forecast to decelerate sharply to below 4 percent in 2001 from 6.8 percent in 2000, and to recover to over 5.1 percent in 2002 (comparative forecasts for these countries are shown in Figure 1.5).

Driven by domestic demand growth, the PRC economy is forecast to slow somewhat, but still grow by over 7 percent in 2001 and 2002 led by strong performance in the industry and services sectors. Inflation is likely to be modest, investment rates high, and foreign investment strong. Export growth should slow as the global economy weakens and imports accelerate during the time that entry into the World Trade Organization brings a more liberal trade policy environment in its wake.

Growth in India will depend largely on the performance of agriculture and on the continued efficiency gains in the industry

Box 1.3 Effects of a US Slowdown on DMC Exporters

A slowdown in the US economy might have a significant effect on DMC exports beyond the impact measured by the proportion of total exports destined for the US market. This is because many of the DMCs are heavily involved in intraregional trade in electronic components. In the recession of 1991, when US GDP fell by 0.5 percent, its imports from Asia fell from a high of 9.8 percent growth (year on year) in the second quarter of 1989 to a contraction of 2.7 percent in the first quarter of 1991. Will the current slowdown in the US economy have a similar effect? The changes in the intervening decade to the structure of Asian exports to the US should be considered. The major exports from DMCs to the US are now manufactured goods, a large portion of which are electronics. These products fall within three broad classifications: industrial electronics (mainly microchip testing equipment), electronics components and parts (mainly semiconductors and microprocessors), and consumer electronics (predominantly personal computers). The box table gives the shares of electronics in total exports and of these three classifications in electronics exports. Except for the PRC and Indonesia, where electronics exports are a small fraction of total exports, the economies shown are strongly linked to the global and US electronics cycle.

In seven of the nine Asian economies reviewed, at least two thirds of electronics exports are in electronics components and parts. Only the PRC and Indonesia are concentrated in consumer electronics (85 percent) while Hong Kong, China; Korea; Singapore; and Taipei,China have 10–18 percent in industrial electronics. Thailand is roughly split between consumer electronics and electronics components. Forecasts for the next three years suggest that electronics components will continue to grow at a healthy rate but growth will fall from close to 40 percent in 2000 to 20–30 percent a year in 2001 and 2002. The growth in consumer electronics has been much slower, and is also likely to fall in the next two years.

Simulations of possible slowdown scenarios in global demand for these three subsectors suggest that export growth in Malaysia and the Philippines will be most adversely affected by a slowdown in the global demand for electronics, as they are heavily focused on electronics components. The PRC and Indonesia would be the least vulnerable, since electronics represent a smaller share of total exports. Taipei,China and Korea, followed by Malaysia and Singapore, would suffer the biggest reductions in GDP growth.

Box Table: Sector Distribution of Electronics Industry, Selected DMCs, 1999 and 2000
(percent)

Economy	Share of electronics exports in total exports[a]	Share in electronics exports		
		Industrial electronics[b]	Electronics components and parts[b]	Consumer electronics[b]
Singapore	64	10	89	1
Philippines	61	0	66	33
Malaysia	58	2	70	28
Taipei,China	46	15	80	5
Korea	38	18	78	4
Thailand	36	0	43	57
Hong Kong, China	33	12	70	18
PRC	24	0	15	85
Indonesia	14	0	15	85

[a] January–August 2000.
[b] 1999.

Source: CEIC Data Company Ltd.

sector as a result of policy reforms. While somewhat shielded from the global economic slowdown, exports will still be adversely affected. Assuming normal weather conditions and relaxed monetary policy, GDP growth in India for 2001 and 2002 is forecast to remain in the 6–7 percent range. In most of the other countries, the outlook is for slightly slower growth. Growth for South Asia as a whole should remain unchanged in 2001, at about 5.8 percent, improving somewhat in 2002.

In the Central Asian republics, Azerbaijan, and Mongolia, economic growth is expected to slow in 2001 and 2002 as oil prices soften somewhat and as demand slackens in the Commonwealth of Independent States for these countries' exports. This forecast assumes that the various governments will adopt further policy reforms to support growth and further liberalize their economies. Growth is projected to be in the range of about 3–5 percent in 2001 and 2002.

In Cambodia, Lao PDR, and Viet Nam, growth will depend on strength in agriculture, export prospects for garments, and a furtherance of stabilization measures to contain fiscal deficits and maintain stable prices. Growth is forecast at about 5–7 percent in 2001 and 2002.

In the Pacific DMCs, a gradual return to normalcy in the Fiji Islands and Solomon Islands and improved prospects for Papua New Guinea should provide a foundation for more sustained growth. The subregion is expected to grow by 3–5 percent in 2001 and 2002.

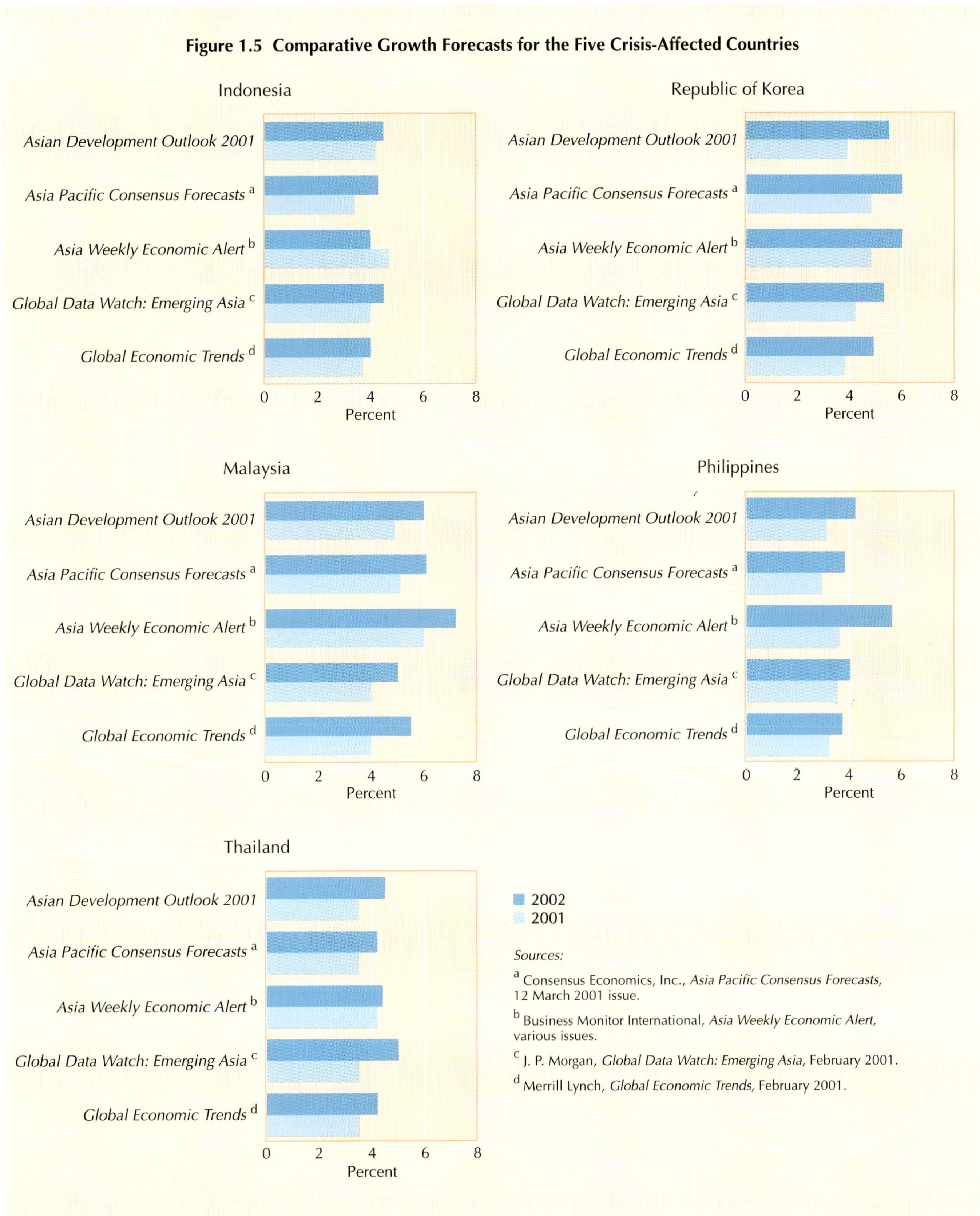

Figure 1.5 Comparative Growth Forecasts for the Five Crisis-Affected Countries

Sources:

[a] Consensus Economics, Inc., *Asia Pacific Consensus Forecasts*, 12 March 2001 issue.

[b] Business Monitor International, *Asia Weekly Economic Alert*, various issues.

[c] J. P. Morgan, *Global Data Watch: Emerging Asia*, February 2001.

[d] Merrill Lynch, *Global Economic Trends*, February 2001.

RISKS AND UNCERTAINTIES

The above projections are subject to a number of risks and uncertainties. The main external risks for DMCs in 2001 and 2002 relate to the prospects for the US economy. For some time, a key question has been the manner in which the US would make the transition from very rapid growth rates toward more moderate rates of expansion, often cast in terms of a "hard" or "soft" landing, and what a hard landing would imply. This question was central during 1998 and 1999 when the US economy was the main locomotive of global growth, given weakness in much of Europe, Japan, and the developing world. A sharp US slowdown at that time risked plunging the world into recession with adverse implications for many countries, including DMCs struggling to grow out of the 1997/98 financial crisis. In view of the broadening of the global recovery in 2000, the risks in this area have clearly receded, but have not entirely disappeared given the size and importance of the US economy and some fragilities in the rest of the world.

As noted earlier, key assumptions underlying the projections are that the current slowdown in the US will not be very severe—and that the other major industrial economies have sufficient momentum to keep the world economy growing at a satisfactory pace in 2001 and 2002 as the US recovers from its current weakness. Each of these assumptions can be considered in turn.

The expectation that the US slowdown will not be very severe or long-lived is based on the judgment that the macro-economic fundamentals in the US are strong and that the economy has very flexible product and factor markets. More-over, according to some observers, recent high levels of invest-ment in high technology there have permanently and significantly boosted the economy's potential growth rate. In an extreme version of this view, the current slowdown is essentially a modest "hiccup" and relatively rapid rates of growth will return quickly once current small inventory imbalances have been worked off and confidence returns.

There is some merit to this view. But there is also considerable uncertainty about the size of the "new economy" effects and the extent to which US productivity growth has been permanently raised. In addition, questions remain about the sustainability of continued very high valuations in the US stock market and the prospects for the dollar (in light of the large US current account deficit). It is possible that imbalances in these areas are small and could be reduced gradually, especially if new economy effects are very important. But the argument might also be plausibly made, based on historical experience, that the necessary adjustments could be large and disorderly with significant adverse effects on growth.

Partly in response to these uncertainties, the projections for the near-term outlook for the US economy have been made from the middle ground. On the one hand, it is assumed that the slowdown will be sharper and longer-lived than the hiccup assumed by new economy advocates. In addition, although the US growth rate over the medium term has been marked up to reflect new economy effects, a return to the relatively rapid growth rates of recent years is seen as unlikely. On the other hand, the projections assume no deep or long recession, such as might occur if the US economy faced a significant further stock market correction or if the dollar came under severe pressure. In the event of a more severe downturn, the US authorities have indicated their intention to apply monetary and fiscal measures to stimulate recovery. This might help provide a floor to US growth in 2001.

The other key assumption—that the other major industrial economies have sufficient momentum to keep the world economy growing—is based on the judgment that growth in Europe, and especially the euro area, has become sufficiently self-sustaining to withstand a slowdown in US imports. Various reasons for optimism can be put forward. Most important, the euro area is considerably more dependent on domestic demand than exports as a driver of growth, given the relatively low ratio of exports to GDP. In addition, reflecting significant structural reforms in recent years, the region has been enjoying an expansion led mainly by domestic demand, with generally impressive growth in consumption and investment and large reductions in unemployment rates. Beyond this, planned tax reductions in 2001 in the euro area, worth a little more than a net 0.5 percent of GDP, should help sustain domestic demand.

An important concern for the euro area, however, would be a sharp correction in the euro/dollar exchange rate due, for example, to unwillingness of investors to continue to finance the US current account deficit. Were the resulting appreciation of the euro to be very large and rapid, this could harm export competitiveness and growth. Although this is an important risk, it should not be exaggerated as some of the funds that previously financed the US deficit would no doubt move to the euro area. This would help boost European financial markets, offsetting somewhat the adverse implications of euro strength for external competitiveness. In addition, a stronger euro would provide the European Central Bank with additional room to lower short-term interest rates without compromising inflation objectives.

Although recent data for Japan suggest some faltering of the recovery in 2000, it is premature to conclude that the economy will slip back into recession. Indeed, the projections suggest that the recovery will remain largely on track in 2001—albeit at a slightly lower rate than in 2000—before picking up momentum again in 2002. There are, however, risks if the US economy makes a hard landing. Macroeconomic policies in Japan will need to remain accommodative and structural reform must be urgently accelerated.

Turning to the DMCs, the main external risks relate to the effects of slower growth in the US. Although the projections already take account of a US slowdown, the size of its effect is uncertain, given both the key role that the strong recent expansion in the US played in helping DMCs grow out of the 1997/98 financial crisis and the fragility of some of the recoveries in DMCs. In addition, there is uncertainty about the implications of the US slowdown for the terms and conditions of DMCs' access to international capital markets. The possibility of an increase in risk aversion and tighter terms for external financing cannot be excluded, especially if major stock markets remain volatile. This would have negative spillover effects on Asian financial markets and net capital flows.

As background, the 1997/98 financial crisis gave an important lesson to many DMCs on the risks of financial integration. Not surprisingly, therefore, concerns have been raised as to whether such a crisis could happen again in the event of a sharp deterioration in the external environment. As currencies and stock markets in a number of DMCs tumbled in the latter half of 2000, many commentators wondered whether the region was seeing a repeat of the earlier crisis.

There are several reasons for believing that the current situation is fundamentally different from that of 1997/98, and that another crisis is, therefore, extremely unlikely.

- First, and most important, the external shock that the region faces this year is primarily a real rather than a financial shock, related to the slowing in one of the regions' major export markets. Although export slowdowns played some role in triggering the 1997/98 crisis, the key factor at that time was a significant confidence-induced turnaround in the capital account following a period of strong capital inflows. Moreover, much of the turnaround in DMC capital accounts may already have taken place in 2000 as the effects on the region of the US slowdown started to become apparent.

- Second, reflecting policy reforms and adjustments since the financial crisis, many DMCs have considerably stronger external situations than a few years ago. In particular, in the case of the five economies most affected by the crisis, balance of payments on current account are in surplus, short-term external debt levels have been reduced in relation to international reserves, and international reserve positions are generally quite comfortable.

- Third, the structure of capital flows to many DMCs has changed since the mid-1990s with portfolio flows and relatively stable FDI largely replacing volatile short-term bank loans. Although portfolio flows also tend to be volatile, swings tend to be reflected to a significant degree in the prices of assets (equities and bonds) rather than in the capital flows themselves. They, therefore, generally have different implications to pullbacks of short-term bank credit that need to be repaid at face value.

- Fourth, many DMCs—including several with relatively open external capital accounts—have adopted more flexible exchange rate arrangements. In these cases, the exchange rate is able to play a larger role in adjusting the economy to external shocks. More flexible exchange rate arrangements also provide greater scope for monetary policy to moderate a growth slowdown.

- Fifth, many DMCs have embarked on comprehensive reform programs to enhance the safety and soundness of their financial systems and strengthen corporate sectors.

- Sixth, transparency has been improved considerably in many DMCs, making unlikely the reappearance of the kind of regionwide negative surprises that figured prominently in the 1997/98 crisis.

- Finally, the degree of leverage and the activities of investment hedge funds have been cut back in the last few years, making the intense speculative pressure that was evident in the earlier crisis less likely.

Against this background, the current situation appears quite different from that of 1997/98. Yet, this does not imply that DMCs should be complacent about the outlook for 2001. Even though the situation has improved considerably, some DMCs have new and different weaknesses from those in 1997/98 that might be important during any slowing of their recoveries. In this connection, it is useful to note some vulnerabilities that may have implications for how DMCs can be affected by the slowdown, such as:

- high dependence of recoveries in some DMCs on export growth (despite recent pickups in domestic demand);

- concentration of some DMCs' exports in a relatively few product groups, such as technology goods that are currently slowing sharply as the US weakens;

- incomplete progress in financial sector restructuring as reflected in either continued relatively high levels of NPLs and/or inadequate provisioning for bad loans;

- inadequate progress in corporate restructuring as reflected in poor profitability and/or continued high leverage ratios;

- unbalanced recoveries in which some domestic sectors (such as construction) and certain demand components (such as investment spending) have remained relatively weak, even with rapid GDP growth; and

- political difficulties and uncertainties that may impair DMCs' ability to deal effectively with the problems created by a growth slowdown, and that may hinder the pace of economic recovery and reform.

The extent of these vulnerabilities as well as their implications vary significantly across and within country groups in the region. Perhaps the most vulnerable countries are among the five most severely affected by the 1997/98 crisis. To varying degrees, these five countries have been undergoing a sharp "V-shaped" rebound in the last three years and recording, in many cases, very impressive growth. Initially, the recovery was driven mainly by exports, as domestic demand remained very weak due to difficulties in domestic financial and corporate sectors. Subsequently, domestic demand has tended to pick up as recoveries have matured, especially in those DMCs that have made significant progress in financial and corporate restructuring. However, domestic demand has in some cases been largely driven by spillovers from the export sector, rather than autonomous factors.

Moreover, even though consumption spending has risen in some of the five DMCs, fixed investment has generally remained weak and, in many cases, is below precrisis levels. The ability of these five DMCs to sustain growth will depend on their capacity to strengthen domestic demand and increase exports to the faster-growing regions of the world. While there may be room for fiscal stimulus in some cases, that room has generally become more limited given the high budgetary costs of financial sector recapitalization. In these circumstances, it will be important for these five DMCs to move ahead with needed structural reforms to facilitate a "crowding in" of private domestic demand, including investment spending. Where appropriate, this can be supported by an easing of monetary conditions. Although there is some uncertainty about how some of these DMCs will cope with the slowdown, the situation is manageable in all five cases.

The other DMCs likely to be significantly affected by the US slowdown are Hong Kong, China; Singapore; and Taipei,China. For the most part, however, the situation in these economies is very different from that in the five crisis-affected countries. These three NIEs were less severely affected by the Asian financial crisis and thus are not undertaking the kinds of broad recovery programs adopted by the other five. Moreover,

these three economies generally have much stronger and sounder financial systems, as they are not in the process of being nurtured back to good health. Like the five countries, however, recent growth has generally been heavily dependent on exports, including technology items, and their exports are generally expected to slow sharply in 2001, contributing to lower GDP growth that year before a rebound in 2002. In particular, in the cases of Hong Kong, China and Taipei,China, expected continued strong growth in the PRC will help moderate the slowdown.

Finally, the PRC and India will obviously be affected by the US slowdown given the importance of exports in their recent expansions. In addition, each economy, to varying degrees, has benefited from the technology boom. At the same time, however, each country has a substantial nontraded sector and domestic demand has been driven significantly by the implementation of economic reforms and supportive domestic macroeconomic policies. If exports slow rapidly, growth could be sustained in these countries through the implementation of domestic structural reforms and, to the extent that medium-term sustainability is not compromised, through continued supportive fiscal policies. In general, the ability of these two countries to sustain growth is likely to be much greater than in the case of the five crisis-affected countries. And indeed, by maintaining domestic demand growth, the PRC and India can help provide economic stability to the region.

The effects of the US slowdown on DMCs will depend heavily on the behavior of intraregional trade. This has grown significantly over the last decade and can play a role in reducing the region's vulnerability to external factors, such as a slowdown in the US. Whether intraregional trade will, in practice, play such a role will depend on its composition and the factors driving its growth. Hence, for example, if it has been driven mainly by autonomous demand in the region, it might be expected to provide a significant buffer to an external slowdown. Conversely, if outsourcing of production for the region's exports has driven its growth, then it may be less resilient. Based on available data, a sizable share of intraregional trade seems to involve intermediate inputs. Even though this implies that, if such trade will not necessarily be a major buffer to a US slowdown, it does not rule out a stabilizing influence, especially if the PRC and India show continued strong domestic demand growth.

PART II

Economic Trends and Prospects in Developing Asia

Newly Industrialized Economies

Growth in the newly industrialized economies (NIEs) accelerated to 8.4 percent in 2000 from 7.9 percent in 1999 as the subregion further recovered from the Asian financial crisis. Rapid export growth led the expansion, supported by strong investment spending and a moderate increase in consumption. The economic performance of the four economies was more consistently broad based relative to 1999 as Hong Kong, China; Republic of Korea (Korea); and Singapore all recorded similar growth rates of about 9–10 percent.

Exports were boosted by robust demand from the US. For the subregion, the rate of growth in shipments increased to 19.6 percent in 2000 from 5.5 percent in the previous year. The rapid increase in demand for exports triggered a surge in domestic investment, especially in the electronics sector. Gross capital spending was particularly strong in Korea; Singapore; and Taipei,China. In the latter two economies, investment spending rose strongly after very weak performance in 1999. Private consumption spending rose as consumer confidence increased, labor markets tightened, and property prices firmed.

On the supply side, the industry sector performed well in Korea; Singapore; and Taipei,China, buoyed by production in the high-technology sector, particularly electronics. In Hong Kong, China supply-side growth was led by the services sector, while the relocation of manufacturing to nearby mainland provinces continued.

Despite a rise in interest rates in industrial countries in the first half of 2000, monetary policy was basically neutral and there was little interest rate volatility. Korea and Singapore maintained relatively flat rates throughout the year, while Hong Kong, China generally kept pace with interest rate developments in the US. Fiscal policy was tightened during the year, partly because rapid growth brought in more taxes than anticipated. The fiscal surplus increased in Singapore; the deficit fell in Taipei,China; and the deficit turned into a surplus in Korea.

Inflation remained subdued in the subregion, though some upward movement toward the end of the year was seen in response to higher world oil prices. However, capacity utilization rates remained comparatively low in contrast to the years before the financial crisis and had a moderating effect on inflation, as did generally tighter fiscal policy. In Korea, for example, the rate of capacity utilization was around 70 percent. In Hong Kong, China, fierce competition in the retail sector led to price deflation.

Although net exports made a positive contribution to growth in the NIEs, the size of this contribution diminished, from a peak of around 7 percentage points on average in 1998, to about 2 percentage points in 2000. This is primarily because imports also grew quite rapidly, reflecting a combination of restocking of intermediate inputs and, increasingly, of rising demand for consumer goods, as domestic demand conditions improved. The onset of the global electronics downturn in the last quarter of 2000 further weakened the contribution of net exports to overall growth, and was a factor in the modest reduction in the subregional current account surplus. Nevertheless, the surplus remained substantial at $40 billion or 4.7 percent of GDP. The export boom was aided by a modest amount of currency depreciation (aside from Hong Kong, China where the rate is fixed against the US dollar) ranging from just over 4 percent in Taipei,China to nearly 7 percent in Korea (December to December).

As the NIEs are small open economies with a substantial international trade share of GDP, their prospects depend largely on external developments in industrial countries. As early as October 2000, softness in global electronics demand had already begun to have an effect: in Singapore and Taipei,China industrial production slowed, while in Korea the deceleration started a month later. As external demand weakened in the last quarter of the year, equity price indices for three of the NIEs ended the year lower in 2000 than in 1999. The Hang Seng Index finished 11 percent weaker, while the Taiwan Weighted Stock Exchange Index and the Singapore Straits Times 55 Index dropped by 36 percent and 22 percent, respectively.

In 2001, GDP growth is likely to fall back to just over 4 percent for the group. Slower export growth will be the main cause of this: from 19.6 percent in 2000, it is projected to fall to 7.5 percent. Slower export growth translates into a slowdown in domestic consumption and investment. The inventory cycle will also play a role in taking investment lower as firms work off excess inventories as external demand softens. Nevertheless, some additional investment in the high-technology sector is expected as the NIEs invest in new equipment and processes to enhance productivity and to take advantage of developments in the new economy. Of particular interest are the general increases in investment in research and development; the greater investment in human resources in the technology area; the growth of technology parks in both Hong Kong, China and Singapore; the expansion of information and communications technology (ICT) infrastructure in Korea; and the attraction of higher value-added firms in the electronics industry to Singapore. Furthermore, the strong performance of the People's Republic of China and its strong trade linkages with Hong Kong, China and with Taipei,China should provide a partial buffer for these two economies. Governments are also likely to adopt appropriate macroeconomic policies to soften the downturn. Across the NIEs, monetary policy is expected to ease more and interest rates may fall further. Fiscal stimulus is more likely in Korea and Singapore than in Hong Kong, China and Taipei,China.

Economic restructuring will continue in the NIEs as they make the transition toward higher value-added and technology-intensive products and services. This will involve additional investment in new plant and equipment and in research and development. Sophisticated services-based activities and broad-ened diffusion of ICT pose challenges to those workers with fewer skills and lower education. Further upgrading of the workforce will be needed, particularly at the post-secondary level. Greater investment in physical infrastructure, particularly in the ICT sector, will also be required.

In the financial sector, especially banking, the NIEs face a variety of challenges, from overcrowding, low profitability, and growth of nonperforming loans in Taipei,China; to the continued problem of restructuring of financial and corporate institutions in Korea; to the development of domestic capital markets in Singapore; and to the strengthening of the regulatory framework and increasing efficiency through greater competition in securities and futures markets in Hong Kong, China. To meet these challenges, flexible policies will have to be developed to deal with a rapidly changing and potentially volatile external environment.

Hong Kong, China

Hong Kong, China's high rate of economic growth in 2000 was broad based, characterized by a surge in external demand and a significant rebound in domestic demand. Prospects over the longer term will be influenced by the accelerating trend toward globalization fueled both by technological advances and by economic developments after the accession of the People's Republic of China to the World Trade Organization.

Recent Trends and Prospects

The modest recovery of 1999 accelerated in 2000, to yield real GDP growth of 10.5 percent, compared with 3.1 percent growth in 1999 and a contraction of 5.3 percent in 1998. The underlying momentum was brought about by a buoyant external sector, which was partly responsible for expansion in both private consumption and domestic investment.

Private consumption rose by 5.4 percent in real terms in 2000, due to improved real income flows and employment expansion. Overall investment spending picked up by 8.8 percent in 2000 after contracting by 17.4 percent in 1999, on the back of private sector machinery and equipment acquisition, which rebounded sharply by 27.4 percent in real terms, and steady replenishment of inventories. These improvements were supported by strengthening investment sentiment as business prospects brightened. Public investment expenditure on building and construction declined, partly due to a scaling back of the public housing program. Private investment spending in this area was constrained by property market slackness that began in the third quarter of 1998.

The decline in manufacturing production moderated to an estimated 1 percent in 2000, based on stronger domestic exports. In the first three quarters, output of wearing apparel and textiles both rose by 3 percent in volume terms. Output from fabricated metal products and plastic products declined by 18 percent and 11 percent, respectively, reflecting the ongoing relocation of manufacturing to nearby mainland provinces and rising world oil prices. The dominant services sector strengthened. The upturn in external trade boosted growth in the transport and trade sectors, while an improvement in inbound tourism led to growth in hotels and communications. In the first three quarters of 2000, business receipts of the banking sector rose moderately by 4 percent in value terms, due to reduced mortgage interest income in line with a contraction in the real estate sector and keen competition in the mortgage market, while the nonbanking financial sector surged by 56 percent, benefiting from renewed net inflows of foreign capital.

In spite of the strengthening economic recovery, prices continued to fall. The Composite Consumer Price Index declined by 3.7 percent in 2000. Fierce retail price competition, a fall in apartment rents, and the continued freeze in government fees contributed to the sustained fall in the Index. Another element was the decline in the prices of retained imports of foodstuffs and consumer goods. The rise in international oil prices and local transport prices, particularly in the third quarter, brought in some inflationary pressures, but not enough to push the economy away from the deflationary environment of the previous year.

The residential property market was constrained in an environment of weak demand and expanding supply. Yet sentiment improved somewhat in this market over the middle months of the year, on the announcement of a program of adjustment by the Housing Authority, favorable mortgage loan packages, and an expanded mortgage insurance program. Nevertheless, property prices and rentals in 2000 remained about 50 percent and 30 percent lower, respectively, than their peaks prior to the onset of the Asian financial crisis in 1997.

Generally, financial sector growth improved. Under the linked exchange rate system, the Hong Kong dollar moved closely with the US dollar against other major currencies. Nominal interest rates were on a general upward trend, reflecting US interest rate hikes during the first half of 2000 and the upsurge in international oil prices. The volume of Hong Kong dollar and foreign currency deposits rose by 5 percent and 15 percent, respectively, reflecting increased US interest rates and export receipts. However, total loan demand continued to fall, by 12 percent in 2000, with the contraction in foreign currency loans for use outside the local market. The proportion of classified loans (i.e., substandard and doubtful loans, and losses) in total loans fell to 7.3 percent, because of the economic recovery and the write-offs of loans by banks. The capital adequacy ratio remained healthy, averaging 18 percent.

With a bullish outlook on telecommunications and technology stocks, the Hang Seng Index reached an all-time high of over 18,000 in late March 2000, and then began to decline because of interest rate hikes by the US Federal Reserve, the oil price surge, and corrections in other major stock markets. Overall equity prices, as measured by the Hang Seng Index, fell by 11 percent during the course of 2000.

The fiscal balance unexpectedly moved to a surplus of HK$10.0 billion in fiscal year (FY) 1999/2000, with strong earnings growth on fiscal reserve investment amid a buoyant stock market recovery in 1999. Nevertheless, the operating budget has experienced deficits since FY1998/99. The operating deficit is now expected to be at HK$19.2 billion in FY2000/2001, lower than the HK$25.0 billion originally estimated.

Partly the result of the previous economic contraction, successive operating deficits have raised concerns about the tax system. The base appears to be narrow and shrinking. In June 2000, the authorities launched a review of public finance to assess whether the operating deficits are cyclical or structural in nature. Studies on the tax base and new broad-based taxes to provide more stable revenues are also being conducted.

Total exports of goods attained growth of 16.1 percent in 2000. This reflected mainly a broad-based strengthening of import demand in major overseas markets, and improved price competitiveness of exports following the downward adjustments in prices and production costs in the local economy. Fueled by significant reexport growth and an expansion of retained imports, merchandise imports rose markedly by 18.5 percent, which more than offset the growth in merchandise exports. Services exports remained robust in 2000, rising by 13.3 percent, amid continued increases in exports of trade-related and other business services, offshore trading activities,

and inbound tourism. Services imports registered modest growth of 2.1 percent over the year, reflecting the relatively slower recovery of domestic demand. The deficit of trade in goods increased to US$11.4 billion, while the surplus of trade in services increased to US$19.1 billion. Taken together, the combined goods and services trade account still showed an appreciable surplus, at US$7.7 billion in 2000 (including an estimate of imports of gold for industrial use), though smaller than US$8.5 billion in 1999.

With the sustained pickup in overall economic activity, labor demand further strengthened, and greater employment levels in services and construction more than compensated for declines in manufacturing. The seasonally adjusted unemployment rate continued on a decline from its peak of 6.3 percent toward mid-1999 to 4.4 percent at end-2000. Nominal wages and earnings rebounded modestly to positive year-on-year growth by the second quarter of 2000, having stayed virtually flat over the previous 12 months or so.

The economy is expected to slow, to 4.0 percent growth in 2001, as the US economy slows. With more government infrastructure projects scheduled to start and stronger growth in private sector investment propelled by the development of the knowledge-based economy and the accession of the People's Republic of China (PRC) to the World Trade Organization, gross fixed investment will probably accelerate more rapidly during the next two years. Continued economic recovery will allow further employment generation.

Prices are likely to increase in 2001 by 1.0 percent, largely as a result of continued expansionary monetary policy. Real

Table 2.1 Major Economic Indicators, Hong Kong, China, 1998–2002
(percent)

Item	1998	1999	2000	2001	2002
GDP growth	-5.3	3.1	10.5	4.0	5.5
Gross domestic investment/GDP	29.0	25.1	27.5	26.2	29.0
Gross domestic savings/GDP	30.1	30.5	32.2	32.7	30.0
Inflation rate	2.8	-4.0	-3.7	1.0	4.0
Central government budget/GDP	-1.8	0.8	-0.9	-0.2	-0.1
Money supply (M2) growth	11.8	8.1	8.8	10.0	12.0
Merchandise export growth[a]	-7.5	-0.1	16.1	5.3	8.5
Merchandise import growth[a]	-11.6	-2.7	18.5	4.7	9.0
Services export growth[a]	-5.9	4.4	13.3	6.4	7.0
Services import growth[a]	1.0	-0.8	2.1	0.9	5.0

[a] Based on GDP series, in nominal US$.

Sources: Government of Hong Kong Special Administrative Region; staff estimates.

interest rates are likely to fall in 2001, due to eased deflationary pressure in the local market and interest rate cuts by the US Federal Reserve. The improvements in the external sector should continue, though at a slower rate, as growth of neighboring economies remains solid.

Issues in Economic Management

The forces of globalization and technological advancement that are shaping the financial landscape are having a profound influence on the long-term development of Hong Kong, China. The dismantling of entry barriers to markets, the availability of low-cost, high-speed transport, and the dramatic impact of advances in information and communications technology (ICT) have challenged the effectiveness of domestic market regulations.

The task facing the authorities is to strengthen the effectiveness of the regulatory framework as traditional boundaries melt away and to improve efficiency and innovation through a more open environment conducive to competition with safeguards to ensure continued stability of the financial sector. In banking, the authorities have developed policies to remove unnecessary market entry restrictions, improve transparency, and deregulate the rules for setting interest rates. The first phase of interest rate deregulation for short-term time deposits was implemented in 2000, while the restrictions on savings deposit interest rates will be lifted in 2001, depending on the economic and financial conditions at the time. This will encourage efficiency in pricing and provide incentives for bank mergers and acquisitions to enhance competitiveness. Measures to enhance stability were also undertaken. The Hong Kong Monetary Authority clarified its role as lender of last resort. A study to improve depositor protection was completed in 2000. Although a depositor protection scheme would provide a safety net for the banking system, the financial costs and the risk of moral hazard associated with the scheme would need to be carefully considered.

A three-pronged reform to enhance competitiveness and strengthen risk-based supervisory regime in securities and futures markets was announced by the authorities in 1999 in the face of global changes. The reform includes (i) enhancing market infrastructure, (ii) modernizing the market structure through the demutualization and merger of the two exchanges and three clearinghouses, and (iii) modernizing and rationalizing the legal framework for the regulatory regime. On market infrastructure enhancement, a number of short-term measures have already been completed, which among other things, enable the electronic submission of returns by intermediaries to the regulator. The Steering Committee on the Enhancement of the Financial Infrastructure is considering the possibility of introducing straight-through processing, scripless trading, and a single clearing system for securities transactions. In terms of market structure modernization, the exchanges and clearinghouses were demutualized and merged under the name of Hong Kong Exchanges and Clearing Limited on 6 March 2000. The merged entity was listed on the stock exchange on 27 June 2000. The merger has produced a new market structure that should achieve greater efficiency, cost reduction, and better risk management, and facilitate development of new products and services. As regards regulatory reform, the Securities and Futures Bill that consolidates and modernizes 10 existing pieces of legislation governing the securities and futures market was introduced into the legislature in November 2000. The Bill seeks to provide a more transparent and coherent regulatory regime in line with international standards and practice.

A US dollar clearing system was developed in 2000. It is expected to promote the issuance and trading of US dollar-denominated stock and debt securities in Hong Kong, China and to support its position as an international financial center.

All these structural changes are expected to deepen liquidity and investor participation in the market, reinforcing Hong Kong, China's position as the PRC's main window for international capital raising. Continued policy initiatives that enhance effective management by the banks themselves as well as careful monitoring by banking supervisors will also be needed. The financial sector reforms, which aim at enhancing competitiveness and tapping the enormous opportunities brought about by globalization and the knowledge-based economy, will further support Hong Kong, China's long-term vision of itself as a global financial center.

Policy and Development Issues

The economy began its transition in the 1980s when manufacturing activities moved across the border after the PRC opened to foreign investment. The share of manufacturing employment in total employment fell from 38 percent in 1982 to only 7 percent in the first three quarters of 2000. In contrast, the proportion of employment in the services sector went up from 51 percent to 82 percent of the total over the same period, mirroring both the accelerated trade flow between the PRC and the rest of the world, and the continued orientation of the economy toward services.

The impact on employment of these structural adjustments was aggravated by the financial crisis. Weaker reexports caused by lower regional trade volumes, falling property values, and slowing private consumption raised unemployment in the services and construction sectors. In more recent years, as the economy underwent restructuring toward services- and knowledge-based activities, unemployment for low-income workers stayed at relatively high levels. As part of this restructuring, deregulation in banking and telecommunications initiated competition, that led to an increasing emphasis on efficiency and high value-added economic activities performed by high-skilled labor. The rapid rise of the knowledge-based economy, especially ICT, has led to great demand for well-trained talent with specialized skills required for technological development and application. However, the majority of the low-income workforce lack the skills and educational background to adapt to the new economy. Statistics show that the lowest paid 20 percent of the employed population suffered a fall in employment earnings of 18 percent in real terms between 1990 and 1999, with much of this decrease occurring in the late 1990s during the financial crisis. The top 10 percent (in earnings terms) of the employed population, however, enjoyed a 43 percent increase in earnings in real terms during 1990–1999, partly because they appeared relatively less affected by the crisis due to consistently strong demand for workers with greater skills and a better education.

To relieve the shortage of ICT talent in the short run, the authorities may need to formulate a policy for importing professionals. The attraction and maintenance of a concentration of highly skilled and motivated immigrants from all parts of the world could be a crucial component of a comprehensive strategy to maintain a dynamic economy. If the economy is to emerge as one of the world's technology centers, existing entry barriers in immigration policy need to be removed.

However, the long-term policy strategy to address these problems at the source should include reform of the education system and curriculum to enhance labor flexibility and skill levels. The Education Commission proposed a comprehensive reform package in 2000, covering education from early childhood to continuing level. The proposed measures include broadening the spectrum by updating the school curriculum, improving the format and content of public examinations, and revising the systems of admission for primary and secondary schools. In addition, the Government has set a target of enabling 60 percent of senior secondary graduates to have access to higher education opportunities, including degree and subdegree programs.

The long-term development of the economy and its competitiveness will depend critically on the success of these education reforms and the adoption of a proper set of educational priorities and strategies. The authorities should consider the involvement of more private initiatives in the provision of education facilities to supplement those supported by public funding. The Education Department should decentralize decision making further to individual educational institutions, including selection of students, choice of instructional medium, and specific subject curricula. These measures are essential for the ongoing transformation of Hong Kong, China into a knowledge-based economy.

Republic of Korea

The strong pace of the 1999 economic recovery continued into early 2000. However, the rate of economic growth began to ebb in the second half of the year as optimism about the pace of reforms started to fade and external demand growth slowed. Real GDP grew by an estimated 8.8 percent in 2000, but is expected to slow to 3.9 percent in 2001 before picking up in 2002. Long-term stability depends crucially on continued and steadfast implementation of financial and corporate restructuring.

Recent Trends and Prospects

In 2000, the economy of the Republic of Korea (Korea) continued its impressive recovery from the 1998 recession, led by rapid growth in the value of both total exports and equipment investment. Real GDP expanded by a robust 8.8 percent in 2000, moderating from the very strong 10.9 percent rate of growth in 1999. Yet this strong annual performance masked a significant weakening in the economy in the fourth quarter of 2000. Because of a rapid fall in the expansion of external demand, annual growth in total export value (in dollar terms) fell from 26.6 percent in September to 1.4 percent in December. Changing external conditions, labor strife, and slow corporate restructuring eroded investor and consumer confidence. Annual equipment investment is estimated to have dropped from 38.1 percent growth in August to a contraction of 2.1 percent in December, to give a figure for the year of 29.3 percent. Growth in real final consumption expenditures fell steadily throughout the year, with consumption of durable goods contracting in the fourth quarter.

The industry sector led the economic expansion in 2000. The industrial production index, which tracks manufacturing activity, increased by 16.6 percent, below the 24.2 percent pace of 1999 because of the sharp slowdown in manufacturing growth in the fourth quarter (see Figure 2.1). Construction activity contracted for the third year in a row, though the rate of contraction slowed toward the end of the year. Electricity production rose to 12.0 percent from 9.1 percent in 1999 as industrial and residential demand grew.

Wholesale and retail trade growth moderated throughout the year, matching the slower growth of consumption. The transport and communications sector continued its rapid double-digit expansion in 2000, fueled by the greater popularity of mobile phones and Internet services. Growth of value added in financial, insurance, real estate, and other business services was slower than in 1999 and declined throughout the year.

On the external side, the current account was in surplus for the third year in a row, but narrowing from 12.7 percent of GDP in 1998 to 6.0 percent in 1999 and to 2.4 percent in 2000 as the recovery brought rapid growth of imports in both 1999 and 2000. Merchandise exports grew by 21.1 percent in 2000 but merchandise imports surged by 36.3 percent, cutting the trade surplus to $16.6 billion from $28.4 billion in 1999. Heavy industry products (including chemicals, machinery, electrical and electronic products, semiconductors, and automobiles), which account for over 70 percent of exports, accelerated to over 20 percent growth in 2000 compared with 15 percent in 1999. This, combined with a partial recovery in light industry exports (about 20 percent of exports by value) of about 2.5 percent growth from the previous year's 8.5 percent contraction, accounted for the surge in exports.

The capital account, which experienced a deficit of $3.2 billion in 1998 as a result of capital outflows, improved to show a surplus of $2 billion in 1999. With sustained high growth, the capital account continued in surplus throughout the first three quarters of 2000 but fell into deficit in the fourth quarter as investor confidence slipped. Overall, the capital account surplus was estimated at $11.7 billion in 2000. As a result of the combined current and capital account surpluses, foreign exchange reserves rose from $74 billion in late 1999 to about $96 billion at end-2000. Reflecting the fourth quarter deterioration, the monthly average exchange rate of the won depreciated against the dollar by 6.5 percent between December 1999 and December 2000. After strengthening to W1,110 per dollar in April, the exchange rate weakened to W1,216 per dollar in December 2000 due to the slowdown in growth, delayed structural reforms, and the rapid increase in world oil prices.

Reflecting high economic growth, unemployment dropped from an annual average of 6.3 percent in 1999 to 4.1 percent in 2000. However, much of this improvement took place in the fourth quarter of 1999, in which the seasonally adjusted annual GDP growth rate peaked at 14 percent. On a seasonally adjusted basis, the unemployment rate stood at 4.4 percent in January 2000, bottomed out at 3.7 percent in June, and rose back to 4.0 percent in December. The growth rate of nominal wages slowed to the high single digits in 2000 compared with a 12.1 percent increase in 1999. In contrast, annual average consumer price inflation, at about 5.5 percent during 1994–1998, rose from a low of 0.8 percent in 1999 to 2.3 percent in 2000. This was a result of the combination of the external influence of rising oil prices and the internal influence of rising agricultural prices reflecting poor, weather-affected harvests.

Monetary policy was generally tight in 2000. With an inflation target of 2.5 percent, the Bank of Korea raised short-term interest rates in February and October 2000 to lower the spread between short- and long-term rates in an effort to reduce the concentration of funds at the short end of the market. This was done despite concerns about liquidity problems faced by large corporations. The Bank of Korea was concerned about signs of a rising core inflation rate (i.e., excluding oil and food). The overnight call rate was raised from 4.74 percent a year in January to 5.31 percent in December, while the three-year treasury bond rate fell from 9.3 percent to 7.16 percent. Although the supply of broad money (M2) grew at a fairly rapid pace of about 26 percent through the year, M3, which includes various financial market instruments, expanded by 5.5 percent, much slower than the rate of economic growth.

Fiscal policy tightened in the second year of high growth as the consolidated government budget recorded a surplus for the first time since 1996, at 1.1 percent of GDP. This was achieved through a 23.7 percent increase in total revenues, while the growth of total expenditures plus net lending was contained at 5.8 percent. In particular, income, profit, and capital gains tax collection showed a 40.3 percent gain in 2000, as corporate income tax payments surged with the economic revival and the resulting increase in corporate income. On the other side of the account, current expenditures increased more rapidly than capital expenditures due to a 9.4 percent increase in transfers to local governments, nonprofit institutions, and households. Current expenditure represented about 65 percent of the current budget.

Real GDP growth is forecast to fall sharply to about 4 percent in 2001, before recovering to perhaps 5.5 percent in 2002. Private consumption is projected to experience low single-digit growth in 2001 as a result of lower consumer confidence, higher unemployment, and negative wealth effect of a weaker stock market (in which average prices fell by about 9 percent in 2000). Equipment investment is expected to contract in 2001. However, net exports will be relatively strong in 2001, since the won is still undervalued in terms of its real effective exchange rate and foreign demand is likely to remain fairly buoyant despite the anticipated slowdown in the US. The Bank of Korea's inflation target is 3.0 percent for 2001 to allow for an accommodative monetary policy. Fiscal policy is expected to be expansionary in 2001.

Issues in Economic Management

The Government is currently implementing a coordinated, two-pronged reform program that aims to restructure the financial and corporate sectors simultaneously. The financial sector program was designed in two phases to strengthen enforcement of prudential regulations and capital adequacy requirements in the financial sector, so that financial institutions will in turn put pressure on firms to accomplish debt-reduction and business-restructuring measures. In the first phase, which began after the 1997 Asian financial crisis, the Government initiated and

Table 2.2 Major Economic Indicators, Republic of Korea, 1998–2002
(percent)

Item	1998	1999	2000	2001	2002
GDP growth	-6.7	10.9	8.8	3.9	5.5
Gross domestic investment/GDP	21.2	26.7	28.7	29.0	29.5
Gross domestic savings/GDP	33.9	32.7	30.9	31.0	30.0
Inflation rate (consumer price index)	7.5	0.8	2.3	3.0	2.5
Money supply (M2) growth	27.0	27.4	25.7	27.0	24.0
Fiscal balance/GDP	-4.2	-2.7	1.1	-1.0	-0.1
Merchandise export growth	-4.7	9.9	21.1	9.0	10.5
Merchandise import growth	-36.2	29.1	36.3	8.0	13.0
Current account balance/GDP	12.7	6.0	2.4	1.9	1.1

Sources: Bank of Korea; staff estimates.

implemented measures designed to (i) restructure the financial industry, (ii) liberalize and augment the capital market, and (iii) strengthen prudential regulation and supervision. Through this program, the number of banks has fallen from 33 to 22 through mergers, closures, and nationalization. In addition, with W100 trillion in public funds, the Government has raised capital adequacy ratios to above 8 percent and reduced their nonperforming loan ratios. However, weak loan classification standards may be masking the real extent of the problem.

The second phase of financial sector restructuring began in late 2000 with the creation of financial holding companies and the decision to inject an additional W40 trillion into the banking sector. The Government is also encouraging mergers among the better run banks that have had no injection of public money to enlarge bank size and strengthen their competitiveness.

To ensure that public money is efficiently used, the Special Law on the Management of Public Money was promulgated on 20 December 2000. However, improving efficiency of the banking system will be difficult since it requires strong independent management expertise in a banking system that is accustomed to accommodating government policy directives. To sustain balance sheet gains following financial restructuring, banks will have to improve business practices, particularly with respect to evaluating potential borrowers and analyzing risk. The Government's large equity holdings should eventually be replaced by private sector equity, including that from abroad.

The second plank of the economic reform program—corporate sector restructuring—also started right after the financial crisis began. It focused on three aspects: (i) improving management transparency and corporate governance structure, (ii) allowing financial institutions to assume the lead role in corporate sector restructuring, and (iii) restructuring the *chaebol* (conglomerates). The introduction of "forward-looking criteria" as an element in asset classification put banks' potential nonperforming loans on their balance sheets. Consequently, banks' credit monitoring has been strengthened, and some of their troubled debtor companies were forced to close in 2000. Also, based on a credit inspection of companies conducted in November 2000, the Government has made specific plans for 52 firms on the brink of bankruptcy, including liquidation, court receivership, and sale of the firms.

However, the restructuring of larger companies has been difficult and the corporate sector remains weak. The failure of the planned acquisition of Daewoo Motor had a large negative impact on the stock market. Also, Hyundai Construction has continued to receive new credit despite concerns that the company is financially weak. Debt-equity ratios in the corporate sector are still high, profitability is low, and the level of nonperforming loans remains high. Thus, the corporate sector is particularly vulnerable to the slowing of the economy and the associated reduction in profit growth.

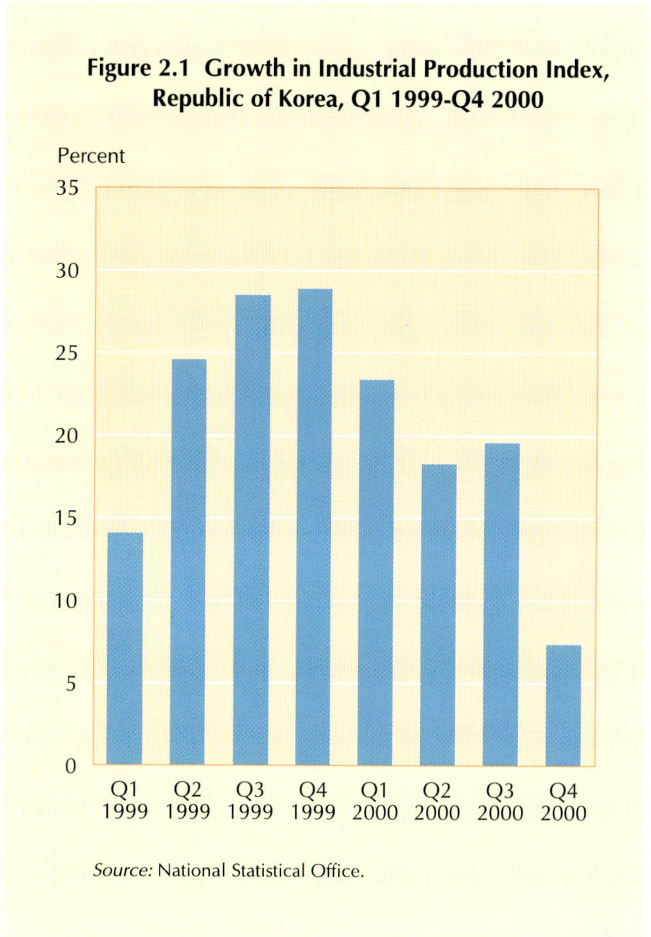

Source: National Statistical Office.

Policy and Development Issues

In the longer term, the Government recognizes that it must take on the task of redefining its role in promoting economic growth. Recent events indicate that, in the financial and corporate sectors, the Government is finding this task difficult. Around the time of the financial crisis in 1997/98, a large number of corporate bonds were issued and most of them will mature in 2001. To prevent them from paralyzing the bond market when corporations attempt to roll them over, the Government provided investment trust companies with credit guarantees to ensure that the maturing bonds are purchased. The Korean Industrial Bank was directed to purchase a significant portion of the bonds. However, this policy has drawn criticism because six of the initial companies to receive support from the Korean Industrial Bank in January 2001 consisted of four Hyundai subsidiaries, and two cement companies. Two of the subsidiaries and the two cement companies are in a weak financial condition. This raised the specter of moral hazard created by using public money to support failing companies.

While it attempts to disengage from the financial and corporate sectors, the Government has been promoting information and communications technology (ICT). Korea is already one of the world's largest producers of ICT products for export. At the same time, the Government has been encouraging the development of the domestic market. The dramatic increase of Internet access has largely been the result of government initiatives, such as sponsoring research and development on ICT, strengthening infrastructure by laying more high-speed telecommunications lines, encouraging foreign investment in ICT, deregulating telecommunications, and simplifying procedures for Internet startup firms.

The proportion of Internet users in Korea is estimated now to be about 35 percent of the population, one of the highest rates in the world. As demand for Internet services has surged, the number of Internet service providers has also soared, from about 23 in 1998 to more than 80 in 2000. Because the industry is relatively new, turnover is still high among the small and medium-sized Internet service and content providers, reducing consumer confidence. Moreover, ICT firms tend to be concentrated in Seoul. To help balance ICT development geographically, the Government intends to set up what it calls "information technology towns". A super high-speed telecommunications network will link the information technology towns.

To further develop its ICT infrastructure, the Government plans to expand its ICT-related investments from the current 1.2 percent of GDP to 3.0 percent over the next five years in an attempt to raise national competitiveness to the level of the industrial countries. This is part of its overall aim to weave the use of the Internet into many areas of the economy so as to spur national competitiveness. However, the Government should plan these investments with care given the recently demonstrated volatility of the global ICT market.

Singapore

After strong GDP performance in 2000 on the back of an export boom in electronics, growth momentum is likely to moderate in 2001. However, with a strong fiscal position and a highly competitive economy, Singapore is expected to weather the slowdown in world economic growth well. After this, its investments in education and telecommunications infrastructure as well as liberalization measures should enable the economy to continue robust expansion.

Recent Trends and Prospects

In 2000, Singapore's real GDP growth surged to 9.9 percent from 5.9 percent in 1999 as growth in real total demand (i.e., domestic demand plus exports) more than doubled to 14.0 percent from 6.5 percent. Stronger external demand accounted for nearly 80 percent of the growth because of strong global demand for manufactured exports, particularly integrated circuit boards, and because of a rising volume of trade flowing through Singapore's ports, fueling a rapid rise in services exports. Domestic demand also accelerated as investor and consumer confidence rose. Real gross fixed capital formation recovered from two years of contraction with a 5.9 percent improvement, while consumption spending, benefiting from rising income, expanded by 10.3 percent. By sector, the percentage contributions to real GDP growth were largest in manufacturing (3.9 percentage points), due primarily to electronics exports, and in retail and wholesale trade (2.5 percentage points), largely because of entrepôt trade.

Associated with strong GDP performance, total employment creation in June 2000, at 110,700 jobs, returned to precrisis levels. Both manufacturing and services made job gains of, respectively, 26,200—the highest increase since 1988—and 82,700. The seasonally adjusted unemployment rate continued to fall throughout the first three quarters of 2000 to 2.5 percent in September 2000 before rising modestly in the last quarter. The average rate of unemployment fell to 3.1 percent in 2000 compared with 3.5 percent in 1999. With accelerating economic growth and falling unemployment, inflationary pressures began to emerge as the average consumer price level, which had been unchanged in 1999, rose by 1.3 percent, primarily because of the effect of rising world oil prices on housing and transport costs.

In the midst of a rapid expansion, macroeconomic policy in 2000 was conservative. Fiscal policy was more restrictive as strong economic performance and surging car sales led to a further widening of the fiscal surplus to 3.5 percent of GDP from 2.6 percent in 1999. Operating revenues increased by

17.1 percent while total expenditures rose by only 12.3 percent. The generally strong economy pushed up collection of income tax by 15.5 percent to 40 percent of operating revenues, and that of the goods and services tax by 26.3 percent to 6.7 percent of operating revenues. A 60.6 percent increase in the number of new cars that the Government allowed for registration led to a surge in new car sales and thus in motor vehicle tax collection and customs and excise receipts, which together accounted for 11.8 percent of operating revenues in 2000. On the other side of the account, a 35.9 percent rise in operating expenditures, in part because of salary increases, was mitigated by lower development expenditures as a large waste-management system was completed.

The Monetary Authority of Singapore (MAS) voiced its intention in July 2000 to permit a modest and gradual appreciation of the trade-weighted Singapore dollar but it is likely to wait until world economic trends are clearer before moving to a more restrictive monetary policy. The MAS adopted a broadly neutral stance with respect to the exchange rate in 2000, acting only occasionally to support the Singapore dollar when its value was eroded by the general weakness of most Asian currencies. Exchange rate movements were mixed in 2000 as the Singapore dollar depreciated by about 1.7 percent against the US dollar and by 6.6 percent against the yen, while appreciating by 13.6 percent against the euro. Interest rates moved very little in 2000, with the prime lending rate remaining at about 5.8 percent. Broad money supply (M2) shrank by 2.1 percent, despite an 11.0 percent increase in checking accounts associated with robust income growth, as savings deposits declined, perhaps as a result of low interest rates and a switch to alternative savings vehicles such as insurance policies.

At the heart of the strong economy, export growth in 2000 in current Singapore dollars accelerated to 22.4 percent from 5.7 percent in 1999 (see Figure 2.2). A 30.7 percent surge in reexports, from virtually no growth in 1999, accompanied the acceleration of domestic export growth from 9.8 percent in 1999 to 16.9 percent in 2000. Rapid strengthening of global demand for electronic products, particularly semiconductors for which sales grew by over 30 percent worldwide in 2000, stimulated domestic exports and increased the volume of trade flowing through the ports. Although the value of office machinery exports fell in 2000, while the value of electronics components and parts exports rose, both have expanded rapidly in the last decade to become major non-oil export earners. Total imports rose by 23.4 percent compared with a 10.8 percent improvement in 1999, with retained imports growing by 18.3 percent, largely due to rising demand for intermediate inputs for the electronics industry.

The current account surplus narrowed to 23.6 percent of GDP in 2000 due to faster growth of imports and a fall in net income. The capital account deficit shrank from 22.0 percent of GDP in 1999 to 12.5 percent in 2000 as the 1999 banking sector net outflow was reversed with the repayment of external loans. The overall balance-of-payments surplus strengthened and official foreign reserves expanded to about S$139 billion, sufficient to cover about seven months of imports.

Economic growth is expected to moderate to about 5 percent in 2001 as the US economy slows and the electronics boom subsides, while export growth is expected to slow markedly to about 5 percent. In line with a general cooling of the economy, private consumption growth is likely to ease. However, gross fixed capital formation should continue to grow, based on manufacturing's higher levels of fixed investment commitments in 2000 than 1999. Electronics exports should slow in the second half of 2001 since new US orders in this area showed some signs of declining in 2000. Much of the downside risks to the forecasts are due to the uncertainty surrounding the magnitude of the slowdown in intraregional and US imports of semiconductors and personal computers.

Issues in Economic Management

If the global economic slowdown is deeper or longer than presently expected, or both, the Government may need to take steps to counter an extended loss of export earnings. Given the high degree of openness of the economy, external shocks feed through to domestic demand and price pressure quickly. Fortunately, given its strong fiscal position, the Government has latitude to ease fiscal policy to cushion the economy against an adverse external shock. Indeed, it is already moving to modestly reduce corporate, property, and income tax rates in 2001, while planning for a small increase in revenues, in part based on the contributions of past budget surpluses in the form of net investment income. However, planned operating and development expenditures plus special transfers are to remain roughly constant so that the Government expects a continuation of the budget surplus in 2001.

The Government has less scope to use monetary policy to stimulate the economy, with rising inflation and generally low interest rates relative to other markets such as the US. Price

---

Table 2.3 Major Economic Indicators, Singapore, 1998–2002
(percent)

Item	1998	1999	2000	2001	2002
GDP growth	0.1	5.9	9.9	5.0	6.0
Gross domestic investment/GDP	32.6	32.4	31.3	32.0	32.5
Gross domestic savings/GDP	52.4	51.8	49.8	51.0	52.0
Inflation rate (consumer price index)	-0.3	0.0	1.3	1.5	2.0
Money supply (M2) growth	30.2	8.5	-2.1	4.0	6.0
Fiscal balance/GDP[a]	2.5	2.6	3.5	2.5	2.5
Merchandise export growth[b]	-1.0	5.7	22.4	5.0	10.0
Merchandise import growth[b]	-13.6	10.8	23.4	8.0	13.0
Current account balance/GDP[c]	24.8	25.9	23.6	24.0	25.0

[a] Operating revenues less operating expenses and development expenditures.
[b] Includes both domestically produced exports and goods that are imported and not retained but reexported. All import and export growth rates are calculated from levels quoted in current Singapore dollars on a customs trade basis.
[c] Derived from the balance-of-payments accounts quoted in current Singapore dollars on a customs trade basis.

Sources: Ministry of Trade and Industry, *Economic Survey of Singapore 2000*, February 2001; staff estimates.

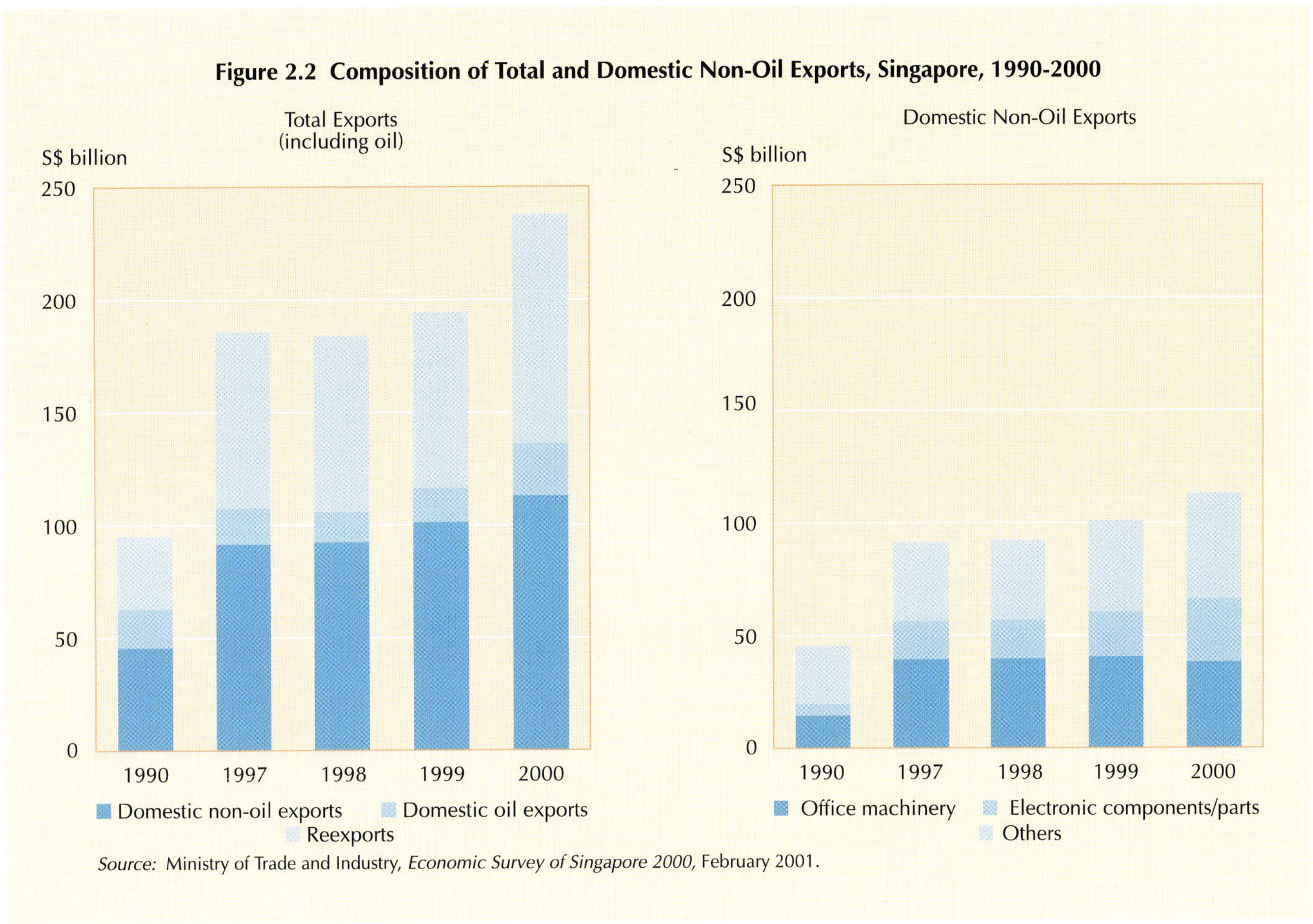

Source: Ministry of Trade and Industry, *Economic Survey of Singapore 2000,* February 2001.

stability remains the primary goal of monetary policy. Thus, as it has previously signaled, the MAS would likely tighten monetary policy if consumer price inflation edges above 2 percent, resulting in a strengthening of the trade-weighted exchange rate. This could exacerbate the weakening in external demand caused by softer information technology spending in the US. Thus, the Government is likely to proceed cautiously in allowing the exchange rate to appreciate.

Policy and Development Issues

In the longer term, the Government is eager to retain Singapore's distinction of having one of the world's most competitive economies. It continued its efforts in 2000 to improve the business environment by divesting its holdings in companies, by expanding opportunities for foreign direct investment, and by facilitating development of selected economic sectors. Sales of government interests in transport companies were initiated, while preparations to reduce state interests in leading firms in other sectors progressed. However, the Government is unlikely to markedly reduce its holdings in private firms in the near term. Restrictions on foreign investments are being

relaxed, most notably in communications, media, insurance, and banking, which should enable foreign companies to enter these areas. The Government continues to invest selectively in priority areas such as information technology infrastructure, biotechnology, and worker training. This is to encourage the economy's transition from a base for manufactured exports to a fully networked, knowledge-intensive economy and a hub for Asian finance, information technology, and transport.

The Government is also promoting competitiveness through liberalization of key economic sectors, particularly finance, telecommunications, and energy. To promote the financial sector in particular, the Government has been taking steps since 1998 to soften its policy of discouraging internationalization of the Singapore dollar, which was intended to protect its capital markets against excessive volatility. In late 2000, to further facilitate the development of domestic capital markets, primarily for bonds and loans, new guidelines were issued to permit banks to lend to nonresidents in Singapore dollars for investments in equities, bonds, and real estate in Singapore, as well as for offshore activities under certain conditions. This will broaden the customer base for local banks and retain the investor base for bonds denominated in Singapore dollars.

Before the new guidelines were announced, nonresident investors were discouraged by the requirement to raise foreign currency to finance their investments in Singapore, which made them vulnerable to exchange rate risk. Although it is hoped that the new guidelines will help attract not only more foreign investors but also more foreign bond issuers, leading to a larger and more efficient bond market, as of the end of 2000, the size of the Singapore bond market was only S$30 billion. Thus, the Government may have to consider further measures for boosting liquidity in the financial sector.

Another way in which the Government is strengthening the economy's competitiveness is by promoting diversification of exports. Office machinery is showing signs of decline, despite its current importance as an export earner. The Government has been successful in attracting higher value-added semiconductor producers. However, this has mixed implications for future economic performance. The semiconductor industry is still in its infancy with respect to its ability to build complete wafer-fabrication plants or produce the inputs to the process of fabrication. It will have to rely heavily on imports for them over the medium term, which implies that the overall effect of this restructuring may be to reduce the contribution of net exports to GDP growth over the next few years.

In the interim, the Government is working to address the mismatch between availability of local talent and the demands of the higher value-added industries for highly skilled personnel. The Government forecasts that in the next 10–15 years, at least 65 percent of the workforce will need an education beyond secondary school; the current rate is 35 percent. The fiscal budget for the 2001 financial year reflects a two-pronged approach to this challenge. First, an enlarged education budget of S$6.3 billion is intended to ensure that new labor force entrants are well prepared. Second, a S$30 million Manpower Development Assistance Scheme and a S$1 billion Lifelong Learning Endowment Fund will emphasize skill upgrading for the existing workforce.

Taipei,China

The economic recovery of 1999 continued in 2000 due to a strong performance of exports and export-related private investment that benefited from surging global demand for electronic goods. However, performance of traditional industries was weaker and unemployment remained at historic highs. During 2001, reflecting a slowdown of the US economy, growth is likely to slow.

Recent Trends and Prospects

The economic recovery of 1999 further strengthened in 2000, with growth in real GDP accelerating to 6.0 percent from 5.4 percent in 1999. The major contributing factors were a jump in exports of more than 20 percent and export-related private investment, both of which benefited from strong global demand for semiconductors and telecommunications equipment. The rapid pace of growth, however, slackened later in the year as political uncertainty undermined consumer and investor confidence considerably, and aggregate demand tapered off.

Private investment expanded by 13.7 percent, compared with a contraction of 0.7 percent in 1999. It rose sharply in the first two quarters, by 18.4 percent and 27.1 percent, respectively, as companies, responding to the boom in electronics demand, expanded and upgraded production facilities. It moderated later in the year, however, because of the anticipated slowdown in the global economy. Investment in traditional industries such as textiles, construction, and real estate remained weak. Public sector investment, on the other hand, shrank by 8.3 percent, as the implementation of state projects was sluggish. Total fixed investment grew by only 7.8 percent.

Private consumption picked up to 5.6 percent in 2000 from 5.4 percent in 1999. It rose by 7.7 percent year on year in the first quarter, stimulated by campaign funding in connection with the presidential election in March, a vigorous stock market, and a low base in the previous year. Political weakness in dealing with economic issues after the election had an adverse effect on the stock market, and largely as a result of the negative wealth effect of this decline, subsequent private consumption growth fell to around 5.3 percent. State consumption increased by a mere 1.9 percent as a result of attempts to rein in the fiscal deficit that had snowballed after a strong earthquake in 1999.

Led by the robust performance of high-tech industry, the industrial production index grew by 7.7 percent compared with 7.5 percent in 1999. While electronics production surged, production in traditional industries remained sluggish. Production in light industries such as food, wood, and rubber fell by 0.8 percent and construction contracted by 4.2 percent. Agricultural production fell by 1.3 percent due to unfavorable weather conditions. In the services sector, telecommunications served as the main engine of growth, while the financial sector and state services remained weak.

Export growth jumped to 22.3 percent from 9.9 percent in 1999. Recovering Asian economies and booming global demand for electronic, information, and communications products were the main driving forces. Imports also soared by 27.3 percent, from 6.2 percent growth in the previous year. The rapid growth of private investment stimulated a sharp increase in imports of capital goods, while the current account surplus narrowed as imports rose faster than exports.

The unemployment rate has risen gradually in recent years, from a low of 1.4 percent in 1993, to 2.6 percent in 1996, to 2.9 percent in 1999. At the end of 2000, unemployment was 3.0 percent. The downturn of traditional industries, the slowdown of the financial sector, and the influx of foreign workers are the main reasons for the high rate.

The budget deficit, which had swollen from 3.4 percent of GDP in 1998 to 6.0 percent in 1999, fell to 4.8 percent of GDP in 2000. Improved budgetary revenues—thanks to a healthy economy—and a slowdown in current expenditure were the major factors. Despite an easing of the monetary stance earlier in 2000, money supply (M2) growth slowed later in the year, to give M2 growth of 6.5 percent for the whole year. This was lower than the 8.3 percent in 1999 and was due mainly to outflows of foreign capital.

Prices rose in 2000 due to rising world oil prices and the depreciation of the currency. Consumer price inflation was 1.3 percent, an upswing from 0.2 percent in 1999, while wholesale inflation reached 1.8 percent, in contrast to 4.5 percent price deflation in 1999. Import prices rose by 4.6 percent. However, compared with other economies in Asia, inflation remained low.

In 2001, real GDP growth is projected to moderate to just over 5 percent as the global economy slows. Export growth is forecast to be weaker due to anticipated softer global demand. Domestic demand will also likely be softer than in 2000. Private consumption growth is projected to decelerate to around

Table 2.4 Major Economic Indicators, Taipei,China, 1998–2002
(percent)

Item	1998	1999	2000	2001	2002
GDP	4.6	5.4	6.0	5.1	5.8
Gross domestic investment/GDP	24.9	23.4	22.8	23.4	23.5
Gross domestic savings/GDP	26.0	26.1	24.8	26.1	26.6
Inflation rate (consumer price index)	1.7	0.2	1.3	1.7	1.8
Fiscal balance/GDP	-3.4	-6.0	-4.8	-4.3	-4.7
Money supply (M2) growth	8.8	8.3	6.5	7.0	6.7
Merchandise export growth	-9.5	9.9	22.3	11.8	9.8
Merchandise import growth	-7.4	6.2	27.3	10.8	9.5
Current account balance/GDP	1.3	2.9	2.4	2.5	3.0

Sources: Directorate-General of Budget, Accounting and Statistics, Executive Yuan; staff estimates.

4.6 percent. Private investment growth, closely linked with the external sector, will also slow to around 7.4 percent. Imports, however, are expected to continue growing, albeit more slowly, as market-opening measures are implemented when Taipei,China joins the World Trade Organization. Continued robust growth of the economy in the next few years requires economic restructuring, especially in the financial sector and in traditional industries.

The authorities will probably adopt a more relaxed monetary policy in 2001 to attempt a soft landing for the economy. The budget deficit is projected to shrink to 4.3 percent of GDP, as the authorities keep a tight grip on expenditure and implement plans to raise revenues, such as reforming the tax system and privatizing state-owned enterprises. The authorities have little room to use fiscal policy to stimulate the economy since, in 2000, they pushed to the legal limit the amount of debt that they can issue. As a result, the currency is expected to depreciate further and prices will likely rise moderately due to weaker aggregate demand and to deflationary pressures from market-opening measures adopted in preparation for World Trade Organization membership. Unemployment will probably rise even higher, to 3.4 percent.

Issues in Economic Management

Traditional industries, such as textiles, construction, and real estate, as well as agriculture, have recently plunged into a structural downturn. These industries, dominated by small and medium-sized enterprises (SMEs), face serious challenges. Their profitability has persistently decreased with rising fixed costs and wages. Their production modes, however, are too inflexible to accommodate rapid changes in market demand and their technology has yet to develop to compete with large international companies. Moreover, a tumbling stock market have curtailed banks' willingness to lend, thereby restricting these SMEs' access to bank credit and so aggravating their financial distress.

Consequently, it is high unemployment in these industries, particularly among unskilled and older workers, that has pushed unemployment higher over the last few years. Official statistics show that unemployment among unskilled and semi-skilled workers in traditional industries reached 3.3 percent in the second quarter of 2000, compared with an economy-wide unemployment rate at that time of 2.8 percent.

Since most SMEs in traditional industries have low levels of knowledge and capital, it is very difficult for them to restructure their business. Therefore, restructuring led by the authorities would be more realistic, and this should include effective and stronger policy measures to upgrade workers' skills and make the labor market more flexible.

Policy and Development Issues

The banking sector has suffered from overcrowding and surging volumes of nonperforming loans (NPLs). In 2000, more than 450 financial institutions, including 47 domestic banks and 314 credit departments of farmer and fisherfolk associations, were operating. The excessive competition and limited market share dragged down aggregate profitability. Moreover, the downturn in traditional industries, and flagging real estate and stock markets, raised the NPL ratio of financial institutions to 5.5 percent by the end of October 2000. The NPL ratio of cooperative associations and credit departments of farmer and fisherfolk associations surged to 15.6 percent.

The authorities moved to solve the overcrowding problems and improve the quality of bank assets through a range of measures. One was an amendment to the Banking Law, passed in October 2000, which relaxed restrictions on banks' investment activities and raised the ownership ceiling in other banks or financial companies from 15 to 25 percent. The authorities also passed the Merger Act of Financial Institutions in December 2000 to encourage mergers, including those by foreign financial institutions. In addition, the central bank cut the average reserve requirement ratio from 7.7 to 6.4 percent in 1999 and lowered the gross business revenue tax for banks from 5 to 2 percent, then eliminated it altogether in November 2000.

Though these financial restructuring measures have tackled several weaknesses, concerns remain. For example, the authorities recently urged banks to roll over loans to troubled traditional industries. However, this will only worsen the bad debt problem. The authorities' decision to relax restrictions on banks' investment activities will make banks even more vulnerable to stock market volatility. The weakening real estate market also raises uncertainties about the pace of restructuring. To activate the market, the authorities may introduce both a real estate price monitoring system to reduce price distortions and a real estate secondary market.

The information and communications technology (ICT) industry has grown substantially over the last several years, serving as the main engine of economic growth. Production of computer hardware, growing by over 40 percent a year in 1995–2000, amounted to around $50 billion in 2000. Despite the weak performance of the domestic economy, hardware's rapid expansion was brought about partly by the authorities' various incentives and the flexibility of local SMEs in adapting to global market trends. Exports of software are smaller than hardware, but this subsector also registered very strong growth of 30 percent a year in 1995–2000. Output of domestic communications and Internet-related products has also increased, at about 10 percent a year over the same period.

Given that the ICT industry in Taipei,China is highly cyclical and sensitive to market shocks, the industry still has to overcome several challenges if it is to prosper in international markets. First, most SMEs in the ICT industry spend only a small percentage of their turnover on research and development, and are not therefore ready to quickly adjust to new market trends. For example, traditional makers of wire for telecommunications equipment—most of them SMEs—did not adapt to the surging demand for mobile phones and wireless products and were, therefore, forced to withdraw from the international market due to lower sales. Second, Taipei,China's ICT industry still relies heavily on the US and Japan for its key components and technology. Third, the economy's main trading partners are these two countries and the People's Republic of China. Policymakers must, therefore, provide a policy and institutional environment in order to (i) enable the ICT industry to adopt rapid technological change to meet continually evolving market conditions, (ii) encourage research and development and support the transfer of technology to domestic firms, and (iii) diversify exports to more destinations to enable the industry to better weather any downturn in the economies of its major trading partners.

Central Asian Republics, Azerbaijan, and Mongolia

$\mathbf{T}$he group of countries comprising the Central Asian republics, Azerbaijan, and Mongolia all face challenging geographic and economic circumstances, including the relatively small size of their economies; remoteness from world markets; long-term isolation from global technology and capital flows; heavy dependence on primary production of energy, minerals, and other commodities; continuing vulnerability to external shocks arising from volatility in international oil and commodity prices; dependence on the Russian economy (which is still the single largest market for their exports); and an industrial structure from the Soviet era that is hardly compatible with an open economy. These formidable economic challenges are further exacerbated by problems of systemic transition and the severance of Soviet fiscal subsidies that have resulted in a sharp decline in human development indicators and emergence of widespread poverty. Recently, the appearance in some of these countries of social, religious, and ethnic strife, which perhaps lay dormant under the strictures of the earlier centrally controlled regime, has added to the uncertainty, affecting the investment climate and growth prospects of these economies.

Faced with such adverse circumstances, the various governments have implemented a large-scale and wide-ranging program of structural reforms, though with significant variations across countries. On the basis of these reforms and with external circumstances finally turning favorable in 1999, most of these economies—with the exception of Mongolia—are now recovering from the economic downturn that lasted, for most of them, from the breakup of the former Soviet Union until the mid-1990s when the decline in GDP was arrested and positive growth was achieved. This recovery was nearly derailed as a result of the Russian crisis of August 1998 that followed in the wake of the Asian financial crisis.

The improvement in the Russian economy since 1999 and the rise in international energy prices have helped generate strong aggregate GDP growth of nearly 5 percent in 1999 for these countries as a whole; this growth improved further to almost 8 percent in 2000. The growth performance would have been better if the agriculture sector had not suffered a severe drought that affected the cotton crop, a major export item, and food grain production in some countries.

More creditably, the improved growth performance has been achieved along with overall macroeconomic stability. The aggregate level of inflation in these seven countries remained high at around 15 percent in 2000. This reflected the positive effects of exchange rate stability and tighter monetary policies. Higher revenues from the oil sector and efforts at improving public expenditure management and tax administration have seen the countries' fiscal balances improve. Taking advantage of high international oil and gas prices and greater access to pipelines and other supply outlets, the export earnings of the group increased from virtually zero to about 25 percent in 2000 (excluding Azerbaijan and Turkmenistan). This enabled some of these countries to improve their external account balances as reflected in the buildup of international reserves and the significant improvement in external debt-service ability. The Kyrgyz Republic and Tajikistan, though, face an unsustainable external debt-service burden in the short term. This has prompted a multilateral review of their external debt liability and bilateral negotiations for rescheduling their debt-service flows.

Although the positive aggregate economic performance hides wide variations across countries, the economic outlook for this group is upbeat. Economic growth will remain positive, though lower than in 2000 as oil prices are expected to soften and demand from the Russian Federation and other countries in the Commonwealth of Independent States slackens as a result of a slowing of these economies. Agricultural performance is expected to remain weak if the adverse weather forecasts for the next two years are proved right. Even with strong and sustained GDP growth as achieved in the last two years, per capita income levels in these countries are not expected to return to the levels of the late 1980s for the next few years. Determined policy efforts will be needed to ensure that market-based economic growth does not cause equity disparities to rise further and that growth is inclusive.

For generating sustained growth in per capita incomes and for reducing poverty levels, the countries, to greater or lesser degrees, need to vigorously pursue their structural reform programs. The focus has to be on generating pro-poor growth while maintaining macroeconomic stability. This will require liberalizing the economies further, in keeping with individual country conditions; removing any significant price distortions and controls on the current account; privatizing state enterprises and setting up a regulatory mechanism to ensure fair competition and consumer protection; establishing the institutional framework for private sector-led growth; ensuring that the poorer segments of society participate in the growth process;

Box 2.1 Azerbaijan

Economic performance was strong in 2000, with real GDP growth estimated to have accelerated to 11.0 percent from 7.4 percent in 1999. The major contributing factor was the 20-plus percent upsurge in the oil and oil-related sectors in the first half of 2000, which benefited from rising world oil prices. The agriculture sector, however, grew more slowly in 2000, by about 6 percent. Growth in other labor-intensive sectors is estimated to have remained weak. Consequently, the level of unemployment (hidden and open) is estimated at 18 percent in 2000, similar to the 1999 level.

The current account deficit improved significantly in 2000 to 0.9 percent of GDP ($43 million) from 15.0 percent ($600 million) in 1999 primarily because of a stronger trade balance, on which a surplus of $400 million (8.0 percent of GDP) was posted in 2000 compared with a deficit of $408 million a year earlier. Among the contributing factors were growing oil exports and a smaller increase of imports due to the slowdown in oil equipment imports. Gross foreign exchange reserves increased slightly from $676 million in 1999 to $680 million in 2000, equivalent to about six months of imports. Total external debt rose to $1.2 billion, from $962 million over the same period.

The Government adopted a tight fiscal stance in 2000. The total fiscal deficit is estimated to have been reduced to 2.3 percent of GDP in 2000 from 5.4 percent in 1999. Improved budget revenues and a lower level of public expenditures were the main reasons for this. On the monetary side, an eased policy stance that began in mid-1999 continued. Inflation (measured by the consumer price index) is estimated at 2.2 percent in 2000 compared with deflation of 8.5 percent in 1999. Without jeopardizing currency stability, the Government has continued its flexible exchange rate management approach. The local currency, the manat, depreciated gradually by 7.8 percent to an average level of 4,474 manat in 2000 from 4,126 manat in 1999.

To better manage the expected increase in oil revenues, the Government is aiming soon to put into operation the State Oil Fund, which was established in November 1999. In addition, progress has been made in implementing policy reforms, such as the passage of a civil code (effective 1 September 2000) and an amended tax code (effective 1 January 2001). However, structural reforms, particularly in the banking sector, have lagged behind. Crucial reforms are needed in this sector to improve supervision and strengthen enforcement of prudential regulations in line with international best practice.

The economic outlook for 2001 appears to be promising in view of positive prospects in the oil-related industries and indications of improved performance in agriculture in the second half of 2000. However, real GDP growth in 2001 may be lower than in 2000, due to a softening in world oil prices and a slowdown in foreign investment. In the short term, the Government is expected to maintain its current tight fiscal and slightly loose monetary policy mix. The fiscal deficit has been budgeted at 2.0 percent of GDP for 2001. Improved value-added tax collection and the adoption of the amended tax code will help in this. However, it remains a challenge for the Government to lift much-needed social expenditures, while keeping the fiscal deficit under control. After significant deflation during 1998–1999 and a moderate rate of inflation of 2.2 percent in 2000, inflation in 2001 will likely continue to rise. In view of slowing foreign capital inflows, the manat will be subject to greater pressure to depreciate further.

To maintain investor confidence, the Government needs to make a serious effort in implementing structural reforms. Important areas include privatization, financial sector restructuring, and good governance to establish institutions and the rule of law conducive to a market-based economy. The increasing dependence on oil exports is a concern, and the development of non-oil sectors will be crucial to achieving a balanced external account position and sustainable growth. Understanding this, the Government made the issue of non-oil sector development a priority in its recent development strategy.

---

and putting in place a social safety net that will protect the poor and vulnerable from the adverse impact of cyclical economic downturns.

The seven economies continue to be characterized by a weak banking and financial sector. This prevents the effective mobilization of investment resources. The small and medium-sized enterprise sector—often the most dynamic sector for creating new competitive industrial capacities and trading ventures—especially suffers from a relative lack of access to financial resources. Particular attention is needed for the development of the financial sector to facilitate the emergence of small and medium-sized enterprises and to help in channeling resources to the rural sector, both of which contribute to pro-poor growth. Human resources development now requires a combination of public and private sector initiatives and resources for meeting the needs of a market economy.

In each of these countries, the government may need to actively intervene to try and diversify the economy so as to reduce its vulnerability from volatility in international energy and commodity prices and to generate employment. Given the geographic isolation of these economies and their relatively small size, any strategy for sustained growth, rapid industrialization, and economic diversification will be facilitated with the emergence of a subregional market. This requires an active program of economic cooperation that will promote the free flow of goods and services and permit the establishment of viable and internationally competitive production capacities. The infrastructure, which was developed in the past to connect these economies individually to the Russian markets, also needs to be revamped so as to permit more efficient resource allocation.

Recognizing these imperatives, and because of the collapse of the Soviet trade system, the various governments have actively searched for viable cooperation ventures among themselves. The establishment of the Interstate Council of Kazakhstan, Kyrgyz Republic, and Uzbekistan (later joined by Tajikistan) is a notable example. In addition, most of the governments have conducted negotiations on the trade in energy, and have taken steps toward cooperating on resolving the environmental problems of the Aral Sea area. These activities reveal an underlying commitment to economic cooperation, and an understanding and appreciation by the governments that solutions to their common problems must be found.

Kazakhstan

Economic performance in 2000 improved considerably, mainly due to a favorable external environment. However, to promote sustainable long-term growth and maintain macroeconomic stability, the Government needs to ensure greater diversification of the economy.

Recent Trends and Prospects

Economic performance was vigorous in 2000. The economy, which in the second half of 1999 began to recover from the recession caused by weak world commodity markets and 1998's Russian crisis, experienced even stronger growth in 2000. GDP grew by 9.6 percent compared with 2.7 percent in 1999 (see Figure 2.3). The rapid growth was primarily due to favorable external factors, including rising world prices for oil, natural gas, and metals (the major exports) and the robust recovery in the Russian Federation, Kazakhstan's main trading partner.

Growth of industrial output accelerated to 14.6 percent in 2000 from 2.8 percent in 1999, mainly because of sharp increases in the production of crude oil, natural gas, and metals. As a result of high world prices, the value of crude oil and natural gas output expanded by 15.8 percent and 23.2 percent, respectively. The manufacturing sector, which accounts for half of total industrial output, rose by 15.6 percent due to increased government investments. The Government regards import substitution of capital and intermediate goods as the key to achieving rapid industrialization, and has therefore allocated sizable resources to this area.

Agricultural production contracted by 3.3 percent in 2000, largely because the output of grain fell by 18.2 percent to 11.6 million tons; this was due to unfavorable weather conditions. Despite the decline, grain production was not only adequate for domestic consumption but also generated a surplus of about 4 million tons that were exported to Iran, Turkmenistan, and Ukraine. In contrast, the output of cotton rose by 15.0 percent, due to an extension of the sown area.

Official statistics show that the services sector expanded by 7.9 percent in 2000, due mainly to a growing private sector. However, official data still do not fully cover the private services sector. Trading, restaurants, hotels, information technology, and construction have grown significantly over the past few years as a result of small-scale privatization and the Government's policy of encouraging private sector development.

After a modest increase of 3.8 percent in 1999, capital investment rose steeply by 29.4 percent in 2000, driven by both the public and private sectors. The major areas of capital investment were oil and gas, transport and communications, and construction. In particular, activities in the oil and gas and construction subsectors were strong, as reflected by work on an export pipeline in the Caspian Sea area and the continuing building of Astana, the country's new capital.

Savings grew sharply in 2000 as a result of improved economic performance. Gross domestic savings as a proportion of GDP increased to 20.8 percent in 2000 from 16.9 percent in 1999. Better collection of revenues and a prudent fiscal policy contributed to higher public savings, while rising profits in the corporate and financial sectors, particularly among oil companies, stimulated private savings. Since domestic savings grew more rapidly than domestic investment, a resource surplus equivalent to 3.8 percent of GDP emerged in 2000, compared with a resource gap of 1.1 percent of GDP in 1999.

Economic growth contributed to an increase in wages and a marginal decline in official unemployment. Average nominal monthly wages at the end of 2000 were T14,174 (equivalent to $97.5), a rise of 19.6 percent over the 1999 level. This represented an increase in the real average monthly wage of 5.7 percent. The official registered unemployment rate at the end of 2000 was 3.8 percent, slightly lower than the rate of 3.9 percent at the end of 1999. Employment generation was led mainly by the expansion of the services and education sectors. Growth in manufacturing and mining had little impact—and so unemployment remains a major problem with the actual level estimated at 13.5 percent of the labor force, much higher than the official unemployment rate.

The fiscal situation continued to improve in 2000, helped by strong economic growth, higher revenues from exports of oil and minerals, as well as the Government's efforts to strengthen tax collection and administration and to improve public expenditure management. For the first time since independence in 1991, Kazakhstan achieved a budget surplus, equivalent to 0.1 percent of GDP. Total government revenues rose to 23.1 percent of GDP from 21.1 percent in 1999. Tax revenues accounted for 20.2 percent of GDP, up from 17.1 percent in 1999. As a result of its rationalization efforts, government expenditures declined to 23.0 percent of GDP in 2000 from 24.6 percent in the previous year, but despite this decline, the shares of development investment and social sector spending in total public expenditures in 2000 remained relatively high. Social assistance accounted for 28.7 percent of total expenditures, followed by education (14.2 percent) and health (9.1 percent). However, interest expenses accounted for 6.0 percent of revenues in 2000, with external public debt amounting to $4.0 billion. To reduce the volatility of budgetary revenues, which are highly dependent on earnings from oil exports, the Government plans to establish an offshore state oil fund to maintain stable resource flows to the budget and preserve national wealth generated from the oil sector for future development.

The National Bank of Kazakhstan (the central bank) pursued an expansionary monetary policy to stimulate growth. This included reducing the refinancing rate from 18 percent in 1999 to 14 percent in 2000, and lowering the reserve requirements for commercial banks from 10 to 8 percent of demand and short-term time deposits. As a result, the monetary position eased and growth of monetary aggregates continued. Money supply (M2) and bank credits increased by 45.9 percent and 85.6 percent, respectively, in 2000. Because of financial sector reform, depositors have regained their confidence in the banking system. The reforms included the adoption of international banking standards and depositors' insurance for household deposits, and the application of a law on banking secrecy and confidentiality. Largely as a result, bank deposits rose sharply by 60.2 percent in real terms in 2000.

Despite the relaxed monetary policy stance, inflation by the end of 2000 had fallen to 9.8 percent, from 17.8 percent 12 months previously, due mainly to increased productivity, an improved fiscal position, and a stable currency. The national currency, the tenge, which had depreciated sharply against the dollar after the authorities floated it in April 1999, was relatively stable in 2000, fluctuating in a range of T138.25–T145.40 to the dollar, and depreciated by only 5.2 percent against the dollar during the year.

The balance-of-payments situation improved significantly in 2000. The current account achieved a surplus equivalent to 3.8 percent of GDP in 2000, compared with a deficit equivalent to 1.1 percent of GDP in the previous year. This resulted mainly from a doubling of exports (largely oil and metals) as a result of higher world prices, increased oil export quotas through the Russian Federation's pipeline, and the positive effects of the currency devaluation in 1999.

With the beginning of a turnaround in investor confidence after the Russian crisis, as reflected in the increase in foreign direct investment (FDI) inflows to $1.6 billion in 1999 from $1.1 billion in 1998, in April 2000 the authorities issued the country's fourth Eurobond in an amount of $350 million. In addition, due to improved economic performance, in July 2000 Standard & Poor's raised its long-term foreign currency and local currency ratings, which will further boost investor confidence in the economy.

Strong export growth, renewed inflows of FDI, and the issuance of the Eurobond helped strengthen the gross interna-

Table 2.5 Major Economic Indicators, Kazakhstan, 1998–2002
(percent)

Item	1998	1999	2000	2001	2002
GDP	-1.9	2.7	9.6	4.0	7.0
Gross domestic investment/GDP	14.3	17.9	17.1	17.3	16.9
Gross domestic savings/GDP	14.9	16.9	20.8	20.3	20.4
Inflation rate (consumer price index)[a]	1.9	17.8	9.8	5.5	4.9
Money supply (M2) growth	-14.1	84.3	45.9	21.3	21.6
Fiscal balance/GDP	-4.2	-3.5	0.1	-2.2	-1.2
Merchandise export growth	-14.9	2.0	52.6	1.3	12.9
Merchandise import growth	-7.0	-15.4	-10.5	50.2	15.0
Current account balance/GDP	-5.4	-1.1	3.8	3.3	2.4
Debt-service ratio	22.4	27.3	24.6	17.3	19.4

[a] End of period.

Sources: State Statistical Agency; National Bank of Kazakhstan; staff estimates.

tional reserves position, which improved to $2.1 billion (equivalent to 3.3 months of imports) at the end of 2000, the highest level since independence. External public debt fell from $4.1 billion (24.1 percent of GDP) at the end of 1999 to $4.0 billion (21.8 percent of GDP) at the end of 2000, mainly because of debt repayment to the International Monetary Fund ahead of schedule. The debt repayment requirement, particularly debts accumulated by joint ventures in the oil and gas sector, rose in 2000. As a result, despite a doubling of export revenue, the debt-service ratio declined only moderately from 27.3 percent in December 1999 to 24.6 percent one year later.

The economic outlook for 2001 remains positive, though GDP growth is projected to slow to about 4 percent, mainly due to an anticipated leveling-off of world prices of crude oil and minerals. Industrial production is forecast to improve by 8 percent as production of these commodities continues to surge on the back of growing FDI and the expansion of oil export capacity (largely due to increased quotas in the Russian Federation's pipeline network). The fiscal balance will likely switch to a deficit of 2.2 percent of GDP, despite the Government's commitment to achieving medium-term sustainability of public finance.

Inflation is forecast to further decline to about 5.5 percent, provided the central bank keeps tight control of credit growth and money supply. Slower inflation will likely lead to a further reduction in the refinancing rate to 8–10 percent. The current account should remain in surplus in 2001, although it is projected to decline to about 3 percent of GDP as imports are likely to grow more rapidly than exports. Total external debt is expected to decrease, as the Government is committed to repaying a large portion of its outstanding external debt in 2001. The debt-service ratio is forecast to further decline during the year.

Issues in Economic Management

In 2000, to achieve macroeconomic stability, the Government made great efforts to strengthen fiscal management, including raising revenue collection and rationalizing public expenditures. A new tax code, designed to broaden the tax base, was submitted to Parliament. A program to improve collection of excise taxes on oil products and cigarettes was introduced, and a government decree was issued in March 2000 converting specific tariffs into ad valorem rates (except for alcohol) to strengthen excise tax collection. The Government implemented measures to closely monitor medium-sized and large corporate taxpayers and to simplify tax declaration procedures for small businesses. These helped raise tax collection by nearly 40 percent. The Government also conducted intensive training of tax collectors and officers. In the area of public expenditure, it focused on reducing current expenditures by undertaking civil service reform to reorient and downsize the bureaucracy, by limiting transfers to loss-incurring state-owned enterprises, and by better targeting social sector spending.

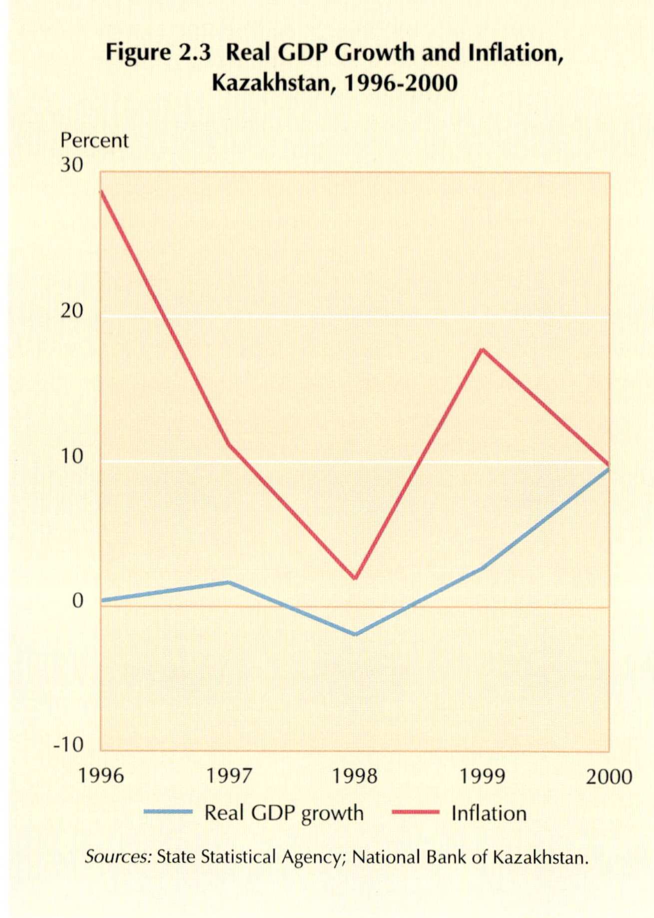

Sources: State Statistical Agency; National Bank of Kazakhstan.

Despite such progress, the Government needs to make further efforts to restore the fiscal balance; for example, by ensuring that the new tax code is implemented effectively, and by improving collection of value-added tax on imported goods, excise tax on gasoline, and royalty payments in the oil and gas sector. It also needs to strengthen tax and customs enforcement systems through closer monitoring of taxpayers, computerization of tax and customs administration, mandatory preshipment inspections, postrelease control, and improvement of customs legislation. Privatization of large state-owned enterprises should be accelerated to generate greater revenue. Given limited domestic resource mobilization and debt repayment capacity, further government efforts are needed to reduce current spending and to prioritize capital expenditures. Finally, the Government needs to pay special attention to restraining the growth of public sector wages, phasing out subsidies through administered price adjustment and improved operational efficiency, and limiting sovereign-guaranteed borrowing.

Policy and Development Issues

Despite the recent economic achievements and positive short-term prospects, the economy faces a major development issue with regard to globalization. Globalization has had a twofold impact on the economy: positive development trends in the world economy, favorable world commodity markets, and a recovery in regional demand have led to its strengthening through expansion of external trade and rising inflows of FDI.

On the other hand, the economy is highly dependent on production and exports of a few commodities such as crude oil, natural gas, and metals. Together, they account for about 70 percent of industrial output, nearly 90 percent of exports, about 60 percent of FDI, and about 30 percent of budgetary revenues. Such an economic structure raises not only the risk of Dutch disease, but also makes the country vulnerable to commodity price fluctuations, as in 1998 when weak world commodity markets tipped the economy into recession. A broad-based economic structure is essential to minimizing the risks related to globalization and to achieving sustainable development.

The Government has taken some initial steps to diversify economic activities, especially in nonextractive sector development, but greater efforts must be made to further this process and broaden the economic base. The Government needs to address three policy areas. First, it should develop a national strategy for economic diversification, based on an analysis of the country's development priorities, strengths, and resource availability. In particular, decisions to develop any new sectors or industries must take into account financial affordability and economic viability to ensure the achievement of maximum development impact.

Second, the Government needs to adopt policies for facilitating the development of nonextractive sectors that have been identified as priorities by the national strategy. Public investment should be increased and private investment, both domestic and foreign, attracted through favorable incentives. These should include reduction in, or exemption from, taxes and duties in the initial period of operation; permission for the establishment of foreign firms and remittance of their profits abroad; improving the terms for foreign investors with regard to land use; security of property and contract rights; and simplified entry and exit procedures.

Third, the Government needs to promote production of processed products in the resource-based sectors (e.g., petroleum and petrochemical products), which are less affected by world price fluctuations and which have greater value added. Kazakhstan is in a good position to expand output of these processed products because of its rich natural resource endowments and its relatively high level of human capital.

Kyrgyz Republic

Economic growth improved in 2000 despite extensive crop damage. Foreign trade recovered, price and exchange rate stability were in large measure restored, and a modest fiscal consolidation was achieved. However, in the immediate future, a heavy external debt repayment burden threatens to hamper the stabilization process.

Recent Trends and Prospects

The economy appears to be recovering from the adverse impact of the 1998 Russian crisis. In 2000, GDP growth accelerated to 5.0 percent, from 3.7 percent in 1999. The agriculture sector performed well during the first half of 2000 with 9.6 percent growth. But early snowfall in the latter half of the year caused extensive crop damage to an estimated 12.2 percent of the cropped area. This resulted in lower agricultural growth of 3.9 percent for the year compared with 8.2 percent in 1999. Industry recorded 6.0 percent expansion, led by power generation, light manufacturing, and chemical industries. Strong export demand for leather products, and a revival of cotton processing and pharmaceutical units contributed to the improvement of light manufacturing and chemical industry output. The construction sector expanded by 5.9 percent in 2000, aided by externally funded public investments.

The Government followed a tight monetary policy in 2000 in an attempt to achieve low inflation and stabilize the exchange rate: broad money grew by 12.3 percent in 2000, while exchange rate stability was restored to a degree—the som depreciated by 18.2 percent against the dollar in 2000. Interest rates also declined. To improve the central bank's ability to pursue monetary policy effectively and fairly independently of the Government's debt operations, "Notes of the National Bank" were introduced in June 2000. These will have shorter maturities and larger face values than treasury bills and are expected to reduce fluctuations in the expansion of the money supply.

Inflationary pressure abated significantly in 2000, with an average annual price increase of 18.7 percent against 35.9 percent in 1999. This was the result of a relatively stable som and strong farm output growth in the first half of the year despite increases in the administered prices of utilities, communications, and social services (especially health care), as well as a rise in food prices in October.

Although the official rate of unemployment in 2000 increased only marginally to 3.1 percent from 2.9 percent in 1999, the main issue is that the quality of employment is deteriorating due to regressive changes in occupational structure.

The decline of the industry sector after independence in 1991 led to a substantial shift in workforce composition: the share of agriculture in the total workforce rose from 33 percent in 1990 to 47.3 percent in 1995. This movement from (relatively) high-wage sectors to low-wage agriculture drove down real wages and impoverished many people. The process was briefly reversed by economic revival during 1995–1997, resulting in an improvement in average real wages, but the growth in non-farm employment was still too weak to raise real minimum wages and reduce poverty. Since 1998, the migration of labor to agriculture has reemerged, raising the share of the workforce in agriculture to 51.6 percent in 1999. The significant fall in real wages and an increase in food prices in 1998 sharply pushed up the poverty ratio by about 12 percentage points to 63.9 percent. Further food price rises and erosion in real wages marginally raised the poverty incidence to 64.1 percent in 1999. Preliminary trends for 2000 indicate a continued fall in real wages, suggesting a further deterioration in the poverty situation.

The fiscal deficit is estimated to have fallen from 12.0 percent of GDP in 1999 to 9.4 percent in 2000, but this may not be enough to meet official targets. Fiscal consolidation is being hampered by lower than expected tax revenues and the reduced scope for public expenditure cuts. In part, this was because the Parliament elected in March 2000 failed to approve the Government's efforts to raise additional resources through a comprehensive revision of the commodity tax code. Neither did Parliament approve the proposed increases in land tax rates to raise additional resources from the undertaxed agriculture sector. It did, however, enact a law to tax profits earned in free economic zones if these profits are invested outside the zones.

With significant erosion in the real incomes of government staff since 1997, in some cases to below the poverty line, the Government was compelled to implement a 20 percent increase in nominal wages and pensions in August 2000. Yet even this failed to fully offset the erosion in real wages.

Foreign trade improved. Aided by a substantial depreciation of the som in 1999, exports rose by 9.1 percent in 2000 while imports grew by only 1.4 percent. Exports of electricity, nonprecious metals, machinery, and chemicals were the principal contributors to export growth. The trade deficit fell sharply to $50.1 million in 2000, from $84.3 million in 1999.

The Government brought down tariff rates significantly in 2000, reflecting its commitment to World Trade Organization (WTO) requirements. The new structure is expected to yield an average tariff of 5.2 percent. The central bank's international reserves shrank in November 2000 to $256.7 million and are expected to have fallen further to around $250 million by the end of 2000, mainly due to foreign debt service.

Issues in Economic Management

The Kyrgyz Republic has made solid progress in overcoming transition problems, yet several tasks are unfinished, clouding considerably the country's medium-term prospects. The economy has the potential to grow faster than the 5.0 percent attained in 2000 if the Government achieves a sustainable level of internal balance and if financial sector reforms are implemented properly. Although the fiscal situation improved in 2000, it remains fragile. The Government needs to pay greater attention to raising additional tax and nontax revenues to service its debt while maintaining the necessary public expenditure levels. High external debt and the bunching of debt-service payments over the next five years will make macroeconomic management difficult in the absence of strong measures to restore the internal balance. Generation of adequate budgetary savings is the only way to maintain the current level of public investment, which is imperative to sustain economic growth and maintain a minimum level of social services.

The Kumtor gold mine, on which exports and the economy depend heavily, will gradually lose its importance ahead of its scheduled closing in about seven years. The economy will have to diversify its export base in terms of both commodities and markets to offset the impending fall in gold exports. If it does not, declining exports and the heavy debt repayment burden will put considerable pressure on the balance of payments. In short, medium-term growth prospects depend on (i) how fast and effectively the Government can implement broad-based economic and financial reforms and (ii) how it can handle the spikes in debt service through effective management of public sector resources.

The agriculture sector has shown considerable dynamism, driven mainly by the 62,000 private farms created since 1995. These farms, which now account for about 49 percent of the cropped area, are over 20 percent more productive than state farms, and produce profitable cash crops. Yet their output is still far below potential because current levels of productivity are low. Several institutional, social, and economic factors are preventing them from realizing their potential, including excessive regulation of agro-based industry, irrational taxation, obsolete technology in farm-based industry, poor input supply policies, and inadequate promotional support. However, by lifting the ban on the sale and purchase of land and authorizing the establishment of registry offices, Parliament has recently taken a critical step to improving farm productivity and prospects.

Though the Government has privatized over 60 percent of enterprises in manufacturing, the private sector faces an uncertain future in an unfriendly policy framework. A radical

Table 2.6 Major Economic Indicators, Kyrgyz Republic, 1998–2002
(percent)

Item	1998	1999	2000	2001	2002
GDP growth	2.1	3.7	5.0	5.0	5.2
Gross domestic investment/GDP	15.4	18.0	—	—	—
Gross domestic savings/GDP	-6.1	3.2	—	—	—
Inflation rate (consumer price index)	10.5	35.9	18.7	9.1	7.2
Fiscal balance/GDP	-9.5	-12.0	-9.4	—	—
Money supply (M2) growth	17.2	33.9	12.3	—	—
Merchandise export growth	-15.2	-13.5	9.1	—	—
Merchandise import growth	17.0	-27.6	1.4	—	—
Current account balance/GDP	-22.6	-14.8	-9.4	-9.3	-7.8
Debt-service ratio	7.0	8.3	—	—	—

— Not available.

Sources: National Statistical Committee of the Kyrgyz Republic; International Monetary Fund; staff estimates.

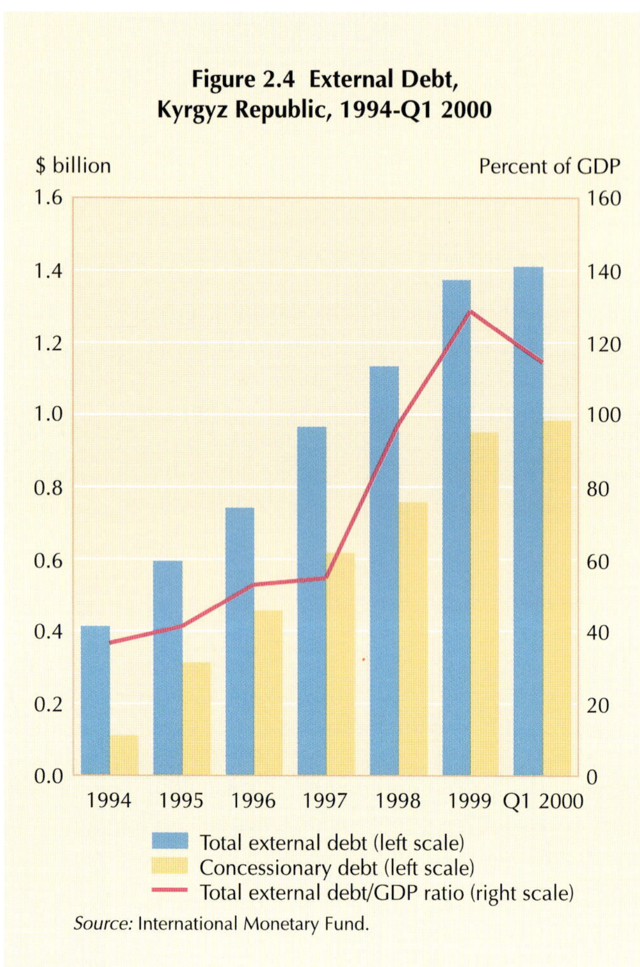

2005 because practically all nonconcessionary debt must be repaid and the grace periods for many concessional loans will end. About 38 percent of government revenue in 2001 is expected to be used for servicing debt; this figure is projected to remain well above 20 percent in the medium term. Rescheduling of bilateral debt will be required in the coming years to smooth out spikes in repayment burdens. The non-concessionary loans are principally from the Russian Federation and Turkey, and include some guaranteed by the Government on commercial terms for the Kumtor gold mine. Bilateral talks are under way to reschedule repayments of the non-concessionary debt. The Government is reviewing its $675 million externally funded public investment program, which is unsustainable at current levels, so as to classify projects on the basis of their social and economic impacts. After classification, public investment in these projects will be reprioritized.

The Government needs to take radical decisions to improve its fiscal consolidation efforts through additional mobilization of tax and nontax revenues to restore fiscal balance. There is scope for raising these revenues with better administration and base broadening since the revenue-to-GDP ratio is low. Pursuit of public sector reforms, particularly in the energy, telecommunications, and transport sectors, is needed to better price the output from these sectors to generate additional internal resources for investment.

Policy and Development Issues

The Kyrgyz Republic is a small open economy, with exports amounting to about 40 percent of GDP, and has made rapid progress in trade liberalization. It joined WTO in December 1998, the first of the former Soviet republics to do so. The present tariff structure is simple: it has four groups with an average rate of 5.2 percent and a maximum rate of 20 percent. Nontariff barriers are few, mainly in the form of quantitative restrictions on and licenses for sumptuary goods, such as alcohol and tobacco, and sensitive items, such as military goods, explosives, and poisonous substances. Export licenses are required for several products. Subsidies are not provided for exports except, to a limited extent, for the units in the free economic zones. The economy is yet to reap the full benefits of WTO market access arrangements as four out of its six largest trading partners are non-WTO members and three of them are neighbors. These three neighbors have also applied for WTO membership and their accession could ease some of the country's current bilateral trade difficulties with them. Pursuance of good subregional trading relationships and finding new trading partners, which inevitably happens with a lag, could provide new opportunities for substantial improvement in foreign trade. In accordance with WTO membership conditions, the Kyrgyz Republic will have to align its economic policies and standards of governance with international benchmarks to help create a vibrant market economy.

improvement in the business environment, and strong support from the Government, are needed to promote entrepreneurs. In particular, the weak financial sector and underdeveloped legal and regulatory institutions are major constraints to rapid private enterprise growth. The restructuring of public enterprises, which will help improve the fiscal situation and general business environment, has been slow but is expected to pick up in the near future.

The economy has a high debt burden, which presents serious risks to macroeconomic management in the short to medium term. Total external debt stood at $1.37 billion (129 percent of GDP) at the end of 1999, rising to $1.41 billion at the end of the first quarter of 2000 (see Figure 2.4). Of this, 69.8 percent (in net present value terms) was concessionary, supplied mostly by multilateral agencies. Persistently high fiscal deficits in excess of 9 percent of GDP since 1993, a shortage of domestic savings to finance public debt, and a sharp devaluation of the som contributed to the sudden increase in outstanding debt. In 1999, debt service absorbed 18 percent of government revenues and amounted to 2.8 percent of GDP. The debt-service burden will increase substantially in the years to

As in most other transition economies, the financial sector and capital markets are still at an early stage of development. The economy has a very low level of financial intermediation. Even at its best, in 1998, the ratio of bank deposits to GDP was low at 6.3 percent; it fell further to 5.4 percent in 1999, reflecting much weaker public confidence in the banking sector after the Russian crisis. This can be compared with figures of 43–99 percent for some countries in Southeast Asia in 1999.

The first round of financial sector reforms began in 1996 and introduced the Basle Committee of Banking Supervision norms for capital adequacy, prudential income recognition, risk exposure, and transparency. The bank supervision capacity of the central bank was also enhanced. While these reforms established a solid regulatory framework, they did not adequately address the inherent weakness of the banking system. Efforts are under way both to reform the banking system by addressing larger corporate governance and restructuring issues as well as legal reforms, and to strengthen the regulatory capacity of the central bank.

However, restructuring of banks and the introduction of stringent entry and regulatory norms are complex processes fraught with political difficulties and financial constraints. The country has 23 licensed commercial banks with an average asset size of $4 million; this is too many banks for a population of 4.7 million. The proliferation of small banks has been due to lax entry norms. Besides significantly increasing the central bank's supervisory burden, this has led to fragmentation of capacity and uneconomic scales of operation. Consequently, the banks work on wide interest rate spreads. Lending rates are high and profit margins thin. High interest rates also increase the risk of default. Poor corporate governance has compounded these problems. At present, six banks, which hold 24 percent of bank deposits, are insolvent, and the finances of the remaining profit-making banks are weak.

Tajikistan

Economic performance in 2000 improved despite a severe drought. Politically, the successful conclusion of the peace process that ended the civil war bodes well for an improvement in the general economic climate, and should help attract much-needed foreign investment and benefit the ongoing privatization process. Careful management of the heavy external debt burden will be necessary to maintain economic stability and support efforts to reduce poverty.

Recent Trends and Prospects

Economic growth accelerated to 5.0 percent in 2000 from 3.7 percent in 1999, despite the worst drought in 74 years (see Figure 2.5). Growth was led by the industry sector, which expanded by 10.3 percent compared with 5.0 percent in 1999. Aluminum production, rising by 30 percent still, dominates the sector. World prices for aluminum rose by 18 percent in 2000, spurring a 44 percent increase in the dollar value of aluminum exports. The services sector also continued to expand, as did small-scale crafts and trade.

Agriculture remains a key sector of the economy, contributing 20 percent of GDP and accounting for 60 percent of employment. A devastating drought resulted in a severe food deficit in 2000, compelling the Government to appeal to the international community for emergency food aid and related assistance. The Government allocated $30 million from the budget to purchase seeds. However, the important cotton sector was less affected because irrigation makes it much less dependent on seasonal weather patterns.

Labor markets remained weak because the country began its transition to a market economy later than other former Soviet republics. Moreover, the narrow base of economic growth has limited employment opportunities. However, they are increasing in the emerging private sector, especially in services, small-scale crafts, and trade. Although official unemployment in 2000 was 3.1 percent, the actual rate was about 30 percent. The official figure does not include unemployment and underemployment in inactive state-owned enterprises (SOEs), and many of the unemployed do not register because of low unemployment benefits.

The fiscal position improved in 2000 due to higher tax collection resulting from economic growth, better compliance, an expanding tax base, and continued rationalization of expenditures. Revenues increased marginally to 13.7 percent of GDP from 13.5 percent in 1999, while expenditures declined to 14.4 percent of GDP from 16.6 percent. As a result, the 2000 deficit narrowed to 0.7 percent of GDP from 3.1 percent in

1999, despite higher drought-related expenditures. However, the fiscal performance is somewhat overstated because some transfers to loss-incurring SOEs were made as directed credit from the banking sector rather than as allocations through the budget. Importantly, the Government has continued its policy and practice of avoiding arrears on government wages, pensions, and social benefits. This policy will soon have a statutory mandate, having been included in the 2001 budget law.

Since June 1997, the authorities have pursued a tight monetary policy to combat inflation. Consequently, inflation dropped steeply from 164 percent in 1997 to 2.7 percent in 1998. A number of external factors, including the Russian crisis, the resulting depreciation of Tajikistan's currency, and increases in the prices of key imports, pushed inflation to 31.0 percent in 1999. There was slippage in the authorities' tight monetary stance in the first half of 2000, resulting in broad money supply (M2) increasing by 30.0 percent in 2000. Monetary expansion, a food price rise of 30 percent due to the drought, and a 90 percent increase in fuel prices resulted in an inflation rate of 24.0 percent in 2000. The currency continued to depreciate, falling by about 30 percent against the dollar in 2000. On 30 October 2000, the somoni replaced the Tajik ruble as the national currency at a rate of 1 somoni to 1,000 Tajik rubles.

The economy's external position is fragile. External balances face substantial instability due to lack of diversity of exports and volatility of prices. Over three quarters of Tajikistan's export earnings come from aluminum and cotton, prices of which fell substantially in 1998 and remained low in 1999, exacerbating the external position. Although prices of these goods rebounded in 2000, by 18 percent and 13 percent, respectively, the current account deficit worsened because the price of imported oil also increased while the drought necessitated significantly higher volumes of imported food: it stood at 5.7 percent of GDP in 2000, compared with 3.5 percent in 1999. The balance of trade also deteriorated in 2000 as imports rose by 13.6 percent and exports expanded by 11.4 percent. Export earnings were led by aluminum, which accounted for

Table 2.7 Major Economic Indicators, Tajikistan, 1998–2002
(percent)

	1998	1999	2000	2001	2002
GDP growth	5.3	3.7	5.0	5.0	6.0
Inflation rate (consumer price index)[a]	2.7	31.0	24.0	12.4	11.0
Money supply (M2) growth	30.7	29.2	30.0	25.2	24.0
Fiscal balance/GDP	-3.8[b]	-3.1[b]	-0.7	-1.0	0.5
Merchandise export growth	-21.4	13.6	11.4	10.8	8.3
Merchandise import growth	-9.7	-4.5	13.6	9.2	6.8
Current account balance/GDP	-9.3	-3.5	-5.7	-6.5	-5.6
Debt-service ratio	11.4	7.6	13.0	14.0	13.0

[a] End of period.
[b] Includes extrabudgetary funds.
Sources: State Statistical Agency; International Monetary Fund.

55 percent of the total. Cotton export earnings fell by 5.4 percent, despite higher prices, because of the poor harvest at the end of 1999. Gross international reserves stood at 1.9 months of imports at the end of 2000, up from 1 month at the end of 1999, but this is still too low. The small increase occurred because capital inflows in the form of concessionary lending from international financial institutions offset the deteriorating current account balance.

External debt was 117 percent of GDP at the end of 2000, and the economy's debt-service burden is fiscally unsustainable. Including repayment of principal, debt service in 2000 was estimated as a proportion of government revenue at 44 percent, and as a proportion of exports at 13 percent. About 35 percent of the outstanding public debt at the end of 2000 was owed to multilateral institutions. The two largest bilateral creditors, the Russian Federation and Uzbekistan, accounted for almost half the public external debt. Virtually all multilateral debt is concessionary, but most bilateral debt is not, and is of a short-term nature. The Government has ongoing negotiations to resolve remaining external debt issues with several bilateral creditors. The Government of the People's Republic of China converted Tajikistan's bilateral debt to a grant in June 2000, but further debt rescheduling agreements with other bilateral donors will be required to prevent the debt-service burden from worsening in the future.

After four consecutive years of economic growth, the outlook continues to improve, but risks and uncertainties remain. A continued tight monetary policy, including a prohibition on directed credits by the central bank, will contribute to achieving a stable macroeconomic environment conducive to growth and poverty reduction. GDP is expected to grow by 5–6 percent in 2001 and 2002, led by faster growth in newly privatized businesses and farms. Manufacturing output is also likely to rise in response to rising domestic demand and excess capacity. However, high world oil prices, food shortages, and the continued depreciation of the currency suggest that the rate of inflation, though slower, will remain quite high over the next two years and that the balance-of-payments position will remain precarious.

The country's large external debt is a major concern and severely constrains the Government's ability to establish a meaningful poverty reduction program. Over the next five years, the external debt could strain the balance of payments as the grace periods for rescheduled debt expire. Debt service is projected to peak at 48 percent of government revenue in 2001 before falling to 30 percent by 2004, while as a proportion of exports it is forecast to rise to about 14 percent in 2001 before falling to around 12 percent in 2003. Managing the debt burden successfully will require the Government to continue negotiations to reschedule the nonconcessionary debt from bilateral creditors, as well as to increase fiscal revenues to about 17 percent of GDP by 2005. Fiscal performance should improve as the value-added and excise tax bases continue to expand and tax compliance improves with the strengthening of the inspectorate dealing with large taxpayers and computerization of tax administration. These gains should more than offset the revenue reductions resulting from a lower sales tax on exported cotton.

Issues in Economic Management

In 2000, the successful conclusion of the peace process that began with the peace agreement of 1997 marking the end of the

Box 2.2 Turkmenistan

GDP declined sharply by almost 50 percent during the years following Turkmenistan's independence in 1991. Despite significant terms-of-trade gains following the move from administered prices to world prices, the economy was unable to take full advantage of rising energy prices due to the inability of several countries of the Commonwealth of Independent States to pay for their imports of natural gas from Turkmenistan. As a result, payment arrears mounted and natural gas output declined. Since 1997, however, the economy has steadily improved. For the first time since independence, real GDP grew by 7 percent in 1998 and by 16 percent in 1999. These increases were due to stronger production of cotton, wheat, gas, and oil. Industrial output rose by 1 percent and 16 percent in 1998 and 1999, respectively, while agriculture expanded by an impressive 24 percent and 26 percent over the same two years.

While GDP growth has resumed, the economy is growing from an extremely low base. In addition, the recovery is fragile as the economy remains vulnerable to external shocks as a result of its almost total reliance on the natural resources of oil and natural gas, and cotton. Furthermore, deep structural problems remain, casting further doubt on the sustainability of the economic recovery in the medium term.

Year-on-year consumer price inflation was at 11 percent for the first five months of 2000, despite a considerable loosening of the Government's monetary stance since the beginning of the year. This is partially explained by pervasive price controls on oil products, building materials, public services, passenger transport, and telecommunications. In addition, water, gas, fuel, and flour, as well as social services, are made available at almost zero cost to consumers. While the policy of providing goods and services free or at very low prices has served to alleviate the conditions of the poor, it reduces incentives to conserve and maintain service infrastructure, distorts the ability of enterprises supplying and receiving such commodities to operate on a market basis, and damages the environment, for example, through wasteful use of non-economically priced water.

On the fiscal front, the situation appears to be under control as data released by the Finance Ministry in early July 2000 showed a budget surplus equivalent to 0.3 percent of GDP for January–June 2000. However, the official figures do not include the large structural deficit reflected in the accumulation of a high level of debt by the ministries and numerous off-budget funds.

Against a background of volatile growth and export performance, the Government has adopted a policy of tight foreign trade and exchange regulations to manage its limited foreign exchange reserves. The economy has a dual exchange rate regime. Since December 1998, when the authorities closed the commercial banks' foreign exchange window, the spread between the official and black market exchange rates has consistently widened. In November 2000, the black market rate reached 20,000 manat per dollar against an official rate of 5,200 manat.

The external position reached dangerous levels in 1998 with a current account deficit of 33 percent of GDP, mainly due to a very difficult export situation. This deficit fell sharply to about 0.2 percent of GDP in 1999 (according to International Monetary Fund estimates), with the resumption of natural gas exports to the Russian Federation. Despite a pronounced improvement in the trade balance, which recorded a $400 million trade surplus for the first nine months of 2000, the current account is expected to have remained with a small deficit in 2000, mainly as a result of a growing deficit on the services account. Turkmenistan's costly state-led investment program (mostly involving infrastructure projects in the capital, Ashgabat) relies on the use of foreign companies, which will consequently require payments in, largely, hard currencies. Given the relatively low levels of foreign investments and the absence of multilateral assistance (mainly due to the very slow pace of economic reforms and the lack of progress toward a more pluralist and democratic political system), Turkmenistan is likely to be faced with increasing difficulties in meeting its debt-service obligations.

---

civil war was of crucial importance to stability and the country's potential to continue its economic recovery. In February and March 2000, members of a new parliament were elected. The subsequent dissolution of the National Peace and Reconciliation Council, in accordance with the 1997 peace agreement, officially concluded the peace process. Continued peace, stability, and security are clearly prerequisites to promoting economic recovery and attracting foreign investment.

Because of the long civil war, Tajikistan's economic reforms were delayed. However, substantial progress in structural reforms has been made since the signing of the peace agreement. The reform process, including privatization, accelerated in 2000. In the first nine months of the year, an additional 60 state-owned farms were privatized. Hence, by the end of

September, 290 of the 600 state farms had been restructured into about 14,000 private farms with marketable land-use rights. Moreover, the Government issued a decree in October to ensure that contracts between private farms and their marketing agents are not controlled by central or local governments. Between April and September, the country's 19 remaining state-owned cotton ginning mills were privatized and paid for. Furthermore, 265 out of some 700 medium and large state-owned enterprises had been sold by August, with full payment received for 214, against December 2000 targets of 280 sold with full payment for 250. Plans were also being developed to restructure and reequip the Tursonzoda aluminum smelter with the assistance of the International Finance Corporation. Hence, after an initial slow start in implementing its privatization pro-

The stock of external debt surged to 54 percent of GDP in 1999 while in 1998 the debt-service ratio reached 98 percent of total exports. The latter was reduced to 55 percent in 1999 following the sharp increase in export revenue. The country's net external debt position is not so bleak if the total amount owed to it for gas exports is taken into account. However, the probability of repayment is not very high. On the other hand, gross official reserves had been built up to about 14 months of imports at the end of 1999.

GDP growth is expected to have risen further to 17 percent in 2000, resulting mostly from the resumption of large-scale gas exports to the Russian Federation. Agricultural growth is likely to have been more limited due to a severe drought. Nevertheless in 2001, GDP growth is forecast to remain strong at 9 percent.

Overall, the Government continues to gradually pursue transition to a market-based economy, primarily with the goal of minimizing the negative impact on living standards of the population. The Government has been fairly successful in maintaining living standards of the very poor. It is estimated that in 1998, 7 percent of the population lived below the poverty line. People are mostly kept out of absolute poverty through a large number of subsidies that are untargeted and perhaps potentially unsustainable. About three quarters of the poor live in rural areas.

The main challenges facing the Government are to consolidate the budget and improve public resource management, unify and liberalize the exchange rate, and further reduce the role of the State in commercial and productive activities. The economy has a good long-term potential for development given its rich resource base, but reaching this potential requires a significant change in policies and careful management of debt and public expenditures. With respect to poverty reduction, the dynamic growth of the agriculture sector seems especially important, and in this regard, the management of water is crucial, as current agricultural practices are extremely wasteful of this commodity, and have contributed to salinization of land and the consequent reduction in yields.

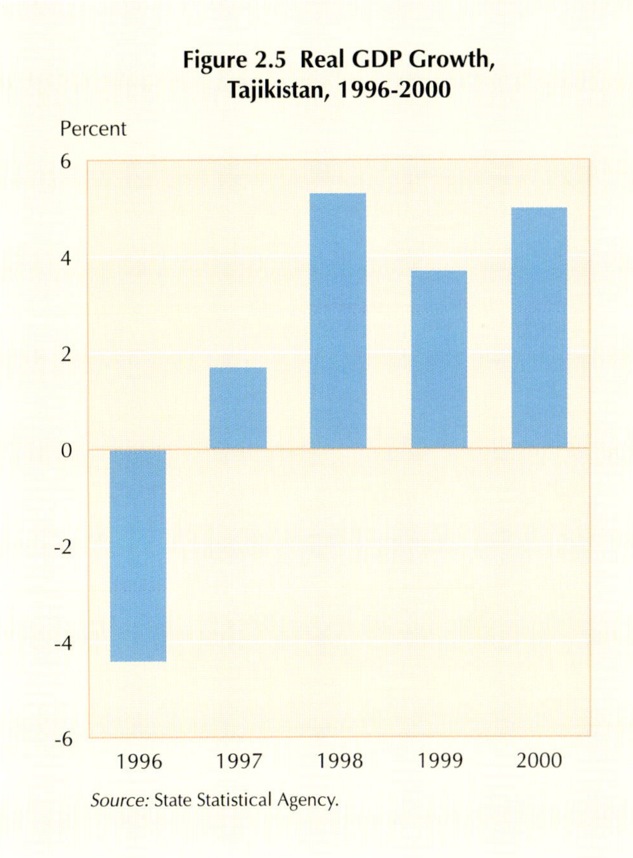

Source: State Statistical Agency.

is 83 percent; the existing social safety net remains inadequate and poorly targeted, and must be strengthened urgently. The Government has already committed itself to reducing poverty, and to this end devoted 42 percent of its 2001 budget to education, health, pensions, and a cash compensation program. In addition, in October 2000, it completed an interim national poverty reduction strategy, which sets out a broad framework for reducing poverty, promoting employment and economic growth, and reforming the social safety net. A final version of this strategy is due to be completed in early 2001. A pilot program to provide an allowance to the poorest 20 percent of schoolchildren began in September 2000. If successful, it will be implemented nationwide in 2001.

Policy and Development Issues

The banking sector performed poorly after independence because of weak management skills, directed credits, an inadequate legal and regulatory framework, and the country's political and macroeconomic instability. Given the importance of this sector, particularly in supporting newly privatized farms and businesses, the authorities are implementing a program to restructure it and rebuild public confidence in it. Under the restructuring guidelines, the Government will only recapitalize a commercial bank if it has restructured its operations, estab-

gram, the Government is largely meeting the program targets. While this is commendable, reports of continued lack of transparency in some privatization activities, resulting in insider sales of farms and enterprises to vested interests, suggest that steps are needed to ensure a more open and fair privatization process. Some local authorities also continue to interfere in the production decisions of privatized farms. More generally, governance and public sector management need to be strengthened to reduce the scope for misuse of public resources and to promote structural reforms that create an environment promoting private-sector-led growth.

Because of the sharp economic contraction since independence in 1991, the Government's ability to provide basic social services has been severely strained. The estimated poverty rate lished a professional management team, developed a business plan to achieve the required capital adequacy ratios and profitability level, and attracted private capital. In May 2000, the four largest commercial banks, which account for over 90 percent of the country's savings and loans, signed restructuring agreements with the central bank. The agreements include reducing staff headcounts and branch numbers, improving recovery of bad loans, limiting new credit expansion, enhancing credit administration and internal controls, and preparing preliminary business plans. Some of these banks have already improved loan recovery rates.

Implementation of banking reforms has been uneven, however. In 2000, the central bank continued occasionally to extend directed credits to some state-owned enterprises, in violation of its stated policies and International Monetary Fund conditions. Moreover, the central bank's loan collection performance was poor. While some of this weakened performance was brought on by the urgent needs resulting from the drought, the authorities need to redouble their efforts to implement sound central banking policies. In the commercial banking sector, lending to insiders is still common, and loan collection remains inadequate. Hence, to further improve supervision, the central bank created a Problem Bank Unit in late 2000 that will be responsible for monitoring and inspecting banks that systematically violate prudential standards. At the same time, the central bank created a Bank Liquidation and Loan Recovery Unit responsible for liquidating failing banks. Moreover, the central bank's Legal and Bank Supervision Department and the ministries of finance and justice are reviewing banking legislation to identify inconsistencies, deviations from international best practice, and impediments to prudent banking. Areas of the legal framework that need to be improved include reducing the cost of repossessing collateral, making loan-loss provisions 100 percent tax deductible, and making the accounting principles in the tax and banking laws consistent with each other.

Finance to the agriculture sector was severely limited in 2000. Most of it was provided to the cotton sector, while financing for newly privatized farms was virtually nonexistent. There were exceptions: a few isolated microfinance schemes led by nongovernment organizations, and pilot credit unions set up in association with newly privatized farms in selected districts. However, these programs have limited outreach, depend on subsidies from donors, and their operations are unsustainable. In 2000, the authorities began to address the need for sustainable rural financial institutions by working with nongovernment organizations to begin developing a framework to encourage the expansion of microfinance services. The need to expand, deepen, and strengthen rural financial institutions will be a crucial component of a general program to reduce rural poverty.

Although distortions in the foreign currency exchange market have lessened, the spread between the official exchange rate and the curb rate remained substantial, averaging 9 percent in 2000, after averaging 22 percent in 1999. In order to further reduce these distortions and to create an efficient market, the operations of the Tajik Interbank Currency Exchange, by which the central bank auctioned foreign currency, were suspended in July 2000, and the central bank lost its role as the sole supplier of foreign exchange. Competitive interbank markets were established to replace the old system. The central bank now quotes the official exchange rate based on a weighted average of the interbank market exchange rates.

Uzbekistan

The economy recorded its fifth year of consecutive GDP growth in 2000. This was at a slower pace than in the previous year, mainly due to a severe drought that hit agricultural production. Overall, the macroeconomic situation remains fairly stable but fragile, with the Government initiating long-awaited currency and trade liberalization reforms.

Recent Trends and Prospects

Economic growth decelerated in 2000 to 3.0 percent from 4.4 percent in 1999; the official target for the year was 4.2 percent. This was mainly the result of slower rates of expansion in agriculture and industry. A poor cotton harvest was caused by drought, while the stagnant growth in industrial output was due to the sharp drop in foreign direct investment and continuing structural problems in the economy.

The growth rate of agricultural output declined to 3.2 percent in 2000 from 5.9 percent in 1999. Grain production reached only 61 percent, and cotton 77 percent, of the target; cotton production was only 3.0 million tons compared with 3.7 million tons in 1999. Overall, the drought destroyed more than 300,000 hectares of sown land, including 50,000 hectares of rice and 30,000 hectares of cotton.

Industrial output slowed slightly to 5.8 percent in 2000 from 6.1 percent in 1999, which was attributed mainly to a lack of investment in the gold and energy sectors and a decline in the production of machinery and equipment. In contrast, ferrous metals, textiles, clothes, and footwear performed relatively well.

The services sector grew by 13.0 percent in 2000 compared with 12.6 percent in 1999 as the sector benefited from the effects of a flurry of private sector activities in wholesale and retail trading, restaurants, bars, hotels, and taxi services. The level of gross domestic investment declined to about 15.9 percent of GDP in 2000 from 17.1 percent in the previous year (see Figure 2.6). Meanwhile, the foreign share of the total volume of capital investments decreased to 22.7 percent in 2000 from 24.4 percent in 1999. Investors seem to have adopted a wait-and-see attitude ahead of the completion of the macroeconomic reform program (discussed below). In particular, very restrictive currency regulations remain a major disincentive to foreign investment.

Economic recovery since 1996 has contributed to employment growth, mainly in the private sector. Nevertheless, unemployment remains high. While the official unemployment rate was only 0.6 percent in 1999, the data mask considerable hidden unemployment in state-owned enterprises (SOEs) and in rural areas. SOEs and collective farms often retain surplus employees to avoid massive layoffs. Labor force participation rates tend to be lower in poorer regions and in rural areas.

Average annual inflation was reported at 28.2 percent in 2000 compared with 29.1 percent in 1999. The inflation target of 20 percent set by the authorities at the beginning of 2000 was exceeded due to a 51 percent increase in wages, the increase in fuel prices (which came into effect on 1 August 2000), and the depreciation of the sum (which fell by 70 percent against the dollar over the first half of 2000). Partly as a result of the government-initiated reforms, the difference between the official and curb market rates was reduced to about 2.5 times by the end of 2000, compared with about 3.5 times during certain periods of 1999.

The current account situation improved, with a surplus equivalent to 0.7 percent of GDP in 2000, compared with a 0.1 percent deficit in 1999. While export earnings declined in 2000 due to lower gold prices and falling cotton export volumes, imports fell even more due to increased import compression and intensified import-substitution policies, because of depreciation and import controls. Gross official reserves grew from $1.24 billion (5.8 months of imports) at the end of 1999 to $1.34 billion (5.2 months of imports) in 2000, while the external debt increased from 26.4 percent to 35.1 percent of GDP over the same period. Most of this debt was raised through the presale of gold and cotton. The debt-service ratio increased from 16.7 percent in 1999 to 28.7 percent in 2000.

With an improvement in tax collection and expenditure control, the state budget outcome was a small deficit of 1.2 percent of GDP at the end of 2000 compared with the 2.8 percent deficit targeted at the beginning of the year. The increase in revenues came from higher valued-added tax and excise tax receipts. Total government revenues remained virtually unchanged at 30.6 percent of GDP while total expenditures declined to 31.8 percent of GDP in 2000. Priority was given to expenditures relating to the development of key economic sectors and the financing of state and national programs. Additional expenditures were also made from contingency funds to help in drought relief, but at the cost of lower social safety net

Table 2.8 Major Economic Indicators, Uzbekistan, 1998–2002
(percent)

Item	1998	1999	2000	2001	2002
GDP growth	4.4	4.4	3.0	3.0	3.0
Gross domestic investment/GDP	20.9	17.1	15.9	—	—
Gross domestic savings/GDP	16.5	17.3	16.5	—	—
Inflation rate (consumer price index)	17.7	29.1	28.2	22.5	22.0
Money supply (M2) growth	28.1	32.1	27.1	25.2	25.2
Fiscal balance/GDP	-3.4	-2.7	-1.2	-3.3	—
Merchandise export growth	-18.0	-2.7	-5.9	9.4	4.7
Merchandise import growth	-22.0	-11.9	-8.0	3.5	3.8
Current account balance/GDP	-0.8	-0.1	0.7	2.1	3.3
External debt/GDP	23.7	26.4	35.1	39.7	41.4

— Not available.

Sources: Ministry of Macroeconomics and Statistics; International Monetary Fund; staff estimates.

expenditures, which declined from 3.0 percent of GDP in 1999 to 2.4 percent in 2000.

Monetary policy remained relatively loose, with interest rates still sharply negative in real terms and growth in money supply (M2) estimated at 27.1 percent in 2000. Credit to the economy from the banking system has increased significantly in real terms over the past couple of years. Yet overall, the country's financial sector, including its equity and bond markets, is still at a very early stage of development.

Annual GDP growth is projected to remain at about 3 percent in 2001 and 2002. Development prospects for agriculture remain bleak, mainly due to the persistence of drought, the existing inefficient and inequitable state order system, and the lack of effective water management policies. Industry is likely to continue experiencing difficulties in the short to medium term, as SOE reforms will probably lead to more downsizing and closure of nonviable SOEs. On the other hand, the chemical industry is expected to grow significantly as the Government is implementing an ambitious state-led development program in the sector. The services sector is also expected to develop faster due to the almost complete privatization of SOEs in this sector and increasing demand.

The fiscal deficit is forecast to widen to more than 3 percent of GDP in 2001. While government revenues are projected to be maintained at around 30 percent of GDP, total expenditures are projected to rise to about 33 percent of GDP, as outlays on education, health, and social security increase further.

Real interest rates are expected to move up in 2001 and 2002, given that the Government is slowly weakening the exchange rate as part of a painful move toward sum convertibility. However, positive real interest rates could strain the Government's fiscal stance further by increasing its cost of borrowing. In addition, a tight monetary policy might lead to bankruptcies. Therefore, over 2001–2002, the monetary stance is likely to remain loose with a targeted inflation rate of about 22 percent.

The balance-of-payments situation is projected to improve gradually over the medium term mainly because of the anticipated better export performance, caused by the depreciating sum, and greater inflows of foreign direct investment (FDI), as the Government's efforts toward unification of the multiple exchange rates (see below) gather momentum. The current account surplus is projected to improve to about 2–3 percent during 2001–2002.

The economy faces several short- and medium-term risks, namely: (i) high dependence on exports of two major products, gold and cotton, making it vulnerable to adverse movements in world prices or the vagaries in the weather, as was the case for cotton in 2000; (ii) vulnerability to an increased debt-service burden as a result of the recent sharp rise in external debt; and (iii) constant threats to political and territorial security from terrorist groups in the border areas, and consequent high defense spending.

Issues in Economic Management

While the economy has good long-term potential for growth (e.g., a relatively high level of human capital and rich natural resource endowments), economic performance is likely to be modest. The Government must take further steps toward exchange rate unification and trade liberalization to re-attract FDI flows and spur the growth of the economy. Existing foreign trade restrictions include the following: (i) mandatory registration of import contracts with the Ministry of Foreign Economic Relations (MFER); (ii) an obligation on importing enterprises to obtain a foreign exchange license from the Central Bank of Uzbekistan; (iii) an obligation on any importing enterprise to obtain a license from the MFER to conduct import operations; (iv) centralized exports of gold and cotton; (v) exporters' obligation to surrender 50 percent of foreign exchange at the less preferential overvalued official exchange rate; (vi) import quotas through the tender system for basic foodstuffs; and (vii) import tariffs and excise duties set at high levels compared with international norms. It is crucial that economic policies and decisions are increasingly driven by price signals, and that the Government gradually moves away from being a dominant figure in all economic decisions to playing a regulatory and supportive role to growth led by the private sector.

Overall, however, the issue of current account convertibility is the main item on the economic reform agenda for 2001. Despite the first steps taken by merging the official and commercial bank exchange rates in May 2000, the unified official exchange rate remained substantially overvalued, administratively determined, and accessible to the same limited set of economic agents. Exchange rate unification by itself is not sufficient to achieve current account convertibility. Real liberalization of access to foreign exchange for all current account transactions as well as lifting exchange restrictions on current account transactions should accompany the process. Concessionary and commercial foreign capital inflows are likely to increase if the Government commits itself to a genuine liberalization policy. Any such policy should include: (i) implementing current account convertibility; (ii) lifting foreign trade restrictions; (iii) reforming the banking sector; (iv) developing a market infrastructure for capital, commodity, and real estate markets; (v) eliminating bureaucratic obstacles to establishing and operating private businesses; (vi) removing the state order system for cotton and wheat that will improve incentives in the agriculture sector; and (vii) switching from an import substitution to an export promotion policy that will build on the country's dynamic comparative advantage.

Unemployment and poverty also present important concerns over the medium term. Currently, there is considerable hidden unemployment and underemployment in SOEs and collective farms. Deepening of SOE and agricultural reforms will lead to downsizing or closing of inefficient industrial units and collective farms, and the resulting surplus labor will pose a major challenge to policymakers. Possible responses include initiating wide-ranging reforms that will attract private sector investment for creating new employment opportunities and further developing small and medium-sized enterprises so as to help absorb redundant workers and new entrants to the labor force. Currently, there is a mismatch between the supply and demand for various skills in the labor market. One of the impeding factors is the slow pace of reform. Additional steps have to be taken to increase labor mobility, which has traditionally been very low, but which is crucial due to the seasonal factor in labor demand.

Policy and Development Issues

One of the priority reforms in the short and medium term is the restructuring of the financial sector, currently dominated by a few large banks. The Government recognizes the importance of having a strong financial sector to ensure sustained growth, an orderly transition to a market economy, and efficient delivery of credit to small and medium-sized enterprises. The banking system is highly concentrated, with five major state banks controlling 90 percent of total banking assets in the country. Banks do not compete with each other but maintain their sectoral focus, as in the early post-independence years. The

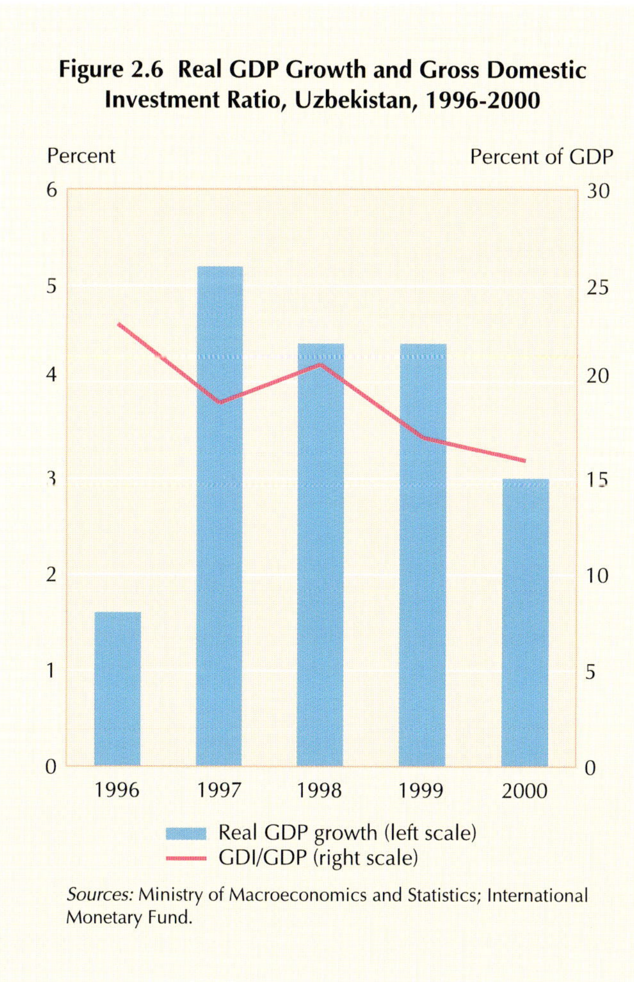

Figure 2.6 Real GDP Growth and Gross Domestic Investment Ratio, Uzbekistan, 1996-2000

Sources: Ministry of Macroeconomics and Statistics; International Monetary Fund.

most important commercial banks are still state owned and follow credit policies set by the Republican Monetary Policy Commission, in pursuance of the Government's agricultural and industrial strategies. Banks also facilitate revenue collection for the Government. In the transition toward a market economy, the banks have helped the Government fund its budget through timely collection and transfer of taxpayers' funds. To improve public trust in banks and to allow their proper functioning as financial intermediaries, the institutional basis for tax collection as a government function should be strengthened, and kept distinct from the responsibilities of a commercial bank.

Some major steps in banking sector reforms have already been taken. Recognizing the need for better depositor protection and confidentiality, and for increased interbank competition, the Government passed a resolution in January 1999 to regulate the use of bank accounts for tax purposes and gradually phase out restrictions pertaining to the number of bank accounts used by a legal entity. Further, to extend efficient banking services to small depositors and small private entrepreneurs, it has attached high priority to developing efficient and stable privately owned banks: so far, 10 fully privately owned banks have been established. The Government has also moved to restrict the issue of guarantees for bank lending to public investments refinanced by foreign multilateral or bilateral lenders and to priority production activities in sectors such as agriculture and pharmaceuticals. To facilitate these reforms, it is strengthening banking regulation and supervision, providing training for financial sector personnel to improve their managerial and technical capabilities, restructuring banks with poor loan portfolios, and developing other capital market institutions. The Government has a stated policy objective to move the banking sector into a market-oriented environment, to allow the banks independence in banking activities, and to diversify their corporate sector activities. Therefore, it has placed a high priority on speeding up the processes of financial sector liberalization, restructuring, and privatization. To initiate the privatization process, it has created a bank privatization agency and nominated five banks (National Bank of Uzbekistan, Asaka Bank, Uzjilsberbank, Tadbirkorbank, and Zamin Bank) for the first round of privatization.

Mongolia

The economy continued performing much below potential in 2000, with meager economic growth, an increase in inflation, and a slight deterioration in the current account balance. However, with the resumption of stabilization and reform measures after the installation of the new Government, prospects for stronger economic performance have improved.

Recent Trends and Prospects

The economy saw another year of below-potential performance in 2000. GDP grew by a mere 0.5 percent, following 3.6 percent average annual growth during 1997–1999. The country experienced its most severe winter in three decades in 1999/2000, when nearly 10 percent of livestock was lost, affecting the livelihood of about 20 percent of the population. The Government adopted expansionary fiscal and monetary policies, with one eye on the July 2000 elections, leading to the persistence of a substantial fiscal imbalance and a steep rise in the money supply. The fiscal deficit, at 10.8 percent of GDP, breached the 8.5 percent target for 2000 agreed under the Poverty Reduction and Growth Facility of the International Monetary Fund. Money supply (M2) was growing at an annualized rate of about 32 percent by December 1999, and averaged about 35 percent in the first 10 months of 2000, but fell to a more modest 17.6 percent by December 2000.

The expansionary policy stance had three adverse consequences: an increase in domestic inflation, a worsening of the current account balance, and a continued buildup of external debt. The declining trend of inflation was reversed: having fallen from about 37 percent in 1997 to 7.6 percent in 1999, it rose to 11.6 percent in 2000. The increase in food prices was particularly sharp, with the price of meat alone rising by about 30 percent. This had an adverse effect on the living standards of the urban poor, who spend most of their income on food. The current account deficit remained high at close to 15 percent of GDP in 2000. Large current account deficits in recent years have led to a rapid accumulation of external debt, which almost doubled from $532 million in 1996 to about $935 million in 2000, or from 46 percent of GDP to close to 100 percent of GDP. About 53 percent of this debt is owed to multilateral institutions, 40 percent to bilateral institutions, and the remainder to commercial sources.

The landslide victory of the Mongolian People's Revolutionary Party in the general elections of July 2000 ended the political instability that had characterized the country since 1998. This should reverse the economic policy drift of recent years. The new Government has made a modest beginning at macroeconomic stabilization with a budget for the year 2001 that plans to reduce the fiscal deficit from about 11 percent of GDP to 7.4 percent in 2001. As the economy stabilizes, Mongolia should be able to lay the foundations for faster and sustained economic growth over the medium term. GDP growth is likely to pick up to about 3 percent in 2001 and to about 4 percent in 2002. While gross domestic investment is expected to stabilize at a more sustainable rate of about 25 percent of GDP, gross domestic savings should gradually rise from about 19 percent of GDP in 2000 to about 22 percent in 2002. Both these elements should contribute to a decline in the current account deficit to about 10 percent in 2002. In addition, the external economic environment is likely to be slightly more favorable in 2001 and 2002 than in the recent past. The prices of copper and cashmere, two of the most important export items, have improved in the international market, which should reverse the deterioration in the terms of trade that the economy has experienced since 1999, thus easing the balance-of-payments situation. Moreover, growth in the Russian economy has accelerated, which should provide a positive external impetus. With the reduction in the current account deficit, growth in the country's external debt is likely to be contained to modest levels. The stabilization measures should also lead to a decline in inflation to about 8 percent in 2001 and about 6 percent in 2002. Higher growth and lower inflation should enable some dent to be made in the unemployment and poverty figures.

Issues in Economic Management

Any improvement in the economic outlook depends on the Government's commitment to effective economic management, which in particular should focus on progressively reducing the fiscal deficit to levels that concessionary foreign sources can finance, and on strengthening the country's agriculture sector.

Fiscal consolidation is required to bring aggregate demand in line with aggregate supply, and is the most pressing need for macroeconomic stability. Although the 2001 budget plans a significant reduction in the fiscal deficit, it makes very little effort to contain government spending, where the key challenge is to contain current expenditures, especially wages, goods, and services (which together constitute about 17 percent of GDP), and indirect subsidies to state enterprises. While direct subsidies to nonfinancial state enterprises have largely stopped, indirect subsidies through preferential input pricing, noncollection of debts, and exemptions from import duties have increased in recent years. The Government needs to make a concerted effort to contain these costs.

Strengthening agriculture is likely to minimize supply-side shocks to a predominantly agricultural economy, and requires immediate attention from the new Government. Bad weather over the past two years has caused severe harm to the sector and to the people who depend on it. Although the Government has taken measures to promote broad-based agriculture—including deregulation of agricultural prices, privatization of livestock, and liberalization of agricultural trade—the sector faces various constraints. Many of the new private owners have little knowledge of how to manage their assets in a market economy. The supply of critical support services, previously organized and controlled by the Government, has deteriorated and left a vacuum that the private sector has not yet adequately filled. Inadequate rural finance and marketing facilities have further hampered the sector's development.

Policy and Development Issues

The main task facing the Government is to bring down the high poverty rates, in part caused by the low-growth environment of recent years and by a weakened social safety net. The collapse of the command economy and the subsequent steps in the transition to a market economy, including privatization, led to severe unemployment, as well as to reduced public provision of health, education, and other social services, weakening the scope of the social safety net. In response, the Government made some attempts to develop alternative approaches, such as social insurance and health insurance programs. Despite these measures, the social safety net remains inadequate for the many people who have lost their jobs. Since 1995, the proportion of people living below the official poverty line has remained high at about 36 percent, while both the depth and severity of poverty have increased. The poor, especially small livestock herders, the urban poor, and street children, are highly vulnerable to even minor external shocks, adverse weather patterns, and negative effects of the transition process. Besides fiscal consolidation and restoration of macroeconomic stability, progress in poverty reduction over the medium term will depend crucially on the Government's success in generating faster economic growth and employment, and in strengthening overall standards of governance.

A strategy of generating faster growth and hence employment over the medium term should rely primarily on improving the productivity of investment, both in the public and private sectors. At more than 25 percent of GDP, Mongolia's investment rate compares favorably with that of many developing countries with similar incomes. However, the productivity of that investment (as measured by the capital-output ratio) is low and falling. Investment in Mongolia is only about two thirds as productive as investment was in the fast-growing Asian economies before the financial crisis. Domestic investment is roughly

Table 2.9 Major Economic Indicators, Mongolia, 1998–2002
(percent)

Item	1998	1999	2000	2001	2002
GDP growth	3.5	3.2	0.5	3.0	4.0
Gross domestic investment/GDP	25.0	27.0	26.0	25.0	25.0
Gross domestic savings/GDP	18.5	20.0	19.0	21.0	22.0
Inflation rate (consumer price index)	9.4	7.6	11.6	8.0	6.0
Money supply (M2) growth	-1.7	31.6	17.6	14.0	12.0
Fiscal balance/GDP	-14.3	-11.9	-10.8	-7.4	-6.0
Merchandise export growth	-12.1	4.7	15.0	15.0	13.0
Merchandise import growth	9.5	2.9	17.1	12.0	10.0
Current account balance/GDP	-13.2	-14.1	-14.8	-11.0	-10.0
Debt-service ratio	7.3	9.7	5.3	5.1	5.0

Sources: Bank of Mongolia; Ministry of Finance; International Monetary Fund; staff estimates.

split between the public and private sectors; about half the public sector investment is made by the national Government and the remainder by state enterprises.

Efforts to improve productivity of public investment should start with state enterprises, especially in the copper, coal, and power sectors. A combination of low energy prices, production inefficiencies, and inadequate application of commercial principles in financial relationships between enterprises has led to a massive buildup of operational deficits that are financed by interenterprise arrears and borrowings from the domestic banking system. To improve investment returns, restructuring these state enterprises is crucial, and the new Government has committed itself to this, including some privatization. The medium-term strategy to reform them should concentrate on improving technical efficiency, strengthening internal enterprise governance, and imposing market discipline.

Improved productivity of private investment requires the reforming and restructuring of the financial system. Despite recent measures to strengthen the banking system, including the liquidation of two large insolvent banks, the doubling of minimum capital requirements, and the revocation of licenses of banks that do not meet minimum capital requirements, further measures are needed. These include curtailing public sector borrowing from the banks, phasing out the Government's role as owner of the banking system, and reinforcing its role as an arm's length banking regulator.

Efforts to strengthen overall governance standards should focus primarily on reforming the civil service and improving public sector management, and establishing a legal infrastructure to support the private sector and a market economy. At present, the structure and functioning of the civil service are highly centralized, with pay and benefits centrally determined and a single annual entrance examination. New management methods and regulations are required, in particular a more performance-based approach. Recognizing this, the Government has embarked on a 10-year program of public administration reform.

Compared with other small transition economies, Mongolia has made significant progress in laying the foundations for the development of a private sector, which now accounts for about 60 percent of GDP. Despite this progress, the lack of clearly defined property rights, especially with regard to land-ownership, is constraining private sector efficiency. The fact that land leases are not transferable impedes infrastructure development on leased land. Similarly, the prohibition of private ownership of cropland impedes investment in agriculture. Over the medium term, measures to reform the land tenure regime need to focus on amending the Land Law to allow for the transfer of leases, establishing a national land information system, and approving the draft Land Privatization Law and the Land Ownership Law (which were submitted to Parliament in 1997 but have yet to be approved).

People's Republic of China

People's Republic of China

Three straight years of expansionary fiscal and monetary policy have helped the economy contain the adverse effects of the Asian financial crisis, maintain a stable exchange rate, and achieve robust growth. The main challenges now are to maintain a high growth rate of aggregate demand in a less expansionary fiscal and monetary environment, and to establish a sustainable social security system.

Recent Trends and Prospects

GDP growth accelerated to 8.0 percent in 2000 from 7.1 percent in 1999, due to an improvement in industrial growth to 9.6 percent from 8.1 percent. The profitability of both private and state-owned enterprises (SOEs) improved as a result of increased consumption demand and reform measures such as debt-equity swaps. The services sector likewise improved, posting 7.8 percent growth in 2000, compared with 7.5 percent expansion in 1999. The agriculture sector, on the other hand, suffered from a severe drought and a decline in retail food prices. Grain output fell by about 9 percent in 2000.

Growth in 2000 was driven mainly by domestic consumption and investment. After slowing for five consecutive years, retail sales grew by 9.7 percent, up from 6.8 percent growth in 1999. A combination of fiscal stimulus packages and a recovery in private investment led to 9.3 percent expansion in 2000 in domestic fixed investment. An accommodative monetary policy boosted domestic demand: the prime lending rate was 5.9 percent from June 1999, compared with 11 percent in mid-1996. Since June 1999, the domestic bank lending rate has been lower than the comparable rate on dollar-denominated assets in the international market.

The deflationary trend of the previous two years was largely arrested in 2000: the consumer price index increased by 0.4 percent. However, excluding oil-related goods and one-time price adjustments for some service products, the index declined slightly in 2000, mainly because of lower prices for agricultural products.

The official estimate of urban unemployment in 2000 was about 3.1 percent of the urban labor force, the same level as in the previous year. However, this estimate covers only those registered with the Ministry of Labor and Social Security. It does not include about 7 million *xiagang* workers (i.e., those who were laid off as part of ongoing SOE reforms) who have not found alternative employment. When *xiagang* workers are included, urban unemployment rises to about 7 percent.

Fiscal policy in 2000 remained expansionary (see Figure 2.7). An additional Y50 billion stimulus package was announced in August 2000. Revenue collection was 16.9 percent higher than in 1999 because of improved performance in industry, recent fiscal reform measures including those against smuggling, and strong growth of external trade. Despite this, the fiscal deficit in 2000 widened to 2.8 percent of GDP compared with 2.1 percent in 1999. Broad money supply grew by 12.3 percent in 2000, slightly lower than in 1999.

To prepare the economy for membership of the World Trade Organization (WTO), the People's Bank of China, the central bank, is considering mechanisms to gradually allow a greater role for market forces in determining interest rates. As a first step, interest rates on foreign currency loans and foreign currency deposits of more than $1 million were liberalized in the third quarter of 2000.

With the recovery of the countries affected by the Asian financial crisis and strong growth in the US economy, exports from the People's Republic of China (PRC) surged in 2000 by 27.8 percent to $249 billion. Imports soared by 36.8 percent to $217 billion. Exports to the Russian Federation, the Republic of Korea, and countries of the Association of Southeast Asian Nations grew by over 40 percent. Imports of primary products, such as crude oil, metal, wood, timber, and paper, increased by 82 percent. The current account surplus in 2000 amounted to $14 billion or 1.5 percent of GDP, compared with $15.6 billion or 1.6 percent of GDP in 1999.

Actual foreign direct investment increased by 4 percent in 2000, while contracted foreign investment rose by 51 percent. With foreign exchange reserves of $165 billion and an external debt of $156 billion, the external payments situation remained comfortable.

Driven by domestic consumption growth, the economy is forecast to maintain annual GDP growth of 7.3 percent and 7.5 percent in 2001 and 2002, respectively. Both the industry and services sectors should grow at about 8 percent in this period, and the agriculture sector at about 3 percent. Domestic consumption is projected to remain strong as the general domestic economic environment improves. With the pickup in domestic consumption and economic growth, the deflationary trend in prices will be reversed. Furthermore, the impact of rising world oil prices will push up production costs. In addition, food prices may rise slightly in the first half of 2001 because of the reduction in grain production in the second half of 2000. Given significant excess capacity in many industries, including several consumer industries, the net result is that inflation is likely to be about 2–2.5 percent in 2001–2002. Urban unemployment could further rise as more workers are laid off as SOE reforms continue.

Export growth is forecast to decline to about 10–15 percent in 2001–2002, reflecting a slower global economy and the high base of 2000. With the PRC's entry into WTO and the liberalization of trade policies, including fewer tariff and nontariff barriers, imports will continue to grow faster than exports in the next few years. As a result, the current account surplus will gradually decline. However, the fall in the current account surplus will be offset by larger inflows of foreign investment, as the Government further opens up the economy to foreign participation. Consequently it is expected that the PRC will have an overall balance-of-payments surplus of about $10 billion–$12 billion in the next two years. Some of this surplus will be used to build up foreign exchange reserves. Therefore, despite a reduction in the current account surplus, official foreign exchange reserves will have increased to nearly $185 billion by the end of 2002. It is projected that this level of reserves should be sufficient to cover eight months of imports, the entire external debt, and several times the level of short-term external debt. The exchange rate is expected to remain stable over the next two years.

Issues in Economic Management

In the aftermath of the Asian financial crisis, the Government followed an expansionary fiscal policy. Fiscal stimulus packages totaling Y360 billion were used to increase investment in infrastructure and pump-prime growth in 1997–1999. As a result, the fiscal deficit rose from 0.8 percent of GDP in 1996 to 2.1 percent in 1999. While the fiscal deficit in 2000 was 2.8 percent of GDP, it does not give a full picture of potential fiscal vulnerability, as it does not take into account: (i) the quasi-fiscal expenditures needed to resolve the problem of nonperforming loans (NPLs) of the state-owned banks and the recapitalization of those banks, (ii) the unfunded pension liabilities of the Government, and (iii) the expenditures necessary to finance social security obligations. Some estimates show that, if these quasi-fiscal expenditures had been included, the public sector deficit in 2000 would have been about 8 percent of GDP. The fiscal implications of resolving the legacy of the NPLs and reforming the social security system suggest that the public sector deficit may increase to about 10 percent of GDP by 2003. Therefore, further improvement of fiscal management will be required to make the fiscal balance sustainable. This is a challenging task, especially since government expenditures, as a percentage of GDP, have grown faster than revenues in recent years.

While the world oil price increases in 2000 had some negative impact on the PRC's economic growth and balance of payments, the magnitude was much less than in other Asian economies. The ratio of net oil imports to domestic oil consumption was about 22 percent in the PRC compared with 55 percent in Thailand, 60 percent in the Philippines, and

Table 2.10 Major Economic Indicators, People's Republic of China, 1998–2002
(percent)

Item	1998	1999	2000	2001	2002
GDP growth	7.8	7.1	8.0	7.3	7.5
Gross domestic investment/GDP	37.4	37.0	37.1	37.0	37.2
Gross domestic savings/GDP	39.8	38.0	38.0	38.2	38.5
Inflation rate (consumer price index)	-0.8	-1.4	0.4	2.0	2.5
Money supply (M2) growth	14.9	14.7	12.3	13.0	14.0
Fiscal balance/GDP[a]	-1.2	-2.1	-2.8	-2.3	-1.8
Merchandise export growth	0.5	6.1	27.8	10.0	15.0
Merchandise import growth	0.3	15.8	36.8	20.0	15.0
Current account balance/GDP	3.1	1.6	1.5	1.2	1.0

[a] Central and local government finance.

Sources: National Bureau of Statistics; International Monetary Fund; staff estimates.

100 percent in Japan. The PRC has been a net oil importer since the early 1990s. Its net oil import bill in dollar terms doubled in 2000 from the 1999 level, and may rise further in 2001. To reduce the burden on state finances, domestic fuel prices were increased on seven different occasions since November 1998, and the Government has since decided to adjust fuel prices every month. In the future, the economy will become heavily dependent on imported oil. Its demand for crude oil is projected to grow annually by 4 percent in the next decade, while the ratio of domestic supply to its total demand for oil, including refined products, is forecast to fall from the present 78 percent or so to 71 percent in 2010 and to 62 percent in 2020. Unless the economy can improve its energy efficiency, develop new domestic supplies, and diversify to other energy sources, oil imports will eventually become a heavy burden on the balance of payments.

Policy and Development Issues

Issues that the Government must resolve in the coming years include strengthening the financial system, addressing urban poverty, adjusting the economy to WTO rules, and reducing income disparities between regions. The establishment of four asset management companies (AMCs) to resolve the problem of NPLs in the banking system in 1999 was a major milestone in financial sector reform. About Y1.3 trillion ($157 billion) of NPLs, equivalent to about 10 percent of the total assets of the four big state-owned commercial banks, were transferred to the AMCs by June 2000. Most often, the AMCs used debt-equity swaps to resolve the NPL problem, signing contracts worth about Y200 billion, an amount equivalent to about 15 percent of the total assets of the AMCs, with 228 enterprises. Many of the problems in the financial sector that are related to ailing SOEs account for a large portion of bank NPLs. Two of the most difficult SOE reform issues are developing alternative methods to provide social security services traditionally provided by SOEs and generating employment for workers made redundant by SOE reforms.

While the transfer of a significant proportion of NPLs to AMCs will improve the financial position of the banks, the ultimate success of the AMCs will depend on the rate of recovery from NPLs. For the AMC initiative to succeed, debt-equity swaps must be accompanied by meaningful enterprise restructuring. This will require (i) providing legal powers to the AMCs to restructure the management and operations of the enterprises in which they become stakeholders, including the ability to replace managers when necessary; and (ii) enhancing creditors' rights by revising the bankruptcy law and establishing procedures for the valuation and disposal of state assets.

The Government has made significant efforts to restructure many nonbank financial institutions. However, as the proportion of NPLs held by these institutions becomes greater than that held by the banks, the Government must increasingly ad-

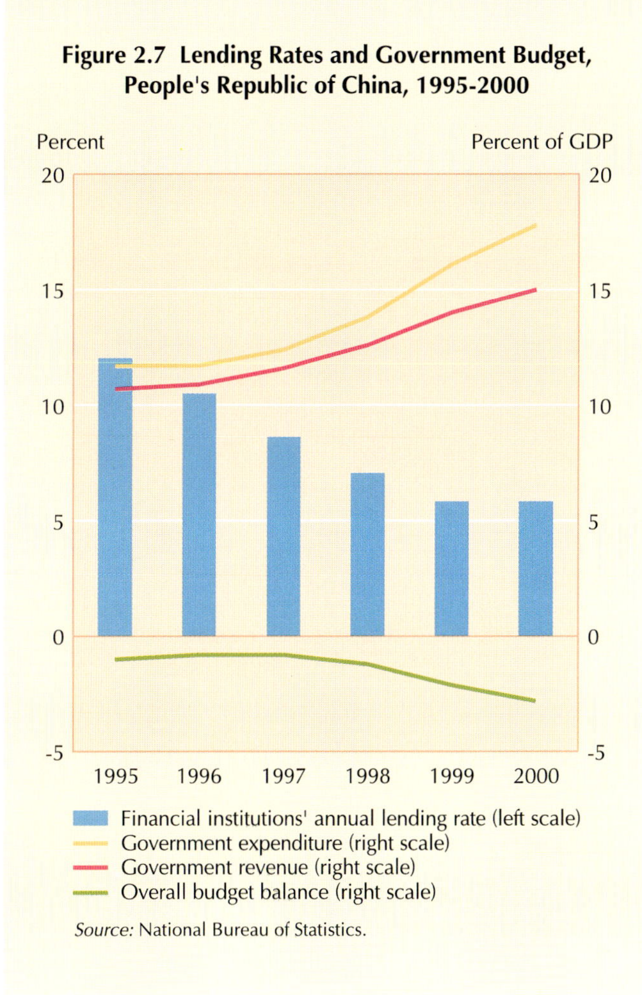

Figure 2.7 Lending Rates and Government Budget, People's Republic of China, 1995-2000

Source: National Bureau of Statistics.

dress their NPL problem so that systemic risks will not be transmitted to the rest of the financial sector.

The PRC's accession to WTO and its associated commitments to cut tariffs, liberalize trade and investment, and open domestic sectors to foreign participation will lead to significant efficiency gains, more competition, and wider consumer choice. However, some of these benefits will take time to make themselves felt. During the early years, membership in WTO will pose several challenges, including substantial structural adjustment across a wide range of sectors (e.g., agriculture, automobiles, banking, insurance, and telecommunications). The Government has amended three laws relating to foreign investment (on foreign joint ventures, foreign cooperatives, and wholly owned foreign ventures) in preparation for WTO entry. These changes will generally help foreign firms compete equally with domestic companies. The Government is also committed to revising over 1,000 laws and regulations, including a patent law, to make them consistent with WTO rules.

As a result both of redundancies among workers and rural-urban migration, urban unemployment and urban poverty

Box 2.3 Role of the Private Sector in Economic Development in the People's Republic of China

The emergence of a significant private sector in the People's Republic of China is one of the most important aspects of the market-oriented reforms in the past 20 years. The domestic private sector (including domestic private enterprises and self-employed individuals) accounted for at least 13 percent of PRC's GDP in 1998. If a broader concept is used—including companies listed on stock exchanges, joint ventures with foreign participation, private agriculture, and nominal collective companies, which are collective in name but truly private companies—the private sector accounted for 50 percent of GDP.

Private sector development has helped the economy absorb a growing component of the labor force. Since 1994, the domestic private sector has taken in an average of 8.2 million workers every year. Aside from joint ventures with foreign participation, the domestic private sector is the only sector that has provided jobs to unemployed workers from state-owned enterprises and redundant rural laborers in the past five years. The sector currently employs 83 million people, or 12 percent of the workforce, which is equivalent to the number employed by the Government and state-owned enterprises.

Private sector development has also had a significant impact on poverty reduction. Provinces and cities that have a high share of private sector activity usually have much lower poverty. A recent unpublished Asian Development Bank study shows that the relationship between per capita GDP and the share of private sector employment in total employment in 30 provinces clearly indicates the contribution of private sector employment to the level of income (see box figure). On average among provinces, for every 1 percent increase in the share of private employment, there is a corresponding increase of Y164 ($20) in per capita GDP.

In spite of the rapid development of the last two decades, the general environment for the private sector needs to be further improved: market distortions, strict regulations, limited access to finance and public service, and high operating costs due to rent seeking and bureaucratic procedures of some local governments should be removed. General weaknesses of governance and transparency of private firm operations are also apparent. The Government needs to overcome these constraints.

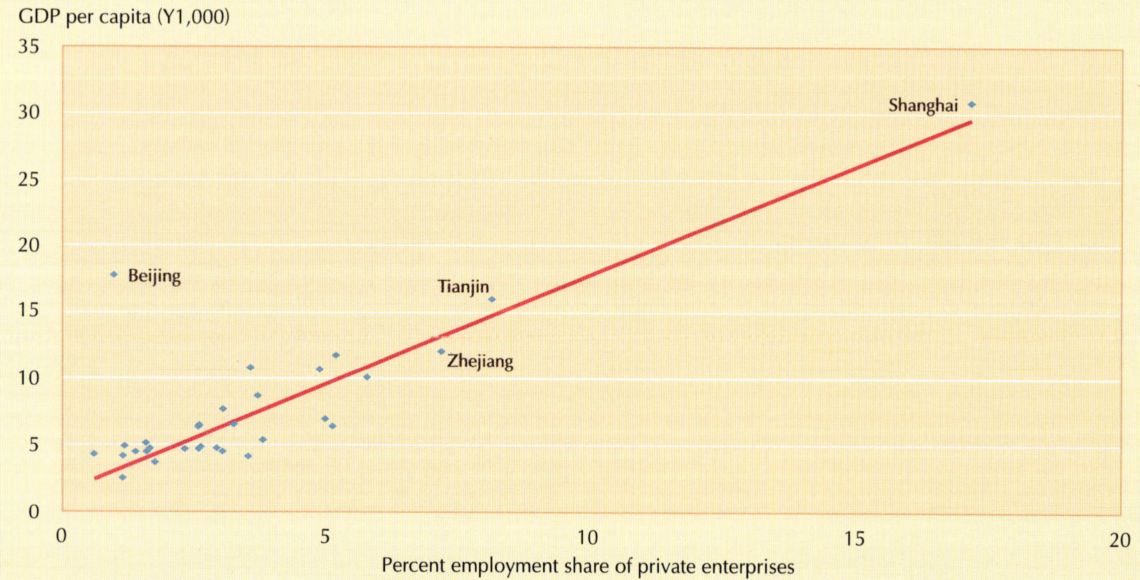

Box Figure: Relationship between per Capita GDP and the Employment Share of the Domestic Private Sector in the People's Republic of China, 1999

Note: The data include 30 provinces, municipalities, and autonomous regions excluding Beijing. GDP per capita in Beijing was Y19,800 ($2,400), but the employment share of private enterprises was only 1.3 percent.
Source: China Statistical Yearbook, 2000.

increased in the second half of the 1990s. The Government has responded to rising urban unemployment by facilitating job creation through promoting the private sector, especially small and medium-sized enterprises (SMEs), and by initiating reforms of the social security system to establish a social safety net. It has also adopted measures to create a more favorable environment for the private sector, including amending the constitution in March 1999 to give greater legal status to the private sector. The Government has passed several economic laws to develop the type of legal and regulatory framework required for the efficient functioning of a market economy. It has also sought to improve SME access to credit by setting up credit guarantee schemes in more than 70 cities. Commercial banks have been requested to establish SME departments to improve their services to these enterprises. In addition, the Government has initiated a social security reform program to reduce the social costs of SOE reform, the key objectives of which are to help transform the existing arrangements into a multifaceted and financially sustainable system, broaden coverage, and establish an enabling environment that will support the long-term viability of the system. Starting in 2001, a large-scale pilot project on social security reform will be implemented in Liaoning province and in several cities. A minimum living standards support system for urban residents has also been established to help those in urban areas with incomes below the poverty line.

Coupled with the Government's antipoverty programs, sustained economic growth and macroeconomic stability have helped reduce poverty. The number of rural people with incomes below the official poverty line declined from 42 million (4.8 percent of the rural population) in 1998 to 34 million (3.8 percent of the rural population) in 1999. The number of rural poor declined further to about 26 million (3.1 percent of the rural population) in 2000. However, the official poverty estimate is based on a very low annual income, which is just enough to meet basic food and clothing requirements. Also, the Government's poverty data do not cover urban areas. Estimates of poverty levels based on internationally comparable norms and covering both rural and urban areas are much higher. About 230 million people (18.5 percent of the population) still live below the $1-a-day poverty level (based on per capita consumption norms at 1985 purchasing power parity rates). The incidence of poverty in the interior provinces is much higher than the national average, especially in the western regions. Education and health conditions in the interior provinces are also far below the national average. In addition, roughly half the children in households at or below the poverty line are at least mildly malnourished.

In the past 20 years or so of reform, substantial disparities in regional living standards have emerged. Per capita GDP in the western regions is about two thirds of the national average and only one third of that in the coastal regions. The Government has, in fact, made efforts to promote development in the poorer interior provinces. The March 2000 session of the National People's Congress endorsed the "go west" policy, a proactive policy to promote growth and development in the western regions. It is a priority in the Tenth Five-Year Plan. Developing infrastructure, both physical and social, and improving natural resource management constitute the core of the policy. The Government has also announced a package of preferential measures to facilitate development in the western regions, including: (i) raising the central Government's budget allocation for large-scale projects in these regions and increasing fiscal transfers to them for social development; (ii) allocating the central Government's poverty reduction funds mainly to these regions; (iii) encouraging international financial organizations, bilateral agencies, and state banks to invest more in the western regions; (iv) encouraging economic cooperation of these regions with neighboring countries; (v) giving foreign-funded firms participating in the economic development of the western regions the same preferential policies as those in the coastal economic zones; and (vi) encouraging foreign-funded enterprises in the coastal areas to reinvest profits in the western regions.

Southeast Asia

GDP growth in Southeast Asia improved to 5.1 percent in 2000, from 3.1 percent in 1999 as the economic recovery that began in 1999 continued to broaden and deepen. The driving force behind the momentum was robust external demand for the subregion's products and a slight increase in domestic demand. These overall trends, however, masked significant variations among countries, with GDP growth ranging from 8.5 percent in Malaysia to 3.9 percent in the Philippines. Moreover, toward the end of the year, economic growth seemed to lose some of its momentum with export growth, particularly of electronic products, declining sharply. This tracked increased signs of a slowdown in the US economy and a corresponding weakening in global demand for electronic goods.

While exports across the subregion received a boost in 2000 from strong US growth and recovery elsewhere in Asia, domestic demand growth has been underpinned in a majority of countries by expansionary fiscal and monetary policies. While public consumption and investment have substantially increased since the Asian financial crisis, private consumption remains relatively subdued despite rises in public sector wages and tax breaks. However, the distinction between cyclically advanced and less advanced economies is important. In Malaysia, private consumption has grown strongly on the back of greater consumer confidence resulting from higher export revenues, employment levels, and real wages, and low interest rates. On the other hand, in Indonesia, Philippines, and Thailand, consumer sentiment remained downbeat in 2000, due to weakening currencies and uncertainty over the sustainability of recovery.

Although renewed investment in export-oriented industries has led to a recovery in private capital formation from the crisis-induced contractions of 1998 and 1999, the overall level of gross fixed capital formation in 2000 remained considerably below precrisis levels. Private investment activity (especially foreign direct investment) remained slack owing to a combination of factors that included excess capacity in non-export industries, weak corporate sector profitability, and incomplete corporate and financial sector restructuring. Moreover, in Indonesia and the Philippines, this has been compounded by political uncertainty, civil unrest, and a perceived lack of transparency in business practices. These factors, together with a lack of market orientation, have also hindered private capital formation in Cambodia, Lao PDR, and Viet Nam.

Low interest rates, made possible by subdued inflation, helped balance sheet restructuring in the corporate and banking sectors and limited the growth of public debt-service payments. However, weak loan growth across the subregion due to concerns by banks over their asset quality has tended to reduce the effectiveness of an accommodative monetary stance. Moreover, in Indonesia and the Philippines, the authorities pushed up interest rates during 2000 to defend weakening currencies in the face of persistent doubts over their resolve to implement needed structural reforms.

Despite a pickup in subregional inflation during the last quarter of 2000 as a result of higher oil prices, overall inflation during the year remained low and relatively stable due to moderate food price inflation and continued excess capacity in certain production sectors.

Current account surpluses throughout the subregion narrowed during the year due to a recovery in imports, in spite of robust export growth. This owed much to higher domestic economic activity, the import-dependent nature of manufactured exports, and (except for Indonesia, Malaysia, and Viet Nam) higher oil prices.

Immediate prospects for the subregion have been clouded considerably by less hospitable external and domestic environments. The outlook for the US economy has deteriorated: a relatively sharp slowdown in GDP growth is expected in the first half of 2001 before activity picks up in the second. This is likely to have a significant negative impact on Southeast Asia's exports in general and electronic products in particular, as the US remains the subregion's largest export market, accounting for some 20 percent of total exports. Individual country exposure to electronics exports varies from 14 percent of total exports for Indonesia to around 60 percent of total exports for Malaysia and the Philippines. The slowdown in the US is also likely to adversely affect exports within the subregion, given that a large proportion of these form part of linked production sites that ultimately feed final demand for goods from industrial countries.

In terms of domestic demand, consumption growth is also likely to remain weaker in 2001 than in 2000. Although lower US interest rates have provided some flexibility for lowering domestic interest rates (especially in the context of generally low domestic inflation), fiscal options remain more constrained (especially in Indonesia and Thailand). Slower export growth will also hold back domestic consumption and investment in the subregion. Moreover, investment activity in 2001 is likely to remain subdued owing to incomplete corporate sector restructuring in Indonesia, Malaysia, and Thailand. A perceived nontransparent investment environment in Indonesia, Philippines, and Viet Nam, and ongoing political uncertainty and civil unrest in Indonesia are other factors that are likely to hinder inward investment into the subregion.

Even in the worst-case scenario of a harder landing and longer downturn for both the US and global high-technology sectors, the risk of a renewed crisis in the subregion remains small. Unlike 1997, Southeast Asia is not in the midst of a financial bubble, interest rates remain relatively low (and could fall further in 2001), current account balances remain healthy, and reliance on short-term foreign funding has been greatly reduced. Subregional economic growth is expected to slow to 4.0 percent in 2001 before picking up to 4.8 percent in 2002 as the US economy recovers and the electronics cycle turns positive. In Cambodia and Viet Nam, which are less dependent than most other countries in the subregion on electronics exports, GDP growth is likely to remain stable or even increase in 2001 due to a recovery in agricultural production, after the effects of severe droughts in 2000.

Export growth (in US dollar terms) is likely to slow considerably in 2001 in Southeast Asia due to lower demand for manufactured goods as well as a lower price for crude oil (which will hurt the oil exports of Indonesia, Malaysia, and Viet Nam). This is, however, likely to be accompanied by faster import growth (relative to exports) and a further narrowing of the current account surplus in the subregion in 2001.

In the medium term, high growth in Southeast Asia can only be sustained if governments step up the pace of structural reforms. In the countries worst affected by the financial crisis, although substantial progress has been made in corporate and financial sector restructuring, some items on the reform agenda remain: nonperforming loans are unacceptably high, and the pace of restructuring of heavily indebted companies is slow. In the Lao PDR and Viet Nam, as well as pursuing banking sector reform, the governments should play a less active role in the economy while enhancing their regulatory and supervisory capabilities to promote greater competition. These governments also need to expedite trade liberalization by dismantling existing quantitative restrictions. In addition, throughout the subregion, governments need to enhance human resources development to provide greater flexibility to take full advantage of the opportunities that globalization presents.

Cambodia

Due to severe seasonal flooding, economic growth slowed slightly in 2000 to 4.5 percent. With greater political and macroeconomic stability, the Government is focusing on accelerating socioeconomic development. Future prospects depend on expanding tourism, the area under cultivation, and the garment sector.

Recent Trends and Prospects

Severe seasonal floods hampered otherwise good economic performance in 2000, slowing real GDP growth to an estimated 4.5 percent from 5.0 percent in 1999. A contraction in agricultural production is estimated in 2000. This was due to loss of crops in the floods as well as poor forestry performance, which stemmed from the reduction in the legal limit of timber that could be felled. Strong growth in industrial value added is estimated on the basis of rapid expansion in garment exports, primarily to the US. Robust growth in tourism continued in 2000, contributing to an estimated moderate expansion of the services sector.

Since 1997, droughts, political volatility, and the Asian financial crisis have hindered broad-based economic development. Average real per capita GDP growth during 1997–2000 amounted to about 1 percent a year. In addition, growth was somewhat uneven, with average real growth in value added during 1997–2000 of about 14.1 percent in industry, 2.3 percent in agriculture, and 1.2 percent in services. Recent economic performance has been too low and urban-biased to bring about broad-based poverty reduction or to create enough jobs for a rapidly expanding labor force. The proportion of the population below the absolute poverty line remained at about 36 percent during 1997–1999, while the wages of unskilled labor fell in real terms by 5–10 percent in the same period. (The absolute poverty line is defined as the food poverty line—sufficient income to buy a food basket equivalent to 2,100 calories a day—plus a nonfood allowance.)

Macroeconomic conditions were stable in 2000. The Government's domestic debt fell and inflation remained low. The Government generated public savings of about 1.7 percent of GDP in 2000 as revenues increased to an estimated 12.0 percent of GDP in 2000 from 11.7 percent in 1999. Expenditures rose to an estimated 17.4 percent of GDP in 2000, from 16.1 percent in 1999. The fiscal deficit is estimated at 1.7 percent of GDP in 2000, up from 1.5 percent in 1999. However, concessionary financing more than covered this deficit with the result that domestic government debt to the central bank fell.

Average consumer price inflation fell from 4.0 percent in 1999 to register price deflation of 0.8 percent in 2000, despite rising fuel prices. This is because the prices of food items that dominate the consumer price index, particularly rice, were lower in 2000 than in 1999, partly because of low world prices. The riel was generally stable against the dollar in 2000. Total liquidity increased by about 28 percent, yet did not fuel inflation as the velocity of money fell. Foreign currency deposits and private sector credit grew rapidly, reflecting increased confidence in the political and economic situation.

Vigorous growth of merchandise exports of about 31 percent in dollar terms and of tourist arrivals of 34 percent, as well as higher capital inflows, produced an overall balance-of-payments surplus, raising gross official reserves to about $492 million in 2000 from $422 million in 1999. However, the current account deficit is estimated to have risen to 4.6 percent of GDP as the value of imports increased by about 33 percent, in part because of higher world oil prices.

Economic growth in the range of 5–6 percent in 2001–2002 is possible. Weather permitting, modest agricultural growth is achievable because of expansion of the area cultivated to annual crops and because of increased investment in rural development. Over this period, the garment sector should continue to lead the expansion of industry, while tourism is likely to remain a source of employment and income growth, foreign currency earnings, and government tourism income (e.g., from the Angkor Wat temple complex). Because the effects of a post-conflict baby boom are now expanding the labor force more rapidly, significant poverty reduction will require better economic performance than that seen in 1997–2000.

Issues in Economic Management

To accelerate socioeconomic development, the Government is undertaking comprehensive fiscal reforms. This includes measures to increase revenues, which grew from less than 5 percent of GDP in 1993 to an estimated 12.0 percent in 2000, and steps, such as a military demobilization program, to shift public expenditures from defense and security—where spending fell

Table 2.11 Major Economic Indicators, Cambodia, 1998–2002
(percent)

Item	1998	1999	2000	2001	2002
GDP growth	1.8	5.0	4.5	5.0	6.0
Gross domestic investment/GDP	12.0	18.4	18.8	20.0	22.0
Gross domestic savings/GDP	5.4	7.3	6.6	6.8	6.9
Inflation rate (consumer price index)	14.8	4.0	-0.8	5.0	5.0
Money supply (M2) growth	15.7	17.3	28.5	24.0	20.0
Fiscal balance/GDP	-2.7	-1.5	-1.7	-3.5	-3.1
Merchandise export growth (domestic)	13.0	17.9	31.3	15.0	12.0
Merchandise import growth (retained)	1.6	21.4	33.1	14.5	13.0
Current account balance/GDP	-0.3	-1.7	-4.6	-5.0	-5.1
Debt-service ratio[a]	2.1	1.8	2.4	4.1	3.9

[a] Excludes payments to the Russian Federation.

Sources: Ministry of Economy and Finance; National Institute of Statistics; National Bank of Cambodia; International Monetary Fund; staff estimates.

from 4.3 percent of GDP in 1998 to an estimated 3.6 percent in 2000—to health, education, and rural development—where spending rose from 1.4 percent of GDP to an estimated 2.5 percent over the same period.

The Government needs to improve public expenditure management, particularly budget planning and execution. To protect aid-financed public investment projects and maximize their development impact, the Ministry of Economy and Finance, working closely with the Ministry of Planning, will initiate a three-year rolling medium-term expenditure framework in 2001. This will provide estimates of incremental recurrent costs based on planned investments identified in the three-year rolling public investment program. These recurrent costs can then be incorporated into budget plans. To streamline the budget process and improve budget execution, the Ministry of Economy and Finance created the Budget Strategy and Enforcement Center in 2000. The Center will facilitate bid screening and cash disbursement, particularly in health, education, agriculture, and rural development.

Policy and Development Issues

Refined budget planning and a sharper focus on target outcomes are critical to successful implementation of the (second) Socioeconomic Development Plan 2001–2005, which the Government is currently preparing. The Plan's proposed poverty reduction agenda, based on the October 2000 Interim Poverty Reduction Strategy Paper, has three principal policy objectives. First, to expand economic opportunities for the poor, the Government will promote broad-based, equitable, and sustainable economic growth, aiming to (i) maintain a stable macroeconomic environment; (ii) improve public sector efficiency; (iii) develop the supporting infrastructure and institutions for the private sector; and (iv) promote employment creation in light manufacturing, tourism, and agriculture.

The second main objective is to improve the ability of the poor to take advantage of this wider range of economic opportunities. The Government and international aid agencies are already beginning to devote more public resources, historically skewed toward infrastructure and urban development, to social and rural development. The recently formed state-owned Rural Development Bank is expected to significantly increase the supply of loan funds to rural areas over the next five years by providing wholesale funding to microfinance institutions in rural areas. Access by the rural poor to traditional community forestry and fisheries resources has been increasingly threatened over the last few years by abusive commercial exploitation. The Government is, therefore, canceling some concessions and improving oversight of concession management.

Third, to protect the most vulnerable groups against any adverse effects of accelerated structural transformation, the Government will work toward the provision of a limited social safety net. Many nongovernment organizations and bilateral aid programs offer some social protection to vulnerable groups. However, it is important for the Government to begin developing a more comprehensive and sustainable basic safety net.

Indonesia

Economic growth recovered in 2000, due to increased external demand for manufactured goods and natural resource-based products. Although growth is forecast to continue in 2001 and 2002, the fragility of peace and order, high levels of public and private debt, slow progress in governance reform, and a weak banking system, cast a shadow over future economic prospects.

Recent Trends and Prospects

Economic growth resumed at a rate of 4.8 percent in 2000 after a sharp recession in 1998 when GDP contracted by 13.1 percent, and 0.8 percent growth in 1999. The major area of strength was exports, which rebounded strongly in 2000 from a decline in 1998 and weak growth in 1999 when exporters struggled with a lack of financing and general banking services in the wake of the Asian financial crisis (see Figure 2.8). In contrast to surging exports, domestic spending by businesses, households, and the public sector recorded only modest growth. Household income recovered from the recent recession, but weaknesses in the labor market and in agriculture continued to hold back spending. Agricultural output was affected by poor weather, natural disasters, and civil unrest.

The uncertain political situation also hindered investment, though there are some signs that enterprise spending is recovering from the low point of the recession. New foreign direct investment (FDI) commitments in 2000 rose by 60 percent above 1999 levels. However, despite the sharp increase in 2000, FDI is still nearly one third below precrisis levels and is largely confined to export-oriented areas. The huge depreciation of the rupiah against currencies such as the dollar and yen provided large incentives for exports of garments, as well as of agricultural and natural resource-based products. To provide a broader perspective, Indonesia may have been the only country in the region to experience "negative FDI" or net divestment in 1998 and 1999. In addition to political uncertainties, foreign investors cite corruption and complex tax and regulatory systems as discouraging to investment. Domestic investment is also running at a small fraction of the precrisis level.

On a national income basis, gross domestic investment—covering plant, equipment, infrastructure, and inventories—stabilized in 2000 at 17.9 percent of GDP. This is well below the over 30 percent share preceding the financial crisis. Reflecting the strong trade surplus, gross domestic savings are estimated to have amounted to 22.0 percent of GDP in 2000.

Spending in fiscal year (FY) 2000 (which covered the period April to December to allow for a transition to a calendar-based fiscal year in 2001) reflected the need to contain the budget deficit—necessitated by the increasingly difficult debt burden—with maintaining aggregate demand and encouraging a more sustainable recovery. Budgeted spending (including transfers to local governments) in FY2000 increased from the previous fiscal year by slightly more than 4 percentage points to 21.6 percent of GDP. Against this, revenues improved by approximately 2 percentage points to 16.8 percent of GDP. The overall budget deficit worsened to 4.8 percent of GDP in FY2000 from 2.3 percent in FY1999.

The largest single public expenditure component consists of interest payments on domestic debt. In FY2000, these amounted to 4.2 percent of GDP, accounting for nearly one fifth of total expenditures. In contrast, interest payments on external debt are less than one half the domestic debt burden. The emergence of a serious public debt burden reflects the costs of the financial crisis, especially the use of public funds to recapitalize the banking sector.

Personnel expenditures and subsidies are the next largest items of central government spending, both accounting for 3.4 percent of GDP. Personnel expenditures increased by more than 21 percent in FY2000, reflecting efforts made to raise civil service compensation. Among subsidies, the largest item is for petroleum products, while smaller amounts are given for food and electricity. The subsidies stem from earlier programs to contain the cost of living for the poor. It is generally acknowledged that the subsidies have been ineffective in reaching the poor and they are being phased out.

Social sector spending fell a little in FY2000. Education expenditures declined from 7.3 percent of total central government expenditures in FY1999 to 6.0 percent in FY2000. This is quite worrisome because Indonesia has historically devoted a smaller fraction of the national income to education than Malaysia, Philippines, and Thailand. Expenditures for health, population, and social welfare also declined.

On the revenue side, the slight impovement in domestic resource mobilization largely stemmed from greater tax efforts. In FY2000, total domestic tax collection was 10.5 percent of GDP—the largest elements being income and value-added taxes.

Much of the year-to-year increase resulted from higher oil and gas earnings, which strengthened by 30 percent in nominal annualized terms, due to higher world oil prices. The Government is committed to further increasing domestic resource mobilization; however, the major obstacle to this is weak tax collection. Government officials acknowledge that only long-term civil service and judicial reform can deal with this serious problem.

The impact of higher debt service payments on the overall fiscal balance becomes apparent when one considers that the primary fiscal balance—before interest payments—was a positive 1.2 percent of GDP. Around 43 percent of the overall budget deficit was financed by foreign borrowing, nearly all of which comes from official development assistance. Roughly an equal amount was financed by asset sales—largely by the Indonesian Bank Restructuring Agency.

Monetary policy faced the same problem as fiscal policy— treading carefully between supporting recovery and maintaining macroeconomic stability, especially price stability. On balance, the net result was to lean on the side of supporting recovery. Monetary aggregates tended to grow faster than targeted and, at the end of 2000, inflation was also higher than targeted. Growth in monetary aggregates has come largely in demand for currency and more liquid bank deposits, i.e., demand deposits rather than time deposits.

Interest rates rose somewhat over the year: the one-month Bank Indonesia Certificates rate increased from 12.5 percent at the end of 1999 to 14.5 percent at the end of 2000. One-month treasury bill rates moved marginally above three-month rates, testifying to the premium on liquidity. The demand for liquidity reflected renewed lack of confidence in short-term prospects of the rupiah against the dollar as well as continued concerns over the health of the banking system.

Merchandise exports in 2000 surpassed the precrisis high of $56.3 billion to reach an estimated $65.7 billion, marking a rise of 28.2 percent during the year. Most of the increase was in non-oil and nongas exports. The sharp depreciation of the rupiah since the onset of the crisis has stimulated a wide range of exports, including in 2000 electrical equipment, textiles, and some natural resource products, particularly aluminum and nickel. (In nominal terms, the rupiah depreciated by 75 percent against the dollar from the beginning of 1996 to the end of 2000.) Agricultural products suffered from some weakness in international prices, but often showed strong volume increases. Imports rose faster than exports, but from a much smaller base, paced by raw materials purchases. Capital goods imports have yet to pick up, reflecting the lack of widespread investment spending. Overall, the merchandise trade surplus improved in 2000 to $24.9 billion. This led to a corresponding increase in the current account surplus from $5.8 billion in 1999 to $7.8 billion in 2000.

The capital account saw continued capital flight, reflecting both negative FDI as well as continued outflows of portfolio capital. Capital flight was only partially offset by higher levels of official development assistance. As the capital account deficit was smaller than the large current account surplus, net official reserves increased.

With the exception of some brief stability in the third quarter, the rupiah weakened over the year, falling to Rp9,500 to the

Table 2.12 Major Economic Indicators, Indonesia, 1998–2002 (percent)					
Item	1998	1999	2000	2001	2002
GDP growth	-13.1	0.8	4.8	4.2	4.5
Gross domestic investment/GDP	16.8	12.2	17.9	15.0	17.0
Gross domestic savings/GDP	26.5	20.2	22.0	20.9	21.3
Inflation rate (consumer price index)	58.5	20.7	3.8	9.0	6.0
Money supply (M2) growth	62.3	11.9	15.6	11.8	12.4
Fiscal balance/GDP[a]	-3.7	-2.3	-4.8	-3.7	-3.0
Merchandise export growth	-10.5	1.7	28.2	8.1	11.2
Merchandise import growth	-30.9	-4.2	33.3	15.4	17.3
Current account balance/GDP	4.3	4.1	5.1	2.9	1.3

[a] For the years up to 1999, fiscal year refers to 1 April–31 March. For 2000, fiscal year refers to the nine-month period, 1 April–31 December 2000. Thereafter, fiscal year refers to the calendar year.

Sources: Central Bureau of Statistics; Bank Indonesia; International Monetary Fund; staff estimates.

dollar in December 2000 from Rp7,100 one year earlier. Business confidence in rupiah-denominated investments remained limited.

According to data provided by Bank Indonesia, Indonesia's external public debt increased from $56.3 billion at the end of March 1997 to $81.5 billion at the end of June 2000 before moderating to $75.3 billion by the end of September. The sharp rise in debt reflected the public assumption of privately contracted debt following the government bailout of the financial sector and the continuing need for external funds to finance the budget deficit and meet external debt-service obligations. The fall in external public debt in the latter half of 2000 led to a corresponding decline in total external debt outstanding to $130.8 billion at the end of 2000 from $150.0 billion at the end of 1999.

Paris Club debt restructuring, through an agreement on 13 April 2000, provided significant easing of anticipated debt-service obligations. Official creditors rescheduled approximately $6 billion in principal repayments, originally falling due through early 2002. This facilitated additional rescheduling by London Club creditors. The agreements are, however, contingent upon successful annual International Monetary Fund reviews.

Average annual inflation fell considerably in 2000 although the end-December 8.7 percent increase in the consumer price index was significantly above the comparable 1.9 percent increase in 1999. Inflation was particularly noticeable in the last few months of the year as renewed rupiah weakness was matched by domestic price increases. In addition, higher fuel costs, resulting from the Government's program to reduce subsidies, were also a factor in higher inflation. Although clearly showing progress relative to 1999, the end of year inflation rate was over the target of 5–7 percent of the International Monetary Fund-sponsored stabilization program.

Unemployment figures in Indonesia are generally lower than in many developing member countries—the relatively flexible labor market tends to provide a high level of employment. Even during the crisis, on an annual basis, the number of people reported as working increased. Changes in aggregate economic activity, even severe changes such as during the crisis, tend to be reflected in real wages rather than in aggregate employment. During 1998, a sharp decline in purchasing power occurred as price rises for basic goods outpaced wage increases. The initial impact of lower real wages helped push many near-poor people below the poverty line. As the economy recovered in 1999, greater macroeconomic stability was achieved, purchasing power and real incomes rose, rice and other food prices stabilized, and poverty rates fell back somewhat. In 2000, preliminary data suggest that real wage increases observed in late 1999 and early 2000 did not continue throughout the year. The recovery will likely have to become broader and deeper to have a significant and continued impact on poverty.

GDP growth is expected to slow slightly from 4.8 percent in 2000 to 4.2 percent in 2001 before improving to 4.5 percent

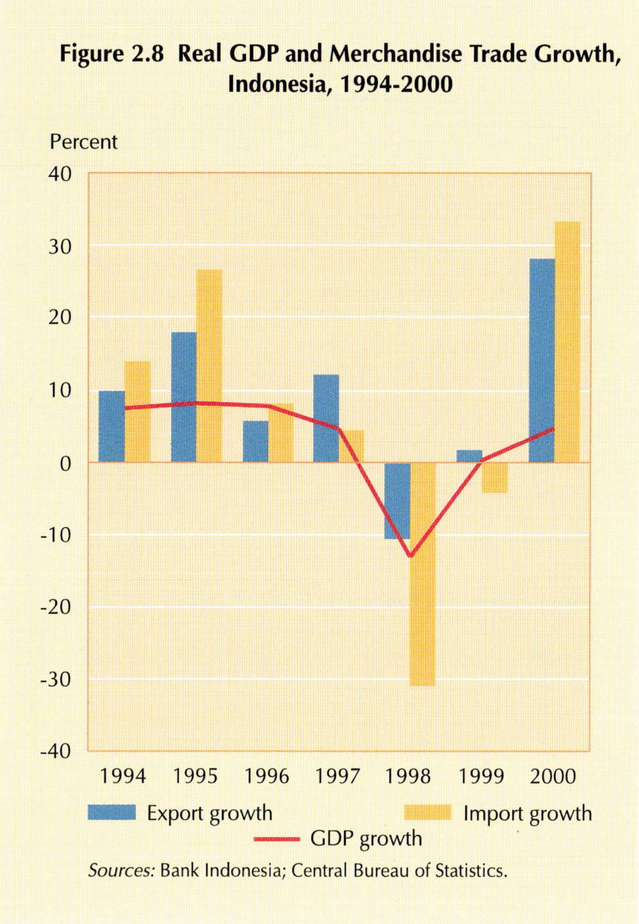

Sources: Bank Indonesia; Central Bureau of Statistics.

in 2002. In the near term, the recovery is likely to be constrained somewhat by a less favorable domestic and external environment. Domestic demand will remain relatively weak because of low disposable incomes, sluggish credit growth, and relatively high interest rates, especially if civil unrest continues. On the external front, export growth will be adversely affected by the slowdown in the global economy. This will partly offset the positive impact of a depreciated rupiah on export competitiveness.

Toward the end of our forecast period, export growth is likely to pick up due to a recovery in global demand. Investment and construction are expected to gradually strengthen, partly on export gains. Investment, however, is likely to continue to be narrowly based and construction is unlikely to reach its precrisis robustness. Household spending will increase with improved income and employment opportunities. However, continued weakness in the banking sector, the debt overhang in both the private and public sectors, and political uncertainties limit a faster pace of recovery.

The Government projects a declining fiscal deficit trajectory from 4.8 percent of GDP in 2000 to a near balanced budget in 2004, based on relatively optimistic assumptions. The

Box 2.4 Social Safety Net Scholarship Program in Indonesia

In response to the Asian financial crisis and fears of mass school dropouts, the Government, with the financial assistance of the Asian Development Bank and the World Bank, instituted a scholarship program. This ongoing program provides financial assistance to poor households with children in school. The amount generally covers the cost of school fees (Rp10,000, Rp20,000, and Rp30,000 per month for primary, lower secondary, and upper secondary school students, respectively) and can be used for that purpose or other expenses.

Funds were first allocated to schools so that "poorer" schools received proportionally more scholarships. School committees (consisting of the school head teacher, the chair of the parents' association, a teacher representative, a student representative, and the village head) then allocated scholarships to individual students. School students in all but the lowest three grades of primary school were eligible. Participating students were to be from the poorest backgrounds. If there were too many eligible students for all the poor students to receive a scholarship, then additional indicators were to be used to identify the neediest students. The additional indicators were those living far

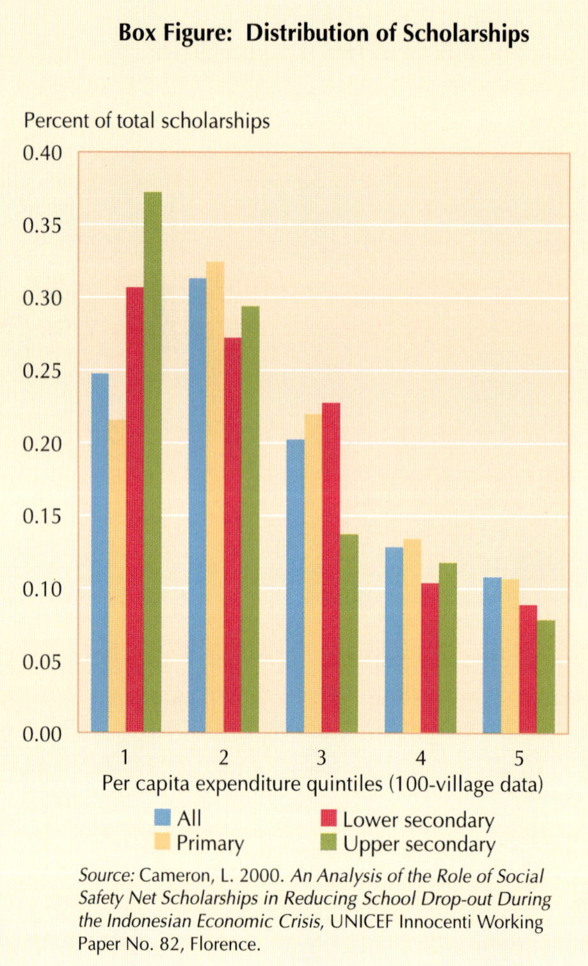

Box Figure: Distribution of Scholarships

Source: Cameron, L. 2000. *An Analysis of the Role of Social Safety Net Scholarships in Reducing School Drop-out During the Indonesian Economic Crisis,* UNICEF Innocenti Working Paper No. 82, Florence.

from school, those with physical handicaps, and those coming from large or single-parent families. Also, a minimum of 50 percent of scholarships, if at all possible, were to be allocated to girls.

The monitoring of the program was done independently of the Government by a team under British Council management with units in each province (contracted to nongovernment organizations) collecting the data through site visits. The combination of (i) schools deciding who received the scholarships, (ii) direct funds transfer to the beneficiary, and (iii) independent nongovernment organization monitoring helped to ensure more efficient targeting and transparent use of resources.

Qualitative evidence on the impact of the program indicates that it has been well received in the villages, has been reasonably well targeted, and has played a role in keeping at least some children in school. This is backed up by quantitative evidence. The figure shows the targeting of the scheme within a random sample of 100 relatively poor villages. The scholarships seem to have been effective in reducing dropout rates by about 2.4 percentage points at the lower secondary school level.

---

recently revised budget for 2001, projecting a deficit of 3.7 percent of GDP, is consistent with this plan. Tight fiscal spending within the context of a large public debt service burden will limit public expenditures on health and education. Maintaining public infrastructure will also be much more difficult. These issues make it more important that the Government has a development strategy ensuring efficient use of limited resources.

The ongoing process of decentralization of both administrative and fiscal responsibilities has implications for budgetary allocations in general and development support in particular. In the 2001 budget, transfers to other levels of government will represent 25.4 percent of total outlays by the central Government, a rise of roughly two thirds from 2000.

Issues in Economic Management

A healthy banking system is a prime requirement for reducing the vulnerability of the economy to external shocks and for enabling long-term private sector growth. As in the rest of the crisis-affected Asian countries, the most severe macroeconomic impact of the crisis was felt in the financial sector. In June 1997, the banking sector in Indonesia consisted of 238 commercial banks, but by mid-2000, 66 banks had closed, 13 had been nationalized, and four of the seven state banks had merged. To support restructuring, as of October 2000 the Government had issued bonds valued at Rp650 trillion. Much has also been done to strengthen prudential regulation and banking supervision. Banks, however, remain minimally capitalized and are reluctant to lend. Current levels of lending remain far below those needed to support a vigorous recovery.

Further financial sector reforms are needed to reduce overdependence on the banking system, through the development of nonbank financial institutions such as bond and equity markets. Reforming nonbank financial institutions, including those dealing with pensions and insurance, is also important in establishing fiscally sustainable social protection and social insurance mechanisms that can play an important role in long-term antipoverty development.

Reforms also need to be enacted to strengthen the independence of the central bank, which has been weakened by continued political infighting over loans made during the crisis to private banks. The loans were made ostensibly to maintain liquidity in the face of depositor panics; however, an investigation by the state auditor suggested that as much as $15 billion of the loans were inappropriately made. The outcome of these reforms needs to be the reassertion of central bank control over monetary policy and the strengthening of prudential regulations to prevent such practices from reoccurring.

Policy and Development Issues

Indonesia's record in reducing poverty in the years preceding the crisis was exceptional. From a country with widespread poverty, it rose to rank as a middle-income country in two decades. The incidence of poverty fell from 40.1 percent in 1976 to 11.3 percent in early 1996. The crisis threatened to undo these long-term gains. Using a new methodology for measurement, poverty incidence soared from 17.7 percent in February 1996 to a peak of 24.2 percent in late 1998, when perhaps 15 million more people had fallen below the poverty line. The sharp descent into poverty of so many in just over a year shows the vulnerability of the poor to economic shocks. As the recession receded, the situation improved: a survey in August 1999 showed a decline in the overall incidence of poverty to near precrisis levels of 18.2 percent. The incidence of poverty is, nevertheless, high and new programs have to be developed to address these issues (see Box 2.4).

The incidence of poverty varies significantly across the country, and is notably higher in rural than urban areas. Metropolitan Jakarta, for example, with its infrastructure and its role as a center of manufacturing and high value-added services, has broader access to basic services and a much lower poverty incidence than other areas. In sharp contrast, Irian Jaya has a poverty incidence more than 10 times that of Jakarta. These disparities need to be addressed in new legislation on poverty.

Poor people living in rural areas often depend on coastal, fishery, marine, or forest resources. Excessive stress on the ecosystem has reduced income for the present generation and sharply reduced potential income for future generations. In addition, many of the poor live in environmentally sensitive areas prone to pollution, erosion, floods, and landslides, and have inadequate sanitation and clean water facilities. Efforts must be undertaken to act more decisively and effectively to manage environmental and natural resources in a sustainable fashion. Failure to do so will severely weaken the potential for poverty reduction in the coming decades.

Lao People's Democratic Republic

Sharp reductions in the rates of inflation and monetary expansion accompanied moderate economic growth in 2000. The outlook is for this improvement to continue, provided that the Government sustains its commitment to macroeconomic stability and refocuses on structural reform, particularly in the banking system.

Recent Trends and Prospects

Supported by improvements in macroeconomic management, real GDP rose by an estimated 5.5 percent in 2000. This was accompanied by an increase in trade as both imports and exports expanded rapidly. As macroeconomic conditions improved, larger foreign direct investment and official loan disbursements enhanced capital inflows, improving gross official reserves to cover about 2.4 months of imports in 2000 from 2.1 months in 1999.

Agriculture, accounting for over 50 percent of GDP, continued to show a solid expansion because of extensive public irrigation investments made during 1997–1999. In services, accounting for about 26 percent of GDP, the robust trend of growth in real value added, which averaged over 6 percent in 1996–1999, persisted as tourism earnings continued to strengthen. The industry sector averaged about 8 percent growth over 1997–2000, continuing to lag average performance of 13 percent growth during 1993–1996 for two main reasons. First, Thailand's 1997 financial crisis delayed the start of several hydropower investment projects in the Lao People's Democratic Republic (Lao PDR) intended to produce electricity for export to Thailand. This reduced large-scale construction activity, although anecdotal evidence suggests that greater small-scale construction activity occurred in 2000 than in 1998 and 1999. Second, the EU withdrew preferential access for Lao PDR garment exports in late 1995 and reinstated it in late 1997. The garment sector is only now gradually recovering.

Macroeconomic management improved markedly in 2000. Revenues (excluding grants) grew strongly from 10.6 percent of GDP in fiscal year 1999 (1 October 1998–30 September 1999) to 12.7 percent in fiscal year 2000. However, a steep fall in grants contributed to the increase in the fiscal deficit relative to GDP. The growth rate of the money supply fell from 72.4 percent in 1999 to 45.7 percent in 2000. This was the primary factor both in reducing the rate of inflation from 128.4 percent in 1999 to 23.2 percent in 2000, and in slowing the annual average rate of depreciation of the kip against the dollar from 53.6 percent to less than 13.5 percent over the same period.

The outlook for 2001 and 2002 is for some improvement in economic growth despite the adverse impact of flooding on agriculture in late 2000. Industrial growth should accelerate as garment exports to the EU continue expanding, and gold and copper mining operations commence in Savannakhet Province. If the large Nam Theun II hydropower project proceeds as planned, investment, construction activity, and the current account deficit will increase significantly, beginning in 2002. As economic growth gradually accelerates, inflation is likely to fall, along with the rate of growth of the money supply. The fiscal improvement is likely to be sustained as the Government continues to enhance revenues, while containing expenditures in conjunction with a possible new International Monetary Fund program currently under negotiation.

Policy and Development Issues

Since mid-1999, the Government has taken decisive steps to reduce its fiscal deficit and contain monetary expansion so as to restore macroeconomic stability after the volatility of 1998 and 1999 when fiscal deficits and monetary expansion led to soaring inflation and rapid exchange rate depreciation. However, to ensure continued macroeconomic stability and to accelerate economic development, the Government needs to undertake the structural reforms necessary to restore investor confidence and strengthen the economy's ability to withstand external shocks. Perhaps the most pressing problem is the weakness of the banking system, which was aggravated by the extremely high inflation rates of 1998 and 1999.

A decade earlier, in 1988, as part of its moves toward a market-based economic system, the Government established a two-tier banking system. By 1991, seven state-owned commercial banks (SOCBs) managed by the Bank of the Lao PDR (BOL), which also acted as the monetary authority, dominated banking. Because of weak supervision and regulation, about 35 percent of SOCB loans were nonperforming loans (NPLs) in 1994, and the Government recapitalized the banks. Despite several new laws designed to improve supervision and regulation, audits of SOCB accounts in 1996 and 1997 revealed still-high levels of

NPLs. Then, in the midst of the Asian financial crisis, with fiscal revenues and foreign financing falling, the Government turned to the banks to finance its rising fiscal deficit, delaying reform and accelerating the deterioration of SOCB balance sheets.

The Government prepared a Financial Sector Note with the Asian Development Bank and the World Bank in 2000, as part of its moves to strengthen the banking system. The SOCBs dominate the banking system with 80 percent of total bank deposits, of which about 85 percent are in foreign currencies (reflecting the lack of confidence in the kip). Deposits account for about 60 percent of bank resources, with debt to BOL constituting as much as 10 percent of bank liabilities and invested capital for only about 15 percent. Loans account for about 30 percent of bank assets; about 75 percent are in foreign currencies and about 50 percent are to the public sector. With an NPL ratio perhaps as high as 60 percent, adequate provisioning and subsequent recapitalization of SOCBs to achieve an adequate capital adequacy ratio would cost about $50 million, or 4 percent of GDP.

However, as the 1994 recapitalization demonstrated, it would be advisable for the Government to ensure that appropriate banking regulatory measures and institutions are in place prior to investing such a substantial amount. The high level of NPLs is partly the result of insufficient human resources at BOL and the SOCBs, preventing these institutions from setting up the necessary systems to assess general lending conditions, evaluate risks, and establish guidelines for lending practices. Many NPLs, for example, originated because borrowers with no foreign exchange earning potential were permitted to take out loans in foreign currency. When the kip depreciated rapidly, many of them defaulted.

Another problem is the Government's frequent recourse to the banking system to finance public sector activities. Thus, even if the banks had the capacity to adopt prudential practices, they would find it difficult to do so. BOL's mandate does not focus only on the maintenance of a healthy financial sector, but also requires it to ensure financing for the Government's development priorities. When inflation began to accelerate in 1998, the Government capped the interest rate on treasury bills at 20 percent to limit interest expense. The negative real interest rate made the treasury bills unmarketable and the Government began to rely more heavily on bank credit to finance budget deficits as well as off-budget spending priorities. However, in 2000, it ceased borrowing from BOL.

The banks have also been frequently called on to give credit to state-owned enterprises (SOEs), even to those defaulting on existing loans (though recent government policy statements suggest that this practice is ending). Despite progress in the early 1990s in privatizing SOEs, several key enterprises remain under government control. Some of these SOEs account for many of the NPLs at SOCBs. Commercializing SOE operations can reduce their reliance on easy credit from SOCBs.

Table 2.13 Major Economic Indicators, Lao People's Democratic Republic, 1998–2002
(percent)

Item	1998	1999	2000	2001	2002
Real GDP growth	4.0	5.2	5.5	6.0	6.5
Gross domestic investment/GDP	24.9	22.7	20.4	21.6	22.2
Gross national savings/GDP	14.8	16.4	14.6	15.0	15.5
Inflation rate (consumer price index)	90.0	128.4	23.2	9.0	7.5
Money supply (M2) growth	120.7	72.4	45.7	20.0	20.0
Fiscal balance/GDP[a]	-9.6	-4.0	-5.1	-5.0	-4.9
Merchandise export growth	7.6	-10.3	8.3	7.5	9.0
Merchandise import growth	-14.7	0.3	6.6	10.6	10.0
Current account balance/GDP[b]	-10.0	-11.2	-5.8	-6.6	-6.7
Debt-service ratio	9.9	9.6	11.2	11.4	11.3

[a] On a fiscal year basis, ending 30 September.
[b] Excludes official transfers.

Sources: Bank of the Lao PDR; Lao People's Democratic Republic, "Macroeconomic Policy and Reform Framework," September 2000; Asian Development Bank, *Country Assistance Plan: Lao People's Democratic Republic 2001–2003,* December 2000; International Monetary Fund; staff estimates.

Malaysia

Malaysia has achieved an impressive economic recovery since the Asian financial crisis, and has made considerable progress in financial sector restructuring. The short-term growth outlook is somewhat clouded by the slowing US economy, while in the medium term, several corporate sector issues need to be resolved to sustain high growth rates.

Recent Trends and Prospects

Despite a progressive slowdown in quarterly GDP growth rates in 2000 (on a year-on-year basis), GDP for the year is estimated to have risen by 8.5 percent, compared with a 5.8 percent expansion in 1999. The performance in 2000 was underpinned by robust external demand for manufactured goods, especially electronic and electrical products, buoyant consumer demand, and a recovery in gross fixed investment.

Reflecting the stronger fiscal stimulus in 2000, public investment is estimated to have risen by 21.7 percent compared with an increase of 15.9 percent in 1999. Private investment activity also rose sharply, in a turnaround from the crisis-induced contractions of 1998 and 1999, and mirroring higher capacity utilization following economic recovery. Despite this improvement in both public and private investment, the level of gross fixed capital formation in 2000 is likely to have remained considerably below precrisis levels (see Figure 2.9). Private consumption demand, however, stayed at relatively high levels due to improved consumer confidence, resulting from both an increase in disposable incomes and low interest rates.

On the aggregate supply side, higher growth was spearheaded by manufacturing, due to increases in the output of electronic products, electrical appliances, and transport equipment. While the overall improvement in economic performance led to a pickup in services subsectors such as wholesale and retail trade, increased manufacturing activity and stronger exports stimulated a recovery in the transport, storage, and communications subsectors. Construction saw a moderate improvement due to increased public spending on physical infrastructure and higher demand for low-cost housing. Agricultural output also rose marginally, as moderate growth in crude palm oil production and sawn logs was largely offset by a decline in rubber output.

The budget deficit for 2000 is officially estimated at RM18 billion or 5.5 percent of GDP. Although this represents a steep rise over the 1999 actual deficit of RM9.5 billion (3.2 percent of GDP), the actual outturn is likely to be smaller due to stronger tax revenues resulting from higher economic growth.

The continued economic recovery led to a decline in the rate of unemployment to 2.9 percent of the labor force in 2000, from 3.0 percent in 1999. The number of job vacancies during 2000 increased by 14 percent, whereas the number of retrenched workers decreased by 32 percent compared with 1999. Although wage pressures have remained fairly modest, the tightening labor market has led to quite high wage settlements in some areas of manufacturing.

After averaging 2.8 percent in 1999, consumer price inflation decreased during 2000 to average 1.6 percent, despite a pickup in the last quarter of the year due to higher energy prices and bus fares. Overall inflation remained subdued due to moderate food price increases, minimal imported inflation, and the persistence of excess capacity in certain sectors of the economy. With inflationary pressures muted, the Government continued with its accommodative monetary policy stance, maintaining low interest rates and its fixed exchange rate regime. During 2000, the central bank's three-month intervention rate (used by commercial banks to fix their base lending rate) was unchanged at 5.5 percent. This intervention rate had earlier been cut in several steps from a high of 11 percent in February 1998 to the current level in August 1999. The commercial banks' base lending rate stayed within a tight range of 6.75–6.79 percent, down from a high of 12.3 percent in June 1998. Loan growth, however, remained subdued.

Preliminary trade data for 2000 indicate robust export growth and even stronger import growth. The trade surplus narrowed to a still sizable $19.6 billion in 2000, from $22.8 billion in 1999. Export growth was buoyed by continuing strong growth in the country's main export market (the US), buoyant global demand for electronic goods, and ongoing recovery in Asia. The surge in international oil prices also helped Malaysia, a small exporter of crude oil and liquefied natural gas. Import growth was stimulated by strong demand for intermediate and capital goods, reflecting the strength of demand from the import-dependent, export-oriented manufacturing sector. Available data suggest that a lower trade surplus was accompanied by a higher services and income deficit due to the economy's dependence on trade-related services imports

Table 2.14 Major Economic Indicators, Malaysia, 1998–2002
(percent)

Item	1998	1999	2000	2001	2002
GDP growth	-7.4	5.8	8.5	4.9	6.0
Gross domestic investment/GDP	26.6	22.3	27.0	25.0	26.2
Gross domestic savings/GDP	48.5	47.3	46.9	44.9	46.1
Inflation rate (consumer price index)	5.3	2.8	1.6	2.6	2.8
Money supply (M2) growth	1.5	13.7	5.3	7.9	11.5
Fiscal balance/GDP[a]	-1.8	-3.2	-5.5	-4.6	-3.4
Merchandise export growth	-7.3	16.9	14.5	11.8	14.8
Merchandise import growth	-26.6	13.0	25.2	23.7	27.5
Current account balance/GDP	13.1	15.9	8.8	5.5	3.2

[a] Fiscal balance is federal government only.

Sources: Department of Statistics; Ministry of Finance; Bank Negara Malaysia; staff estimates.

and greater outflows of profits and dividend payments from an improving national economy. These developments led to a fall in the current account surplus from 15.9 percent of GDP in 1999 to an estimated 8.8 percent in 2000. A smaller current account surplus and a deficit in the overall capital account— due to lower inflows of public long-term capital, higher nonfinancial public enterprise investments overseas, smaller inflows of foreign investment, and higher repayments of short-term debt—led to a considerably smaller balance-of-payments surplus. This in turn contributed to a decline in external reserves to $29.9 billion (or 4.5 months of retained imports) as at end-December 2000, compared with a reserve figure of $30.8 billion 12 months previously. The external debt position improved in 2000 due to higher repayments of short-term debt. The debt-service ratio correspondingly decreased from 6.0 percent at the end of 1999 to 5.0 percent at the end of 2000.

GDP growth is likely to slow to 4.9 percent in 2001 before accelerating to 6.0 percent in 2002 due to an expected sharp slowdown and subsequent pickup in US growth. Weaker net exports will increasingly exert a drag on GDP growth over these two years, which will be sustained, however, by relatively high private consumption resulting from an increase in disposable incomes due to higher wages and a reduced incidence of taxation. Fixed investment is also likely to pick up as capacity utilization increases. Although the expansion in public investment will remain solid as the Government continues to stimulate domestic demand, private investment may not reach precrisis levels despite a sharp increase in both domestic and foreign investment applications. Private investors' lack of confidence is explained partly by uncertainty over the impact of the current

US slowdown on Malaysia's exports and the reduced attractiveness of countries in the Association of Southeast Asian Nations due to political uncertainties and incomplete corporate restructuring.

Consumer price inflation is likely to rise gradually and average 2.6 percent in 2001 and 2.8 percent in 2002, as stronger domestic demand, due in part to higher real wages, is reinforced by a recovery in non-oil commodity prices. While slower export expansion will, to some extent, be offset by slower growth in intermediate imports for the country's import-dependent export industries, growth of imports is nevertheless likely to exceed that of exports as a result of greater capital goods imports. The trade surplus is, therefore, likely to narrow further. This will probably be accompanied by a widening of services and income deficits. As a result, the current account surplus will likely narrow to 5.5 percent of GDP in 2001 and to 3.2 percent in 2002.

Issues in Economic Management

The Government remains committed to pursuing expansionary fiscal and monetary policies for consolidating economic recovery and strengthening domestic demand so as to make the economy more resilient to external shocks. Toward this end, the fiscal deficit for 2001 is projected at RM16 billion, or 4.6 percent of GDP, moderately lower than the RM18 billion deficit estimated for 2000. However, government financial support for loss-incurring privatized companies risks straining national finances at a time when the economy is projected to slow and when domestic debt is already high.

Reflecting higher levels of economic activity, new loans approved and disbursed by the banking sector amounted to RM360.7 billion and RM133.0 billion, respectively, in 2000, representing increases of 27.5 percent and 13.4 percent, respectively, over the 1999 levels. Loan growth has nevertheless been restrained compared with precrisis levels. Total loans outstanding in the banking system at end-December 2000 amounted to RM453.0 billion, an increase of 5.4 percent on the end-December 1999 figure of RM429.7 billion. This rise has been variously attributed to a higher level of loan repayments and to banks' lingering concerns over their asset quality. It could, however, also signify a generally lower level of loan demand following the economic downturn of 1998, and a greater reliance on retained earnings by companies attempting to clean up their balance sheets by reducing leverage. The latter would have been a definite option for export-oriented manufacturers experiencing strong growth.

In 2000, the Government introduced significant regulatory changes to simplify and expedite the issuance of private debt securities, in order to reduce overreliance on the banking sector as a source of finance and thereby lessen systemic risks. Although net issues of private debt rose rapidly in 2000, the amounts raised were small. The market remains fairly underdeveloped and secondary trading is thin. The development of a corporate bond market is a long-term issue and bank financing is unlikely to diminish in importance in the foreseeable future. Loan growth, therefore, needs to improve to sustain economic recovery in the medium term.

The Government is likely to maintain the ringgit peg at its current rate of RM3.80:$1 for the remainder of 2001 on the basis that it affords stability and predictability in an environment of volatile foreign exchange markets. The pegging of the ringgit to the dollar at this rate in September 1998 led to the ringgit's undervaluation in 1999 against the currencies of its main regional competitors, after the latter had bounced back following their precipitous declines in the second half of 1997 and 1998. This initially helped improve the price competitiveness of Malaysian exports. In 2000, however, in tandem with the appreciation of the dollar, the ringgit appreciated slightly against the yen and the euro, and much more against regional currencies. This overvaluation of the ringgit is likely to continue. Persistent overvaluation could, in turn, lead to an erosion of price competitiveness of exports.

The main risk, however, facing Malaysia's short- to medium-term growth prospects is a sharper than anticipated slowdown in the US economy. The US is Malaysia's biggest export market, especially for the electrical and electronic goods that account for around 60 percent of the country's exports. If the US economy slows much more than envisaged, the current export-led growth momentum could be severely affected.

Policy and Development Issues

Despite considerable progress in financial and corporate restructuring, the reform agenda has yet to be completed. As at end-September 2000, Danaharta, the agency set up to purchase the financial sector's bad debts, had a total of RM46.8 billion in nonperforming loans (NPLs) in its portfolio, of which RM38.2 billion had come from the banking system. The latter figure constituted 43.2 percent of the NPLs in the banking system. Danaharta is now focusing on loan and asset management activities, and by the end of September 2000 had restructured and disposed of loans and assets worth RM35.3 billion, achieving an average recovery rate of 74 percent. Danamodal, the special purpose organization for recapitalizing and strengthening banks, has injected a total of RM7.6 billion into 10 troubled banking institutions since it was created in August 1998. As of 8 January 2001, seven financial institutions had already repaid their loans in full, with the remaining three owing Danamodal a total of RM3.7 billion. Progress has also been made in merging the country's banking institutions to build stronger organizations able to withstand the eventual liberalization of the sector. Although not all banking institutions were able to meet the 31 December 2000 deadline to complete the merger process, at that date, 50 of the country's 54 financial

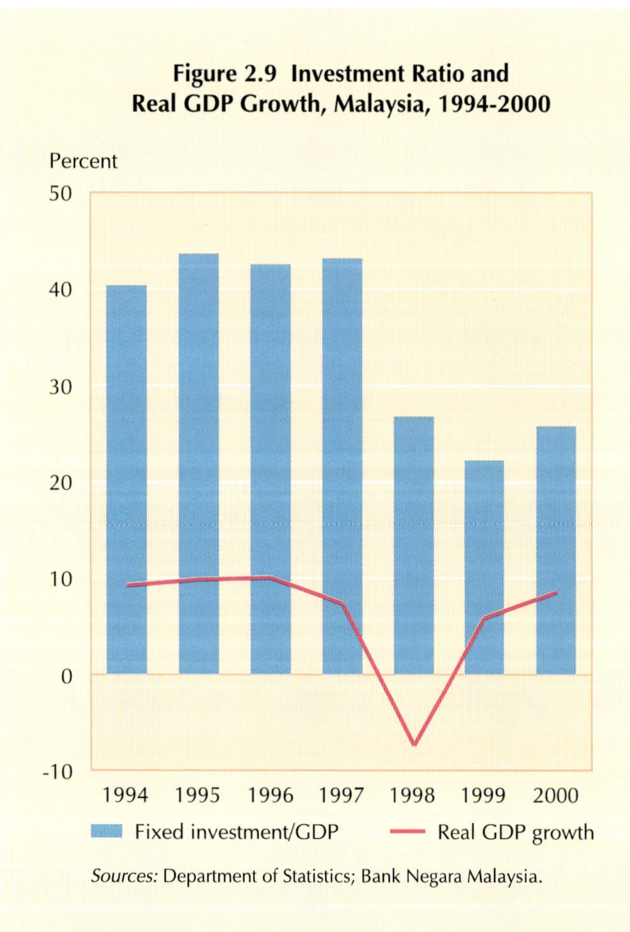

Figure 2.9 Investment Ratio and Real GDP Growth, Malaysia, 1994-2000

Sources: Department of Statistics; Bank Negara Malaysia.

institutions had consolidated into 10 core groups. Faced with increased global competition, it is likely that this consolidation process will continue.

However, progress in lowering the level of NPLs in the banking system is slow. On a three-month arrears basis, central bank figures indicate that the NPL ratio decreased from 11.0 percent of total outstanding loans at the end of 1999 to 9.5 percent at the end of November 2000. This ratio is, however, computed on a net basis, after the netting-out of interest in suspense and specific provisions from both total NPLs and total outstanding loans. If these omissions are included in both total NPLs and total outstanding loans, the NPL ratio would only have been reduced from a high of 19.9 percent at the end of December 1999 to 19.1 percent 12 months later. The slow pace of reducing NPLs could signify problems in restructuring the heavily indebted corporate sector. The lack of corporate restructuring, in turn, could undermine recovery over the medium term.

The Corporate Debt Restructuring Committee, which oversees voluntary corporate debt workouts, had restructured debts of 28 companies worth RM23.1 billion as of 17 October 2000. However, a range of corporate issues are still unresolved. Many Malaysian firms, including privatized entities, remain heavily indebted and are unable to service their debt obligations. The weakness of the Kuala Lumpur Stock Exchange in 2000 also hindered corporate sector restructuring as it adversely affected plans to swap debt for equity. The Government continues to support firms that it considers strategically important. While this assistance has mainly taken the form of helping firms extend their repayment periods, the Government has also resorted to buying assets of heavily indebted privatized firms at prices well in excess of present market valuations. This is preventing an early resolution of corporate sector indebtedness. Moreover, the apparent lack of transparency in such asset purchases, the retention of considerable government influence in the management decisions of such firms, and a reluctance to let foreign investors own controlling stakes in these strategically important companies have clouded the investment environment. It has also prevented these firms from entering into strategic partnerships with foreign investors, which many commentators believe is the only way to ensure their long-term viability. Although established foreign investors are likely to increase investment in existing plants (especially in export-oriented manufacturing ventures) in the short term as capacity utilization improves, new investors are not likely to regard Malaysia as an attractive investment destination. This should be of some concern to top government officials in a country where current levels of private investment in general, and foreign investment in particular, are well below those seen before the financial crisis, and where significantly higher volumes of investment are required to meet the Government's objective of achieving developed country status by 2020.

Myanmar

In 2000, the economy sustained the double-digit growth rate of 1999. This was underpinned by strong agricultural performance due to good weather and the expansion of the area under cultivation. To fully exploit the economy's potential, the Government needs to address certain critical structural and policy issues.

Recent Trends and Prospects

According to official estimates, GDP grew by about 11 percent in 1999. On the basis of preliminary estimates, this growth performance was maintained during the first three quarters of 2000. Real growth in the agriculture sector is estimated to have exceeded 11 percent in 1999 as a result of good weather and expansion of the area under cultivation. Agriculture sector performance remains the most important factor in GDP growth and socioeconomic development. Real growth in manufacturing is reported to have been about 15 percent in 1999.

Inflation was high in the mid-1990s, largely because of rising food prices and excess liquidity; it has since subsided. In 1999, it stood at 11.4 percent and is estimated to have declined further in 2000.

Official data indicate that, in 1997, there were about 22.5 million persons in the labor force and 14.2 million persons employed, out of a total population of 47.2 million. This yielded an unemployment rate of 4.1 percent that year, which some economists have suggested is an underestimate. The employment structure reflects agriculture's predominance in the economy, with 56.5 percent of total employment.

The consolidated budget comprises the union government, state enterprises, and cantonment development committee budgets. On the revenue side, union government budget revenues as a proportion of GDP declined from 7.2 percent in 1998 to 4.9 percent in 1999. The decline is attributable to a narrow tax base, significant undervaluation of imports, and a large number of tax exemptions. Public expenditures declined from 6.9 percent of GDP in 1998 to 5.8 percent in 1999. Current and capital expenditures accounted for 46.3 percent and 53.7 percent, respectively, of union government budget expenditures in 1999. The fiscal balance moved from a surplus of MK4.5 billion in 1998 to a substantial deficit of MK20.2 billion in 1999.

One major source of the budget deficit has been financing for loss-incurring state-owned enterprises. Subsidies for some

commodities, including rice, fuel, and services such as transport for state employees, have been another. For example, the subsidized selling price of rice is estimated to be only about 15 percent of the state procurement price. The public sector deficit has been financed mainly by the issuance of treasury bills and bonds.

Monetization of the economy is still at a relatively low level with total liquidity at around 30–40 percent of GDP. Money supply has been increasing by 30–40 percent a year in recent years, the same rate as domestic credit. The share of currency in broad money has been decreasing. Since the central bank started granting banking licenses to the private sector in 1995, private banks have grown rapidly and now account for more than 60 percent of total banking sector deposits. Credit outstanding to the private sector expanded significantly throughout the 1990s and now accounts for more than 30 percent of total domestic credit. Real interest rates have been negative with the central bank lowering its discount rate from 15 to 12 percent in April 1999 and further to 10 percent in April 2000, to encourage investment and to minimize the impact of high interest rates on inflation. Despite the interest rate reduction, the volume of deposits continued to expand in 1999. Foreign currency deposits have increased in recent years and, at the market exchange rate, account for almost 30 percent of total liquidity.

According to official figures, total imports amounted to $2.4 billion in 1999, comprising about 40 percent capital goods, about 17 percent intermediate goods, and the remainder consumer goods. The Government has recently adopted several measures to further clamp down on nonessential imports to bring down the trade deficit. Total exports stood at $1.1 billion in 1999, consisting mainly of primary products but with an increasing share of garments and agro-based manufactured goods. Border trade with neighboring countries accounts for nearly 30 percent of total exports but only about 10 percent of total imports. While the trade deficit amounted to $1.3 billion in 1999, the current account registered a smaller deficit of $494 million because of surpluses on the services account and

2000 refers to fiscal year 2000/01, ending 31 March.

transfers. After adjusting for capital account transfers, Myanmar posted a net balance-of-payments deficit of about $145 million in 1999. At the end of March 2000, gross foreign exchange reserves were reported at about $240 million or 1.6 months of imports, reflecting the fragile state of the external balances.

The foreign exchange market remains highly distorted, with the parallel market rate of MK460 per dollar cash, as compared with the official rate of about MK6 per dollar. Trade in the state sector, still recorded at the official exchange rate, is reported to account for about 30 percent of total trade.

At the end of March 2000, total debt outstanding was reported at about $6 billion, almost all as medium- and long-term debt. At that time, the economy had arrears totaling about $2 billion, of which about 70 percent was owed to bilateral sources, about 20 percent to private creditors (including suppliers' credit), and the rest to multilateral sources.

After quite a successful period of growth following the initial liberalization of the economy in 1988, progress has slowed because of ongoing structural and policy distortions as well as resource and technology constraints. Unless more comprehensive and consistent structural reforms are undertaken and additional domestic and external resources are mobilized, economic growth will remain sluggish and vulnerable to exogenous factors such as the weather, the regional economic environment, and fluctuations in global commodity prices.

Issues in Economic Management

To fully exploit the potential of the economy, the Government needs to tackle certain critical structural and policy issues. First, investment and savings ratios, which are around 12–13 percent of GDP, need to be lifted. Second, the budget deficit has to be reduced, but not by further lowering the already very low levels of public expenditure. Instead, the tax-to-GDP ratio, currently among the lowest in any developing economy, needs to be raised. Third, exports need to be promoted and, in this context, it may be important to abolish the public sector monopoly on rice exports. Fourth, the policy of multiple and widely divergent foreign exchange rates has to be given up and unification of the exchange rate implemented as soon as possible. This will remove both an existing distortion in resource allocation and a strong disincentive to investment. Lastly, the banking sector needs to be further strengthened, including the supervisory and regulatory capacities of the central bank.

Policy and Development Issues

Myanmar currently ranks number 125 out of 174 countries in the United Nations Development Programme's Human Development Index of 2000, slightly above Cambodia and the Lao PDR. All three are at the lower end of the group of countries considered to have "medium human development". The country's social indicators have improved over the last few decades and frequently reveal better social conditions than expected given the per capita income. According to official statistics, the poverty incidence is 23 percent, quite low in comparison with other countries at similar levels of per capita income. While cases of severe poverty are reported in the border regions, the incidence of poverty has a fairly low gender and regional bias. Life expectancy was around 60 years in 1997/98. According to statistics consolidated by the Department of Labor, the infant mortality rate is about 48 per 1,000 live births and the maternal mortality ratio is about 150 per 100,000 live births. These figures are lower than indicated in reports from major international organizations. Accessibility to health services needs to be improved as only about 50 percent of villages have health centers. Although adult literacy is high at around 90 percent and the gross primary school enrollment rate is also around 90 percent, the primary school completion rate is only about 50 percent while the gross enrollment ratio at middle school is less than 40 percent.

The most urgent challenge facing the Government is to achieve rapid economic growth to reduce poverty. If it can initiate a program of policy reform measures and external aid agencies can provide assistance, the economy has the potential to maintain broad-based growth.

Philippines

Economic growth picked up somewhat to 3.9 percent in 2000, and inflation fell. However, the fiscal deficit came to more than twice the 2000 budget target because of poor revenue collection. The looming slowdown in the US economy and slower global demand for electronics exports are risk factors for growth in 2001.

Recent Trends and Prospects

Despite political and economic uncertainties, real GDP grew by 3.9 percent in 2000 after 3.3 percent in 1999, resulting in real per capita GDP growth of 1.8 percent, up from 1.1 percent in 1999. The services sector, in which growth strengthened slightly to 4.4 percent in 2000 from 4.1 percent in 1999, was responsible for more than half the economic improvement. Transport, communications, and storage, and wholesale and retail trade were the strong leaders in this sector. The communications subsector surged by 18.8 percent due to a sharp climb in the number of cellular phone subscribers. Agriculture, accounting for almost 20 percent of GDP, slowed to 3.4 percent growth in 2000 from 6.0 percent in the previous year when a bumper rice crop was harvested.

Relatively slow growth in the industry sector has been symptomatic of economic performance in recent years. Unlike some of its neighbors, the Philippines has lagged behind in shifting its output and employment structure away from agriculture to industry and to services. Industry's share in GDP contracted from more than 40 percent two decades ago to nearly 35 percent in 2000. Nevertheless, industry showed a moderate upswing in 2000 as growth in value added quickened from 0.9 percent in 1999 to 3.6 percent. Manufacturing, which dominates the sector at over 70 percent of industrial value added, was at the forefront of the expansion, spurred by a strong performance in electronics arising from buoyant US demand for semiconductors and other high-technology products. Construction, however, continued to perform poorly, recording a larger contraction in 2000 than in 1999. Overcapacity, and an overhang of nonperforming loans that inhibited growth in bank financing for new construction projects, were the main factors.

Net exports continued to support the recovery, as export growth exceeded import growth. The value of semiconductor exports, the top export earner, grew strongly by 20.7 percent after a small increase of 1.9 percent in 1999. Other major exports showing strong gains in export earnings included electrical machinery (7.4 percent), garments (10.2 percent), and crude coconut oil (126.6 percent). Benefiting from enhanced

purchasing power from such sources as increased net factor income from abroad, private consumption grew by 3.5 percent. Investment growth was sluggish, at 0.8 percent, but a turnaround from the previous year's 1.7 percent contraction. Although fixed capital formation fell by 1.6 percent, pulled down by a 5.4 percent drop in construction, this was offset by a smaller adjustment for changes in inventories, which declined more slowly in 2000 than in 1999. Efforts to improve the investment climate were made harder by the Government's need to raise interest rates in response to exchange rate volatility.

Despite the improvement in economic growth, the labor force participation rate fell between October 1999 and October 2000, from 65.7 percent to 64.3 percent as the number of people aged 15 years and above not in the labor force increased by over 1 million. The unemployment rate rose from 9.6 percent to 10.1 percent over the same period. Thus, the number of unemployed people reached about 3.1 million in October 2000.

Inflation continued to subside, averaging 4.4 percent for 2000, the lowest level in a decade. This was better than the 5–6 percent target set by the monetary authorities, and was achieved in spite of international oil price increases and the weakening of the peso. The lower inflation rate reflected slower money supply growth as well as weaker food prices stemming from slightly higher agricultural production and large stockpiles of grain from the previous season.

Lower than expected inflation allowed the monetary authorities to reduce interest rates in early 2000. But monetary policy was tightened in May and again in September in response to the peso's depreciation (about 5 percent on average against the dollar in 2000), rising US interest rates, and emerging inflationary pressures. The benchmark 91-day treasury bill rate trended upward in the latter part of the year and then reversed itself in December 2000, reflecting the drop in policy interest rates for the month as the exchange rate stabilized. Overall, interest rates were lower in 2000 than in 1999 in nominal terms but were higher in real (inflation-adjusted) terms. For example, the average lending rate for all maturities fell from 11.8 percent in 1999 to 10.9 percent in 2000, while rising in real terms from 5.1 percent to 6.5 percent. Tightening monetary policy was reflected in the reduced rate of money supply (M2) growth, which fell from 19.3 percent in 1999 to 5.2 percent in 2000.

Fiscal performance, particularly revenue mobilization, continues to fall significantly short of expectations. The national fiscal deficit increased from P112 billion or 3.7 percent of GDP in 1999 to P136 billion or 4.1 percent in 2000, substantially higher than the government target of P63 billion or 1.9 percent of GDP. Revenues, at P506 billion, reached only 89 percent of the 2000 budget target because of shortfalls in tax collection and privatization revenues. Despite the shortfalls, expenditures, at P642 billion, slightly exceeded the 2000 budget target as deteriorating economic conditions made the Government reluctant to cut spending. As a consequence, national government debt worsened from 59.3 percent of GDP in 1999 to 61.3 percent as of September 2000.

With merchandise exports growing faster than merchandise imports (in dollar terms), the merchandise trade surplus rose by more than half from $4.3 billion in 1999 to an estimated $6.7 billion in 2000, while the current account surplus increased by only about 19 percent over the same period from $7.2 billion to an estimated $8.6 billion because of smaller levels of net income and current transfers. The capital account deficit was substantially larger in 2000, despite an increase in foreign direct investment, due to much larger outflows of portfolio and other short-term investments. This led to an overall balance-of-payments deficit, and a slight decline in net international reserves from $11.8 billion in December 1999 to $11.3 billion in December 2000, a level equivalent to about four months of imports of goods and services.

In spite of serious political problems in 2000, such as ethnic conflict in the south, and charges of large-scale corruption against the President and his subsequent impeachment trial, the economy nearly achieved the Government's 4 percent growth target in 2000. The improved performance of both economic growth and job creation in services, and the sustained expansion in agriculture, where most of the poor are employed, bode well for poverty reduction, although the continued decline of the construction sector, an important source of employment for the urban poor, is of concern. Real economic growth is forecast to slow to about 3 percent in 2001 before recovering to over 4 percent in 2002, in line with the expected improvement in global economic conditions. Inflation is expected to rise to about 7 percent in 2001 due to the lagged effect of fuel price rises and pre-election spending prior to the May elections. On the external front, a slower US economy and weaker world demand for electronics point to a deceleration of Philippine export growth. (A large part of exports is composed of electronic goods—see Figure 2.10.)

In January 2001, the country resolved its political uncertainties. The early economic manifestations of this resolution were rising stock prices, a stabilizing exchange rate, and a restoration of investor confidence. The improved political climate should contribute significantly to carrying out the pending economic reforms. After the May elections, the Government needs to devote its energies to improve economic governance. A favorable environment needs to be developed to attract foreign direct investment, which is now crucial in a context of anticipated slower export growth and the

Table 2.15 Major Economic Indicators, Philippines, 1998–2002
(percent)

Item	1998	1999	2000	2001	2002
GDP growth	-0.6	3.3	3.9	3.1	4.2
Gross domestic investment/GDP	20.2	18.6	17.6	16.0	19.0
Gross domestic savings/GDP	12.8	14.9	17.0	15.0	15.5
Inflation rate (consumer price index)	9.8	6.7	4.4	7.0	6.0
Money supply (M2) growth	8.2	19.3	5.2	10.0	10.0
Fiscal balance/GDP	-1.8	-3.7	-4.1	-3.5	-2.0
Merchandise export growth	16.9	18.8	8.7	3.0	8.0
Merchandise import growth	-18.8	4.1	2.1	5.0	10.0
Current account balance/GDP	2.4	9.4	11.5	8.0	5.0
Debt-service ratio	11.5	12.4	14.2	14.3	15.3

Sources: National Economic and Development Authority; National Statistical Coordination Board; Bangko Sentral ng Pilipinas; Bureau of Treasury; Department of Finance; International Monetary Fund; staff estimates.

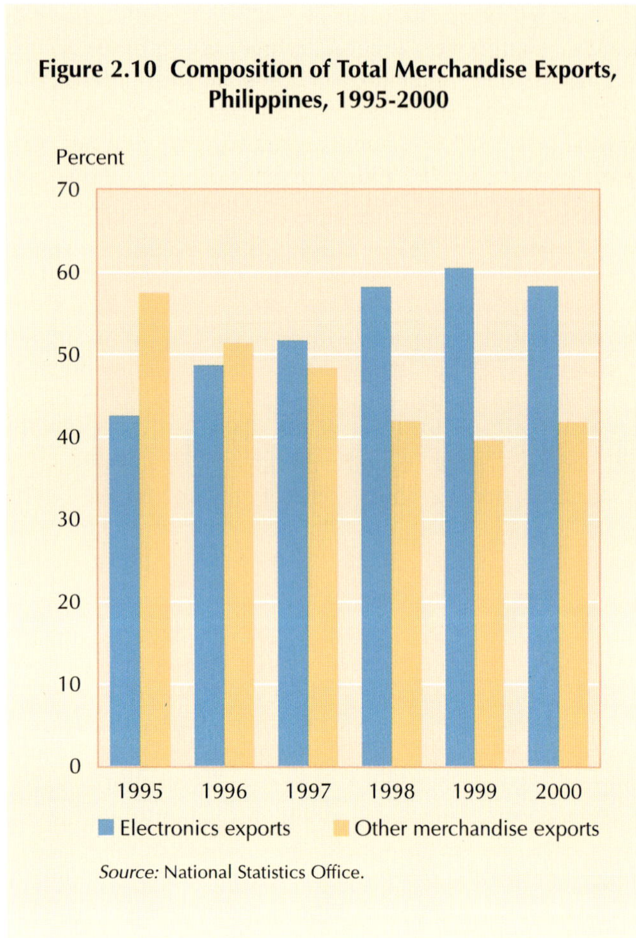

Figure 2.10 Composition of Total Merchandise Exports, Philippines, 1995-2000

Source: National Statistics Office.

terms of promulgating new economic legislation, following the establishment of an Economic Coordinating Council in January 2000, the Government saw some success. Laws enacted in 2000 included the Retail Trade Liberalization Act (liberalizing foreign ownership of retail firms), the General Banking Law of 2000, the Electronic Commerce Act (establishing regulations for and promoting e-commerce), and the Securities Regulation Code (enhancing capital market competitiveness). These laws are intended to create a business environment conducive to domestic and foreign investment, and should help improve investor confidence. However, the political and economic uncertainties that characterized much of 2000 detracted the Government's attention from economic reforms, including implementation of the above laws. The efficacy of these new laws hinges on the Government's success in tackling various investor concerns, including the large fiscal deficit, weak public sector governance, and ineffective implementation of laws. In terms of the fiscal deficit, the emphasis should be on revenue mobilization by streamlining the tax code to reduce the number of exemptions and by strengthening enforcement of tax laws.

Policy and Development Issues

The General Banking Law of 2000 was passed as part of a new banking framework in response to the Asian financial crisis and the changing global economic environment. The new law overhauls the regulatory and supervisory responsibilities of the central bank, Bangko Sentral ng Pilipinas. It updates the classification system of banks to include universal, cooperative, and Islamic banks. It also sets limits on the regulatory scope of the central bank over nonbank financial institutions.

The new law is also designed to restructure the banking system. On bank ownership, it liberalizes the entry of foreign banks to foster competition. The law raises the maximum foreign ownership level of banks to 40 percent of voting stock. Also, under certain conditions, the central bank can allow a foreign bank to own 100 percent of a domestic bank. The central bank will, however, ensure that banks majority-owned by locals hold 70 percent of total resources in the banking system.

The passing of the General Banking Law is expected to strengthen the domestic banking industry and make it better able to withstand internal and external shocks. However, the financial sector still faces several issues. One is the weak credit culture, as the country has one of the lowest degrees of financial intermediation in Asia. The inadequacy of credit to vital sectors of the economy and the inefficiency with which it is provided still need to be tackled. Among other things, this includes reducing or eliminating financial intermediation taxes to lower costs. It also includes promoting competition and encouraging greater foreign entry (addressed by the new law) as well as strengthening public listing requirements to improve corporate governance in the banking industry.

Government's ballooning fiscal deficit. Provided that the Government can revitalize the governance reforms and maintain political stability, the exchange rate, stock prices, inflation, and growth rates should all improve. Continued reform of the financial system is expected in 2001, specifically the drafting of the Implementing Rules and Regulations for the General Banking Law of 2000.

In 2002, any cyclical recovery in global electronics depends on a worldwide recovery of the information and communications technology sector, which will affect the economy's export projections. By this time, it is expected that reform programs such as the Omnibus Power Bill, long delayed by the country's political problems in 2000 and the intervening elections, will be in place. If the anticipated reduction of the Government's fiscal deficit in 2001 is realized, then this enhances growth prospects for 2002, a prerequisite for which, however, is continuing political stability.

Issues in Economic Management

The priority for the Government is to turn its attention to the economic reform agenda so as to restore investor confidence. In

Enhancing the role of capital markets is a long-term policy issue. While private sector borrowing comprises mainly short-term bank credit, the development of long-term bond markets would help stimulate complementary financing through the capital markets. This would contribute to lowering banks' nonperforming loan levels. Parallel reforms in the corporate sector are also important for the health of the banking system, including improvement of corporate governance, reinforcement of regulatory and supervisory arrangements, and expansion of the investor base. Such reforms may include upgrading standards of corporate disclosure and transparency, and adopting formal rules for rehabilitating companies.

Thailand

The economic recovery maintained its momentum in 2000 with real GDP growth of 4.2 percent, despite slower industrial expansion. Exports were the main engine of growth as domestic demand remained weak. Monetary policy stayed accommodative with low interest rates while the fiscal deficit improved. Reducing the level of nonperforming loans and restructuring the corporate sector are critical to continued economic improvement.

Recent Trends and Prospects

Real GDP grew by 5.7 percent in the first half of 2000 but slowed markedly in the second half, to give a figure for the year of 4.2 percent, the same as in 1999. Rapid acceleration in the first half of the year was propelled mainly by strong export performance, by the lagged effects of earlier fiscal stimulus packages, and by accommodative monetary policy. The slower pace in the second half was mainly attributable to the steep rise in world oil prices, the slowdown in the US economy, and the uncertainty surrounding the national election scheduled for January 2001.

During 2000, real value-added growth decelerated in both the agriculture and industry sectors while in services, three years of contraction were reversed. Overall, the industry sector still led the economy with 5.2 percent growth followed by services at 3.8 percent and agriculture at 1.2 percent. In the agriculture sector (accounting for about 10 percent of GDP), excessive flooding reduced crop production.

The slowdown in industrial growth was seen primarily in manufacturing. The manufacturing production index, which covers 62 percent of total value added in manufacturing, rose by only 3 percent in 2000, compared with an 11.5 percent increase in 1999. The deceleration in manufacturing growth was mainly concentrated in domestic-oriented industries (whose share of exports is less than 30 percent of output), which contracted by 7.1 percent. Export-oriented industries (whose share of exports exceeds 60 percent of output) registered a manufacturing production index increase of 20.8 percent. The industrial capacity utilization rate for 2000 averaged just under 56 percent—a decrease from the 60 percent rate in 1999 and still below the average of about 70 percent that prevailed before the Asian financial crisis.

In services (accounting for about 46 percent of GDP), the generally robust expansion in real value added that characterized much of the sector in 1999 continued in 2000. The turnaround in services came as the rate of contraction in financial intermediation services slowed to 7.8 percent in 2000 from 38.8 percent in 1999. The subsector shrank to less than 3 percent of GDP in 2000 from over 7 percent in 1996.

Reflecting the excess industrial capacity, the resource gap (investment less savings) switched from a deficit of 8.1 percent of GDP in 1996 to a surplus of 8.0 percent in 2000, as the rate of investment after the financial crisis dropped off much more steeply than the rate of savings.

The fiscal stance was less accommodative in fiscal year 2000, which ended on 30 September 2000. Despite its critical role in stimulating the economy throughout 1999, fiscal spending began to taper off in the first quarter of 2000, reflecting the Government's policy of gradually reducing the fiscal deficit. For fiscal year 2000, the Government's cash deficit was B115.9 billion, a reduction from B134.4 billion in the previous year. Fiscal expenditure expanded by 3.5 percent, while revenue rose by 5.4 percent. The fiscal deficit fell to 2.2 percent of GDP from 2.8 percent in 1999. Total public debt outstanding was B2.8 trillion at the end of 2000, equivalent to around 58 percent of GDP. This is more than three times its precrisis level of 16.8 percent of GDP in 1996 and is the consequence of four years (1997–2000) of budget deficits.

In 2000, to spur domestic demand, the Bank of Thailand maintained its low interest rate policy, keeping the key policy rate (14-day repurchase rate) at 1.5 percent a year. Yet the average annual growth rate of the money supply (M2) in 2000 was only slightly higher than the 2.1 percent in 1999. Commercial banks remained cautious in new lending, as reflected in the level of bank credit outstanding falling by 10.2 percent at the end of 2000 from the level of the previous year. The poor condition of the credit market reduced the effectiveness of the accommodative fiscal and monetary policies. With banks unwilling to lend, neither government spending nor low interest rates had a strong expansionary effect on domestic demand.

Following a historically low rate of 0.3 percent in 1999, inflation increased to 1.6 percent in 2000. Upward pressures came mainly from supply factors such as the rise in world crude oil prices and the continued depreciation of the baht from an average of 38 to the dollar in 1999 to 40 to the dollar at the end of December 2000. Nevertheless, given excess productive capacity within the economy, slack labor market conditions and weak domestic demand kept inflation subdued. Core inflation (calculated from the consumer price index, excluding raw food and energy items) remained at 0.7 percent in 2000, well within the target range of 0–3.5 percent announced by the Monetary Policy Board in May 2000.

Robust export expansion played a major role in economic performance in 2000. The value of exports rose by 19.6 percent over the 1999 level, although toward the end of the year export growth decelerated. The economic slowdown in the US in the second half of the year particularly affected exports. The value of imports grew much more rapidly than in 1999 at 31.3 percent, with a sharp increase in net oil imports (from 2.7 percent of GDP to 3.7 percent in 2000), raw materials, and capital goods. As a result, the surplus on the current account declined from $12.4 billion in 1999 to $9.9 billion in 2000. International reserves continued to accumulate in 2000, but at a slower rate than in 1999, reaching $34.2 billion by the end of the year, or more than twice the level of short-term debt and equivalent to around seven months of imports.

External debt outstanding continued its downward trend, with the maturity profile shifting toward long-term debt. In June 2000, all external debt figures from 1995 onward were revised upward by the Bank of Thailand following a comprehensive survey that included the nonbanking financial sector. Based on the revised figures, total external debt decreased from $95.6 billion at the end of 1999 to $80.2 billion in December 2000. This was mainly attributable to repayments by the private sector. The share of short-term debt fell from a peak of 52 percent in 1995 to around 18 percent of total external debt in December 2000.

As the economic recovery continued in 2000, the relatively high unemployment rates of late 1998 and 1999 fell. According to labor force surveys conducted in May and August 2000, unemployment, excluding seasonally inactive labor, fell to 3.3 percent of the total labor force from 4.1 percent of the total labor force in 1999. Employment in agriculture rose by 37,000 persons or 0.3 percent year on year while nonagricultural employment increased by 618,000 persons or 3.6 percent year on year.

GDP growth is projected to be around 3.5 percent in 2001 due to sluggish domestic demand and less favorable external conditions. However, economic momentum should strengthen in 2002, provided that external conditions improve and that the fiscal stimulus is maintained. Economic expansion remains vulnerable to domestic political instability, the possibility of weaker than expected economic performance in the US and Japan, and the risk of world oil prices remaining high. Continued progress in financial sector reform and corporate debt restructuring is essential to increasing the level of investment.

Table 2.16 Major Economic Indicators, Thailand, 1998–2002
(percent)

Item	1998	1999	2000[a]	2001	2002
GDP growth	-10.8	4.2	4.2	3.5	4.5
Gross domestic investment/GDP	20.3	19.9	22.0	25.3	27.5
Gross savings/GDP	33.2	30.1	30.0	31.8	33.1
Inflation rate (consumer price index)	8.1	0.3	1.6	2.0	2.6
Money supply (M2) growth	9.5	2.1	3.6	4.0	6.5
Fiscal balance/GDP[b]	-2.4	-2.8	-2.2	-2.0	-1.8
Merchandise export growth	-6.8	7.4	19.6	7.0	11.0
Merchandise import growth	-33.8	16.9	31.3	13.0	14.0
Current account balance/GDP	12.7	10.2	8.2	6.5	5.6
Debt-service ratio	21.4	19.4	15.4	13.4	11.4

[a] Preliminary estimates.
[b] Central government balance on a fiscal year cash basis, ending 30 September.
Sources: Bank of Thailand; International Monetary Fund; Ministry of Finance; National Economic and Social Development Board; staff estimates.

Issues in Economic Management

As export demand weakens, stronger domestic demand will become more important to sustaining the recovery. However, credit expansion is constrained because the financial sector is still plagued by a large overhang of nonperforming loans (NPLs), defined as loans for which payment is at least three months overdue. This could hamper economic growth. Some progress has been made in reducing the proportion of NPLs, which declined from a peak of about 48 percent of total loans in May 1999 to 18 percent in December 2000. However, for two reasons, the resolution of the NPL problem is incomplete and remains a significant challenge to the Government.

First, the sharp decline in NPLs was largely due to the transfer of some NPLs to asset management companies (AMCs), created to remove bad loans from the banks' balance sheets. If these NPLs had been included in the calculation of the NPL ratio, together with new NPLs and reentry NPLs, the NPL ratio would have been around 30 percent (see Figure 2.11). Moreover, as of December 2000, state-owned commercial banks and finance companies had significantly higher NPLs than private commercial banks, averaging around 22 percent and 25 percent, respectively.

Second, as economic growth slows, some restructured loans are resurfacing as reentry NPLs. Many commercial banks were reluctant to accept the losses associated with writing off bad loans and tended simply to reschedule payments. In 2000, reentry NPLs amounted to about B200 billion, reflecting the inability of companies to meet the new repayment schedules on loans restructured in 1999 and early 2000. Meanwhile, despite the overall improvement of the economy, new NPLs continued to emerge, particularly in those industries that were still struggling such as real estate and construction.

The transfer of bad assets to AMCs should allow the banking sector to refocus attention on carrying out day-to-day operations and on developing new lending while the AMCs concentrate on the difficult process of restructuring corporate debt. With some NPLs off their books, banks were able (i) to nearly complete the task of loan-loss provisioning in 2000 (although state banks are lagging behind and some banks may still have significant unrealized losses on their balance sheets due to weak standards of NPL classification) and (ii) to post operating profits. With fresh capital of about B900 billion, the banks have made significant progress in meeting capital adequacy standards, though additional capital may be required as the economy slows and as new NPLs appear.

Policy and Development Issues

Although conditions are beginning to stabilize in the banking sector, much work needs to be done to restore the health of financial institutions and corporations so as to ensure sustained economic growth. The Corporate Debt Restructuring Advisory Committee, formed in 1998, has been monitoring and facilitating the process of debt restructuring for over 2,000 large corporations. In about half these situations, creditors and debtors reached voluntary restructuring agreements while the remainder were sent to the civil courts for reorganization or liquidation, creating a backlog of cases that might last as long as eight years at current court capacity. Several legal and institutional obstacles inhibit the expeditious and efficient resolution of these cases, including a shortage of experienced bankruptcy judges, weak insolvency criteria, and legal difficulties in removing weak corporate management and in implementing liquidation and foreclosure procedures. To speed up the process of debt restructuring and restore financial sector health, these obstacles must be removed or lessened.

Although the pace of corporate debt restructuring quickened in 2000, complete resolution is likely to be a lengthy process. This problem, which is inhibiting the ability of the banking sector to generate new loans and stimulate domestic demand, is related to generally weak corporate governance. Oversight by both the Government and by corporations' boards of directors was ineffective (it also did little to protect minority shareholder interests). Poor accounting, auditing, and financial

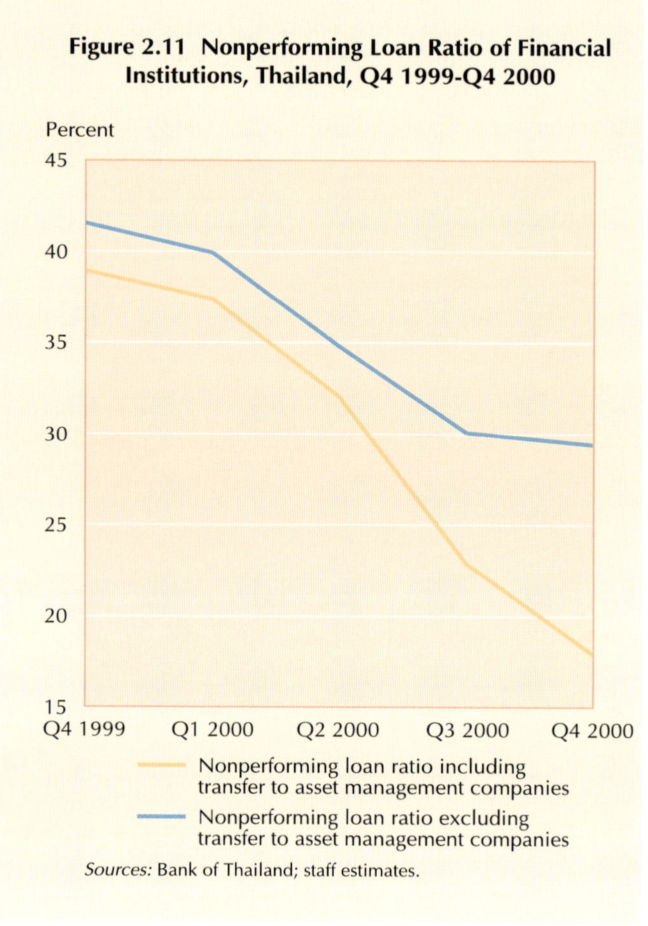

Figure 2.11 Nonperforming Loan Ratio of Financial Institutions, Thailand, Q4 1999-Q4 2000

Sources: Bank of Thailand; staff estimates.

reporting practices compounded the problem. To improve the transparency of corporate management, the Government is amending laws and strengthening regulations to enhance shareholder rights, adopt international accounting and auditing procedures, and ensure adequate government enforcement of regulations on corporate finance and management. The Government must now focus on implementing these new procedures to enhance the ability of Thai corporations to compete in the global environment and contribute to sustained economic growth.

Viet Nam

GDP growth accelerated to 6.1 percent in 2000 from 4.7 percent in 1999, due to a recovery in domestic private demand and robust export performance. The signing of a bilateral trade agreement with the US boosted export prospects, although structural constraints and quality problems remain. The investment rate needs to be raised to reach the Government's target of at least 7 percent annual growth over the next 10 years.

Recent Trends and Prospects

Economic growth improved to 6.1 percent in 2000, following two slow years when growth ranged between 4.4 percent and 4.7 percent. On the supply side, the recovery was led by a strong performance in industry. On the demand side, domestic consumption recovered from a slump in 1998–1999, but the contribution of net exports to GDP growth turned negative.

The sectoral pattern of GDP performance in 2000 saw growth in agriculture of 3.6 percent despite floods in the central and southern regions, and drought in the north. Rice production increased by about 3.8 percent over the 1999 level, but producers saw their earnings dip due to low export prices, increased transport costs (because of higher oil prices), and the limited supply and high cost of credit. Industry turned in a strong recovery with a 9.7 percent expansion in 2000 after two years of slower growth. Within this sector, industrial output surged by an estimated 15.5 percent, led by processed marine products (up by 32.2 percent), electrical machinery (up by 23.3 percent), and cement (up by 19.1 percent). Construction strengthened by 5.0 percent from 2.4 percent growth in 1999. Services sector growth improved to 4.4 percent from 2.1 percent in 1999. Wholesale and retail sales, accounting for over 40 percent of value added in the services sector, rose by 9.2 percent, compared with 2.1 percent expansion in 1999.

On the demand side, real consumption growth increased to 5.6 percent from 1.6 percent in 1999. This pickup reflected the rise in public sector wages and the Government's fiscal stimulus package. The investment recovery has, however, lagged behind. Gross domestic investment as a share of GDP was 23.0 percent in 2000, a modest improvement from 20.1 percent in 1999 but still below 1997's peak level of 28.3 percent. This is because the proportion of foreign direct investment (FDI) in GDP, which had reached 8.9 percent in 1997, has since fallen sharply and is estimated at 3.2 percent in 2000.

The fiscal deficit is estimated to have been 3.0 percent in 2000 compared with 2.8 percent in 1999. The widening of the deficit, financed from domestic nonbank and external sources, reflects the easing of the fiscal stance to spur economic recovery. Revenue receipts as a share of GDP fell marginally to 18.7 percent from 18.8 percent in 1999, continuing the declining trend exhibited since 1994. They should, in fact, have been stronger given robust growth of exports, recovery of imports, and overall economic recovery. That revenue collection did not reflect these developments is in part because oil import tax rates were cut to zero to contain domestic prices of refined oil products, and to protect state enterprises from incurring losses. Also, value-added tax on essential goods and services and on capital goods was scaled back to ensure that these categories could gradually adjust to the newly introduced system for this tax. Of concern, however, is the fact that poor revenue performance poses a risk for fiscal sustainability over the medium term. On the expenditure side, overall spending as a share of GDP is estimated to have increased by 0.8 percent to 22.0 percent in 2000. This was due to a 25 percent wage increase in public sector salaries and higher capital spending, mainly on rural infrastructure.

Consumer prices fell in 2000. As of end-December 2000, the year-on-year percentage fall in the consumer price index (CPI) was 0.6 percent. The drop in world prices of agricultural commodities, particularly rice, led to a decline in the food price index that was only partially offset by higher prices of nonfood items in the CPI basket. Indeed, trends in food prices largely determine the behavior of the CPI as food items make up 61 percent of the basket.

The monetary policy of the State Bank of Viet Nam (SBV) was accommodative. Credit growth, subdued in 1999 at 10.5 percent, surged in 2000 to about 25 percent while broad money supply (M2) grew by 40.6 percent. The latter's rapid rise was due in part to continued growth in foreign currency remittances from abroad and in part to a year-end acceleration of disbursements under state-funded projects that were deposited in banks. Interest rate policies are gradually being liberalized. In August 2000, SBV replaced the monthly ceiling rate on dong borrowings with a prime monthly rate of 0.75 percent. The ceiling interest rates for foreign currency lending were replaced with a rate based on Singapore's interbank market.

On 1 December 2000, SBV raised the reserve requirement ratio for commercial banks' foreign currency holdings from 8 to 12 percent. The move was intended as an incentive to turn dollar deposits into dong, in a bid to curb the growing dollarization of the economy. To check the rising cost of their currency holdings as the reserve requirement ratio increased, local banks have been cutting the interest they pay on their dollar deposits. Furthermore, the general reduction in dollar deposit interest rates has lessened the incentive for local banks to deposit dollars in foreign banks to take advantage of the interest rate gaps that had previously existed between the local and foreign markets. The opening of the country's first stock exchange is as yet only symbolic as just four local firms have officially registered with it.

The current account surplus fell by half to 2.0 percent of GDP, reflecting the recovery of imports (including refined oil products) after a three-year slump. Export performance remained strong in 2000, with growth of 24.3 percent, led by the price-driven surge in crude oil exports, which in value went up by 71.2 percent but in volume by only 4.1 percent. On the capital account, net FDI showed a modest pickup in 2000 from its level in 1999. The signing of the $1.1 billion Nam Con Son sea basin oil and gas exploration project in December 2000 provided a much-needed boost to Viet Nam's FDI prospects. Foreign currency reserves at the end of December 2000 stood at $3.9 billion, representing 13.9 weeks of import cover. The exchange rate was relatively stable until the last quarter of the year when the dong depreciated. The nominal depreciation of the dong against the dollar during 2000 was in the order of 3.3 percent. The external debt position improved after agreement was reached with the Russian Federation in September 2000 in which Viet Nam secured a significant writedown of its outstanding nonconvertible debt.

The global environment is expected to provide some support for consolidation of Viet Nam's economic recovery. The economy is expected to grow by 6.4 percent in 2001 and by around 7 percent in 2002. Growth will be led by manufacturing, which is expected to expand by around 9 percent. The fiscal deficit is expected to widen over the next two or three years to meet the costs of reform, especially in banking and state-owned enterprises (SOEs). Inflation is projected at around 3–5 percent in 2001 and 2002, on the assumption that low world agricultural commodity prices that dragged down domestic prices will recover.

The prospects of higher exports to the US over the medium term have brightened with the signing of a bilateral trade agreement in 2000, but structural constraints and quality problems in the export sector need to be addressed to realize the potential benefits of this agreement. The trade balance will depend to a significant extent on the relative impact that softer oil prices (vis-à-vis 2000) will have on crude oil export revenue and the cost of refined oil imports. Export growth over the next

Table 2.17 Major Economic Indicators, Viet Nam, 1998–2002
(percent)

Item	1998	1999	2000[a]	2001	2002
GDP growth	4.4	4.7	6.1	6.4	6.9
Gross domestic investment/GDP	23.8	20.1	23.0	24.5	26.0
Gross national savings/GDP	19.2	24.1	25.0	24.0	24.1
Inflation rate (consumer price index)[b]	9.2	0.1	-0.6	3.0	5.0
Money supply (M2) growth	25.6	39.3	40.6	30.0	25.0
Fiscal balance/GDP[c]	-2.6	-2.8	-3.0	-3.9	-5.0
Merchandise export growth	2.4	23.2	24.3	12.0	13.0
Merchandise import growth	-1.1	1.1	31.0	16.0	17.0
Current account balance/GDP[d]	-4.6	4.0	2.0	-0.1	-1.9
Debt-service ratio	13.2	10.7	9.2	9.0	8.3

[a] Preliminary staff estimates.
[b] Annual growth rates for 1998–2000 are based on end-of-period CPIs while 2001–2002 growth rates are based on annual averages.
[c] Excludes grants but includes onlending.
[d] Excludes official transfers.
Sources: General Statistical Office; Ministry of Finance; State Bank of Viet Nam; staff estimates.

two years is likely to be around 12–13 percent while import growth is likely to increase faster than exports at 16–17 percent, implying that the current account surplus will become a deficit in 2001.

Issues in Economic Management

Notwithstanding the economic recovery now under way, the investment response has been weak (Figure 2.12). Gross domestic investment increased from about 15 percent of GDP in 1991 to 28.3 percent in 1997. Following the Asian financial crisis, it fell sharply to about 20 percent of GDP in 1999. It rose modestly in 2000 to 23.0 percent, of which the government, SOE, domestic nonstate, and foreign investment shares were 8 percent, 7 percent, 3.5 percent, and 4.2 percent, respectively. The relatively weak investment response is of concern because, to achieve the Government's GDP growth target of about 7 percent or more in the coming years, the investment rate will have to pick up to around 30 percent. The scope for significantly higher levels of investment from government, SOE, and FDI sources is, however, limited, meaning that private domestic investment will have to provide much of the required increase.

Raising private domestic investment is predicated on creating a level playing field for private sector development, which is necessary to improve the expected profitability of investment. In turn, higher profits can become a source of savings for further capital accumulation. Factors that have constrained private investment in Viet Nam include (i) an industrial structure characterized by a very small private corporate sector and the predominance of household enterprises, (ii) low growth of enterprises' retained earnings to finance investment and their inadequate access to term financing, and (iii) inadequate stock of complementary public infrastructure capital.

Broadly speaking, the private corporate sector is constrained by the policy environment. In regard to access to term financing, private investors are constrained by the limited quantity rather than the cost of capital. The available evidence suggests weak effects of changes in interest rate policy and of tax incentives on investment. The volume of credit to the private sector has been curtailed by the practice of preferential credit given by state-owned commercial banks to SOEs. As a result, the private sector has been crowded out. The rising share of nonperforming loans, which have made banks reluctant to lend, is also a factor. The Government's stated objective is to separate policy-based lending from commercial lending, and the establishment of the National Development Assistance Fund is a step in this direction. A potential problem in realizing this objective, however, is that financing for this Fund is inadequate to cover the policy-based lending that is likely to be made to loss-incurring SOEs.

The bias against the private sector extends to the availability of foreign exchange. While the improvement in the external account has allowed the Government to relax import restric-

tions and reduce foreign exchange surrender requirements, private enterprises still continue to experience difficulties in securing foreign exchange.

Another deterrent to private investors is inadequate infrastructure. Viet Nam's infrastructure needs face a large investment gap: while government forecasts indicate that investment of 12 percent of GDP is required over the next three years, the public infrastructure investment program can meet only half this amount. Funding for the remainder will have to come from retained earnings of utilities and private sources, but given that the Government is not expected to raise tariffs, retained earnings are unlikely to be sufficient for this.

Although the scope for significantly higher levels of public investment in infrastructure is limited over the medium term, room exists for raising the efficiency of such investment. This can be accomplished by better targeting (particularly in remote areas where the private sector will not invest), better maintenance of existing public investment, and making public enterprises more efficient. The Government also needs to develop a strategy for build-operate-transfer projects to provide additional funds to the public infrastructure investment program. Foreign investment in infrastructure projects would probably increase significantly if the Government allowed international competitive bidding and took steps to enhance transparency and speed in its decision making in this area.

Policy and Development Issues

Viet Nam's development partners have recognized the significant progress it has made in trade liberalization, while continuing to urge that the remaining agenda for trade reform should be tackled quickly. The measures taken in the last two years include the freeing up of trading rights, removal of export taxes, removal of quantitative restrictions on seven commodity groups, reduction of the maximum tariff rate, and increased transparency and codification of the trade regime. The Government's commitment to trade reform is also signaled by its participation in the ASEAN Free Trade Area, which it joined in 1995, and the bilateral trade agreement with the US, the implementation of which will involve further dismantling of trade barriers.

However, the following issues remain: (i) quantitative restrictions still cover a third of imports and need to be phased out; (ii) the maximum tariff rate has been reduced but, at 50 percent, remains high; (iii) the number of tariff rates (12) needs to be reduced; (iv) the cascading tariff structure requires rationalization; and (v) trading activities that are still concentrated in the hands of a few state trading bodies need to be further liberalized. Over the next few years, however, more significant reductions in tariff levels are to be effected: tariffs on 95 percent of the tariff lines are to be reduced to under 20 percent by 2003, and tariffs on imports from ASEAN countries are to fall to under 5 percent by 2006.

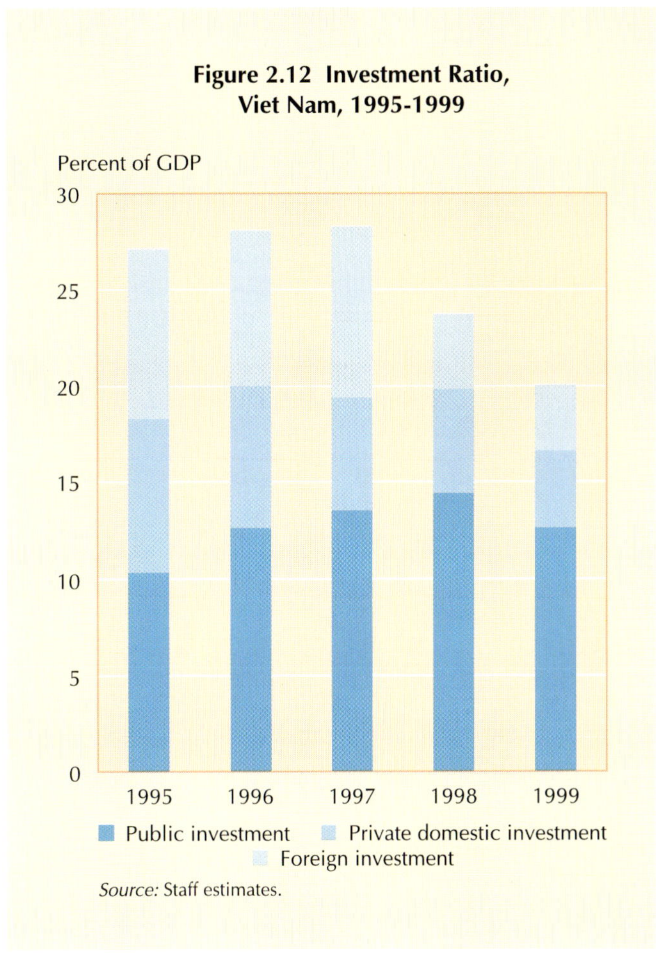

Figure 2.12 Investment Ratio, Viet Nam, 1995-1999

Source: Staff estimates.

that high levels of protection make the cost of doing business in Viet Nam high has also kept many foreign investors away, although they have returned to other regional competitors that have restructured their economies. Consequently, in the changing regional environment, the Viet Nam economy risks being left behind.

The Government must also focus attention on some of the broader ramifications of trade liberalization and the measures needed to mitigate some of the potential adverse effects in designing an appropriate sequence of trade liberalization measures. This means that it will have to minimize the potential negative revenue effects of trade liberalization, and introduce properly structured and administered tariffs that dovetail with a broadening of the domestic tax base.

Viet Nam faces a wide technology gap as it moves toward closer integration with the global economy. It has a weak science and technology base and needs to build up skills and technological capabilities required for competition in the international economy. The problem is compounded on the demand side by the virtual lack of dynamic domestic firms that can draw on the country's scientific and technological resources. So far there is also little evidence that FDI—including that in the industrial zones and export processing zones set up to fast-track industrial development—has served as a vehicle for technology transfer. This is partly because local industry is not yet capable of handling subcontracting and partly because some of the earlier investment was in import-substitution industries. The extent of protection and enforcement of intellectual property rights is also a factor—in industries where these rights are considered critical, weak enforcement may have acted as a deterrent to FDI.

If the economy is to fully realize the benefits of trade and investment liberalization, the Government will need to plan for the acquisition of know-how in those sectors where it is to be imported. It will also have to identify, as well as adequately fund, research and development activities that can be undertaken domestically. Although FDI can serve as a channel for technology transfer, it requires an appropriate and supportive policy environment. At the same time, the Government will need to focus on complementary policies, including human capital accumulation, that enhance the economy's absorptive capacity of technical know-how.

The case for accelerating the pace of trade reform has been made on the grounds that high tariffs and pervasive quantitative restrictions have resulted in a structure that has protected industry. Where the economy does not have a competitive advantage, such as in capital-intensive import-substitution industries, protection should be reduced. At the same time, production in areas such as agriculture and light manufacturing, where the economy has a comparative advantage, should be encouraged. Also, consumers and industries dependent on protected goods for inputs have been penalized. The perception

South Asia

In 2000, the seven South Asian economies achieved generally healthy growth by virtue of a combination of factors, the most noteworthy of which were a strong recovery in agricultural production, rejuvenated export activities, an increase in private sector dynamism, and substantial price stability. India's economy grew at a rate of 6.0 percent in 2000, one of the best performances among developing member countries, led by the service sector which grew at over 8 percent. India continued to make rapid progress in developing the information and communications technology sector, which has played a major role in recent robust growth performance. Pakistan's GDP growth of 4.8 percent in 2000 was the highest since 1997, and was the result of a strong agriculture sector and an increase in exports. The year's outcome was quite encouraging in view of poor performance in recent years. Bangladesh also recovered well from moderate growth in 1999 when floods devastated the country. The pickup was mainly the result of a bumper crop, helping the country achieve self-sufficiency in food grain production for the first time in many years. Other countries in the subregion showed generally strong signs of recovery during the year, attributed largely to higher agricultural growth.

Large fiscal deficits remained a concern in the majority of South Asian countries. The fiscal position of central as well as local governments generally showed no improvement despite continued efforts to stabilize annual budgetary shortfalls and restructure overall revenue and expenditure programs. Pakistan and Sri Lanka saw an increase in the fiscal deficit, mainly due to an overrun in defense expenditures. India's fiscal deficit contracted from 5.5 percent of GDP in 1999 to 5.1 percent.

Inflation was generally kept under control in the subregion, although in India the wholesale price index rose to 7.0 percent in 2000 from 3.3 percent in 1999. Higher world oil prices were the primary cause of this spike. Bangladesh did well in controlling consumer price inflation to only 3.4 percent, compared with substantially higher levels in previous years, thanks largely to greater availability of food items from the bumper harvest. Nepal also exhibited noteworthy stabilization in inflation for the same reason. In Bhutan, price developments were highly dependent on inflationary trends in India, while in the Maldives lower inflation resulted from better fiscal and monetary management.

The export sector played a key role in the subregion's economic recovery. Following moderate growth of about 11.6 percent in 1999, India's exports improved further by about 17 percent in 2000, helped by faster global trade expansion and by depreciation of the rupee. Exports from Bangladesh recovered significantly due to improved foreign demand for ready-made garments and knitwear, its two key products. Sri Lanka's exports increased by 19.8 percent and the growth of exports in Pakistan was also strong at 8.4 percent. Because exports were buoyant in all the countries of the subregion, the majority of them held their current account deficits to around 2 percent of GDP or less.

Macroeconomic forecasts for the next two years are cautiously optimistic, although the slowdown in the US economy will have an adverse impact on both economic growth and export performance. Nevertheless, the impact of the US slowdown will probably be less pronounced in this subregion than elsewhere in Asia, simply because it is less dependent on the US market. India is likely to show GDP growth of 6–7 percent in 2001 and 2002, and Bangladesh, Pakistan, and Sri Lanka of about 4–6 percent over the same period. Inflation is forecast to be modest, barring another steep rise in international oil prices and assuming that weather patterns are normal, contributing to solid agricultural performance. Exports from the subregion, except Bhutan and Sri Lanka are likely to show double digit growth while imports will also be boosted by the import demand of export industries. This should lead to current account positions similar to those of 2000.

The subregion faces many formidable challenges that could have serious repercussions for socioeconomic development if they are not addressed promptly. It has had persistently large fiscal imbalances that are a concern as they are the main reason for the crowding out of financial resources for the private sector, underdevelopment of the financial sector, and high credit costs. It is, therefore, crucial that governments ensure prudent fiscal management by reforming expenditure programs, broadening and modernizing the tax base, and reforming their tax administrations. All these measures have to be accomplished within a rigorously planned medium-term target aimed at a rapid reduction of the fiscal deficits.

Another major issue is pervasive poverty. The subregion is home to more than half Asia's poor people. Poverty reduction efforts have not been successful in the past largely because of high population growth, insufficient GDP growth, low human development, and improper social assistance for the poor. Sustained vigorous reforms to address macroeconomic and social sector impediments are, therefore, critical if the subregion is to improve the people's welfare and accelerate socioeconomic progress. More rapid, equitable, and sustained economic growth should be pursued, since only this can increase the level of per capita income. However, certain microlevel antipoverty programs need to be simultaneously implemented for both rural and urban poor, with recognition of the large differences in underlying circumstances of the two groups.

The countries in the subregion are faced with another major challenge, namely the need for diffusion and adoption of information and communications technology (ICT). While India has made significant efforts to this end in absolute terms, adoption rates are still far below those of many economies elsewhere in Asia. Other countries in South Asia have even further to go. Given that the overall economic activities today are increasingly ICT dependent and that ICT contributes to efficiency and productivity, the subregion needs to strengthen its efforts at adoption. To this end, educational reform, infrastructure development, and adequate financing are crucial.

The seven countries need to strengthen subregional cooperation through higher levels of foreign trade and investment and improving joint natural resource management. Subregional economic relationships have not been cohesive due mainly to political factors, despite the many efforts of various subregional groupings. Stronger economic interaction, particularly among the countries' private sectors, will contribute to trade and industrial upgrading, as well as to economic growth and poverty reduction.

Bangladesh

Economic growth, at 5.5 percent in 2000, depended heavily on agriculture, as it has in the past few years. In 2001, growth is expected to improve marginally due to favorable prospects for agriculture and manufacturing. However, if the country is to achieve higher, sustainable, poverty-reducing growth, the Government needs to pursue comprehensive financial sector and fiscal policy reforms.

Recent Trends and Prospects

In 2000, GDP growth accelerated to 5.5 percent from 4.9 percent in 1999; growth in both years was mainly due to successive record crop harvests. In 2000, the country reached self-sufficiency in food grain. Production was estimated to be just under 25 million tons, or about 1 million tons in excess of requirements (see Figure 2.13). Apart from favorable weather conditions, the adequate supply of key agricultural inputs—fertilizer, diesel, fuel, and seeds—at stable prices boosted food grain output. For agriculture as a whole, value added increased by 6.4 percent in 2000 compared with 4.8 percent in the previous year. Industry sector growth improved to 5.6 percent in 2000 compared with 4.9 percent in 1999. However, growth in this sector remains lower than the growth trend of about 8 percent in the five years prior to 1999. Sluggishness in manufacturing is the main factor, caused largely by growing infrastructure constraints, high costs of doing business (high real interest rates and transaction costs), political uncertainty, scarcity of long-term credit, and loss of competitiveness. The services sector showed expansion of 5.0 percent in 2000, slightly higher than in the previous year.

Remittances from overseas workers were an important factor in raising the level of national savings to 21.4 percent of GDP in 2000 from 20.8 percent in 1999. Gross investment rose marginally to 22.4 percent of GDP in 2000 from 22.2 percent in 1999 due to higher private investment; public investment stagnated.

Export growth recovered to 8.2 percent in 2000, from the flood-affected growth rate of 2.9 percent in the previous year. Two products—ready-made garments and knitwear—accounted for most of the export improvement and 76 percent of total exports. Import growth was relatively low at 4.4 percent, due mainly to reduced food imports. With the trade deficit narrowing from the level of the previous year, and with strong growth (14 percent) in workers' remittances, the current account deficit in 2000 declined to 1.0 percent of GDP from 1.4 percent of GDP in the preceding year. Despite an improvement in the current account, the overall balance-of-payments position remained fragile, and foreign exchange reserves were a mere $1.6 billion (2.3 months equivalent of imports) at the end of June 2000. A substantial residual outflow in the balance of payments under the category "errors and omissions" created pressures on the overall balance. This residual outflow reflected either the lags between shipment of exports and receipt of foreign exchange, or inaccurate recording of some categories in the balance of payments (or a combination of the two). It is also possible that a sizable amount of foreign exchange earnings was retained overseas.

In the 2000 budget, the Government attempted to reverse the deteriorating fiscal trend of the last few years and projected a revenue-to-GDP ratio of 10 percent. Despite this ambitious target, no serious efforts were made to implement key fiscal reforms, rationalize the tax structure, strengthen tax administration, or widen the tax base. As a result, actual revenue mobilization in 2000 turned out to be considerably below budget projections at 8.9 percent of GDP. A delay in introducing a preshipment inspection scheme and sluggish growth in imports contributed to the revenue shortfall. Nontax revenue collection was also less than projected due mainly to reduced profits and dividend income of state-owned enterprises (SOEs). In 2000, losses of nonfinancial SOEs were estimated at Tk31 billion, or 1.3 percent of GDP. As for government expenditure, the rising trend continued in 2000 with total expenditure amounting to 15.0 percent of GDP. As a result of weak revenue mobilization and higher expenditure, the budget deficit increased sharply to 6.1 percent of GDP in 2000, from 4.8 percent in 1999.

At the end of June 2000, the broad money supply (M2) accelerated steeply to 18.6 percent from 15.4 percent in June 1999. Government borrowing from the banking system rose by

2000 refers to fiscal year 1999/2000, ending 30 June.

31 percent, with the central bank accounting for about half of this. Annual growth of bank credit to the private sector declined to 11 percent at the end of June 2000 from 14 percent in the previous year, due mainly to slow growth in the industry sector and the high cost of borrowing. Consumer price inflation declined to 3.4 percent in 2000 from 8.9 percent in 1999. Improved availability of food items (following the two record harvests), weak business activity, excess capacity in manufacturing, and delays in adjusting administered prices contributed toward the low inflation rate.

During 2001, GDP is expected to grow by 5.7 percent despite the dislocation caused by the severe floods in the southwestern region from late-September to mid-October 2000. Another record harvest is anticipated, provided that the weather remains favorable. During 2001, manufacturing output is likely to return to its normal growth trend of over 7 percent due to steady recovery, especially in the export-oriented garment sector. On the external side, though export performance is expected to improve notably, the balance-of-payments situation will likely remain fragile with foreign exchange reserves staying at a critical level of $1.5 billion at the end of December 2000, or equivalent to about two months of imports. In the remaining months of 2001, the pressures on the reserves level and the balance-of-payments current account will depend primarily on the Government's success in preventing large outflows of foreign exchange and in improving investor confidence. The taka's 6 percent devaluation in mid-August 2000 was a delayed response to declining external competitiveness. Despite a mild boost in revenue performance, the fiscal deficit is likely to remain at about 6 percent of GDP during 2001 with sustained

pressures on government expenditures prior to the general elections scheduled to be held by October 2001. The Government is expected to adopt a more prudent fiscal stance once the elections are over, and progress in pushing ahead with sectoral reforms should be considerable.

Over the medium term, growth prospects for the economy should improve. The Government is likely to favorably resolve the issue of exports of natural gas, which will have a positive impact on the balance of payments in subsequent years. In the 2001 budget, total government expenditures are projected to rise further to 15.3 percent of GDP.

Issues in Economic Management

Prudent fiscal management has emerged as a major challenge facing the Government. The ratio of tax revenue to GDP rose from 5.9 percent in 1991 to 7.3 percent in 1993, but since then has remained constant at about 7 percent, reflecting a lack of progress in widening the tax net and in improving the tax administration system. On the other hand, nontax revenues are comparatively small (a little less than 2 percent of GDP), and they too stagnated for much of the 1990s. Over the last three years, government expenditure, both current and capital, has increased rapidly. As a consequence, the fiscal deficit rose to an unsustainable level of 6.1 percent of GDP in 2000.

Fiscal management in recent years has been weak and needs to be improved urgently to restore macroeconomic stability. The Government needs to make serious efforts to strengthen revenue mobilization, contain unproductive expenditure, utilize scarce external assistance in the most efficient manner,

Table 2.18 Major Economic Indicators, Bangladesh, 1998–2002
(percent)

Item	1998	1999	2000	2001	2002
GDP growth	5.2	4.9	5.5	5.7	6.0
Gross domestic investment/GDP	21.6	22.2	22.4	23.3	24.1
Gross national savings/GDP	20.6	20.8	21.4	21.8	22.3
Inflation rate (consumer price index)	7.0	8.9	3.4	3.0	5.0
Money supply (M2) growth	11.4	15.4	18.6	16.0	16.0
Fiscal balance/GDP	-4.1	-4.8	-6.1	-6.1	-5.5
Merchandise export growth	16.8	2.9	8.2	15.0	15.0
Merchandise import growth	5.4	6.6	4.4	8.0	9.0
Current account balance/GDP	-1.1	-1.4	-1.0	-1.5	-1.8
Debt-service ratio	8.6	9.0	9.5	9.3	9.5

Sources: Bangladesh Bank; Bangladesh Bureau of Statistics; World Bank; staff estimates.

address the mounting problems of the banking system (discussed below), and take bold measures to deal with SOE losses and inefficiencies. In mid-August 2000, the Government made upward adjustments to the administered prices of natural gas (15 percent) and various fuel oils (9–20 percent) to reflect changes in international prices. While these measures will, to some extent, help strengthen the Government's fiscal position, it needs to do much more to reduce the fiscal deficit to sustainable levels.

Export diversification remains a major challenge for the Government. The situation is serious because the Multi-Fibre Arrangement, which shields the country's exports of garments and apparel from external competition, is due to end in early 2005. Macroeconomic stability is also necessary for sustained export growth. In addition, a liberal trade regime that gradually eliminates the anti-export bias and supports competitive exchange rate management, is critical. Such management needs to be more flexible, as delayed adjustments often cause considerable uncertainty for exporters. Along with appropriate policy, sound institutional development should be pursued.

Although the economy has received substantial amounts of external assistance, the external debt portfolio has been managed prudently and external debt in 2000 is estimated at 33 percent of GDP, with a debt-service ratio of only 9.5 percent. The external debt is predominantly public or publicly guaranteed, most of it carrying long-term maturities and concessionary interest rates. However, over the medium to long term, debt sustainability could be under pressure due to exposure to nonconcessionary financing, especially suppliers' credit and publicly guaranteed foreign direct investment with significant foreign exchange payment liabilities.

Policy and Development Issues

Despite a few significant policy reforms that the Government has launched in recent years, the financial sector remains shallow and underdeveloped, and while banking has expanded in terms of value added at a reasonable rate, a robust and efficient regulatory system is not yet in place. The capital market is also at a nascent stage, although progress has been made in improving market efficiency. A well-developed long-term savings market has yet to emerge. If the economy is to achieve higher growth and, consequently, poverty reduction, the Government will need to carry out a wide range of policy measures to comprehensively reform the financial sector.

The financial system, dominated by banking, is in distress mainly because of its large nonperforming loan (NPL) portfolio, low recovery rates, high spreads to cover provisioning and management costs, an inadequate legal framework, poor governance, and limited capacity of the central bank to effectively perform its regulatory and supervisory role. Many banks, especially the nationalized commercial banks, are unable to meet the capital adequacy requirements. As of 30 June 2000, bank NPLs

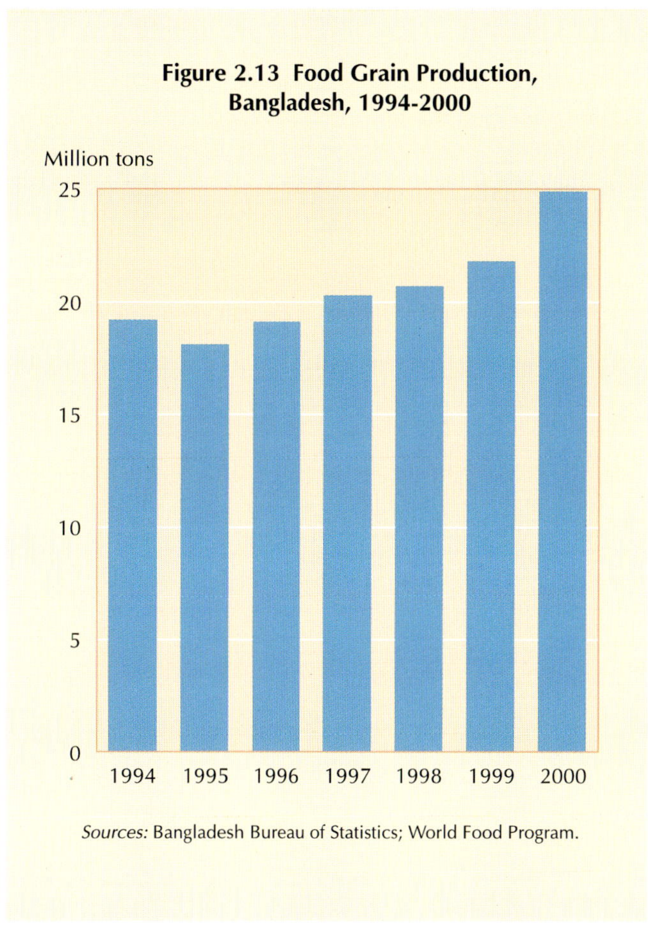

Sources: Bangladesh Bureau of Statistics; World Food Program.

had increased to 40 percent of total loans from 32 percent at the end of 1995. Only the private and foreign commercial banks have been able to reduce their NPLs in recent years. The nationalized commercial banks remain institutionally fragile and are subject to government and political interference. Lending continues through these banks to loss-incurring SOEs. In addition, insider lending has affected the portfolios of several private banks. Slow court settlement is another major impediment to recovering overdue bank loans.

Over the last few years, the Government has taken steps to address some of the financial sector's problems, although progress has clearly been slow. The Bankruptcy Law 1997 was enacted to facilitate the recovery of bad loans. Also in 1997, the Banking Companies Act 1991 was amended to disqualify defaulting directors from remaining on the board of a bank. To hurry up the disposal of default cases, exclusive loan courts and bankruptcy courts have been set up in Dhaka and Chittagong. Recently, steps have been taken to regulate insider lending, restricting the size of such loans and making the process more transparent. Some progress has been made in removing major defaulters from the directorship of commercial banks. The Government is considering amending key banking legislation and policies to improve governance, the legal framework, and the institutional capacity of the banking system. However, banking reforms need to be expedited. In the capital market, the Asian Development Bank has helped the Government strengthen and regulate the system through a reform package via a loan. The Government has taken initiatives to address the fundamental weaknesses of the stock market, including strengthening the Securities and Exchange Commission, upgrading the professionalism of market practitioners, infusing greater transparency in market transactions, and introducing regulations that require higher disclosure and reporting standards of issuers. The old paper-based system of trading on the stock exchange has been replaced by an automated trading system. A central depository company has been established to facilitate scripless trading in corporate stocks. The Government has also taken some steps toward specific reforms for encouraging an increase in the supply of securities to the capital market, including passing legislation for exploring the possibility of investing a portion of the insurance and private provident and pension funds in the capital market.

Bhutan

Economic growth momentum remained strong in 2000 and this is likely to continue in 2001 and 2002. However, institutional and human resources will need to be further developed to enhance steps toward good governance.

Recent Trends and Prospects

Initial estimates suggest that GDP expanded by 6.1 percent in 2000, with the industry and services sectors acting as the main engines of growth (see Figure 2.14). Paradoxically, the heavy rains and flooding during August 2000, which resulted in heavy damage to infrastructure and industry, are likely to have significantly boosted construction activity in restoration and rehabilitation.

Growth in the agriculture sector is estimated to have slowed to 2.4 percent in 2000 from 3.0 percent in 1999. Its share of GDP has declined from over half in the early 1980s to roughly a third today. This sectoral shift away from agriculture toward industry and services partly reflects the rise of hydropower in the country in the late 1980s. Initial estimates suggest that growth in the industry sector slowed to 10.3 percent in 2000. The August flooding forced several major industries to suspend their operations for several months. Manufacturing expansion, as a result, is expected to have slowed significantly.

Growth in services accelerated to 5.6 percent in 2000 from 4.5 percent in the previous year. Transport and communications outperformed the services sector average with a growth rate of 11.8 percent in 2000, which was largely attributable to transport needs generated by hydropower construction. The number of tourist arrivals rose to 7,162 in 1999, roughly a 16 percent increase over the previous year's level.

Given that an estimated 85 percent of the population live in rural areas, agriculture remains by far the largest source of employment, engaging around 75 percent of the employed labor force. Government (public administration and defense), the next largest source of employment, accounted for only 4.7 percent of employees in 1999. The estimated unemployment rate in 1999 was 1.4 percent, and though this seems very low, it is plausible given the overwhelmingly rural population and the predominance of agriculture as a source of employment. Unemployment was higher in urban than in rural areas, and among the young: 15–34-year-olds accounted for 69.1 percent of the unemployed. These figures are particularly worrying given the high rate of population growth, the existing constraints on both agriculture and public sector growth, and the fact that younger people tend to be better educated than their parents. The private sector—the engine of both growth and job creation in most industrial countries—employed a mere 2.9 percent of the workforce in 1999 and its progress remains stunted by a range of structural problems, including a skills mismatch in the labor market.

India is by far Bhutan's largest trading partner, accounting for 94.4 percent of Bhutan's exports and 75.1 percent of its imports in 2000. Driven by a revision of the tariff rate on electricity exports to India (exports to India grew by 7.3 percent), overall exports in dollar terms rose by 6.6 percent in 2000 compared with the previous year. Overall growth of imports, however, markedly outstripped that of exports, strengthening by 12.8 percent, mainly due to a surge in imports of materials and equipment for hydropower projects from India (imports from India increased by 18.5 percent).

The trade deficit with India, which deteriorated by 76.4 percent in 2000 to $33.7 million, was a major factor in the increase in the overall trade deficit of 23.5 percent to $73.4 million. Combined with a large amount of aid-related service transfers—again mainly with India—this resulted in a 27.4 percent increase in the current account deficit to $127.0 million in 2000 from $99.7 million in 1999.

Despite registering deficits on both the trade and current accounts, Bhutan managed to increase its gross international reserves by 13.1 percent to $293.0 million (equivalent to 19 months of imports), largely as a result of official capital inflows. Total debt as a proportion of GDP fell slightly from 40.2 percent in 1999 to 39.6 percent in 2000. The stock of external debt (all concessionary official loans), however, increased by 12.2 percent to $176.3 million, reflecting the Government's continued reliance on external funding

2000 refers to fiscal year 1999/2000, ending 30 June except in the case of GDP, which is on a calendar year basis.

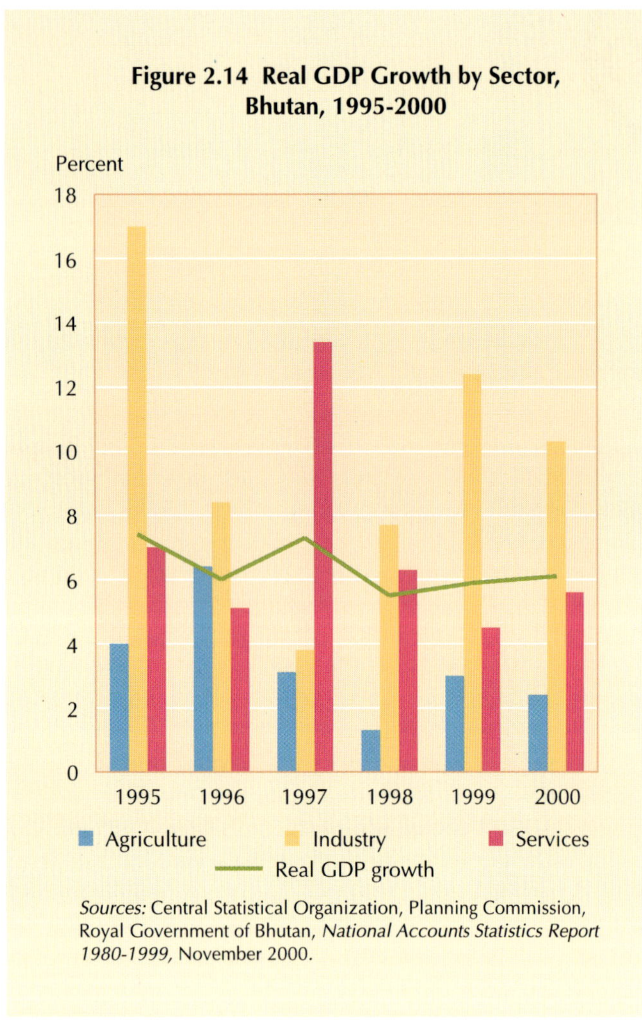

Sources: Central Statistical Organization, Planning Commission, Royal Government of Bhutan, *National Accounts Statistics Report 1980-1999*, November 2000.

large consumer goods, such as vehicles. As a consequence of greater investment and reduced savings, the savings-investment gap widened markedly in 1999, and given the current data, it would seem that it may have widened further in 2000.

Broad money supply remained at 21.4 percent in 2000, the same rate as in the previous year. Inflation, as measured by the consumer price index, fell from 9.2 percent in 1999 to 3.6 percent in 2000, its lowest ever recorded level. The fall was largely attributable to lower edible-oil prices and to stable rice prices.

Current fiscal expenditures in 2000 exceeded current fiscal revenues, despite a widening of the tax base and improved tax administration. Capital expenditure, however, significantly outstripped grant receipts (the conventional source for this type of spending) and the overall deficit grew to 3.9 percent of GDP, from 1.8 percent in the previous year.

Tax revenue, accounting for more than half of total revenue in 1999, surged by 50.6 percent in 2000, from 8.6 percent of GDP to 11.3 percent. This was largely due to the receipt of arrears on excise duties from the Government of India (for 1996 and 1997) and to the greater contribution of corporate income tax from the Chukha hydropower project following the change to the export power tariff. Nontax revenue rose by 4.5 percent in 2000 compared with 1999, mainly as a result of higher dividend receipts from Chukha. The power sector continues to be the leading source of revenue by far, accounting for 44 percent of the total.

The largest allocation in the initial budget for 2001 was for the social sector (26 percent), followed by energy (13 percent), and communications and agriculture (11 percent each). The effects of August 2000's flooding will probably, though significantly, change the overall budget and sectoral shares. The floods are likely to have a double impact on government finances, inflicting a heavy expenditure burden due to the costs of flood-related reconstruction, while cutting projected revenues due to the damage done to infrastructure and industry. The budget deficit is, therefore, expected to widen to 5.9 percent of GDP in 2001.

Growth momentum is likely to continue in 2001 and 2002 at about 5–6 percent a year, on the back of construction related to flood reparations and hydropower projects. However, a higher growth rate and significant job creation will require a takeoff in private sector activity. Prudent macroeconomic management is likely to continue, although the economy remains largely dependent on economic events in India.

The electricity and gas subsector is forecast to grow substantially in the near future with the completion in 2001–2002 of two hydropower projects (Kurichu and Basochu). Their combined capacity of about 120 MW will increase the country's electricity-generating capacity by a third. The Tala hydropower project, with a generating capacity of 1,020 MW, is scheduled to come onstream in 2006 and will make electricity and gas together the largest component of GDP.

for development expenditures. Debt servicing remained manageable, at 5.0 percent of merchandise exports.

Problems with the reliability of savings and investment data for the economy limit analysis to a discussion of broad trends. Changes in the country's savings and investment patterns are, perhaps unsurprisingly, closely linked to the development of hydropower projects, which underlines the economy's heavy reliance on that sector. Prior to the commissioning of the first hydropower project in the late 1980s—Chukha, with current generating capacity of 360 megawatts (MW)—gross domestic savings barely met domestic investment requirements. Government expenditures regularly exceeded revenues. With the income from Chukha, however, government revenues rose significantly. The increase in gross fixed capital formation in 1999 was, likewise, driven largely by the surge in construction activity related to hydropower projects. Private savings fell significantly in 1999 as banks introduced new types of consumer loans and borrowers took advantage of them to buy

Issues in Economic Management

Despite a gradually improving standard of living over the last two decades, some areas of the country face episodic food insecurity, while the nutritional status of women and children needs to be improved. Therefore, enhancing infrastructure is critical to effectively address poverty and disparities that may emerge as a result of development. Necessary institutional and capacity development to produce timely and high-quality data will be essential to properly plan, monitor, and evaluate the impact of development, particularly to target future poverty interventions.

Although the Government is likely to remain reliant on external resources for major development activities over the medium term, it needs to continue exploring modalities for expanding the domestic revenue base. Current preparations for the introduction of personal income tax, user fees for nonessential health services, and appropriate charges for other social services and public utilities will improve fiscal sustainability as well as the efficiency of these sectors.

The pegging of the local currency, the ngultrum, to the Indian rupee and the presence of a large and freely circulating volume of Indian rupees in the economy greatly limit the scope for monetary policy. Consequently, the Royal Monetary Authority of Bhutan has employed conventional instruments of central bank policy mainly to pursue nonmonetary policy goals, such as financial sector development and the setting of prudential norms. Some monetary instruments, such as the cash reserve ratio—introduced for prudential purposes—have proved rather costly to the Authority (e.g., in the case of the cash reserve ratio, through interest payments to commercial banks). Their ineffectiveness as monetary policy tools has led to a reassessment of their value and a consequent move to reduce their use.

Policy and Development Issues

The process of modernization and development is bringing new problems to Bhutan, two of which are urbanization and unemployment. Urban planning has failed to keep up with rapid growth, especially in Thimphu, the capital, and Phuentsholing. As a result, the country now has to contend with unplanned urban expansion and a lack of urban infrastructure. The Government needs to reduce the rate of migration from rural areas by improving village life and to build infrastructure for existing and new urban centers. While urbanization is inevitable, it is important to plan and manage it in a holistic manner in the next five-year development plan, which starts in July 2002.

Recent substantial improvements in access to education have led to greater numbers of graduates entering the labor market every year. The creation of new job opportunities is therefore urgent, but is constrained by the country's nascent private sector. The Government needs to address the requirements of this weak private sector as well as those of a fragile financial sector. It also needs to maintain its efforts to promote an enabling environment through diversification of job opportunities by offering relevant skills training, encouraging competition, strengthening infrastructure, implementing appropriate fiscal policies, and removing bureaucratic constraints for those starting new enterprises.

Efficiency, transparency, and accountability are the goals of the Government's ongoing restructuring exercise. The decentralization process will be accelerated with the adoption of information technology and planning based on village clusters in the next five-year plan. However, the necessary institutions and human resources at national, district, and village cluster levels will need to be appropriately developed to ensure sustained benefits of the restructuring and decentralization efforts.

India

As reforms have slowed, the impulses to economic growth generated by earlier reforms have almost faded. Furthermore, structural impediments have prevented the economy from taking full advantage of the liberalized economic environment. A concerted effort is thus needed to prevent the economy from slipping to a slower growth path of 5–6 percent in the medium term, that is, well below the Government's target of 9 percent.

Recent Trends and Prospects

The optimism that prevailed at the beginning of 2000 over the prospects for economic expansion became more muted in the face of unfavorable weather conditions and sluggish industrial recovery. The real GDP growth rate in 2000 is estimated to have been 6.0 percent, supported by growth of 0.9 percent in agriculture, 6.6 percent in industry, and 8.3 percent in services. With this trend, the average growth rate of GDP during the first four years of the Ninth Five-Year Plan (1997–2002) is estimated at around 6 percent a year, compared with a plan target of 6.5 percent, and an average annual growth rate of 6.7 percent during the Eighth Five-Year Plan (1992–1997). This decline in the growth rate during the current Plan, however, has to be seen in the context of a series of exceptional circumstances in recent years. These include the fallout effects of the Asian financial crisis, economic sanctions following nuclear testing at Pokhran, border conflicts with Pakistan at Kargil, and a sharp increase in international oil prices. Despite these adverse developments, the Indian economy was one of the best performing in Asia in 2000.

Compared with 1999, the Reserve Bank of India (RBI) faced generally unfavorable policy conditions in 2000, characterized by a sharp depreciation of the rupee and higher inflation. Rising US interest rates and the consequent depreciation of the rupee against the dollar prompted the RBI to take reactive measures in July 2000 to prevent a further fall in the currency. The bank rate was raised to 8 percent and the cash reserve ratio to 8.5 percent; this was followed by a hike in prime lending rates by commercial banks. Despite the higher interest rates, though, bank credit to the commercial sector showed steady growth, reflecting the unusually large financing needs of oil companies to cover the high cost of imported oil. Slow growth in net bank credit to the Government and in banks' foreign exchange assets contributed to a deceleration in growth of broad money (M3) during the first half of 2000, though M3 showed a sharp increase in November due to capital inflows linked to the Indian Millennium Deposits (IMD) Scheme designed to raise financing from nonresident Indians.

The inflation rate for 2000, measured by the year-on-year change in the monthly average of the wholesale price index, was 7.0 percent—a marked increase from 3.3 percent in the previous year. This was primarily the result of a rise in oil prices. For instance, the Government raised the administered prices of liquefied petroleum gas and kerosene by 18 percent and 50 percent, respectively, on 1 October 2000. However, the ample supply of agricultural goods and excess capacity in manufacturing helped contain price rises to some extent. Prices of food items increased by only 1.5 percent, and those of manufactured goods by 3.0 percent.

The central Government's direct tax revenues strengthened in 2000. This was due to a broadening of the tax base, an increase in dividend taxes, and a higher corporate tax collection (due to a lower depreciation allowance). The Government announced a number of expenditure control measures, such as retrenchment of surplus staff, cuts in its foreign travel budgets and nonsalary current expenditure, and reduction of subsidies through the use of cost-based user charges for the supply of goods and services. For medium-term management of the fiscal deficit, the 2000 budget proposed to introduce an institutional mechanism, called the Fiscal Responsibility Act. With these initiatives, the actual deficit of the central Government in 2000 has been contained within the budget estimate of 5.1 percent of GDP. Although direct tax collection and nontax receipts were buoyant, the performance of indirect taxes was poor due to sluggish industrial production and a lower growth rate of non-oil imports. In addition, privatization receipts fell short of the budget target because of the slowing pace of divestment.

Despite a slowing economy and rising inflation, the impressive performance of the export sector in 1999 continued

2000 refers to fiscal year 2000/01, ending 31 March.

in 2000. Exports rose by 17.0 percent in 2000 from 11.6 percent the previous year. Exports' strong performance ensured that the balance of payments did not come under pressure: however, imports also grew strongly at 13.0 percent, partly because of a surging oil import bill. This resulted in a 4.0 percent increase in the trade deficit. The current account deficit is expected to have widened to around 1.3 percent of GDP during 2000.

Net capital inflows are estimated to have risen from $10.0 billion in 1999 to $12.0 billion in 2000, with inflows of more than $5.5 billion from the issuance of IMD. Foreign currency reserves rose to $42.1 billion, equivalent to 8.1 months of imports at the end of the year.

The rupee lost almost 7 percent of its value against the dollar between March and December 2000 (from Rs43.5 to Rs46.7 to the dollar). Despite this sharp fall in the nominal value of the rupee, the depreciation of the real effective exchange rate was much more modest—less than 2 percent in 2000. The rupee could experience further volatility in the coming months.

In the medium to long term, the prospects for the economy look favorable as ongoing reforms bring significant gains in supply-side efficiency. Indeed, India's relatively high economic growth over the 1990s was made possible mainly by efficiency gains with little increase in investment rates. Improved economic efficiency was a critical factor in bringing the economic growth rate to over 6 percent at the end of the 1990s, substantially higher than the earlier average of about 3 percent a year in the 1970s and the early 1980s. Furthermore, the reforms are attracting new foreign investment and stimulating new industries based on information and communications technology. India's capabilities in this area are expanding rapidly and the country now offers a range of products, including computer software. Yet skepticism abounds because of India's past record of being very slow to accommodate change. Thus, the Government must remain firmly committed to its reforms, which include improvements in fiscal management.

On the assumption that no major internal or external disturbances arise, such as adverse weather patterns or oil price increases, the economy can sustain real GDP growth rates of 6–7 percent a year in 2001 and 2002. In fact, much depends on the performance of agriculture and progress in industrial recovery. The recent beginning of a slowdown in the US economy will add uncertainty to the overall investment climate and export performance.

The annual inflation rate in 2001 and 2002 in terms of the wholesale price index is likely to fall to around 5 percent. Despite the slowdown in global demand, exports are projected to show steady growth at 12–13 percent. The balance of payments is likely to remain stable, with the current account deficit improving slightly to about 1 percent of GDP in 2002. On the capital account, access to international financial markets will be

Table 2.19 Major Economic Indicators, India, 1998–2002
(percent)

Item	1998	1999	2000	2001	2002
GDP growth[a]	6.6	6.4	6.0	6.2	7.0
Gross domestic investment/GDP	23.0	23.3	23.5	23.8	24.3
Gross domestic savings/GDP	22.0	22.3	22.7	22.8	23.1
Inflation rate (wholesale price index)[b]	5.9	3.3	7.0	5.5	4.8
Money supply (M3) growth	19.4	13.9	16.0	15.0	15.0
Fiscal balance/GDP	-5.1	-5.5	-5.1	-4.7	-4.5
Merchandise export growth	-3.9	11.6	17.0	12.0	13.0
Merchandise import growth	-7.1	16.5	13.0	10.0	9.5
Current account balance/GDP	-1.0	-0.9	-1.3	-1.2	-1.0
Total debt/GDP	24.4	23.5	22.0	21.0	20.2

[a] Based on constant 1993/94 factor cost.
[b] Year on year.

Sources: Central Statistical Organisation, *National Income, Consumption Expenditure, Saving and Capital Formation, 1999–2000*, January 2001; Reserve Bank of India, *Annual Report 1999–2000*, September 2000; Ministry of Finance, *Economic Survey 2000/01*, February 2001; staff estimates.

renewed as international credit ratings improve and as the composition of capital flows continues to shift in favor of nondebt-creating financial flows in response to economic reforms.

Issues in Economic Management

Although the economy has performed well over the past few years, it is not fully utilizing its growth potential. In particular, the deteriorating fiscal health of the central and state governments is significantly undermining the economy's long-term growth potential because of inadequate public investment. In agriculture, wide swings in production and very low productivity have been, to a large extent, the result of declining public investment in irrigation. The rate of capital formation in agriculture declined to 9.2 percent in the 1990s, from about 21 percent during the 1970s and 1980s. So, while agriculture has the potential to grow at more than 4 percent annually, sectoral performance has fallen far short of this.

Industrial growth recovered from its low point of 3.6 percent in 1998 to 6.4 percent in 1999, but insufficient investment in both public and private physical infrastructure remains a major constraint to the expansion of industrial activities in the long run. In particular, the failure of state governments to provide basic infrastructure severely undermines the long-term growth potential of the economy, which is prevented from reaping the full benefits of market reforms and liberalization. In the power sector, new generating capacity during the Eighth Five-Year Plan fell short of the target by 50 percent, due primarily to inadequate investments by state governments. The state electricity boards suffered from a deteriorating financial situation. Similarly, in the road sector during the Eighth Five-Year Plan, only $3.2 billion was provided for state and major district roads, against a requirement of $5.5 billion. The deterioration of state finances suggests that the quality of infrastructure services is likely to get worse (see Box 2.5). Recognizing the severity of the problem, in July 2000 the Eleventh Finance Commission recommended structural reform along with other fiscal changes to help state governments achieve zero revenue deficits by 2005.

While the Government recently announced an economic growth target of 8–9 percent a year, this will require a substantial increase in public and private investment from the current 23.5 percent of GDP. The household savings rate, which is close to 20 percent of GDP, is already high, compared with other developing economies at similar income levels. Thus, the Government needs to make India a favored destination for foreign investment, although it is not possible to fill the resource gap from external resources alone. In order to boost domestic savings, the central Government needs to make a greater effort to mobilize public savings, while state governments must explore the scope for expenditure control at all levels. Politically difficult decisions may be required to reduce expenditure, including serious downsizing of state bureaucracies and cuts in

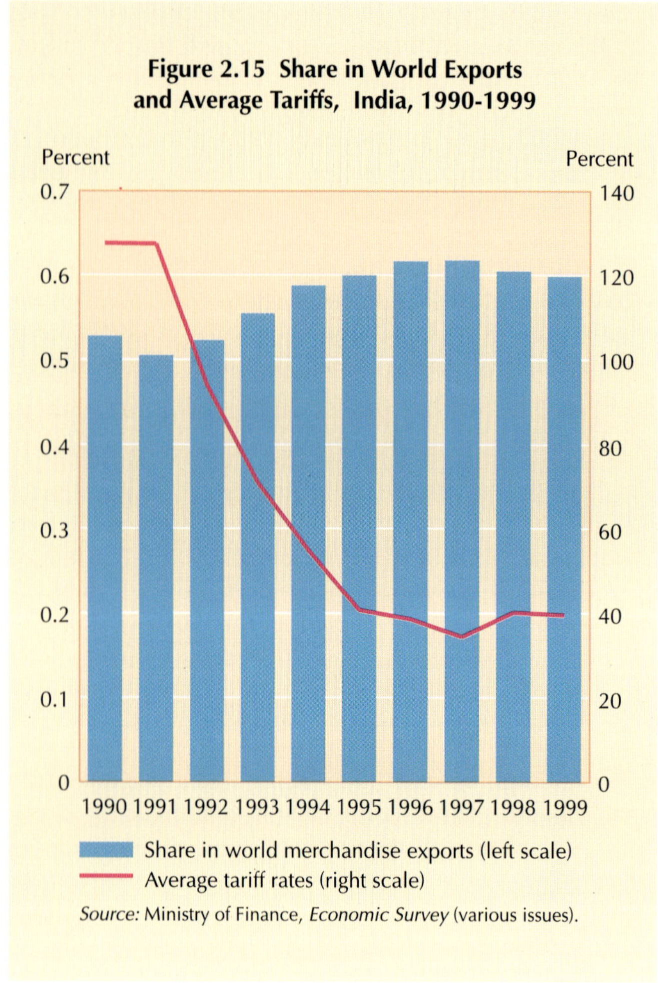

Figure 2.15 Share in World Exports and Average Tariffs, India, 1990-1999

Source: Ministry of Finance, *Economic Survey* (various issues).

subsidies. Privatization will have to be placed at the top of the central Government's reform agenda. The financial waste in public sector undertakings is substantial and must be addressed promptly. On the revenue side, the tax-to-GDP ratio needs to be improved through rationalizing taxes, expanding the tax base, and overhauling tax administration. It is particularly important to bring more services into the tax base because of the increasing importance of the services-oriented economy.

Policy and Development Issues

After the balance-of-payments crisis of 1991, the Government undertook significant structural changes. Reforms included liberalization of trade and gradual opening up of the capital account. The volume of total trade as a proportion of GDP rose from about 15 percent in 1990 to over 20 percent in 1998. The economy has also achieved greater competitiveness in services, particularly in the area of information technology. The opening up of the capital account has spurred capital inflows, leading to greater capital formation in the economy and an increase in

Box 2.5 The Finances of State Governments

Finances of state governments in India continued to deteriorate in the 1990s. The combined fiscal deficit of all states rose from 2.3 percent of GDP in 1993, to 4.3 percent in 1998, and to close to 5.0 percent in 1999. The outstanding debt of the states is estimated to have exceeded 20 percent of GDP in 1999, up from 18.3 percent in 1993. With interest rates on state government borrowings rising during the 1990s, the growing debt stock resulted in higher interest payments. In 1999, the interest burden of the states is estimated to have risen to 20.5 percent of revenue receipts from 15 percent in 1993.

While state governments are responsible for the mismanagement of finances and the consequent deterioration of their fiscal health, structural factors have also played a part. Imbalances between states' revenue-raising powers and spending responsibilities have tended to widen over the years. Under the federal structure, states are responsible for the activities of education, health, infrastructure facilities, maintenance of law, etc. Yet the central Government has been vested with the more buoyant sources of revenue. In the past, sharing of taxes in India between the center and the states was on a tax-by-tax basis. In particular, two central taxes were shared with states, namely, income tax and excise duty. Two other important taxes were not shared with states: corporation tax and customs duty. However, under the 80th amendment to the Constitution in May 2000, the net proceeds of almost all central Government taxes and duties are distributable between the center and the states. The change will widen the sharable revenue base for the states, thereby enabling them to benefit from the aggregate buoyancy of the central taxes, including that of the corporation tax.

One major initiative taken by the central Government to catalyze state financial reforms was to sign a series of memorandums of understanding on fiscal reforms with individual states. In March 1999, the finance minister and representatives of several states resolved that the central Government and states should work together to find a sustainable solution for the states' fiscal imbalances. They requested the central Government to extend an assistance package consisting of accelerated transfer of shared revenues and grants, increased state borrowing limits, and limited rescheduling of loan payments by states. This assistance package is to be linked to appropriate time-bound, medium-term, fiscal reform programs to be developed in consultation with each state. Since then, memorandums of understanding detailing the reform program to be undertaken by each state and the assistance due have been signed by the Government and 11 states (including Assam, Orissa, Punjab, Rajasthan, and Uttar Pradesh). Although the individual memorandums were drawn up separately, a set of common objectives has emerged: downsizing state government; compressing nonplan current expenditure; mobilizing additional resources; increasing user charges; and implementing public sector divestment and restructuring, cash management, debt management, and institutional reform.

States' indebtedness is complicated by the fact that in recent years many of them have been raising funds from the market through state-owned enterprises under state government guarantees. These borrowings are not included in the budget, but debt service and repayment of loans are contingent liabilities of the state government that provides the guarantee. Therefore, these off-budget liabilities must be included in any analysis of state finances. Recognizing the "moral hazard" in excessive use of guarantees by state governments, the Reserve Bank of India introduced a new regulation, effective April 1999, requiring that banks and other financial institutions assign a 20 percent risk weighting (to meet Bank for International Settlements capital adequacy requirements) to state-guaranteed bonds or advances outside the states' formal borrowing programs. If the state fails to pay the interest or principal of these bonds or advances, a 100 percent risk weighting will be assigned.

foreign exchange reserves. The heavier reliance on direct investment has facilitated technology transfer and reduced the risk of another balance-of-payments crisis. The role of external assistance has shrunk, while that of commercial borrowing has increased. Finally, the volume of private transfers has risen significantly, due to the more liberal environment.

India's trade regime was one of the most protected in the world until the beginning of the 1990s, heavily depending on both quantitative restrictions (QRs) and high tariff levels. However, with the introduction of new policies, the share of value added in manufacturing protected by QRs declined from 90 percent in 1990 to 47 percent by May 1992 and to 36 percent by May 1995. In fact, QRs were virtually eliminated for imports of industrial raw materials, intermediate components, and capital goods. However, the corresponding decline was much less steep in agriculture, from 94 percent in 1990 to 93 percent by May 1992 and to 84 percent by May 1995. The import of industrial consumer goods also remains under control because of perceived political sensitivity, although some restricted items are imported freely through transferable special import licenses (SILs). SILs, which can be sold, are granted to selected exporters as export incentives. SIL coverage has been extended significantly since April 1999, with various items removed from the restricted list and put on the SIL list, as well as from the SIL list to the open general license list.

The Government's balance-of-payments justification for using QRs had become untenable given the strong current account, substantial capital inflows, and large foreign exchange reserves during the years following the rupee's devaluation in 1991. India's unrestrained use of QRs was challenged in the World Trade Organization balance-of-payments committee by the EU, US, and other developed economies in December 1995. India lost the case and is required to abolish its QR regime by April 2001 under a bilateral agreement signed with the US in December 1999.

The Government does not provide direct subsidies to exporters. They are provided indirectly through duty and tax concessions, export finance, export insurance and guarantees, and export promotion and marketing assistance. However, the actual effectiveness of this complex structure in enhancing exports is unclear. Though some efforts have been made since 1991 to reduce administrative problems and delays in implementing the various export incentives, the sharp growth of exports during 1993–1995 cannot be attributed to changes in incentives. Rupee devaluation, removal of industrial licensing and other controls over industry, and the opening up of imports of intermediate and capital goods were more proximate causes. The Government plans to phase out income tax exemptions for exports through 2004, as well as expand the use of import duty exemptions.

Prior to 1991, India's import duties were among the highest in the world. The Chelliah Committee (1992) proposed that the average import-weighted duty rate should be reduced from 87 percent in 1990 to 45 percent by 1995 and further to 25 percent by 1998. The Government lowered its average applied tariff rate from 125 percent in 1990 to 71 percent in 1993, to 41 percent in 1995, and to 35 percent in 1997 (see Figure 2.15). The corresponding levels of average import-weighted tariffs were 87 percent in 1990, 47 percent in 1993, 25 percent in 1996, and 30 percent in 1998. The average import-weighted tariff on consumer goods was also reduced from 153 percent in 1990 to 39 percent in 1998. On the other hand, the maximum tariff rate declined from 355 percent in 1990 to 45 percent in 1997 and to 40 percent in 1999. It was reduced to 35 percent in 2000 but has been subjected to a 10 percent surcharge, thus making it 38.5 percent.

In February 2000, the Government took several steps to further liberalize the capital account. Foreign investment played a very limited role in the economy prior to 1991. It was permitted in industries where the Government believed foreign technology to be necessary for economic growth. Foreign equity participation was tightly regulated, usually to a limit of 40 percent of total equity capital. A new industrial policy announced in July 1991 liberalized foreign direct investment, foreign technology agreements, and compulsory industrial licensing. Automatic approval was permitted for investments of up to 51 percent equity in 34 industries. In February 2000, the Government took a major decision to place all items under the automatic route for foreign direct investment except for a small negative list. This was an important step in dispensing with the previous case-by-case approval procedure and in imparting greater transparency to the foreign investment process. Furthermore, subject to sectoral policies and caps, the automatic route would be made available to all foreign and nonresident Indian investors who could secure 100 percent foreign investment.

The Government had already established the Foreign Investment Implementation Authority in 1999 to ensure that the approvals granted for foreign investments actually reached financial closure.

Policies relating to investments by foreign institutional investors and to global depository receipts (GDRs) have undergone various changes since 1991. Indian companies were permitted to raise capital through Euromarket issues of GDRs and foreign currency convertible bonds, and to have access to international capital markets, in 1992. Also that year, certain foreign institutional investors, including pension funds, mutual funds, asset management companies, investment trusts, nominee companies, and incorporated or institutional portfolio managers were permitted to invest in the Indian capital market. These investing institutions need to be registered in their home country or country of origin, and registered with the Securities and Exchange Board of India. The profits from portfolio investment can be repatriated freely subject to India's foreign exchange regulations. Since February 2000, Indian companies no longer needed prior approval from the Government to issue GDRs; the equity ceiling for foreign institutional investors was raised from 30 to 40 percent in the same month.

External commercial borrowings (ECBs) provide an additional source of funds to Indian companies, allowing them to augment domestically available resources and to take advantage of lower international interest rates. From February 2000, ECBs were permitted within a higher annual ceiling, for example, three times average annual export earnings for exporters, or double the previous limit. Other ECB guidelines were relaxed and several procedures were simplified so as to make it easier for Indian companies to borrow abroad.

As discussed above, the Government has substantially liberalized trade-related policies since 1991. However, these policies have covered mainly intermediate and capital goods in manufacturing. Agriculture remains least touched by the trade reforms. Consumer goods imports are also restricted. Although the Government has reduced average import-weighted tariffs significantly over the last decade, India's rates are still among the highest in the developing world. A reduction in import tariffs may lead to some loss in revenues, but this is likely to be made up for when the QRs on consumer goods are dismantled from April 2001. In the long run, there is an implicit agreement among policymakers to phase down Indian customs duties to the 12 percent level of the countries of the Association of Southeast Asian Nations. Trade in services remains another area for future reform. During the 1990s, increased earnings from services and other invisibles helped the economy maintain a strong current account. Opening the services sector to international competition is expected to make it more efficient and to generate additional foreign exchange earnings.

Maldives

The economy slowed in 2000, partly because of weakness in tourism and fisheries. Sustained economic growth requires fiscal consolidation, financial market development, and skill enhancement of the labor force.

Recent Trends and Prospects

The economy decelerated to 4.2 percent growth in 2000, compared with annual average growth of 7–9 percent between 1995 and 1999. The slowdown was general, and affected the leading sectors of tourism and fisheries. The Government undertook development and infrastructure projects to supplement aggregate demand but their impact was limited. Per capita income increased substantially between the early 1990s and 2000. Sound economic management and slower population growth have been largely responsible for this boost in living standards.

The tourism sector was weak. Although total tourist arrivals in 2000 increased by 8.7 percent, compared with the previous year, the impact was partly offset by a decrease in the length of average stay. In addition, the national capacity utilization rate has declined over the past three years because 13 new resorts have been opened. This underutilization of bed space resulted in a competitive reduction in room rates, and therefore the actual contribution of the sector to the economy was stagnant. However, the direct contribution of tourism to fiscal revenue through bed taxes and lease rents increased. The poor performance of the fisheries sector was due to a reduction in the fish catch, which had been exceptionally high in 1998 and 1999.

The fiscal deficit as a proportion of GDP fell marginally from 4.1 percent in 1999 to 4.0 percent in 2000, due to government measures to reduce expenditures coupled with greater than expected revenues from various sources. In recent years, the fiscal deficit has been monetized through borrowing from the central bank. Inflation has been kept in check since sound fiscal management measures were introduced in 1994, and declined from 3.0 percent in 1999 to show price deflation of 1.1 percent in 2000. The key items that contributed to this deflation were food, beverages and tobacco, and clothing and footwear.

Monetary policy in 2000 aimed at facilitating sustained economic growth and maintaining government reserves at a comfortable level. The central bank relied on direct monetary policy instruments such as interest rate controls, credit limits, and a reserve ratio to control money supply growth. Total liquidity increased by 9.1 percent in 2000, but government borrowing crowded out the private sector to a large extent. Continued borrowing from the central bank drove total government debt up to 15.1 percent of GDP in 2000.

In the external sector in 2000, exports rose by 13.2 percent while imports fell by 1.0 percent. Despite falling international fish prices, a substantial rise in export volumes of canned and dried fish generated an increase in exports. Higher world oil prices in 2000 did not affect imports significantly because of the slowdown in the economy. The trade deficit fell from 45.1 percent of GDP in 1999 to 39.1 percent in 2000. On the services account, the increase in tourist arrivals contributed to a surplus. Correspondingly, the current account deficit decreased from 11.1 percent of GDP in 1999 to 4.6 percent in 2000. The overall balance also improved, due to a stronger inflow of foreign grants and loans. Estimates for the end of 2000 indicate that the Government's foreign exchange reserves could pay for 4.3 months of imports of goods and services, compared with 4.4 months at the end of the previous year. The total external debt position improved slightly from 36.6 percent of GDP in 1999 to 36.2 percent in 2000. External debt comprised almost entirely medium- and long-term debt. The debt-service ratio of 3.7 percent in 1999 deteriorated slightly to 3.8 percent in 2000.

GDP growth for 2001 is projected at 5.7 percent largely on the back of tourism expansion. Major marketing and promotional campaigns that were conducted in 2000 are expected to pay off in the next few years. Tourist arrivals in 2001 and 2002 are projected to increase by 8 percent. The excess supply of beds should fall as demand picks up, raising profit margins. The proposed liberalization of the fisheries sector in 2001, including the skipjack fishery that accounts for over 85 percent of the total catch, will encourage competition and enhance efficiency, thereby increasing earnings from the sector. As part of liberalization moves, the monopoly enjoyed by the government-owned Maldives Industrial Fishery Company in exporting canned tuna will be gradually dismantled. These measures are expected to increase both value added in the sector and export earnings. However, if world fish prices remain depressed, the benefits of liberalization will be delayed, perhaps until 2002 or even later.

Although a balanced budget has been proposed for 2001, the Government expects to make considerable savings and to pay back part of the outstanding debt to the central bank. The liberalization of the fisheries sector is likely to increase private sector investment, hence royalty payments to the Government should rise significantly. Revenues from licenses and fees are also expected to improve. In addition, measures introduced in 2000 to control expenditures will be strengthened and this should help minimize pressures on the budget.

Issues in Economic Management

Financial sector reform becomes more critical for sustainable growth as the Maldives becomes more integrated into the world economy. The country has experienced several years of continuous economic growth supported by sound economic management. However, current macroeconomic indicators suggest that the country's future growth performance may be hindered by limitations in long-term credit required for further expansion. Understanding this, the Government, to meet short-term credit needs, is making preparations to issue treasury bills to replace the system of automatic deficit financing through the central bank. To enhance long-term savings, it is pursuing the development of life insurance companies and pension funds. The establishment of a capital market would encourage financing of investment through the issue of long-term bonds and shares. This will ease the current pressures on financing new businesses and commercial undertakings, and stimulate the private sector to take more part in economic development.

Another area that the Government needs to emphasize is the expansion of its revenue base. At present, about 42 percent of its revenue is generated by tourism taxes and import duties. Past deficit financing has increased government debt to undesirable levels. Identifying additional sources of revenue is, therefore, critical if the Government's social and infrastructure development programs are to continue uninterrupted, as its

ability to finance future expenditures in excess of revenues is limited. Several new sources have, in fact, already been identified, such as new taxes on property rental value and corporate income to make the revenue system more resilient to external shocks affecting receipts from tourism taxes and import duties.

Policy and Development Issues

Labor market issues represent a big challenge for the Government. An increase in labor demand accompanying the high economic growth of the last decade has driven the labor market tighter. A recent increase in labor demand has been met by expatriates from neighboring countries, despite more restrictive government measures on foreign recruitment. Currently, over 27,000 expatriates work in the Maldives, more than 75 percent of them in sectors such as tourism and construction that require unskilled and semiskilled workers, where many Maldivians are reluctant to work. On the other hand, a significant number of students are expected to enter the job market in the next few years, and the Government needs to prepare an environment to accommodate them.

Enhancing the skill level of the labor force is one of the key components not only for reducing unemployment, but also for improving economic competitiveness and long-term development goals. The Government has taken several initiatives in this area. To provide cheaper and affordable opportunities for higher education, it has established the College of Higher Education, and is making efforts to affiliate it with recognized international universities in conducting appropriate degree-level programs. It is also trying to enhance the skill level of the workforce through vocational training. In addition, it will start the implementation of a third training and education project to develop human resources, encouraged by the effectiveness of two previous projects in this field.

Nepal

The continued recovery in agricultural production in 2000 boosted the economy's short-term prospects. However, to sustain growth, the Government needs to push forward with its broad-based reform agenda, particularly in the areas of governance and economic reforms. Poverty reduction remains an urgent priority.

Recent Trends and Prospects

Real GDP growth rose to 6.4 percent in 2000 from 4.4 percent in the previous year, led by agriculture and industry (see Figure 2.16). A favorable monsoon season and wider use of fertilizer led to a strong agricultural recovery in 2000 of 5.0 percent growth. This met the projections of the Agriculture Perspective Plan, which details the Government's agricultural development strategy for two decades. However, this rate needs to be sustained, and the annual variation in agricultural performance reduced. Production of food grain increased in 2000, particularly that of rice, which rose by 8.6 percent. The industry sector grew by 8.7 percent, led by manufacturing, which expanded by 13.0 percent. Trade with India, and the tourism, carpet, and garment industries registered strong performance. However, with no large projects undertaken in 2000, electricity and construction growth remained slow.

Consistent with an economy dominated by subsistence agriculture, the labor force participation rate was high and the unemployment rate low. About 86 percent of the working-age population (aged 15 and above) were economically active, with 76 percent employed in agriculture. The unemployment rate for the country as a whole was less than 2 percent, but the rate in urban areas was higher than 7 percent.

Moderated by declines or only slight rises in food prices, inflation rose by just 3.5 percent in 2000, compared with 11.4 percent in the previous year. Favorable monsoon conditions led to stability in prices of food grains and vegetables. A surplus of rice also contributed to lower prices after the main harvest, and the food and beverages index rose by less than 1 percent. Inflation of nonfood items, however, was 7.0 percent, up from 5.8 percent in 1999, because of increases in key administered prices, notably kerosene, electricity, and diesel. High money growth continued with a 4.1 percent increase in inflows of foreign assets. Broad money (M2) expanded by about 21.8 percent in 2000, slightly more than 20.9 percent in 1999.

The budget deficit remained stable at 3.9 percent of GDP in 2000. Domestic revenue collection was lower than budgeted, with actual revenues of about 11 percent of GDP, roughly the same as in 1999. The shortfall in revenues was balanced by the slower than budgeted growth in development expenditures of 17 percent rather than the 48 percent envisaged in the 2000 budget. Even with slower growth, foreign grants and loans financed about 50 percent of development expenditures, a proportion that has remained largely unchanged since the early 1990s.

Nepal's current account balance, which registered a surplus in 1999 of 0.1 percent of GDP, switched to a deficit in 2000 of 1.5 percent of GDP, largely due to strong growth in imports. Non-aid imports increased in 2000. Loan disbursements from aid agencies decreased slightly from the 1999 level, but foreign exchange reserves continued to rise. By the end of the year, such reserves amounted to $981 million (sufficient to cover more than six months of imports). External debt as a proportion of GDP declined slightly in 2000 to 48.0 percent. However, because of the concessionary nature of this lending, the debt-service ratio for external debt declined and remained a manageable 5.3 percent of exports in 2000.

Over the next few years, the economy should remain stable. The country has potential for growth rates exceeding 5 percent a year, but actual performance is still quite vulnerable to changes in the weather and the Indian economy, given India's dominance as a trading partner and Nepal's narrow industrial base. An overall growth rate of 5–5.5 percent, if supported by appropriate policies, is forecast for 2001 and 2002. Agricultural growth may decline somewhat to about 4 percent, depending on weather conditions, but the sector's recovery is expected to continue. Growth in the industry sector will moderate slightly to 7–8 percent, and will be determined by export growth rates. Growth in the services sector will be similar to the past at about 6 percent, boosted by a recovery in tourism revenues but moderated by slower growth in community and personal

2000 refers to fiscal year 1999/2000, ending 15 July.

services. The transport sector, where growth is linked to export performance, should perform well.

In the absence of any external shocks to the economy, inflation is likely to be moderate over the next few years. In 2001, it is projected at 5.5 percent, and is likely to benefit from favorable monsoon weather throughout South Asia. The price of rice, which dominates the price index, will probably decline after the harvest. Nonfood prices, however, are expected to rise. The Nepalese rupee, depreciating against the dollar, is likely to make imported manufactures dearer, while the fuel price has already been raised. The Government can maintain these levels only as long as India, its main supplier, does not alter its prices. Electricity tariffs will also need to be put up to maintain that sector's viability.

Monetary policy will be geared to supporting the exchange rate peg with the Indian rupee. As such, interest and inflation rates need to be kept in line with those in India. Continuing monetization of the economy will provide some leeway in monetary policy, but the 20 percent annual money supply growth rates in recent years cannot continue without fueling inflation. Given projections for real growth and inflation, targets for broad money growth need to be in the range of 12–14 percent in the medium term. To support the central bank's efforts to control inflation and maintain the exchange rate peg, further development of the market for government securities is required to break the link between budget deficits and monetary expansion. Moreover, the limit of NRs1 billion on the Government's overdraft with the central bank needs to be strictly enforced.

The Government's ambitious development expenditure and revenue targets in 2001 will be difficult to achieve, especially since pay rises and a voluntary early retirement scheme were introduced for civil servants. Development expenditures in the 2001 budget are projected to grow by 45 percent. These will be financed mainly by foreign grants, which are forecast to increase by 100 percent. Domestic revenue estimates in the 2001 budget are similarly optimistic, with a projected growth rate of 24 percent. Actual revenue performance will depend on the effective implementation of the value-added tax. The minimum revenue level for firms covered by the value-added tax was lowered from NRs4.5 million to NRs2 million, and the registration of firms was accelerated to widen the tax base. The number of registrations doubled between 1999 and 2000. As in previous years, development expenditures will probably bear any shortfalls in domestic revenues and foreign grants. The fiscal deficit for 2001 is projected to reach 4.5 percent of GDP and rise slightly in 2002.

The current account deficit will rise slightly in 2001 as aid-related inflows continue to increase, particularly if the Government achieves most of its development agenda. Strong economic growth in India will continue to bolster Nepal's exports but probably not to the extent seen in 2000. In exports to other countries, garments have been strong, but are subject

to a gradual removal of quotas in the US as part of the World Trade Organization's (WTO) Agreement on Textiles and Clothing. Another area that is difficult to predict is exports of carpets and *pashmina* shawls as the popularity of these products is based on current fashions. However, business owners are confident of further expansion in the medium term, and estimates of 12–15 percent export growth mirror this view. Depreciation of the Nepalese rupee against the dollar should also help support exports. Imports are expected to grow as rapidly as exports, with some acceleration over time, as domestic growth lifts demand for foreign products and higher public investment raises the inflow of aid-related goods, in particular for a water supply project in Melamchi. Overall, increased aid-related investment inflows will drive the widening of the current account deficit in the coming years. The expanding public expenditure program will lead to higher external debt as a proportion of GDP, but debt service should remain manageable at about 5.5 percent of GDP, assuming that export growth stays strong and given the concessionary nature of the Government's borrowings.

Issues in Economic Management

Nepal still has a predominantly agrarian economy, and the majority of the country's poor people live in rural areas. The Government's continued commitment to the Agriculture Perspective Plan is, therefore, critical, including its ability to coordinate the various government departments properly and monitor implementation. Although the completion of the removal of fertilizer subsidies in mid-2000 was an important step in fostering private sector involvement in the trade in agricultural inputs, it is important that the Government does not reinstate market distortions, but rather, further encourages private sector participation in the agriculture sector.

Given the economy's limited access to foreign capital markets, the savings rate is too low to support the investment needed for sustainable reductions in poverty. Inefficiencies in the financial sector, which is dominated by state-owned financial institutions, hamper the mobilization of domestic resources. The financial sector is, therefore, another key area where extensive reforms are needed, in order to strengthen accounting and auditing standards, deregulate the sector to increase competition, strengthen the role of the central bank, and restructure publicly owned banks.

Commercial banking, the largest segment of the financial sector, is dominated by the state-owned Rastriya Banijya Bank and the formerly state-owned Nepal Bank Limited, which together account for more than half of all commercial bank deposits. However, a recent audit showed them to be technically insolvent. Under government management, these banks had developed extensive, but costly, branch networks and staff resources. For the two banks, reforms are now needed to achieve the following: (i) enhance the commercial orientation, as well as the operational autonomy and accountability, of bank management; (ii) reduce overheads, including measures for staff retrenchment and consolidation of bank branches; and (iii) improve the quality of their portfolios and their loan recovery rates. In addition, the state-owned development banks (Agriculture Development Bank of Nepal and Nepal Industrial Development Corporation) need to be included in the financial sector reform agenda. To do this, independent audits are first required.

To reduce the economy's dependence on foreign assistance for development expenditures, the Government needs to continue its efforts to mobilize domestic resources. While full implementation of the value-added tax is one area that may have an immediate payoff, more broad-based tax reforms are necessary to integrate the value-added tax with income and customs tax administration to produce a more buoyant and responsive tax system. The efficiency of income tax law needs to be improved, and exemptions on income taxes need to be rationalized.

To maintain fiscal stability, reforms must also extend to the expenditure side of the budget. Government expenditure control and better-targeted spending are needed. Preparation of a three-year rolling expenditure plan should be expedited to raise the efficiency of public sector investments.

Nepal has benefited from the quotas on garments imported by the US, but the quotas will be reduced over time and eliminated by 1 January 2005 as part of the WTO's Agreement on Textiles and Clothing. Sudden removal of the quotas would be devastating for this nascent industry, as Nepal would then have to compete directly with garments made in the People's Republic of China and India in this important market. The garment industry must now take steps to be ready for the removal of this protection in 2005.

Policy and Development Issues

With a per capita GDP of $244, Nepal ranks among the poorest countries in Asia. Reducing the level of poverty thus remains the Government's major development challenge. About 42 percent of the population remain below the poverty line, and this rate has not changed significantly in over 30 years, partly because of the high population growth rate in the country (2.4 percent in recent years). Income distribution is skewed in geographical, social, and gender terms. The current Ninth Five-Year Plan (1998–2002) aims to reduce poverty incidence by 10 percent at the end of the plan period. However, the wide scope of the Plan's targets means that the impact on poverty is often lost when the relevant programs are implemented. The Government recently prepared an Interim Poverty Reduction Strategy Paper, which provides a more focused and comprehensive framework for poverty than the Plan. The Paper emphasizes that the Govern-

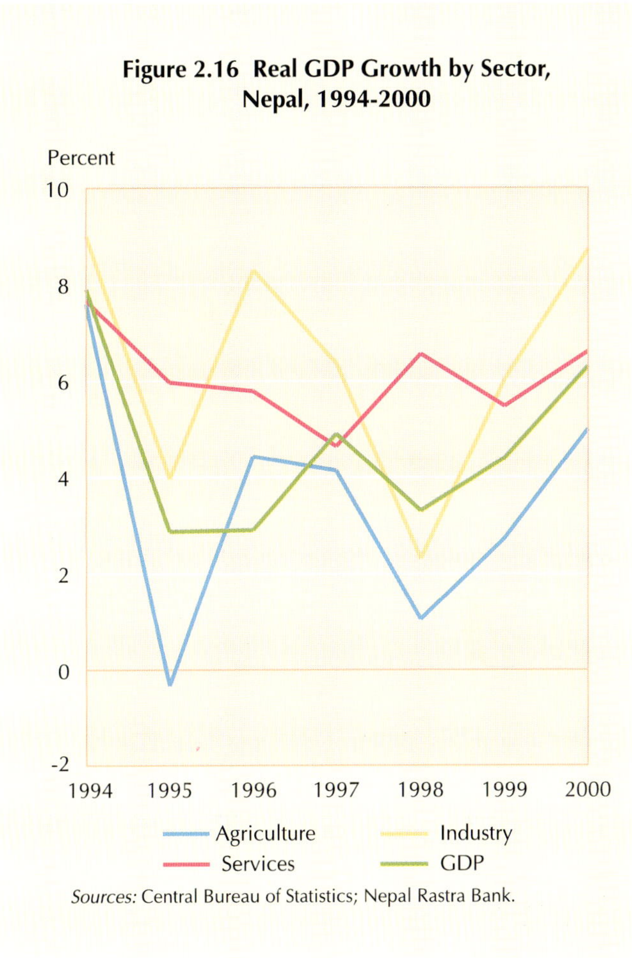

Sources: Central Bureau of Statistics; Nepal Rastra Bank.

ment should consider the impact on poverty when it prioritizes development projects. The Paper will need to be further focused though, and the resulting priorities incorporated into the Tenth Five-Year Plan, for which planning begins in 2001. In addition, improved information for monitoring the impact of specific projects on poverty is necessary for planning purposes.

The Government has indicated its strong commitment to introducing meaningful civil service and governance reforms. It has already reduced the number of ministries, and has indicated that it will also introduce governance reforms to tackle and reduce political interference in the civil service. The Government in the 2001 budget stated unequivocally that Nepal needs a civil service that is both results and people oriented. A coherent approach to improving the performance of the civil service is required, and one that will give the public a voice in determining the services desired and how they will be delivered. Success of this effort will depend both on the degree of consensus that the political leadership can build, and on its own resolve.

Pakistan

Economic performance improved in 2000, to the highest rate of GDP growth since 1996. However, large and unsustainable fiscal deficits and an unstable external situation kept the economy under stress. The medium-term outlook depends on the pace of structural reforms and an improvement in the balance of payments.

Recent Trends and Prospects

Appreciable improvement in agricultural performance, together with a modest acceleration in industry and services, boosted real GDP growth from 3.1 percent in 1999 to 4.8 percent in 2000, the economy's best performance since 1996. A bountiful harvest propelled real agricultural value-added growth from about 2 percent in 1999 to over 7 percent in 2000. Bumper cotton and wheat harvests more than offset a decline in the sugarcane harvest with the result that real value added in crops expanded by 10 percent. Yet the poor sugarcane harvest contributed to a collapse in sugar production that slowed the growth of real manufacturing value added. However, this was more than made up for by a strong recovery in construction and faster growth in electricity and gas so that industrial growth rose from 2.5 percent in 1999 to 3.0 percent in 2000. Real services value-added growth increased to 4.5 percent with stronger improvements in commerce, transport, communications, and public administration.

With a prolonged period of relatively poor economic performance, due in part to political turbulence, the incidence of poverty is estimated to have risen from below 18 percent in 1988 to over 32 percent in 1999. Low economic growth rates in Pakistan, compared with elsewhere in South Asia over the past several years, are linked to rates of savings and investment that are among the lowest in the subregion. As a proportion of GDP, gross investment remained at 15.0 percent in 2000 but still below the 18.9 percent level achieved in 1996. Gross domestic savings increased to 14.0 percent of GDP in 2000 from 12.3 percent of GDP in the previous year.

Large fiscal deficits continue to pose a major challenge to the Government as it strives to lift economic performance. In 2000, total revenues as a share of GDP improved to 17.2 percent from 16.3 percent in 1999. Total expenditures in 2000 rose marginally to 23.4 percent of GDP from 22.4 percent in 1999. This moderate rise in expenditures was achieved by reducing development spending. Current expenditures increased to 20 percent of GDP, their highest share since 1996, primarily because of a larger interest bill (which now represents 34 percent of total expenditures compared with about 24 percent in 1996). Overall, the consolidated budget deficit rose to PRs206.3 billion or 6.5 percent of GDP in 2000, from 6.1 percent in 1999. Nearly two thirds of the deficit was financed domestically. Public debt equaled 92 percent of GDP in 2000.

While growth in the money supply during 2000 was relatively modest, the composition of growth was very different from that expected. Government borrowing was much higher than projected while net lending to the nongovernment sector was reduced sharply during the year, despite an easing in monetary policy as reflected in reductions in the central bank's discount rate and treasury bond yields. Broad money supply (M2) grew by 9.4 percent in 2000, faster than the 8.4 percent pace of nominal GDP growth, but still quite low. This contributed to a further decline in the inflation rate to 3.6 percent in 2000 from 5.7 percent in 1999. Lower non-oil commodity prices also helped keep inflation in check, despite higher fuel prices.

Gross official reserves fell by nearly half from $1.7 billion in 1999 to $0.9 billion in 2000, or about four weeks of imports of goods and services, as large capital outflows swamped an improvement in the current account deficit. The narrowing current account deficit (from 3.9 percent of GDP in 1999 to 1.6 percent in 2000) was attributable to a reduction in the trade deficit and a 35 percent increase in net private transfers. The trade deficit shrank to 2.3 percent of GDP because exports grew strongly while imports were contained. Exports, recovering from a contraction in 1999 and responding to strong external demand, grew by 8.4 percent in dollar terms. Exports of cotton manufactures, which account for about 60 percent of the total value of exports, expanded by over 12 percent. The near doubling of the import bill for petroleum products was offset by reductions in virtually every other category of imports, in part because of lower non-oil commodity prices.

2000 refers to fiscal year 1999/2000, ending 30 June.

The Government's efforts to maintain the value of the rupee relative to the dollar in an environment of falling investor confidence and large-scale private outflows cost the Government additional reserves. In real effective terms, the rupee remained roughly stable on average over the course of 2000. Total external public and publicly guaranteed debt was about 51 percent of GDP in 2000. External debt service on medium- and long-term debt rose as a percentage of exports of goods, nonfactor services, and private transfers, to 30.4 percent in 2000 from 29.4 percent in 1999.

In early 2001, the Government concluded negotiating a program with the International Monetary Fund (IMF) under which various reforms were agreed on. Some reforms have already been implemented, such as the liberalization of the exchange rate in July 2000. Although these measures are expected to boost investor confidence and thus private invest- ment, real GDP growth is forecast to remain sluggish over the next two years. Manufacturing is likely to exhibit robust growth as cotton manufactures continue to expand. However, the agri- culture sector will probably find it difficult to match its 2000 growth rate, particularly with drought conditions in the early part of the fiscal year and a shortage of irrigation water to sustain expansion. GDP growth is, therefore, projected to remain under 5 percent a year in 2001–2002. Nevertheless, as delayed increases in administered energy prices and the effects

of recent rupee depreciation are passed on to consumers, a significant increase in inflation to 6.0 percent is expected in 2001. Under the IMF agreement, the Government is committed to reducing the fiscal deficit to 5.2 percent of GDP in 2001. On the external front, with recent reforms, particularly the rupee depreciation, double-digit export growth is expected in the next two years. Imports are likely to grow at a slower pace than exports, helping contain the current account deficit.

Issues in Economic Management

The new Government that came to power in October 1999 faces a comprehensive reform agenda to reverse a decade of economic malaise, which was due to political instability and which has resulted in rising poverty and socioeconomic inequality. How- ever, containing the fiscal and external deficits is an immediate priority. A prolonged period of budget deficits in excess of 6 percent of GDP has left Pakistan with a huge debt, with debt service accounting for a large share of the budget. While seeking debt relief through the Paris Club, the Government undertook several measures in 2000 to reduce the deficit. These included revenue measures such as expansion of coverage for the sales and income taxes, tax amnesty schemes to encourage compli- ance, and a tax survey and registration program to widen the tax base. On the expenditure side, it reduced the implicit fuel

Table 2.20 Major Economic Indicators, Pakistan, 1998–2002
(percent)

Item	1998	1999	2000	2001	2002
GDP growth[a]	4.3	3.1	4.8	3.8	4.7
Gross domestic investment/GDP	17.3	15.0	15.0	15.5	16.2
Gross domestic savings/GDP	15.4	12.3	14.0	11.6	13.5
Inflation rate (consumer price index)	7.8	5.7	3.6	6.0	4.5
Money supply (M2) growth	14.5	6.2	9.4	11.3	15.0
Fiscal balance/GDP[b]	-7.7	-6.1	-6.5	-5.2	-5.0
Merchandise export growth	4.2	-10.7	8.4	14.6	14.1
Merchandise import growth	-8.4	-6.7	-0.2	9.3	8.8
Current account balance/GDP	-3.0	-3.9	-1.6	-1.7	-1.0
Debt-service ratio	35.5	29.4	30.4	—	—

— Not available.
[a] Based on constant factor cost.
[b] Excludes grants.

Sources: Asian Development Bank, *Country Assistance Plan: Pakistan 2001–2003*, December 2000; Asian Development Bank, 2001, "Pakistan: Recent Trends for 1999/2000 and Prospects for 2001 and 2002", unpublished document; Government of Pakistan, Finance Division, *Economic Survey 1999–2000*, June 2000; State Bank of Pakistan; staff estimates.

subsidy by initiating an adjustment program to ensure that local petroleum product prices reflected actual import prices. To ensure that the target of reducing the deficit to 5.2 percent of GDP in 2001 is met, strict implementation of the new revenue measures is essential, particularly in respect to administration and collection of taxes in the newly covered areas such as agriculture and services. In addition, expenditure controls must include containment of defense spending as well as targeted spending cuts if revenue collection lags.

Another major issue concerns the foreign exchange difficulties that led to the IMF standby arrangement in November 2000, and that, therefore, enabled other multilateral development banks to resume assistance to Pakistan. Exchange rate liberalization was a significant reform, particularly in light of the large fiscal deficits and crumbling investor confidence that drove reserves down to about $1 billion in September 2000, at which level they stabilized. However, the economy's foreign exchange requirements are still large and further debt relief is critical. Under the IMF standby arrangement, the Government will receive $1.5 billion. The Government obtained $1.8 billion through a second round of debt rescheduling with the Paris Club in January 2001. But further assistance from IMF, which is scheduled to be provided in the latter half of 2001 in the form of a Poverty Reduction and Growth Facility loan (such loans have an explicit focus on poverty reduction in the context of a growth-oriented strategy), depends on the progress of the Government's structural reforms, including trade liberalization measures to boost foreign exchange earnings. Under the standby arrangement, for example, the Government has already eliminated several administrative measures that inhibited exports and agreed to continue with tariff reductions that were begun in 2000.

Policy and Development Issues

Longer term, additional reforms to reduce the fiscal deficit or to increase government capacity to facilitate social development is essential if the Government is to achieve its development objectives, including faster economic growth and poverty reduction.

Public expenditure management is weak, partly because it has tended to be associated with expenditure controls, and partly because the rules and regulations are frequently bypassed. Furthermore, interference by political leaders, lack of transparency in public expenditure management, weak institutional capacity, and weak accountability have plagued public expenditure management. Expenditure controls are needed to impose a hard budget constraint, but excessive preoccupation by provincial finance departments with expenditure controls may become an obstacle to smooth and efficient government functioning.

The Government's use of expenditure controls is perhaps a consequence of overcentralized state functions and authority. The Government publicly highlighted the issue of overcentralization as soon as it came to power and stressed that devolution would be a cornerstone of its reform program. A detailed devolution proposal, prepared by the National Reconstruction Bureau, was finalized in August 2000. On 31 December 2000, elections to local bodies were held in 18 districts. In certain regards, however, the devolution plan lacks concrete details, including (i) the fiscal transfer mechanisms between provincial and local governments, (ii) the local governments' revenue base, (iii) the implications of devolution for provincial administrative structures and staffing, and (iv) the details of local government functional responsibilities for social and economic services.

The low level of investment stems partly from high government borrowing, and partly from low savings rates. If recent reform efforts in the financial sector are sustained, savings rates should increase. These efforts include (i) plans for expedited privatization of state-owned banks, (ii) improving the legal and judicial process for enforcement of financial contracts, (iii) centralizing the regulatory authority in the State Bank of Pakistan, (iv) reducing interest rates on National Savings Schemes, and (v) improving the environment for prudential regulations and supervision of financial institutions so as to meet international standards. At the moment though, the financial sector is weak. Despite a recent national loan recovery drive, the banks still carry many nonperforming loans, which need to be reduced.

Sri Lanka

The recovery of the world economy helped boost national economic performance in 2000. However, the ethnic conflict has been a heavy burden on fiscal activities and the balance of payments. The Government formulated a poverty reduction strategy, though a detailed work plan for its implementation is required.

Recent Trends and Prospects

The economy grew by 6.0 percent in 2000, compared with 4.3 percent in 1999. The services sector led the improvement. Telecommunications, stimulated by private sector investment, showed strong growth, while wholesale and retail trade recovered, primarily because of greater external trade. Banking and insurance continued to improve, while the number of buses and train locomotives increased. Tourism receipts, however, fell considerably due to the ethnic conflict in the north. The industry sector also showed strong growth, particularly garments and textiles, which were boosted by the world economic recovery and domestic currency depreciation. The agriculture sector slowed, due to (i) record paddy output in 1999 that resulted in the fall of the paddy price in 2000, (ii) unfavorable weather conditions, and (iii) the fact that the Government drew back from its promise to purchase paddy at a reasonable price, which further discouraged paddy production.

The share of gross domestic investment in GDP increased from the 1999 level: in the private sector, Sri Lankan Airlines purchased three aircraft, although public sector investment declined. The share of gross domestic savings in GDP was lower in 2000 than in the previous year, reflecting an increase in the Government's dissaving. As a result, the resource gap widened in 2000.

The fiscal deficit rose to 9.8 percent of GDP in 2000 from 7.5 percent in 1999 (see Figure 2.17). Expenditure on the conflict was the key factor in the higher deficit. Prior to 2000, defense expenditure had gradually declined from a peak of 6.5 percent of GDP in 1995 to 4.4 percent in 1999. In the initial budget for 2000, it was expected to be as low as 3.9 percent of GDP. However, the worsening of the conflict reversed the trend and defense expenditure increased to 5.1 percent of GDP. In associated measures, the Government raised the national security levy and excise taxes on alcohol and tobacco, and reduced nonessential capital expenditure by about 10 percent.

In order to finance the large fiscal deficit—exacerbated by the delay in the sale of telecommunications shares—the Government turned to domestic financial institutions. This exerted unexpected pressure on credit markets. Consequently, interest rates rose and the private sector was crowded out of the domestic financial market. Utilization of foreign funds was impaired by cumbersome procedures in awarding tenders and the lack of counterpart funds. A decline in public investment and failure to maintain capital assets over the years have seriously reduced the production potential of the economy.

The main aims of monetary policy were to maintain stability in the financial market and keep inflation down. Other objectives included stabilizing interest rates, guaranteeing liquidity in the economy, and preventing volatility in the foreign exchange market. There was pressure to expand domestic credit to finance growing businesses and international trade. On the other hand, the decline in net foreign assets reduced the monetary base and had a contractionary effect on the money supply (M2). The net effect was an overall increase in the money supply of 13.0 percent. The repurchase rate was nearly doubled from 9.25 percent at the end of 1999 to 17 percent at the end of 2000 to take some pressure off currency depreciation. Other market interest rates also increased.

As part of financial sector reform, two state banks were restructured, including a change of management. The consensus built between employees and employers on this matter was a positive step, but implementation of the restructuring may take more time than expected.

Merchandise exports grew by 19.8 percent after a 3.9 percent contraction in 1999. The trend toward diversification of exports away from garments and textiles stalled, as the export growth rate of other industrial products such as ceramics, leather, paper, and other engineering products slowed. Earnings from tea exports increased due to high prices and renewed demand from the Commonwealth of Independent States. However, exports of other agricultural products declined. Merchandise imports surged by 22.4 percent in 2000 after 1.5 percent growth in 1999. Imports of consumer goods, except rice, increased. Intermediate goods imports, representing a little more than 50 percent of total merchandise imports, rose faster than imports of consumer goods and investment goods (excluding aircraft). Imports of petroleum went up by 76 percent.

As a result, the trade deficit widened to 8.7 percent of GDP, while the current account deficit deteriorated to 6.0 percent. The capital account also worsened, because foreign direct and portfolio investment fell and long-term capital flows declined. Reduced inflows of foreign funds required the central bank to draw down on its reserves, with the result that by the end of 2000 official reserves were only sufficient to finance 1.5 months of imports of goods and services.

The level of the exchange rate has been frequently debated over the last few years. The Government has opposed devaluation on the grounds that it would affect the budget deficit by increasing interest and debt repayments. However, a widening of the currency band was a major step toward market orientation of the exchange rate regime. The practice of making daily announcements of the buying and selling rates was discontinued. During the year, the domestic currency depreciated by 7.2 percent. The external debt burden increased marginally, from 57.4 percent of GDP in 1999 to 57.7 percent in 2000.

Inflation increased to 6.2 percent in 2000 from 4.7 percent in 1999, mainly because of price increases of agricultural products, including food. Unemployment remained on its declining trend of the last few years, and fell to about 7 percent in 2000. However, unemployment among new graduates was very high.

GDP is forecast to grow by 4.5 percent in 2001, a lower rate than in 2000, but it should strengthen to 5.0 percent in 2002. Any improvement in the agriculture sector will be limited in 2001, largely due to droughts that affected production in some areas in 2000. Agricultural output should pick up again in 2002, returning to the trend growth rate. Currency devaluation and increases in the administered prices of diesel, gas, and electricity will have a large impact on price levels in 2001, and they are likely to push inflation to about 8 percent in 2001 and to about 6 percent in 2002.

The rate of investment is likely to fall slightly in 2001. The previous decline in investment (excluding aircraft) was due mainly to a lack of investment opportunities and not to high interest rates or economic uncertainties. Because of this, investment cannot recover quickly, though some improvement may be seen in 2002. Domestic savings will likely decline marginally in 2001. The Government has to take strong action to cut expenditures to reduce the budget deficit. The projection is for a slight improvement in the budget deficit in 2001–2002.

It is projected that, in 2001, growth of exports will fall substantially to just over 3 percent; and that of imports to below 3 percent. The slow expansion of trade is the result of a combination of factors, including slower growth in import demand of industrial countries for textiles and garments and a downturn in the import of capital goods. The current account of the balance of payments is forecast to improve in 2001–2002, merely because large import volumes are unlikely. Stronger services sector earnings and steadily increasing private remittances are likely to be contributory factors.

Issues in Economic Management

Although the formation of provincial councils was allowed for by an amendment to the constitution adopted in 1987, national-provincial fiscal relations are still not clearly defined

Table 2.21 Major Economic Indicators, Sri Lanka, 1998–2002
(percent)

Item	1998	1999	2000	2001	2002
GDP growth	4.7	4.3	6.0	4.5	5.0
Gross domestic investment/GDP	25.1	27.1	29.0	27.0	27.5
Gross domestic savings/GDP	19.1	19.8	19.0	18.9	19.3
Inflation rate (consumer price index)	9.4	4.7	6.2	8.0	6.0
Money supply (M2) growth	9.7	13.3	13.0	13.5	11.0
Fiscal balance/GDP[a]	-9.2	-7.5	-9.8	-8.5	-8.3
Merchandise export growth	3.4	-3.9	19.8	3.2	4.2
Merchandise import growth	0.4	1.5	22.4	2.6	1.0
Current account balance/GDP	-1.4	-3.6	-6.0	-3.8	-2.5
Debt-service ratio	13.3	15.2	13.8	13.6	13.4

[a] Excludes grants but includes net lending.

Sources: Central Bank of Sri Lanka; Ministry of Finance and Planning; staff estimates.

due to a lack of understanding about the devolution of powers. The amendment transferred development and many administrative functions to the provincial councils. An arrangement largely mirroring that of the central Government was established in the provinces, and the Finance Commission drew up criteria to allocate funds to the provinces. Nevertheless, some conflicts arose between the center and the provinces.

Many provincial councils, due to lack of experience in handling development activities on their own, failed to use the funds in a rational way, or spent the funds without control on, e.g., vehicles. Since then, some controls have been introduced and central government line ministries have taken over development activities. Provincial councils have not been allowed to take part in many of the line ministries' actions.

Understanding this situation and the weak capacity of the provincial councils, the Finance Commission began allocating funds as special grants to provincial councils in 1997, and issued guidelines for using the funds. However, in the utilization of funds, unwarranted political interference and the lack of commitment to strategic planning were demonstrated again. Beginning in 2000, funds were allocated based on projects developed by the provinces; training is now provided to ensure better implementation. For 2001, the Finance Commission asked the provincial councils to prepare specific development plans. However, certain provincial governments prefer block grants without specifying projects.

Policy and Development Issues

The Government prepared its Framework for Poverty Reduction after a two-year analytical and consultative process involving many government agencies, donors, research institutes, and nongovernment organizations. Based on an analysis of the poverty situation, the Framework advocates a strategy of three main thrusts: reducing poverty by creating opportunities for pro-poor growth, strengthening the social protection system, and empowering the poor and strengthening governance.

The first thrust signals a fundamental shift in the role of the Government with regard to poverty reduction. Its new role is to create an enabling environment for poverty reduction, not to attempt to solve poverty directly through public spending. The Framework provides an array of measures aimed at enhancing opportunities for the poor to participate in the growth process, and seven sets of strategic initiatives were defined.

As part of the second thrust, the Framework calls for social safety net reform to reduce the mistargeting and adverse incentive effects that have characterized past programs, including better protection for those displaced by the conflict and a shift from cash grants to social insurance. The third thrust focuses on the need to transform governance and empower the poor.

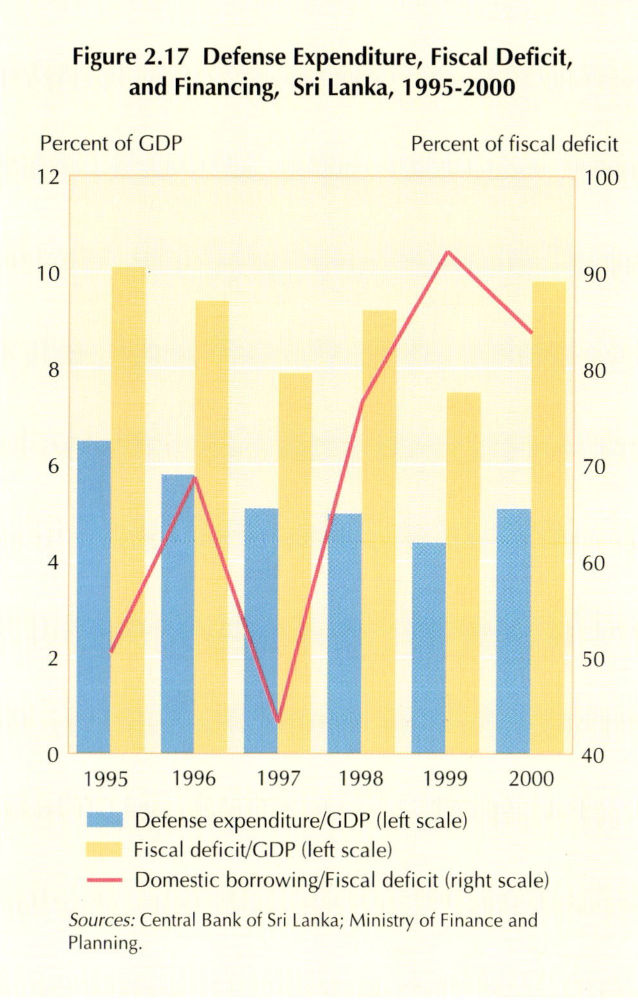

Sources: Central Bank of Sri Lanka; Ministry of Finance and Planning.

Institutional governance is to be strengthened by upgrading management practices in public service. Macroeconomic governance will be improved by tightening financial accountability. Decentralization is to be promoted, while regional fiscal imbalances are addressed and procedures for local government public expenditure management are improved. Community-based initiatives will still be supported, but with greater local cost sharing and in clear response to initiatives articulated by the poor. The Framework also proposes asset redistribution to enable hard-core socially excluded groups to rejoin the economic mainstream.

Specific approaches are outlined in each of the three main thrusts. If successfully implemented, these approaches will greatly improve the impact of the efforts of the Government, international agencies, and civil society to reduce poverty. However, the Framework does not include a work plan for implementing the strategy, nor does it pay enough attention to the link between the ethnic conflict and poverty reduction.

The Pacific

Real GDP of the 12 Pacific developing member countries contracted by an average of 1.8 percent in 2000, largely due to political instability and social unrest in the Fiji Islands and Solomon Islands. Weakening currencies and rising international oil prices caused average inflation to rise to 11.5 percent in 2000. Most governments maintained macroeconomic stability because of their generally prudent fiscal and monetary policies. The medium-term outlook for the Pacific is positive, but this depends on a return to macroeconomic and political stability.

The momentum of economic recovery in the Pacific, begun in 1999, was not sustained in 2000 due to political instability and social unrest in the Fiji Islands and Solomon Islands. Further, growth in the largest economy in the subregion, Papua New Guinea, slowed significantly. Aggregate real GDP of the 12 Pacific developing member countries (DMCs) declined by 1.8 percent in 2000 compared with 4.1 percent growth in the previous year. However, this masks improved growth for some Pacific DMCs, led largely by tourism and construction.

Fiji Islands, Kiribati, Marshall Islands, and Solomon Islands saw their economies contract. While the contraction in Solomon Islands was broad based and affected the entire formal sector of the economy, the nonagriculture sectors, including tourism and garments, were the worst affected in the Fiji Islands. Declines in real GDP in Kiribati and the Marshall Islands were largely due to contractions in the industry sector and weaker domestic demand. Papua New Guinea's growth slowed largely due to a contraction in mining. Cook Islands, Federated States of Micronesia, Papua New Guinea, Samoa, Tonga, Tuvalu, and Vanuatu saw growth in real GDP. While Cook Islands, Tonga, and Vanuatu experienced buoyant growth in visitor numbers due to their weak currencies, promotion activities, and unrest in the Fiji Islands, GDP growth was led by construction activity in Samoa, Tuvalu, and Vanuatu.

Inflation in Cook Islands, Kiribati, Federated States of Micronesia, Nauru, Papua New Guinea, Tonga, Tuvalu, and Vanuatu rose in 2000 as a result of weakening currencies and increasing world oil prices. In contrast, the Marshall Islands — which uses the US dollar as its medium of exchange—experienced deflation of about 2 percent, caused by US dollar strength. Inflation in the Fiji Islands and Solomon Islands declined slightly, largely due to a fall in demand, although it still remained high in Solomon Islands at 6.6 percent due to shortages of local food supplies.

Except for Cook Islands, Marshall Islands, Papua New Guinea, and Vanuatu, Pacific DMCs' overall balance-of-payments positions deteriorated, mainly due to higher oil costs in 2000. The balance-of-payments positions improved markedly due to a stronger US dollar in the Marshall Islands, improved exports in Papua New Guinea, and increased transfers from international aid agencies in Vanuatu. The external debt position improved in 2000 in most Pacific DMCs. However, a few of them, including the Federated States of Micronesia and Nauru, still have very high debt-service ratios.

With a gradual return toward normalcy in the Fiji Islands and Solomon Islands, and the expected response of the Papua New Guinea economy to the reforms currently under way, the medium-term growth prospects are solid for Pacific DMCs. However, subregional macroeconomic stability is fragile, and is vulnerable to internal and external economic developments. Securing and maintaining both macroeconomic and political stability remain crucial for ensuring a strong economic future.

The outlook is for inflation to fall in most Pacific DMCs during 2001 and 2002 in response to a slowing world economy, rebounding currencies, and lower oil prices. The exceptions to this outlook are Fiji Islands, Marshall Islands, and Samoa, with a buildup of some inflationary pressure in Samoa due to strong economic growth being a concern.

Pacific DMCs have only limited opportunities to achieve economies of scale in production due to their small size and geographic fragmentation. Their production base is also narrow. As a result, high external trade ratios and vulnerability to external economic developments are innate to them. In this sense, globalization is not a new concept for the Pacific. Because of a high degree of openness and, in the majority of them, the use of foreign currency as a medium of exchange, Pacific DMCs have to maintain macroeconomic parameters within a narrow range. Over time, these economies have institutionalized mechanisms to operate the macroeconomy under these constraints, while maintaining high external economic interaction. Major economic reforms, which were largely supported by the Asian Development Bank and initiated toward the end of the 1990s, helped the process. Further, despite instabilities caused by external economic events, the Pacific DMCs have recorded

Box 2.6 East Timor

Background

East Timor is situated between Australia and Indonesia, and occupies the eastern part of the island of Timor. The land area of 14,874 square kilometers is largely mountainous, is prone to drought, and has a tropical climate with distinct wet and dry seasons. The economy remains predominantly agricultural, with coffee the most important export commodity. The population is estimated at 780,000, with another 100,000 estimated to be in refugee camps in West Timor.

Following the violence and destruction after the referendum on independence in August 1999, the territory of East Timor was brought under United Nations supervision. The United Nations Transitional Administration in East Timor (UNTAET) was established in accordance with United Nations Security Council Resolution 1272 (1999) of 25 October 1999. On 9 December 1999, a Trust Fund for East Timor (TFET) was established with support from international agencies. TFET grant projects are formulated and supervised by the Asian Development Bank (ADB) and the World Bank. In addition, ADB provided technical assistance grants amounting to $4.8 million in 2000.

Economy

While East Timor was among the poorest provinces of Indonesia, its real GDP is estimated to have grown at an annual average rate of 10 percent during 1994–1996, largely due to heavy spending on roads and construction. In 1996, its real per capita GDP was $430. In 1997, real GDP grew by 4 percent, but contracted by over 2 percent in 1998, largely due to the Asian financial crisis. This was associated with high inflation (of 80 percent) and high interest rates (of 38 percent) in 1998.

Early estimates suggested a 40 percent decline in real GDP in 1999, though the decline is now considered to have been less. The violence and unrest associated with moves toward independence shook the entire foundation of the economy, involving destruction of public and private property, disruption of the agricultural cycle and trade, and devastation to a large part of the infrastructure. Most people avoided starvation through switching to alternative foods such as root crops like cassava, drawing on past savings, securing support from relatives, and obtaining food from aid agencies. At the macro level, the economy functioned temporarily on a cash basis due to the complete breakdown of the banking and payments system, while the system of government collapsed and collection of revenue from all sources stopped.

With a gradual return toward normalcy, the economy has rebounded strongly, albeit from a low base. Real GDP grew by 15 percent in 2000, largely due to initial reconstruction works and the gradual restoration of commerce and basic services. Due to favorable weather, output of maize, rice, and coffee also improved in 2000. Inflation appears to be falling, while regional disparities in the prices of staple foods are becoming less pronounced. Agriculture remains the main employer of the labor force, and although public employment has been growing, unemployment remains high, while the high wages paid by the international aid organizations and the inflexible wage structure of the East Timor Transitional Administration (ETTA) are distorting the labor market.

While the main government functions are being carried out by the ETTA, financial support is also provided by other agencies such as TFET and bilateral donors. The combined budget sources of East Timor for fiscal year 2000/01 (July 2000–June 2001) provide for total revenue of $25.1 million and total expenditure (including net lending) of $183.0 million. The overall deficit of $157.9 million (about 55 percent of GDP) is to be financed largely by external grants.

Early in 2000, the National Consultative Council adopted the US dollar as legal tender, though the Indonesian rupiah continues to be widely used. While residents have begun to deposit funds in commercial banks, these banks have not yet started to make loans to the business community and households.

Exports of coffee were estimated at $8 million in 2000, significantly below the preconflict level of about $25 million. Because of large import components associated with official aid flows, both trade and current accounts deteriorated sharply. Private imports remain low but are gradually rising. In 2000, the current account deficit was 51.7 percent of GDP, and is projected to remain at high levels of about 55 percent and 33 percent of GDP in 2001 and 2002, respectively.

The medium-term outlook for the economy, based on the maintenance of peace and relative stability, is for general growth and improvement in social conditions. The economy is expected to continue its 15 percent growth momentum in 2001 and 2002. Agriculture, construction, and services are likely to be the main engines of growth. Prices are expected to stabilize: inflation, measured by the consumer price index in Dili, is forecast to be 3 percent in both 2001 and 2002.

Policy and Development Issues

While much remains to be done, a basic administrative and legal framework has been established in East Timor. In terms of economic institutions, the Central Payments Office has started to provide basic depository and payment services for the ETTA. Several regulations for the banking and payments system have been enacted. The Central Fiscal Authority has started revenue and budgetary functions.

Setting up the appropriate policy and institutional framework now is a crucial exercise, as this initial framework will profoundly shape the economic future of East Timor. This, together with developing an enabling environment for the private sector, needs to be assigned a high priority: a commercial legal framework, land and property rights, labor laws, and a labor dispute-resolution mechanism need to be established. In addition, a major effort on human resources development is needed for both humanitarian and development reasons.

modest economic growth and improved their human development indicators over the last two decades. However, greater global integration of markets and associated instabilities pose new challenges for them.

The small Pacific DMCs are subject to high variability in government revenue due to their vulnerability to external economic developments, and their heavy reliance on aid, royalties from natural resources, and other irregular or windfall forms of revenue. Some Pacific DMCs have introduced trust funds, or some form of revenue equalization reserve fund, to assist in smoothing government revenues. Success varies: Kiribati, Tonga, and Tuvalu have managed to develop quite substantial funds, though the size of the Marshall Islands fund is still modest.

The rapid growth of information and communications technology (ICT) has opened up new opportunities for both external interaction and internal economic management in the subregion. Pacific DMC governments and the South Pacific Forum were quick to spot the importance of ICT, the growth of which has the potential to solve many problems emanating from remoteness and geographic fragmentation. Many Pacific DMCs have adopted specific policies on ICT—for example, Papua New Guinea's Information Technology Board Strategic Plan 2000—while tele-health facilities are already operating from Hawaii for the Marshall Islands and the Federated States of Micronesia, and from New Zealand for the Cook Islands.

Many Pacific DMCs, particularly Papua New Guinea, Solomon Islands, and Vanuatu, have low human development and high poverty indices. The cost of living in Pacific DMCs is high because of steep transportation costs. Pacific DMCs also face issues related to vulnerability to natural disasters and access to basic services, particularly in the more remote islands. In addition, social and economic inequalities are growing, as are inter-island and rural-urban disparities. In this regard, greater poverty and rapid environmental degradation, due to increasing populations and overexploitation of natural resources, are issues requiring urgent resolution.

Economic reforms initiated near the end of the 1990s were mainly triggered by fiscal crisis. These reforms focused on fiscal discipline, government downsizing, private sector development, and strengthening good governance institutions. In 2000, governments increasingly recognized the need to strengthen public service delivery so as to extend the benefits of reform to the poor and the vulnerable. Further, they placed more emphasis on financial sector development to promote effective mobilization of savings and private sector growth.

Cook Islands

Real GDP improved by 3.2 percent in 2000, led by growth in tourism. The economy is set to maintain this momentum in the medium term. The Government's principal policy issue remains completing the Economic Restructuring Program that began in 1996, and consolidating its achievements.

Recent Trends and Prospects

Real GDP grew by 3.2 percent in 2000 (see Figure 2.18). Tourism receipts amounted to NZ$71 million, representing an improvement of 8 percent as visitor numbers reached a record 64,500. This was partly due to more visitors from the northern hemisphere, reflecting a strong US dollar, and political instability in the Fiji Islands that prompted tourists to switch destination. The black pearl industry and the commercial agriculture sector also showed moderate growth rates of 6 percent and 4 percent, respectively.

Inflation in 2000 was 2.0 percent, a moderate increase from the 1999 rate of 1.4 percent. Inflation rose through the three quarters ending September 2000 to reach 3.5 percent. Employment expanded strongly in 2000, as a flow-on effect of the growth in tourism that stimulated buoyant demand in the retail, commercial agriculture, and restaurant and hotel sectors.

The budget surplus in 2000 was NZ$2.3 million. Tax revenues increased by 15.3 percent, reflecting improved trading conditions for the private sector and settlement of large tax assessments. Government expenditure rose by 7.5 percent to NZ$50 million. Government debt stood at 74.5 percent of GDP in 2000, an improvement on the 1999 level of 77.2 percent. While no official figures are released on the level of debt service, the Government has reported improvements in this regard.

Total merchandise trade for 2000 was equivalent to 65 percent of GDP. It consisted of NZ$9.4 million in exports in a narrow range of primary products (predominantly black pearls), and NZ$89 million in imports (principally food and live animals, machinery, and transport equipment). In comparison, merchandise trade in 1999 amounted to 55 percent of GDP. The trade deficit in 2000 rose to NZ$79.6 million, or 53 percent of GDP, from 47 percent of GDP in 1999. While the trade balance has deteriorated since 1990, the current account has consistently been in surplus because tourism has been a major source of foreign exchange. The current account surplus for 2000 was NZ$9 million, or 5.9 percent of GDP.

In June 2000, the Cook Islands became party to the Partnership Agreement between the African, Caribbean, and Pacific states, and the EU. This may improve access to the EU's trade and tourism market.

The official medium-term forecasts are for GDP growth to remain at slightly over 3 percent a year in 2001 and 2002. These do not take account of several large hotel and aid-assisted infrastructure developments that may occur in the period. Growth may also be larger than forecast if a commercial long-line fishing venture comes to fruition. Inflation is projected to decline in 2001 and 2002 to around 1 percent. The budget surplus is projected to fall to NZ$0.5 million in 2001 from NZ$2.3 million in 2000, largely reflecting higher government spending on infrastructure to support the tourism industry. Net government debt is forecast to decrease slightly to 72.4 percent of GDP by 2002. This is due to stronger projected real GDP growth. However, the debt burden will remain high, even if the Government maintains its commitment to observing manageable debt levels (which are expected to decline to 70 percent of GDP by 2003). The current account balance is forecast to improve in 2001 and 2002 on the basis of increased returns from tourism receipts and investment activities now coming onstream.

Issues in Economic Management

The Government's principal policy issue is to complete the Economic Restructuring Program that began in 1996, and to consolidate its achievements. The numbers of ministries (22) and public servants (1,200) are still too high for a population of around 16,000. The recommendations of the 1998 Political Reform Commission, which included downsizing Parliament, also need to be acted upon. In respect of improving the economic content for the private sector, progress has been made in tax reform and effective promotion of the Cook Islands as friendly to foreign investors. Areas still requiring government attention include tariff reform, privatization (with appropriate attention to the regulatory framework), and a review of laws and

2000 refers to fiscal year 1999/2000, ending 30 June.

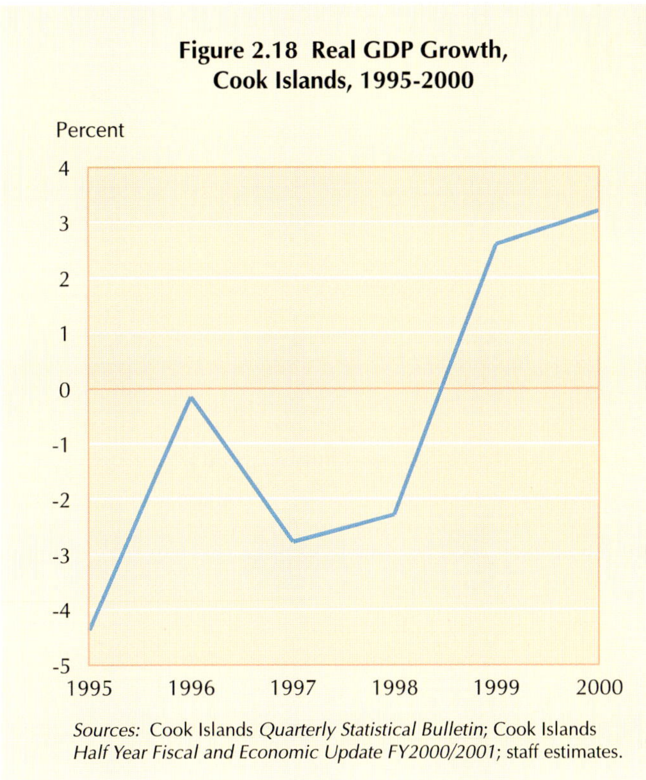

Figure 2.18 Real GDP Growth, Cook Islands, 1995-2000

Sources: Cook Islands *Quarterly Statistical Bulletin;* Cook Islands *Half Year Fiscal and Economic Update FY2000/2001;* staff estimates.

regulations affecting the operation of markets for labor and transport services. Improved environmental management is also needed if growth is to be sustainable.

Another issue, which the Government has indicated as one of its key concerns, is maintaining a skilled labor force. There has been an outward migration of skilled and qualified workers. Residents of the Cook Islands hold New Zealand citizenship and can freely access the New Zealand and Australian job markets as well as those countries' health, education, and social security systems. A lack of suitable staff may hold back expansion of the tourism sector. Continued economic growth may, though, create wage growth and employment demand necessary to encourage Cook Islanders to return home.

Policy and Development Issues

A major issue is devolution, under which outer island councils are given more responsibility for the delivery of social and infrastructure services. To facilitate the devolution process, the Government plans to establish an appropriate legal framework to empower the outer islands, increase their management capacity, and develop management mechanisms to ensure the efficient delivery of goods and services. This important national policy needs to be carried out in line with the Government's commitment to public sector reform and fiscal discipline.

Fiji Islands

Following strong growth in 1999, the economy contracted by over 9 percent in 2000 due to political instability and widespread civil disorder. Despite these difficulties, the management of the economy was commendable. However, medium-term prospects will depend on how the country's internal and external relations evolve.

Recent Trends and Prospects

The economy contracted by 9.3 percent in 2000 (see Figure 2.19), reflecting the impact of political instability in May 2000 and the associated widespread civil disorder and reactions of potential investors, tourists, and the international community. Looting and the destruction of property led to the suspension of operations by many businesses, particularly in the main centers of Suva, Lautoka, and Nadi. The international community's responses included reduced aid flows, imposition of diplomatic and trade sanctions, and travel advisories to tourists. Government activities were also adversely affected, including basic services such as power and water, and the operation of government departments.

After very rapid growth in 1999 of 9.6 percent, led by the sugar and tourism sectors, the contraction in 2000 was seen mainly in the nonagriculture sectors of the economy: manufacturing output fell by 12 percent, construction by 25 percent, and activity in the trade, restaurant, and hotel sector by 15 percent. Tourism shrank by around 30 percent, as arrivals fell from the record level of 410,000 seen in 1999 to about 280,000 in 2000. Hotel occupancy rates were only 20–30 percent in July and August compared with around 80 percent in the same period of the previous year. Several major investment projects, including new tourism facilities, were postponed. Investment had long been weak and declined further in 2000 to less than 10 percent of GDP. The retail sector suffered from a general decline in consumer spending associated with the civil disorder, particularly in Suva; this decline stemmed from high numbers of redundancies, wage cuts, and fewer tourist arrivals.

The main exception to the drastic downturn was agriculture. A very good sugar crop was harvested, after several poor crops largely attributable to drought.

Conditions in the labor market deteriorated in 2000: many people were laid off in the garment, tourism, retail, and construction sectors, while wages fell generally, with pay cuts in the private sector of 15–50 percent.

Total export earnings for 2000 fell by around 20 percent, following exceptionally strong growth in 1999. Garment exports were lower due to the imposition of temporary boycotts by trade unions in Australia and New Zealand, power cuts, and the uncertainties about preferential arrangements under the South Pacific Regional Trade and Economic Cooperation Agreement. Imports declined sharply with the contraction in the economy so that the trade deficit was much lower than normal. The current account still realized a modest surplus, but at a somewhat lower level than a year earlier as tourism earnings declined and outward private transfers increased. The capital account deficit narrowed slightly, largely as a result of capital controls put in place after the political developments of May 2000 and the return of a leased aircraft. The net outcome on the balance of payments was a small deficit.

In response to the sharp fall in revenue following the political crisis, the new Government implemented an interim budget in July 2000. This presented a reduction in expenditure of F\$103 million, or 10 percent lower than originally forecast for 2000. This was to be made up of an across-the-board 12.5 percent cut in government salaries, a 20 percent reduction in operating grants, a 30 percent reduction in other operating payments, and a 30 percent reduction in capital expenditure. The revised deficit target was equivalent to 3.5 percent of GDP in 2000, an increase from the 1.9 percent originally targeted.

At the time of the interim budget, government revenue in 2000 was expected to decline by about 15 percent, or F\$146 million, from the 1999 level. The fall was forecast because poor business profits had lowered corporate tax collection, the decline in employment and pay had reduced personal income tax payments, and revenue from tariffs and value-added tax had weakened. In the absence of corrective action, a deficit of F\$250 million, or 9 percent of GDP, was projected, which would have taken government debt to more than 52 percent of GDP. However, the interim budget helped contain government debt to around 42.9 percent of GDP in 2000, compared with 38 percent in 1999.

The 2001 budget was released in November 2000, and presented a detailed policy response to the crisis. Paralleling some of the policy responses after the coups in the late 1980s, it heavily emphasized business tax cuts. Soon after the political developments of May 2000, the Reserve Bank of Fiji acted to protect foreign reserves and the exchange rate. It set a credit ceiling on commercial banks (to limit lending to levels as of 19 May 2000), put up interest rates (the yield on 91-day Reserve Bank of Fiji notes rose from 2 to 5 percent), and imposed selective exchange controls. By the end of November, reserves had risen slightly to around six months of imports, or F$800 million, and the exchange rate was fairly stable.

Despite the economic downturn, domestic credit grew by almost 11 percent in the 12 months to September 2000, led by lending on real estate. Narrow money and quasi-money grew by 6 percent and 7 percent, respectively, over the same period. The crisis had little impact on prices, with inflation of 1.1 percent in 2000. Even though monetary policy was tightened on 22 May, interest rates remained quite low. The interbank rate rose to just above 7 percent in June, but quickly fell back to below 4 percent. From early September, the Reserve Bank of Fiji relaxed both monetary policy and some exchange controls. By late October, the credit ceiling had been removed.

On the assumption that the crisis will not flare up again, the economy is projected to grow by nearly 5 percent in 2001 and 2002, driven by recoveries in tourism, manufacturing, and construction. Agriculture, forestry, and fisheries are forecast to show slow growth. Weak commodity prices, industrial unrest in key sectors, trade sanctions, the uncertain future of the garment industry, and negative tourism-related publicity are all key elements in these forecasts.

Exports are projected to be weaker in 2001 due to lower garment exports. Imports are expected to strengthen along with the growth in the economy, resulting in a substantial increase in the trade deficit. Higher investment income outflows and larger outward private transfers are also likely in 2001, leading to a much smaller current account surplus. However, net direct investment is forecast to turn strongly positive, in response to measures announced in the 2001 budget, which should help generate a surplus on the capital account and an overall balance-of-payments surplus. Foreign reserves are forecast to reach 5.5 months of import cover in 2001.

Trade prospects are projected to improve in 2002 and the trade deficit to be similar to that of 2001. The current account is expected to improve as tourism receipts grow. Direct investment is expected to weaken but still remain positive as the impact of tax incentives diminishes. A modest deficit is projected on the capital account in 2002. The overall balance of payments is projected to remain in surplus with foreign reserve cover slightly lower than in 2001.

Inflation is projected to be in the range of 3–4 percent in 2001 and 2002 due to expansionary policies. Interest rates are expected to remain at existing levels or to decrease slightly.

Issues in Economic Management

The key issues in the economy include the instability of the sugar industry due to expiring land leases and the expected cessation of the Lomé Agreement, poor productivity in the sugar industry, and uncertainty in the garment industry over the future of preferential trading agreements with Australia.

Although the new Government tightened expenditure in the interim budget, the cuts in expenditure did not match the expected shortfall in revenue and the budget deficit was expected to rise to around 3.5 percent of GDP in 2000. This fiscal stance is to be maintained over the medium term. The 2001 budget presented a deficit estimate of 4.0 percent of GDP in 2001 and 3.0 percent in 2002. Government debt is thus expected to reach 45.0 percent of GDP by 2003. A boost to aggregate demand is important to help support business activity

Table 2.22 Major Economic Indicators, Fiji Islands, 1998–2002
(percent)

Item	1998	1999	2000	2001	2002
GDP growth	1.4	9.6	-9.3	4.8	4.8
Inflation rate (consumer price index)	5.7	2.0	1.1	3.5	3.5
Money supply (M2) growth	-0.3	14.2	-5.7	—	—
Merchandise export growth	-24.1	26.4	-20.1	-4.4	9.4
Merchandise import growth	-25.0	6.3	-26.8	6.4	7.0
Current account balance/GDP	-0.4	1.8	1.6	0.4	1.6
Debt-service ratio	4.1	3.4	2.6	2.2	2.0

— Not available.
Source: Staff estimates.

and to reduce the adverse social impacts of the crisis, such as increased unemployment. But government debt is reasonably high and the budget will soon need to move near balance. This is necessary to stabilize and possibly reduce the debt burden, and reduce the crowding-out of private sector activity.

To help rejuvenate economic activity, the 2001 budget outlined a comprehensive structural reform program. Measures included the adoption of full dividend imputation, lower tariff rates on business inputs, a proposed review of price controls, improved regulation of the financial sector, the removal of the quota system for rice imports, and the pursuance of policies consistent with World Trade Organization guidelines. Another encouraging sign from the budget is the commitment to the Financial Management Reform project (essentially a budget reform program). The budget also emphasizes tax reductions for the business sector, which the Government sees as important for attracting investment. Although the outlook for investment depends heavily on the success of the reform program, political and social stability, and healthy external relations, remain crucial for promoting foreign investment.

Policy and Development Issues

The key to development on a sustained basis is substantially higher private investment. Investment, particularly private, has been very low in the Fiji Islands for many years: private investment averaged only 5 percent of GDP in the 1990s. The 2001 budget noted that a Reserve Bank of Fiji survey identified a lack of clear policy direction, time-consuming bureaucratic procedures, and land issues as factors having adverse impacts on investment. Of the three factors, it seems that uncertainty over property rights and the enforcement of those rights are the primary structural reason for low investor confidence. The reforms to public enterprises proposed in the 2001 budget offer no meaningful strategy to improve their performance on a sustained basis. Consequently, as well as doing more to improve property rights, the Government needs to mark more progress with public enterprise reform.

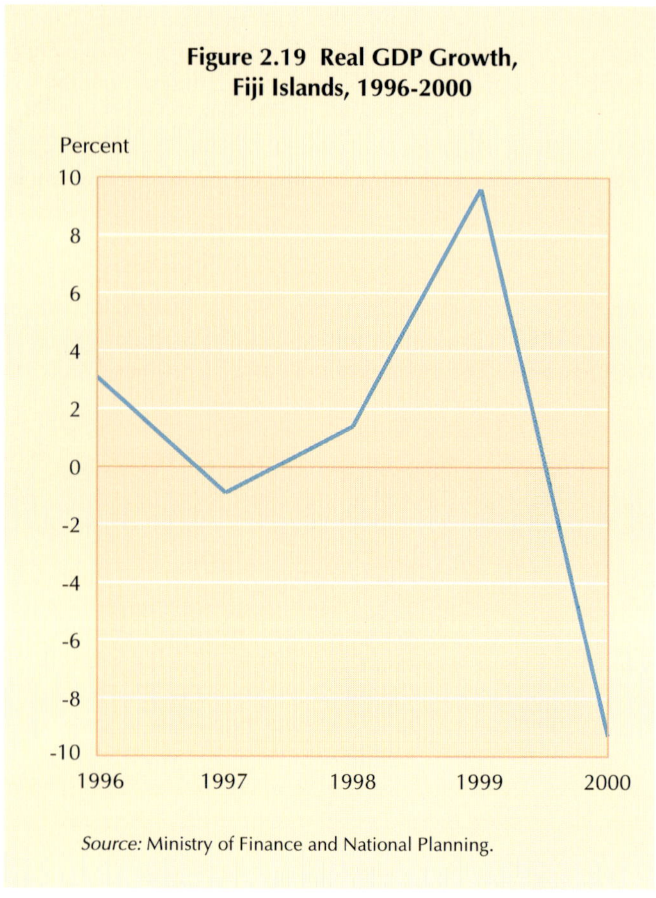

Source: Ministry of Finance and National Planning.

Poverty reduction appears to be reliant on growth and effective government service delivery, especially in health and education. While such a broad strategy has its advantages, it is likely to leave some vulnerable groups behind, such as the aged, female-headed households, and people with disabilities. This contrasts with the approach—widely adopted during the Asian financial crisis—of providing social safety net schemes for the poorest in times of severe hardship, including food and housing support, and school subsidies.

Kiribati

In 2000, GDP contracted by 4.0 percent accompanied by an increase in the government budget deficit. However, the Government reaffirmed its commitment to reforms through the National Development Strategy 2000–2003. Such reforms and private sector development remain critical for the economy's prospects.

Recent Trends and Prospects

Real GDP contracted by 4.0 percent in 2000. This contrasts with growth of 2.3 percent in 1999 and 7.3 percent in 1998 when copra production was higher than normal. The fishing license revenue was also unusually high in 1998. With population growth estimated at 2.2 percent a year, real per capita GDP declined to US$469 in 2000, from US$554 in 1999.

The Revenue Equalization Reserve Fund (RERF), which returns investment income equal to around 33 percent of GDP, continues to underwrite government recurrent expenditure. Fishing license revenue, seamen's remittances, and income from the RERF make up almost half of Kiribati's national income. Consequently, the economy is open and sensitive to international influences.

Current expenditure in 2000 was A$63.8 million, while A$20.8 million was development expenditure. Revenues exceeded expectations as income from fishing licenses was considerably higher than budgeted. The budget deficit was 5.7 percent of GDP. The fiscal deficits in recent years have been financed from external concessionary loans and accumulated balances in the Consolidated Fund. However, if budget deficits grow larger, there is a risk that the real value of the RERF could deteriorate.

The trade deficit deteriorated in 2000 as copra income declined and imports grew. Exports declined by 10.1 percent, while imports increased by 0.8 percent as a result of increased activity in the construction sector. The trade deficit stood at 80.6 percent of GDP while the current account moved to a deficit of 5.0 percent of GDP from substantial surpluses in the previous two years (see Figure 2.20). International reserves are extremely healthy because of the RERF, amounting to around 10 years of import cover. External debt was equivalent to a relatively modest 20.4 percent of GDP in 2000, remaining within manageable levels.

Inflation remained at low levels in 2000, and was broadly in line with the rate in Australia, the nation's main trading partner. General retail prices increased by less than 1 percent in 1999, although a slightly larger rise of around 2 percent was recorded in 2000, mainly as a result of the depreciation of the Australian dollar and higher world oil prices. The broad money supply grew by 5 percent in 2000.

Economic growth in 2001 and 2002 is targeted to return to a positive 2–3 percent, supported by the implementation of several significant development projects, including a sanitation, public health, and environment project of the Asian Development Bank, a sports complex, and a fisheries integration project. Income from fishing licenses is expected to remain low due to continuing normal seasonal conditions and low world tuna prices. The trade deficit is forecast to widen again in 2001 as a consequence of additional funding for development projects, while the current account is also expected to remain in deficit. External debt is set to increase significantly in 2001, but annual debt servicing will be kept within the medium-term performance target of not more than 1 percent of current revenue. Inflation is likely to continue tracking the rate in Australia, which is likely to be around 1.5 percent in 2001.

Issues in Economic Management

In line with the Government's National Development Strategy for 2000–2003, reforms are focused on the Government's provision of core services, and not on competing with the private sector. However, implementing the reform program and divesting public commercial enterprises need to be accelerated in line with the program of private sector development.

Recent government initiatives to improve the investment climate include the introduction of measures to speed up the investment approval process. The Government has indicated that it will further streamline the investment approval process and strengthen the investment promotion and support capacity of the Ministry of Commerce, Industry and Tourism. It also needs to strengthen the tax and tariff systems to support the growth and development of the private sector, assist in the development of a more diversified export sector, and stimulate foreign and domestic investment.

Macroeconomic management requires better data collection and analysis, including more timely economic indicators to provide data for the national accounts. Anticipated

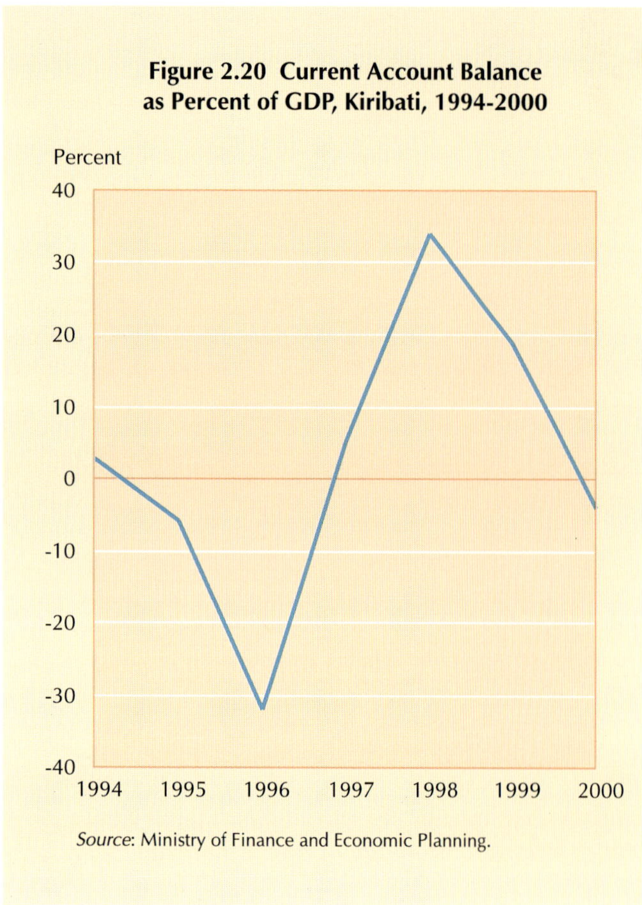

Source: Ministry of Finance and Economic Planning.

bulk of assets in the financial sector. With the recent announcement that Westpac Banking Corporation of Australia intends withdrawing from its joint venture with the Bank of Kiribati, the Government is actively considering the options for providing commercial banking services in the future. The changeover to a new joint-venture partner will provide the Government with the opportunity to update its banking and financial sector legislation.

Growth in private sector credit is constrained by limited investment opportunities, and by the inability of the Bank of Kiribati to use customary land as collateral. As a result, more than three quarters of the assets of the financial sector are invested overseas. The National Development Strategy is, therefore, giving priority to strengthening the banking sector's capacity to utilize domestic savings for private sector development. This can be done with the cooperation of the Development Bank of Kiribati and the Bank of Kiribati.

Underemployment and unemployment levels are high in Kiribati, especially among the younger age groups. Currently, less than 20 percent—8,600 people—of the working-age population are formally employed. Yet, in both the public and private sectors, many job openings remain unfilled because individuals with the appropriate training, education, or experience cannot be found. In the short run, this could mean an increase in youth unemployment as the number of school-leavers exceeds the number of new jobs created. Consequently, the Government has identified human resources development as one of the key platforms of the National Development Strategy.

Employment creation requires an attractive enabling environment for the private sector, which includes attracting foreign investment. This, however, will require a shift in attitudes about foreign ownership. The expected reform of foreign investment regulations will be a first step in this direction.

Outer island development continues to be a priority for the Government, which pushes technical training as a way to help people in those areas and to encourage young people to remain on their home islands rather than seeking employment in already crowded urban areas.

improvements to the collection and compilation of balance-of-payments aggregates will provide a valuable source of macroeconomic performance data to assist in policy development.

Policy and Development Issues

The Bank of Kiribati is the sole commercial bank and, along with four other nonbank financial institutions, accounts for the

Marshall Islands

Due to contractions in trading and transport, primary production, and manufacturing, real GDP declined by about 2 percent in 2000. Along with modest growth prospects in the medium term, the economy faces a major challenge in moving toward greater self-reliance and providing employment for the growing labor force.

Recent Trends and Prospects

Real GDP contracted by 2.3 percent in 2000 after growth of around 0.8 percent in 1999 (see Figure 2.21). Government expenditure grew marginally, while trading and transport, primary production, and manufacturing fell. Due to the strengthening of the US dollar and low demand, and despite the rise in world oil prices, price deflation of 1.9 percent was recorded, compared with inflation of 2.0 percent in 1999.

Exports in 2000 increased by 9.7 percent to $7.9 million, while imports declined slightly to $58.8 million. The trade deficit in 2000 represented 53 percent of GDP, a slight deterioration from the 1999 deficit. The current account in 2000 showed a surplus equivalent to 7.6 percent of GDP. On the capital account, the main item was loan repayments, which absorbed most of the current account surplus.

The budget surplus in 2000 fell by more than half to 5.2 percent of GDP from 10.5 percent of GDP in 1999. Total government revenue of $62.1 million in 2000 was lower than the 1999 figure, mainly due to a reduction in import taxes and despite a 50 percent increase in income from fishing license fees. Government expenditure rose slightly.

Total external debt in 2000 dropped significantly to 72 percent of GDP, from the previous year's corresponding figure of 90 percent. Debt service in 2000 equaled 22.5 percent of GDP. External assistance rose to 70 percent of GDP, from 44 percent of GDP in 1999; the largest component was the payment from the US under the Compact of Free Association. Taipei,China made a large grant of $19 million.

The average rate of interest on savings and time deposits in 1999 was 2.8 percent, marking a decline from previous years, as the banks acquired more deposits than they could lend and inflation stayed low. Lending rates were at 10–16 percent in 1999. These high real rates and the wide spread between deposit and lending rates suggest weak competitive pressure on the banks to increase lending. These trends continued in 2000.

According to the 1999 census, 69 percent of the labor force of 14,700 were employed, including those in subsistence activities. Formal sector employment is estimated to be as low as 54 percent. Around 31 percent of those employed work in the public sector.

The 2001 budget incorporates an 8 percent reduction in expenditure, and a 15 percent increase in revenue, to give an overall surplus equivalent to 15 percent of GDP. Given that the public sector, excluding state-owned enterprises, accounts for about one third of economic activity, it is therefore unlikely that GDP will grow in 2001.

Issues in Economic Management

For many years, payments of interest and principal (debt-service costs) on public sector debt, comprising government and state-owned enterprise bond issues, have run at $25 million to $26 million annually, or about 27 percent of GDP. The biggest of these bond issues will be fully repaid in 2001, relieving the balance of payments, and providing an opportunity for financial stabilization. In fact, this will free up $18 million of annual inflow for the remainder of the first 15-year Compact period—which ends in September 2001—perhaps allowing for some easing of fiscal policy. As a result, GDP is projected to grow at least slightly in 2002. For the past 13 years, the Government has had the benefit of annual grants of around $30 million under the Compact, and its future fiscal position is dependent on the outcome of negotiations on a second compact.

The Public Sector Reform Program, which began in 1997 with the support of an Asian Development Bank loan, has targeted the main economic management issues. Its objectives are stabilizing government finances in the short run, ensuring long-term structural stability, and creating an improved environment for the private sector. Achievements include reducing the government payroll by 30 percent, privatizing domestic shipping services, streamlining Foreign Investment Board License

2000 refers to fiscal year 1999/2000, ending 30 September.

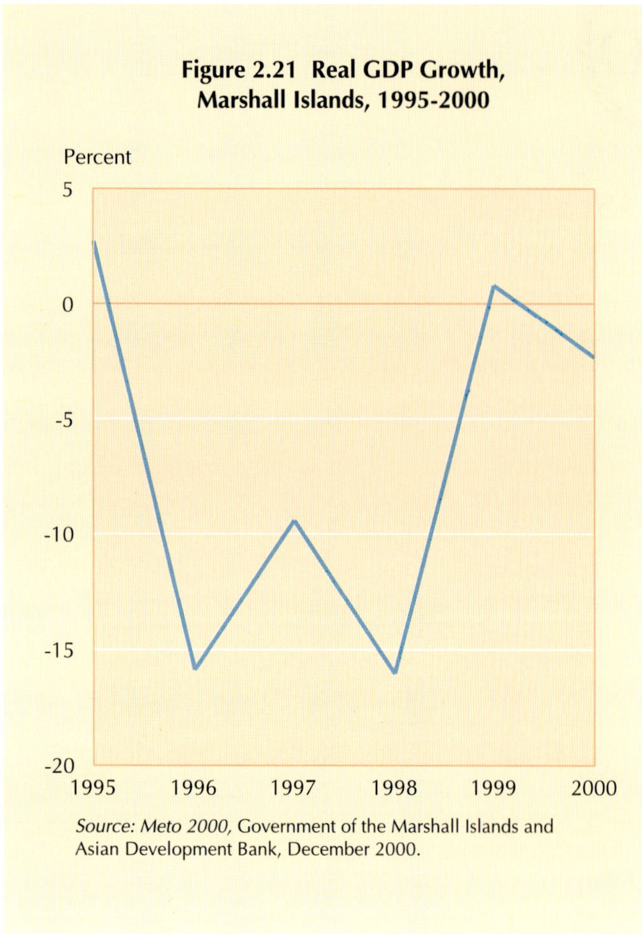

Source: *Meto 2000,* Government of the Marshall Islands and Asian Development Bank, December 2000.

systems of annual and medium-term budgeting, financial control, accounting, internal audit, and reporting to Parliament. Accounting of the capital account of the balance of payments also needs significant improvement.

Policy and Development Issues

About 600–700 new jobs a year are required to broadly keep up with population growth. Thus efforts to attract foreign direct investment must be stepped up, and existing firms expanded. Apart from the problems of remoteness and small size, high local wages make it difficult for firms to compete internationally.

In the last few years, significant positive changes have been made to the process for approving and licensing foreign direct investment. The Government has published a statement on investment policy and amended the law so as to implement easier and quicker investment procedures. It has reestablished the Trade and Investment Division with the aims of promoting investment and trade and supporting small business growth. However, if the economy is to compete effectively, it has to overcome three important structural obstacles: the lack of secure leasehold title to land that can be developed, a complex tax system, and inadequate levels of education for workers in a modern economy.

Action is under way to deal with the first of these, with a draft law being considered to establish registration of "development land" that would be available for lease to investors under government-guaranteed title. The passage of this law and successful establishment of the authority to implement it will go a long way toward removing this first obstacle. Tax reform is currently on the policy agenda, and moves are afoot to conduct a review of tax policy in 2001.

At present, nearly half the teachers in the country have only a secondary school diploma as their highest qualification. The Ministry of Education, with the College of the Marshall Islands, is introducing new regulations for teacher certification, and is encouraging teachers to obtain tertiary degrees. Upgrading the educational system to expand the skill base is important if employment is to move into high-technology areas.

applications, and establishing the Marshall Islands Intergenerational Trust Fund to provide an additional source of revenue for the government budget.

Despite these measures, several issues remain, including low levels of efficiency in public service, weak government financial management, and a slow buildup of funds in the Intergenerational Trust Fund. The Government is developing a program for public finance management reform to establish

Federated States of Micronesia

The economy grew by 2.5 percent in 2000, led by manufacturing, construction, and transport. Recent reforms helped it to return to positive growth in 1999 and expansion is expected to continue in the medium term. Long-term prospects depend on how the economy moves toward becoming more self-reliant.

Recent Trends and Prospects

Real economic growth in the Federated States of Micronesia (FSM) was estimated to have accelerated to 2.5 percent in 2000, from 1.3 percent in 1999 (see Figure 2.22). The Public Sector Reform Program implemented in the latter half of the 1990s facilitated the return to growth in 1999. The largest contributors to the improvement in 2000 were manufacturing, construction, and transport.

The overall consolidated general government balance in 2000 was an estimated surplus of 0.4 percent of GDP. Total revenues were $152.8 million, out of which $96 million (42 percent of GDP) were grants. Further, $79.4 million of these grants were given under the Compact of Free Association with the US.

The value of exports is estimated to have more than doubled in 2000 to $23.5 million, mainly as a result of higher fish exports. Fishing access fees were $16.8 million, similar to the 1999 level. Receipts from tourism changed little. The value of imports increased in 2000 on the back of stronger GDP growth. The trade balance remained at a considerable deficit, rising to an estimated $122.3 million in 2000. Including official transfers, the current account surplus deteriorated from $55.7 million in 1996 to $6.5 million in 2000 due to the second step-down in the Compact funding level in 1997 (the first was in 1992). The country has gradually reduced its external debt from $137 million in 1993 to $85.7 million in 2000. Inflation has, in recent years, been running at generally low levels, with the figure for 2000 estimated at 2.8 percent.

Modest economic growth is expected to continue in 2001 and 2002, led by manufacturing, construction, and transport, and inflation is likely to remain subdued provided that US inflation remains low. The use of the US dollar as the unit of exchange means that, on the external account, the FSM's external debt position is likely to be favorable, with a debt-to-GDP ratio of 21 percent in 2001. The value of fish export receipts is expected to increase in 2001, largely due to anticipated movements in tuna export prices. Overall, however, the short- to medium-term outlook for exports is modest. The debt in 2002 is forecast to be $53.8 million, with a debt-service ratio of 4.5 percent of exports of goods and services. The current account is likely to turn negative in the short term.

Tourism is the sector with the greatest growth potential in the FSM. However, visitor arrivals fell in 1997 and 1998, partly as a result of the Asian financial crisis. The decline continued in 1999 and 2000, with visitor numbers totaling 17,477 and 17,152, respectively. This tourism potential will, however, only be realized once further reforms have made the foreign investment environment more attractive, including, particularly, a transparent, open regime.

Issues in Economic Management

The Government has made concerted efforts to address some of the key economic challenges facing the country, particularly since the second step-down in Compact funding. Yet a range of significant issues remains. Fiscal management at the national level is a serious concern, as the national Government has continued to run fiscal deficits by drawing down from fund balances invested abroad.

As the currency is the US dollar, fiscal policy is the major macroeconomic tool available to the Government. Domestic adjustments in response to lower resource transfers, therefore, are based on cutting government expenditure, reducing public sector employment and wages, and increasing domestic revenues. The Government needs to further adjust public sector taxation and increase its taxation effort. Domestic revenue efforts remain low, although the likely introduction of a value-added tax is expected to provide a nondistortionary broad base for revenue generation. However, further fiscal adjustments will be required.

Renegotiations on the Compact were undertaken in 2000. Their outcome, along with the timing of their completion, are

---

2000 refers to fiscal year 1999/2000, ending 30 September.

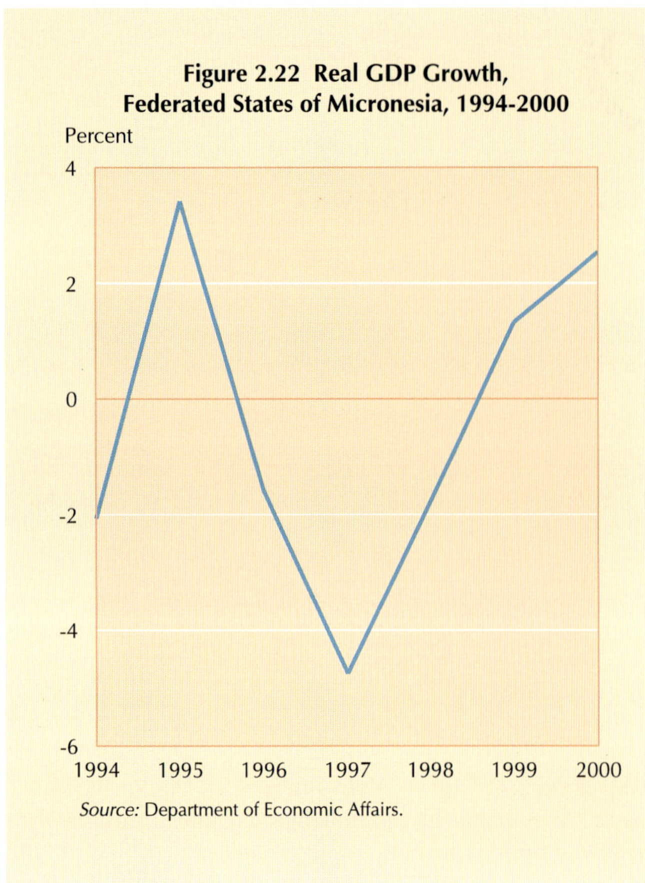

Source: Department of Economic Affairs.

used as a reserve against future shocks and could be used as initial capital for a proposed trust that the Government has asked the US to fund.

Policy and Development Issues

The Government faces several challenges, including the need to ensure strong growth in the private sector. It should, therefore, divest itself of public sector enterprises in the fisheries sector and allow the private sector to identify opportunities and take commercial risks.

The traded goods sectors of commercial agriculture, fisheries, and tourism play a very small role in the economy. Yet these are the sectors in which the economy has some comparative advantage, and which provide medium- and long-term growth potential. Given the objective of achieving financial self-sufficiency, rapid growth in these export sectors must be a focus of government policy, including promotion of foreign direct investment in tourism.

While government employment remains significant, it declined from 6,390 in 1997 to approximately 5,200 in 2000. Formal private sector employment increased over the same period and, in 1999, for the first time exceeded that in the public sector. Overall, however, growth of formal private sector employment remains modest, and the challenge facing the Government is to boost such growth.

Despite some remittances from overseas migrants, the number of low-income households is still high. Although the FSM does not produce a poverty profile as such, recent household income and expenditure surveys suggest that around 40 percent of households could be considered as low income. Furthermore, the lowest-income households are on the outer islands where opportunities for formal sector employment and commercial activities are few. The Government needs to address these disparities.

both significant factors for short- to medium-term economic management. If the negotiations are not complete by November 2001, the Compact provides for a further two years of funding at the level received at the end of the first step-down in 1992. This will result in an increased funding of around $34 million over the two years 2002 and 2003. These funds might best be

Nauru

Real GDP showed only minimal growth in 2000, largely reflecting a fall in profits from phosphate mining. The country faces difficulties on both fiscal and financial fronts, and any resolution will depend on the Government's response to the imminent depletion of primary phosphate deposits and management of government finances.

Recent Trends and Prospects

GDP growth in 2000 was minimal. It expanded moderately in 1999 as a result of increased phosphate exports, the start of construction of Ainabare boat harbor, and an increase in government expenditure. In 2000, profits from phosphate mining fell as the US dollar strengthened, because the impact of changes in the Australian/US dollar exchange rate was greater on the cost of inputs than on revenues. The only major construction project in 2000 was the completion of Ainabare harbor. Revenue from fishing license fees of A$8.5 million represented a 60 percent increase on the 1999 level and this was mainly due to the weaker Australian dollar.

In 2000, the budget deficit was over A$10 million (see Figure 2.24), or around 18 percent of GDP. Government debt increased in both 1999 and 2000. The level of external government debt is estimated at A$280 million. External debt service totaled A$13.3 million in 2000, or around 13 percent of exports of goods and services. However, the Government has significant loans outstanding with government-owned corporations that also have significant levels of external debt, hence the level of external debt service is effectively much greater.

Phosphate prices and volumes have deteriorated in recent years and the Nauru Phosphate Royalties Trust (NPRT), which was established to provide income in the post-phosphate era, has posted poor returns. Aid agencies continue to contribute significantly to current account transfers. It is estimated that prices rose by around 7.5 percent in 2000, in response to the weakening Australian dollar and higher world oil prices.

There is no central bank and Australian currency is the legal tender in Nauru, hence it is not possible to estimate the money supply. However, indications are that it declined in 2000 as a result of the Bank of Nauru's poor liquidity position. During the year, the situation became so serious that it was necessary to ration withdrawals from personal accounts. Because of this problem, the Government recently advised the Nauru Phosphate Corporation (NPC) to pay dividends to the Government after each export shipment, whereas previously it paid at the end of each financial year. This change, in conjunction with the fact that the payments are made in Bank of Nauru cheques, has left NPC with its own liquidity problem, making it difficult for it to undertake necessary capital expenditure. Further, NPC is also the electricity and water supplier, and its relatively poor liquidity position has forced it to buy diesel to run generators on a monthly rather than quarterly basis. In October and November 2000, this resulted in power and water rationing because the monthly delivery of diesel was delayed due to bad weather. Quarterly supplies of diesel facilitate greater reserve storage and reduce the likelihood of such shortages occurring.

Issues in Economic Management

The three main economic problems facing Nauru are the imminent depletion of the primary phosphate deposits, the persistent fiscal difficulties including the mortgaging of assets of the NPRT, and the illiquid state of the Bank of Nauru.

It is expected that the primary phosphate deposits will be exhausted within three or four years, and this underlines the need for further progress in implementing the Government's Fiscal and Financial Reform Program, which was started in 1998. Feasibility studies are being undertaken for mining of secondary and residual phosphate deposits, which could extend mining for an additional 10–15 years. Due to higher extraction costs though, this will not be as profitable as the mining of the primary deposits.

A major concern is that the Government continues to take out loans against future phosphate revenue, and against the assets of the NPRT at a time when the primary deposits are close to exhaustion. Many of the assets owned by the NPRT are heavily mortgaged. The capacity of the financing arm of the Government to take out loans against the earnings and assets of the NPRT represents one of the economy's main structural

2000 refers to fiscal year 1999/2000, ending 30 June.

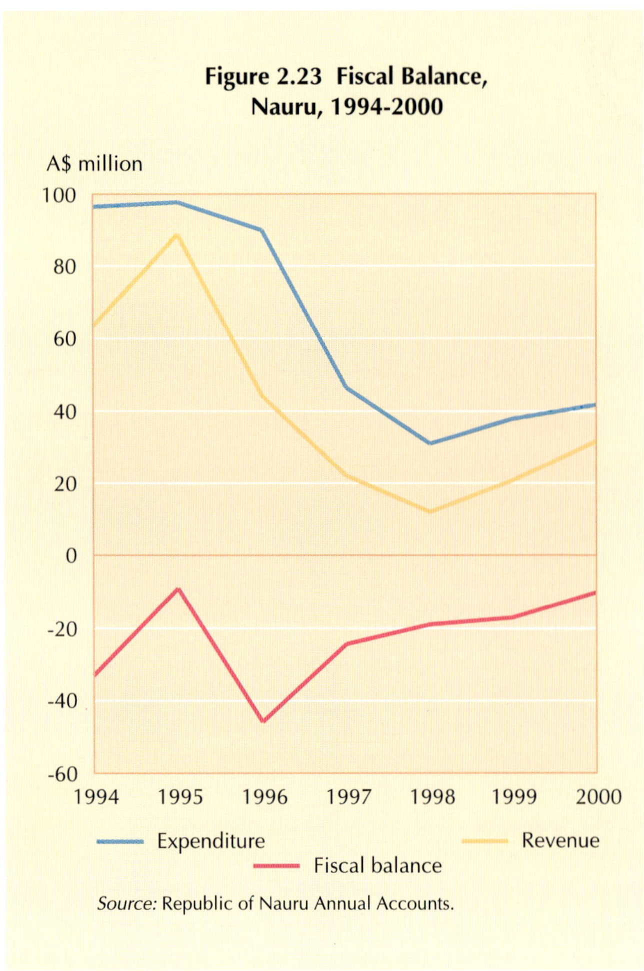

Source: Republic of Nauru Annual Accounts.

fiscal and financial management, operation of government-owned corporations, banking sector reform, the tax regime, and management of the NPRT. This Program, supported by an Asian Development Bank loan, has encountered some hurdles but is now being overseen by the recently formed Committee for Development Planning.

All aspects of the reform agenda need to be tackled more urgently if a satisfactory economic climate is to be created for developing the private sector and if the NPRT is to generate sufficient revenue in the post-phosphate era. The Government is considering options for banking sector reform, including reform of the banking laws. The most likely outcome appears to be closing the Bank of Nauru and replacing it with a foreign bank, though finding one that is interested may well be difficult.

Policy and Development Issues

One of the principal social problems facing Nauru is the extremely high rate of youth unemployment (estimated at 30 percent for males and 55 percent for females). Economic diversification will be required to generate employment opportunities as phosphate-related income tails off. Domestic participation in the offshore fishing industry began in 2000 with the purchase by the Nauru Fisheries and Marine Resource Authority of a long-line vessel, and approval to buy a second vessel. The opening of the Nauru Fish Market in 2000 also provided a source of employment.

Diabetes type 2, a lifestyle-related disease, remains the main health problem, and many Nauruans with the disease are referred to Australian hospitals each year, placing a large drain on the health budget. In fact, overseas referrals account for over half the health budget. The high incidence of the disease is the main reason for Nauruans' low life expectancy: 60 years for females and 55 years for males. Greater preventive efforts, particularly in relation to health education, must be made to reduce pressure on the health budget and improve Nauruans' quality of life.

problems. In addition, loans against the NPRT attract high interest rates (around 16–18 percent).

The Government embarked on the Fiscal and Financial Reform Program following a period of extremely high fiscal deficits in the mid-1990s. The Program focuses on government

Papua New Guinea

The economy slowed in 2000, despite the restoration of macroeconomic stability. The Government followed a tight fiscal and monetary policy during the year. Growth prospects are bright in the medium term, but depend heavily on political stability and continued government commitment to reforms.

Recent Trends and Prospects

According to official estimates, real GDP grew by 0.8 percent in 2000, though the actual figure may be lower. This contrasts with growth of 3.2 percent in 1999 following a period of recession in 1997 and 1998. The agriculture, forestry, and fisheries sector expanded by 0.9 percent in 2000, but mining production fell by 7.9 percent.

Coffee production dropped significantly in 2000 due to a reversal of the traditional wet and dry weather pattern and weak export prices. Copra and copra oil output also declined in response to weak prices. However, cocoa production increased due to renewed production on Bougainville island and better management practices. Logging production improved and prices rose from the 1999 levels, and while palm oil production strengthened, prices weakened significantly. The fall in mining production reflected the ongoing depletion of oil reserves and the impact of a landslide at the important Moran field.

The trade balance improved to $1,155 million in 2000 as exports increased by 7.9 percent and imports declined by 5.5 percent from the 1999 levels. This led to a substantial surplus on the current account of nearly 12 percent of GDP. The capital account was characterized by a significant increase in external aid and a very large rise in private outflows, reflecting, respectively, the drawdown of the first tranche of a structural adjustment loan from the World Bank, and both higher loan repayments and purchases of short-term securities by mining companies. Foreign direct investment was lower. The overall impact on the capital account was to increase the deficit from about 2 percent of GDP in 1999 to over 6 percent in 2000. However, given the sizable current account surplus, the overall balance-of-payments surplus stood at 5.7 percent of GDP. In mid-2000, foreign reserves were equivalent to 2.7 months of total import cover and 3.7 months of nonmineral import cover, considerably higher than a year earlier. Foreign reserves were estimated to have increased to adequate levels in the second half of the year.

The budget deficit in 2000 is estimated to have been about 1.8 percent of GDP, compared with a deficit of 2.6 percent of GDP in the previous year. Both revenues and expenditures were higher than forecast at the time of the 2000 budget: increased tax revenues reflected the impact of higher inflation on incomes and profits, and of higher oil prices; greater expenditure was mainly related to increases in teachers' salaries and higher interest payments.

The improvement in government finances and macroeconomic performance follows a period of lax fiscal conditions and widespread governance problems. With the formation of a new Government in July 1999, fiscal responsibility was restored and a wide-ranging reform program, focusing on improving governance, was formulated and is being implemented.

With no new domestic borrowing and with proposals to retire significant amounts of domestic debt as important features of the fiscal strategy, the authorities expect that the improvement in government finances will facilitate lower nominal interest rates. However, this strategy depends on the generation of significant revenues from the current privatization program and further external concessional financing of at least $45 million—which at the end of 2000 had still not been secured.

Total public debt in 2000 amounted to 60.8 percent of GDP compared with corresponding figures of 63.1 percent in 1999 and 65.8 percent in 1998. External debt rose sharply in 1999, on the basis of both an expanding deficit and the impact of currency depreciation on kina-denominated debt. The servicing of public debt absorbed 18.8 percent of total government revenue in 2000.

The money supply (M2) contracted in 2000, reflecting weaker economic growth and tighter monetary policy. By end-June 2000, credit to the private sector had grown by 5.4 percent over the previous 12 months, while net credit growth to the Government had declined by 8.4 percent over the same period (see Figure 2.24). This decline followed several years of significant growth associated with a period of fiscal difficulties and borrowing from the central bank in excess of statutory limits. In January 2000, the authorities reacted to the buildup in liquidity by selling treasury bills to commercial banks. Despite the tight monetary stance, interest rates moved lower through the year with the treasury bill rate falling from an average of 23.3 percent in 1999 to an average of 18 percent in 2000. To some extent, the reduction in nominal rates reflected lower inflationary expectations and ample liquidity in the banking system.

For 2000 as a whole, the kina weakened by 8 percent against the US dollar, following a substantial depreciation of 19 percent in 1999. The weakness in 1999 reflected problems in securing finance for a growing budget deficit and the impact of political instability on confidence. The slower depreciation in 2000 reflected the impact of a higher trade surplus, international financial assistance, and improved sentiment in the foreign exchange markets. However, the exchange rate varied considerably over the year: in the first half, the kina appreciated strongly against most major currencies, but in the second half it weakened from around $0.40 at the end of July to $0.34 at the end of October. Weakness in this latter period appears to have been related to lower than normal coffee export revenues and the continued strength of imports. A further negative factor may have been the expectation among importers of an even weaker kina. Papua New Guinea does not operate a normal forward currency market and, therefore, when importers seek to obtain forward cover, the effect is felt on the foreign exchange market straightaway as banks purchase the required foreign currency immediately and place it on deposit.

Inflation has been high and rising in recent years, largely reflecting the impact of a general weakening of the kina over the past two years and drought-induced local price increases. For 2000, year-on-year inflation was 17.9 percent. The major factors were the medium-term weakening of the kina, the introduction of value-added tax and increases in other excise taxes, and the flow-on impact of rises in civil servants' wages in 1999.

Real GDP is forecast to increase by about 3 percent in 2001 and nearly 6 percent in 2002. The agriculture, forestry, and fisheries sector is expected to be the major contributor to growth, with coffee exports likely to grow strongly and other agricultural exports to record solid growth. Preliminary work on a nickel mining development in Ramu and a gas pipeline to Queensland, Australia will boost the construction sector. Average consumer price inflation is forecast to fall to below 12 percent in 2001 and to just over 6 percent in 2002 as the kina stabilizes further.

The trade balance is expected to record surpluses of over K2 billion in both 2001 and 2002. These surpluses are considerably lower than the K3.1 billion in 2000 largely because of stronger imports. Import values are expected to increase substantially as the Ramu nickel and Queensland gas pipeline projects get under way. The current account is expected to move to a deficit of around 3.5 percent of GDP in 2001 and 2002, largely reflecting stronger invisibles payments associated with the mining and petroleum sectors. The transfer position is projected to record a modest deficit in 2001 and 2002 as Australian budgetary support is phased out.

Capital flows are forecast to more than offset the current account position, leading to small surpluses on the balance of payments in 2001 and 2002 averaging around 2 percent of GDP. Capital flows in this period will be dominated by finance for new mining projects. Net aid flows are projected to turn negative as receipts decline and repayments increase. The net impact is expected to contribute to a buildup of foreign reserves to $363 million by end-2001, sufficient to provide cover for seven months of nonmineral imports.

Table 2.23 Major Economic Indicators, Papua New Guinea, 1998–2002
(percent)

Item	1998	1999	2000	2001	2002
GDP growth	-3.8	3.2	0.8	3.1	5.7
Gross domestic investment/GDP	17.7	—	—	—	—
Gross domestic savings/GDP	22.4	—	—	—	—
Inflation rate (consumer price index)	13.5	14.9	17.9	11.6	6.2
Money supply (M2) growth	1.8	8.9	-0.7	—	—
Merchandise export growth	-16.1	12.2	7.9	-2.3	-0.4
Merchandise import growth	-27.0	-0.1	-5.5	36.6	-3.9
Current account balance/GDP	1.6	4.0	11.7	-3.5	-3.4
Debt-service ratio	22.5	27.3	16.9	14.2	13.3

— Not available.

Source: Staff estimates.

The 2001 budget aims, in fiscal terms, to continue the trend toward a balanced budget with the deficit for 2001 projected to be 1.3 percent of GDP. It includes the following priority sectors targeted for expenditure: health; education; transport; agriculture, forestry, and fisheries; police and key legal institutions; and the Internal Revenue Commission. It also provides for a large increase in public salaries, which, however, is dependent on savings derived from retrenchments of around 1,400 public servants.

Following a major taxation review completed in October 2000, the 2001 budget is to implement a new personal income tax schedule with a higher tax-free threshold, wider tax bands, and other income and value-added tax simplifications. The overall effect of the income tax changes is revenue neutral, and progressive in terms of income distribution impacts.

Under the 2001 budget, the Government is carrying out a package of reforms for the mining sector, designed to provide a more internationally competitive fiscal regime with greater transparency and improved administration. It has also proposed a draft for a new law guaranteeing stability of fiscal terms in major resource projects and the publication of model fiscal terms for inclusion in agreements made under the law.

Issues in Economic Management

Macroeconomic stability is an important precondition for facilitating broad-based economic growth. In the past, the central bank has normally responded to macroeconomic instability by tightening monetary policy, mainly via higher interest rates. However, the resultant interest-rate volatility is costly for investment and general business activity. To avoid such volatility, the Government needs to prevent fiscal imbalances from emerging in the first place. Its fiscal strategy is, therefore, aimed at reducing debt over time and should thereby contribute to the stability required. It is harder though to select the correct mix of responses in dealing with exogenous shocks, such as the Asian financial crisis, drought, or other natural disasters, due to their very unpredictability.

Policy and Development Issues

The Government has addressed a range of fiscal and governance problems that were contributing to macroeconomic instability and ineffectiveness of public institutions under the old administration. It has restored macroeconomic stability in a fairly short time and is implementing a comprehensive structural reform program, the key objectives of which are to improve governance, sustain macroeconomic stability, improve public sector performance, and remove barriers to investment and economic growth. In 2000, the Government gained endorsement and financial support for its structural reform program from the World Bank via a structural adjustment loan, the International Monetary Fund, and Friends of Papua New Guinea.

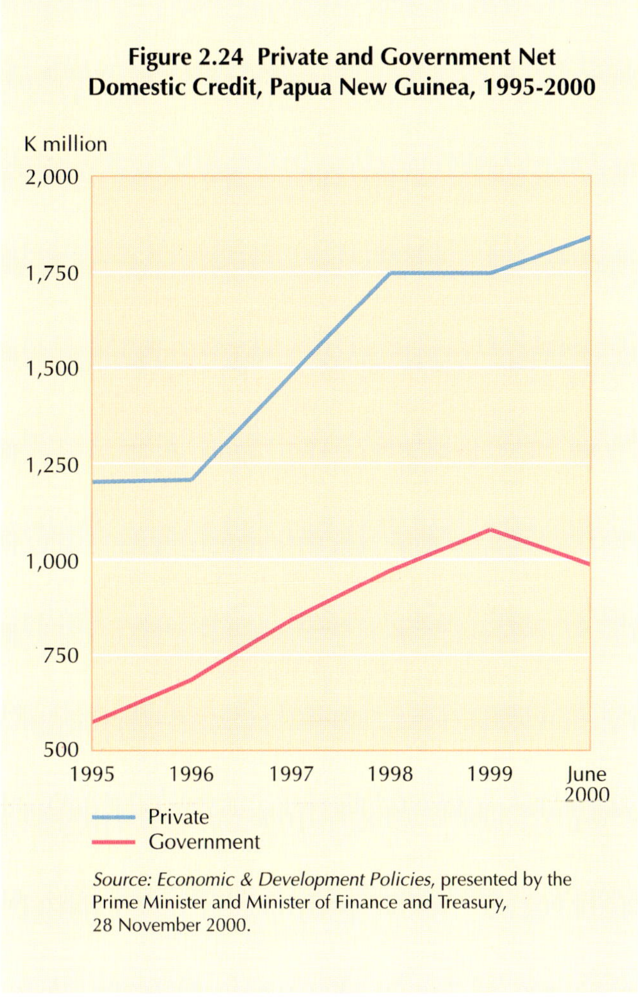

Figure 2.24 Private and Government Net Domestic Credit, Papua New Guinea, 1995-2000

Source: Economic & Development Policies, presented by the Prime Minister and Minister of Finance and Treasury, 28 November 2000.

This reform program is important for laying the foundations of an effective development strategy which, however, also entails the setting of development expenditure priorities. These priorities, contained principally in the National Charter on Reconstruction and Development, are elementary and primary education, primary health care, transport infrastructure maintenance, law and order, and private sector development in rural areas. The 2000 and 2001 budgets increased the allocations to these sectors. The key initiative in the development budget for 2001 is the introduction of the Development Charter Program, which aims to significantly increase the delivery of basic services in rural regions. The program targets health, education, roads, and capacity building. The emphasis on rural regions should help address the incidence of poverty.

The country has wide disparities in income both among social groups and across the country, and a high incidence of poverty. The vast majority of poor people live in rural areas, and nearly two thirds of the poor rely on agriculture as their main source of income. There is consequently a need to diversify production, particularly in the nonmining sector.

Samoa

The economy expanded by 7.0 percent in 2000, largely reflecting the Government's reforms and prudent macroeconomic management. Growth is likely to continue in the medium term, but inflationary pressures and any pause in the momentum of reforms present risks to the strong growth impetus.

Recent Trends and Prospects

The economy is estimated to have grown by 7.0 percent in 2000 with construction, commerce, and hotels and restaurants largely accounting for the buoyant growth (see Figure 2.25). Key projects include the renovation of the Faleolo International Airport, a road-sealing project, and the renovation and construction of several buildings in Apia. The commerce sector has grown at an average of 9 percent for the past three years, with the tariff, tax, and financial liberalization reforms implemented over that period constituting a major contributing factor. The overall level of local food supplies and inflows of remittances increased in 2000. Substantial growth of monetary fishing, as opposed to subsistence fishing, in recent years is a major new development.

Merchandise exports and tourism receipts were slightly lower in 2000 than in the previous year. The main causes of the weakness in the former were coconut products and fresh fish exports, the latter of which now constitute about 60 percent of commodity exports. Annual remittances have been increasing steadily in recent years and are the single most important source of income to the economy. Estimates for 2000 suggest some improvement to the current account. The overall balance of payments remained healthy in 2000, partly reflecting strong capital inflows, while foreign reserves were around seven months of import cover.

The outcome for the fiscal year 2000 (ending 30 June) budget is estimated to be a deficit of 0.7 percent of GDP, after a budgeted surplus of 3.0 percent. This will be the first deficit since fiscal year 1994. Total revenues were lower than budgeted, mainly due to a fall in nontax revenue, particularly receipts from the corporatization of Samoa Communications Ltd. In mid-2000, external government debt fell to around 65 percent of GDP, maintaining the declining trend of recent years. Debt-service costs in fiscal year 2000 were around 7 percent of exports of goods and services, or 6.5 percent of net foreign assets, reflecting the concessional terms of external loans.

By December 2000, annual inflation amounted to 0.5 percent. The money supply was 11.4 percent higher in 2000 than a year earlier, reflecting a booming economy. Monetary policy was unchanged through 1999 and 2000. Substantial government deposits placed in the banking system over the last few years, despite a small reduction in 1999, have provided ample funds for the commercial banks to lend and have been reflected in relatively strong private sector credit growth since 1996. Commercial bank lending rates in 2000 were in the range of 10.25–11.50 percent, slightly lower than before rate liberalization in January 1998. The commercial banks remain strongly capitalized in terms of formal capital adequacy requirements and continue to earn strong profits, with average returns on shareholder funds of 21 percent in 1999.

The recent strong GDP growth performance is expected to continue, but at a slower pace through 2001 and 2002. Expansion in this period will be driven mainly by continuing major infrastructure construction projects. Strong growth is also expected to resume in the fisheries sector, after the weakness in 2000, with the purchase of six new large fishing vessels by the private sector. A recovery in taro production—following a long period when disease had virtually destroyed production—and continuing growth in coconut cream output are expected to boost exports. Tourism is likely to show stronger performance due to better marketing overseas, new hotel development, and some displacement of tourists from the Fiji Islands and Solomon Islands. These factors, and the continuing long-term upward trend of remittances, are expected to support reasonably strong growth in 2001 and 2002 of around 4 percent. Inflation of around 3 percent is forecast, though the outcome may be slightly higher.

The fiscal year 2001 budget has provided for a deficit of over 3 percent of GDP, which is to be financed largely by concessionary borrowing. Total government expenditure is budgeted at around 37 percent of GDP for fiscal year 2001. Current expenditure as a share of GDP is forecast at around 22 percent.

Issues in Economic Management

A major driving force in the strong credit growth of recent years has been financial liberalization, and in particular the easier

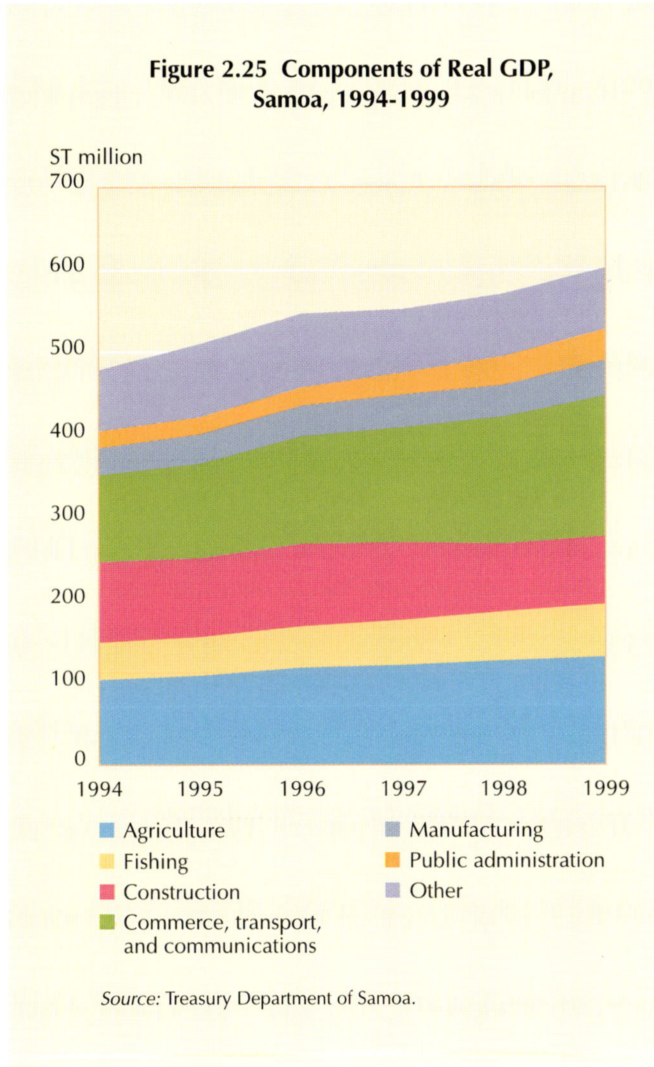

Source: Treasury Department of Samoa.

Another important issue relates to appropriate infrastructure, taxation, and regulation in relation to the rapidly growing fishing export sector. The sector is now making a major economic and social contribution but wharfage, berthing, and refueling facilities are seriously inadequate. Taxation of the sector is very limited and consideration needs to be given to some form of resource rent tax so that the benefits of fishing expansion are reasonably shared with the whole population. There are also concerns about the environmental sustainability of these rapidly growing fishing efforts.

Policy and Development Issues

In 1996, the Government stopped preparing five-year development plans and began issuing a series of biennial statements of economic strategy. The current strategy continues the emphasis on macroeconomic stability, public sector efficiency, improved education and health standards, and measures to support a strong private sector. It also emphasizes agriculture and fisheries, sustainable tourist development, and the importance of a revitalized village economy. An important feature is the extensive and successful consultation that has taken place with stakeholders. A major objective of the strategy is to ensure that the whole community shares in the benefits of the reform program.

Insecure land tenure, inefficient public enterprises, and regulations that make it difficult to transact domestic and international business are important constraints to private sector development. The Government has signaled that it will devise a strategy to improve both access to customary and public land, and utilization of customary land as collateral, but this will be difficult to implement. Similarly, despite the implementation of corporatization and privatization programs, progress has been slow. In addition, an independent and adequately resourced utilities regulator is needed. Other regulatory and administrative requirements that need overhauling include export/import documentation, quarantine requirements, exit permits for residents, and work permits for expatriates. Various legal reforms are also required, including streamlining company and insolvency law, repealing price control provisions, and prohibiting collusion in price fixing.

In education, the priority area is primary education, so as to increase the number of literate and numerate students. Similarly in health, more emphasis is needed on primary health care on a sustainable basis, including health promotion programs aimed at lifestyle-related diseases.

access of households and firms to credit. In light of this, and the current expansionary fiscal stance associated with high world oil prices, the central bank is keeping a close watch on monetary developments, and may tighten monetary policy to ensure that inflationary pressures are kept under control.

For 2001, the Government is proposing to consolidate the tax and tariff reforms, the financial sector reforms, and the initiatives on privatization and public enterprise reform, which have been taken in recent years. However, despite all these measures, there is a perception of less momentum.

Solomon Islands

Civil unrest and ethnic tension were the major factors in the 14 percent contraction of real GDP in 2000. However, a peace accord was signed in October, paving the way for reconstruction and rehabilitation. An early return to normalcy and political stability are vital for reviving the prospects of the near-devastated economy.

Recent Trends and Prospects

Economic and social conditions deteriorated sharply in mid-1999, following an escalation of civil unrest and ethnic tension. The deterioration in the economy was further aggravated by political events in June 2000. As a result of this crisis, the economy contracted by about 14 percent in real terms in 2000. A peace agreement signed in October 2000 opened the way for reconstruction and rehabilitation.

The civil unrest of 1999 resulted in the closure of Solomon Islands Plantations Ltd., the country's largest agricultural enterprise, in June that year. Exports of palm oil and palm oil products fell from SI$97.9 million in 1998 to SI$65.1 million in 1999 and, subsequently, to an estimated SI$6.5 million in 2000. Agricultural output dropped by over 50 percent from the beginning of 1999 to the end of 2000.

Gold and silver from the Gold Ridge mine on the main island of Guadalcanal had begun to make a significant contribution to exports in 1999 and early 2000 before the mine was closed in June 2000. The closure likewise resulted in the loss of employment and export income.

Fish export revenue, which suffered as a result of low prices and civil unrest, sank from SI$195 million in 1999 to SI$45 million in 2000. The sector's contribution to GDP fell by an estimated 42 percent in 2000. Other important sectors in the economy, such as logs, copra, and cocoa, suffered some downturn as a result of the disturbances, although they all continued to export in 2000. Logs are still the principal export commodity in US dollar terms, even though prices, at an average of around US$70 per cubic meter, are low. Copra and cocoa production declined on Guadalcanal, where most of the unrest occurred, but was little affected elsewhere. Copra prices, at around US$300 per ton in late 2000, were down by about 32 percent from the levels seen at the end of 1999. Finally, tourism fell to negligible levels as a result of the disorder.

The Government experienced acute cash-flow difficulties in the second half of 2000 as tax revenues plummeted and most external assistance was suspended (see Figure 2.26). Its response was to suspend public investment and ask employees to take unpaid leave. Repatriation payments to militants following the peace agreement further stretched limited resources. Total government earnings and tax revenues are estimated to have fallen short of budget estimates for 2000 by more than 30 percent, while the overall budget balance for the year is projected to be a deficit equivalent to 4.5 percent of GDP. The stock of central government debt at the end of 2000 reached about 75 percent of GDP, with about 60 percent of this in external debt.

Because of lower domestic demand, inflation has been on a declining trend since the second half of 1999. Over the whole of 2000, it was 6.6 percent, despite higher world oil prices. Total domestic credit increased by 12 percent in the nine months to September 2000; most credit to the private sector had been extended in the first half of the year. Broad money grew by 9.5 percent in 2000. Exports and imports both fell in US dollar terms, by 29.2 percent and 14.8 percent, respectively, because of disruptions to export production and low demand for imported goods. External reserves fell sharply immediately after the June 2000 crisis, but improved subsequently as receipts from log exports improved. Exchange control measures also helped. Gross external reserves were about $33.4 million at the end of 2000, sufficient to cover only about two months of imports; the external position of the country remains fragile.

While some signs of economic revival appeared after the peace agreement, major enterprises in mining, fishing, and agriculture remain closed, and the prospects in the short and medium term will largely depend on how soon the country returns to normalcy. Solomon Islands Plantations will require at least 24 months to resume production once it restarts operations, while gold and silver production will take six months to commence after startup of the Gold Ridge mine. An optimistic scenario might, therefore, suggest growth of about 3 percent in 2001 and 2002. Inflation is likely to decline slightly to 5–6 percent over these two years as the economy begins to recover and local food supplies reach precrisis levels. Debt service will continue to be a concern.

Around 8,000 workers, or 15 percent of the total workforce in the formal sector, were either made redundant or put on unpaid leave as a result of the civil unrest. While some of these workers will be reemployed, employment growth is likely to be stagnant in 2001 and 2002, with youth unemployment remaining at high levels.

Issues in Economic Management

Faced with significant reconstruction challenges, the country needs sound macroeconomic management to facilitate external assistance. In particular, fiscal management that supports price stability and an adequate level of international reserves needs to be established. This will require keeping the government deficit to a level that can be financed by concessionary borrowing. Additionally, government expenditure commitments need to be kept in check so as to avoid further borrowing from the central bank and limit borrowing from commercial banks. At the same time, the Government needs to settle remaining arrears urgently, and avoid falling into arrears with domestic and external creditors and suppliers.

In an effort to stimulate economic recovery, the Government has been granting tax exemptions to selected taxpayers on a discretionary basis. The transparency and efficiency of this policy require urgent review. As an alternative in the short term, a reduction in the goods tax deserves examination.

Policy and Development Issues

To achieve a sound fiscal position in the medium term, the Government needs to raise both expenditure efficiency and revenue, while strengthening customs and tax administration. The privatization of certain government enterprises, such as Solomon Printers and Home Finance, would also help improve the fiscal position, as would introducing a value-added tax to replace the goods tax.

Reduced individual and business incomes, along with fewer employment opportunities, are clearly having a major adverse social impact. Furthermore, the Government's weakened capacity to support health and education services, particularly in more remote areas, has implications for the future of the country. Even prior to the recent disturbances, the Solomon Islands was one of the poorest nations in the Pacific. The crisis has exacerbated the social and economic climate. Responses, to be effective, will require major sustained efforts by the Government and its development partners.

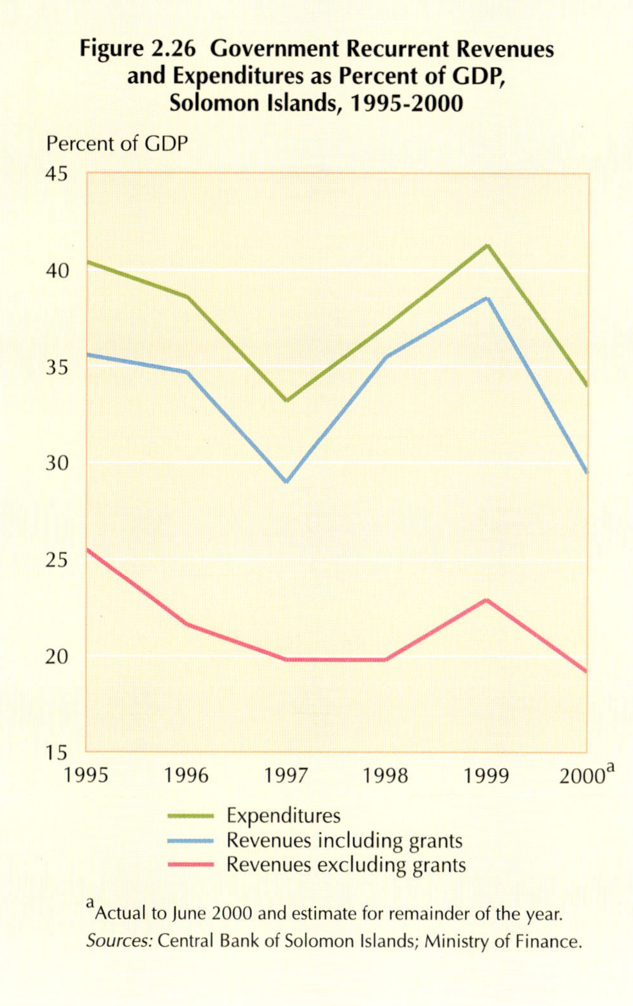

Figure 2.26 Government Recurrent Revenues and Expenditures as Percent of GDP, Solomon Islands, 1995-2000

[a]Actual to June 2000 and estimate for remainder of the year.
Sources: Central Bank of Solomon Islands; Ministry of Finance.

Tonga

The economy recorded robust growth of over 5 percent in 2000, led by tourism. However, the medium-term outlook for growth is modest. Maintenance of an external balance, public enterprise reforms, and support to private sector development are some of the key factors in the growth outcome.

Recent Trends and Prospects

Economic growth is estimated at 5.3 percent in 2000. It was led by a large increase in the trade and services sector related to millennium celebrations, together with the income effect from increased workers' remittances. Growth was also supported by a recovery in agricultural production, which had declined significantly in 1999 as a result of cyclone Cora in December 1998. Inflation rose to 5.3 percent in 2000 due to drought and higher world prices for the country's imports.

Following fiscal deficits in recent years, a surplus of 0.8 percent of GDP was recorded in 2000. The improvement resulted from lower capital expenditure and, to some extent, increased tax revenues due to higher imports. Wages accounted for about 53 percent of current expenditures in 2000, equivalent to 14.4 percent of GDP. Foreign trade taxation accounted for more than 64 percent of tax revenues, or about 50 percent of total revenues. The Government follows an implicit fiscal rule that requires recurrent expenditure to equal recurrent revenue. Consequently, the variation in deficits largely reflects the availability of foreign financing for capital expenditure. Domestic bank financing represented only 0.3 percent of GDP in 2000.

Broad money increased by 8.5 percent in 2000, after 15.0 percent growth in 1999. Monetary conditions were tightened in 1999 and 2000 in response to official reserve losses. The reserve requirement ratio was raised to 15 percent in September 2000, the minimum lending rate was put up to 12 percent, and the Government formalized the imposition of a credit ceiling. The tight policy slowed private sector credit growth to 2 percent in 1999 and 6 percent in 2000 from 18 percent in 1998. Total external debt in 2000 was estimated at US$62.2 million, or 41 percent of GDP, and consists largely of concessionary loans. Domestic debt was equivalent to 6 percent of GDP and is held in the form of bonds, mainly by banks and, to some extent, by the nonfinancial public and private sector. The debt-service ratio in 2000 was 12 percent.

The principal exports in 2000 were squash, fish, root crops, vanilla, and copra, all of which faced increasing international competition. Consumer and intermediate goods accounted for more than 80 percent of imports. Merchandise imports in 2000 increased faster than the growth of GDP as a result of a pickup in imports after the millennium celebrations (see Figure 2.27). A small number of large, one-off imports, including an electricity generator for Vava'u and two fishing boats contributed to this rise, leading to a trade deficit of US$51.7 million for the year. The current account recorded a deficit equivalent to 6.7 percent of GDP. Net current inward transfers improved significantly in 2000 due to an increase in private remittances. Net inward private transfers were recorded at US$40.4 million, while official transfers were US$1.2 million. Outward private transfers also rose, due to increased remittances to meet the living costs of children studying abroad. The capital account deteriorated substantially in 2000, mainly due to declining net private capital inflows. Private capital and investment outflows increased as a result of a number of Tongan business operators making offshore investments. The balance of payments recorded a small deficit. Consequently, foreign reserves declined from US$21.4 million or 3.5 months of import cover by mid-1999, to US$15.5 million or 2.5 months of import cover by mid-2000.

The exchange rate of the pa'anga is pegged to a basket of currencies comprising the Australian, New Zealand, and US dollars and the Japanese yen. Since July 2000, the currency has been allowed to deviate from the rate set by the currency basket by up to 5 percent.

The economy is expected to grow at quite modest rates of around 2 percent in 2001 and 2002. Growth will be supported by continued recovery in agriculture and further expansion of fishing operations. In line with government policy, the budget is expected to remain in balance over the next two years, with small surpluses of around US$0.2 million to US$0.5 million. Inflation is expected to remain at around 5 percent in 2001,

---

2000 refers to fiscal year 1999/2000, ending 30 June.

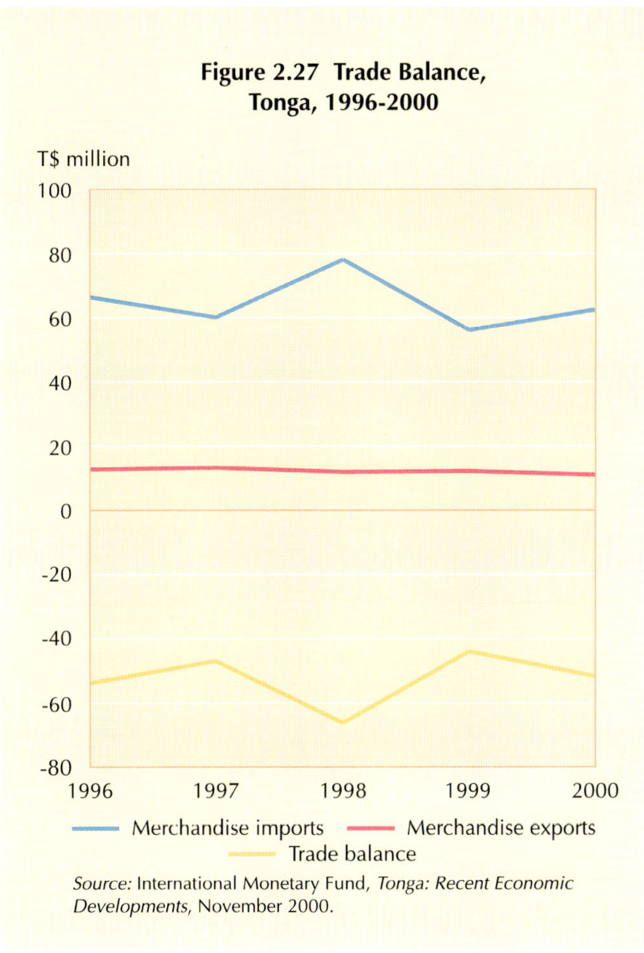

Figure 2.27 Trade Balance, Tonga, 1996-2000

Source: International Monetary Fund, *Tonga: Recent Economic Developments*, November 2000.

The returns from fishing grew steadily throughout the 1990s to a value of US$4.1 million in 2000. Currently, fish exports are mostly high-value products transported by commercial airlines to Japan, Korea, and the US. Although fish exports are held back by a lack of transport facilities, they have the potential for significant expansion with further infrastructure development. The long-line tuna catch can be expanded considerably and still remain an environmentally sustainable industry. However, large investments are required to convert the potential into reality.

The Government has made significant efforts to develop manufacturing over the years. The sector grew steadily in the three years to 2000, but exports reached only US$0.8 million in value. The prospects for manufacturing are limited because of the small domestic market, high operating (including labor) costs, steep duty rates, and shortage of skilled labor.

Policy and Development Issues

While the Government has been promoting tourism and sees it as a promising industry, both the quality and quantity of accommodation are limiting factors to expansion. The prospects for continued growth in tourism are modest in the short to medium term, with the sector likely to be dominated by expatriate Tongans visiting friends and relatives.

Agriculture has also been identified by the Government as an industry with growth potential. However, exports of agricultural commodities are modest (squash exports were valued at US$5.5 million in 2000, with root crop and vanilla exports each worth US$0.5 million). Demand and prices for squash and vanilla have been affected by growing international competition. Root crops rely on sales to Pacific islanders living abroad and are constrained by transport problems as such crops constitute high-volume, low-value commodities. While attempts are being made to diversify into other agricultural commodities, such as kava for the international pharmaceutical market, problems with quality and reliability of supply limit their potential. These commodities may make a useful contribution to exports but the overall outlook for them as exports is unexciting.

The reform of public enterprises has not really begun. This is an important policy issue that the Government should address, given the likely future pressure on fiscal balances due to inefficiencies in the public enterprise sector.

mainly as a result of increasing world prices and some further devaluation of the pa'anga. Remittances will continue to make an important contribution to the economy.

Issues in Economic Management

The public enterprise sector is both large and diverse, with more than 35 enterprises. However, only four pay dividends to the Government. No timetable has been set for their privatization or corporatization, although the Government has signaled its intention to sell some of them. In the meantime, public enterprises need to be more accountable, and this requires the development and implementation of performance guidelines.

Tuvalu

Real GDP grew by 3 percent in 2000. A windfall payment from the lease of the country's Internet country domain address and buoyant returns from the Tuvalu Trust Fund were also realized during the year. However, a possible decline in such revenues and the growth of complacency pose considerable risk to future growth prospects.

Recent Trends and Prospects

Growth in real GDP in 2000 is estimated at 3 percent (see Figure 2.28). Public construction was significantly stronger than in 1999, but expenditure on public administration changed little. As a result of substantial windfall revenue from the lease of Tuvalu's Internet country domain address (".tv"), strong growth in returns from the Tuvalu Trust Fund, and stable revenue from fishing license fees, government revenues totaled around A$44 million in 2000.

The government budget emphasizes the difference between core (recurrent) and noncore (infrastructure and other capital item) revenues and expenditures, with specific allocations to the Tuvalu Trust Fund so that the benefits can be enjoyed in the future. Total government revenues were almost double the budget estimate for 2000 as a result of the lease of the Internet address. Total government expenditures amounted to $22 million, an increase of about $5 million, compared with 1999. Expenditures on infrastructure and other capital projects in 2000 rose to a record A$8.2 million.

In 2000, inflation rose to 5.0 percent from around 1 percent in 1999, partially due to increased costs of imports as a result of higher transport (mainly air) costs. The trade deficit remained high, due to the fact that most agricultural production is consumed domestically, and due to the absence of any significant manufacturing activity. However, the external position is sound overall because of remittances, returns from the Tuvalu Trust Fund, the Internet lease, and aid agency disbursements. Unemployment remains high with less than 20 percent of Tuvaluans employed in salaried positions; over 65 percent of the population are employed in subsistence activities.

The construction sector will see strong growth in 2001, due to the largest civil works project undertaken in the country: the Funafuti roadway will be reconstructed and the airstrip will be repaired. The large scale of these projects, in the context of Tuvalu, suggests GDP growth for 2001–2002 of 5–6 percent.

After a very strong performance in 2000, returns from the Tuvalu Trust Fund are forecast to decline to around A$3 million in 2001. This is based on the expectation that the Australian equities market will experience lower returns associated with an anticipated global slowdown in economic growth. Inflation is likely to ease in 2001 and 2002 to around 1–2 percent, reflecting lower inflation in Australia where most imports are sourced, and lower world fuel prices.

The 2001 budget includes expenditures of A$26.9 million, comprising noncore expenditures of A$8.6 million and core expenditures of A$18.3 million. Revenues are expected to be A$27.2 million, and hence the budget shows a small surplus of A$0.3 million. Also, the budget provides for additional capital projects totaling A$16.6 million, subject to the availability of development funds from aid agencies. Recurrent expenditures of A$16.9 million in 2001 represent an increase of around 20 percent over the 2000 level, due to the opening of an embassy in New York, a 100 percent increase in politicians' salaries, and a 6.8 percent increase in the number of civil servants.

A new policy is being drafted that will lead to the signing of new licensing agreements for fishing in the country's fishing grounds. However, after record revenues in 1999 and 2000 from fishing license fees, these revenues (when translated from other currencies) may decline if the Australian dollar rebounds.

Two further prospects, both uncertain, may also affect government revenues in 2001 or 2002. First, the Government is a significant minority shareholder of the company that leases the Internet country address, with a 20 percent holding of the company's common stock. If the company seeks a public listing, the market value of this holding may well exceed the value of the Tuvalu Trust Fund. Listing the company is likely in either 2002 or 2003 and would clearly represent another—extremely large—windfall gain. Second, the Government is in exploratory talks with an Australian firm on setting up an international shipping registry in Tuvalu, to register merchant vessels under the Tuvalu flag. This too could result in substantial revenues.

Issues in Economic Management

Tuvalu has followed a policy of fiscal restraint in the past, accumulating a series of budget surpluses over the last decade. Although money is available through annual drawdowns from the Tuvalu Trust Fund, the Government is reluctant to rely on it for short-term needs. Each year, the Government reinvests large amounts in the Fund, so it is now the largest contributor in cumulative terms. It aims to maintain the real value of the Fund before distributing returns to the Consolidated Trust Fund account, which can be used for capital expenditure.

There is, however, some concern that the more comfortable financial position of the Government over the last few years is bringing with it a greater tendency for ministries to be less stringent in the application of basic financial management principles. There is also evidence that some core expenditure is being met through the special development expenditure item of the Tuvalu Trust Fund, despite the fact that this was established for development (noncore) activities only. Current trends in the budget are taking the Consolidated Trust Fund account balance well below the level necessary to guard against revenue shocks. The balance in 2001 is expected to fall to A$11.4 million, below the Government's target of A$13.5 million. The Government needs to restore it to the appropriate level as soon as possible. Another concern is the timeliness of government financial reporting. The 1998 and 1999 accounts were prepared only after long delays, making fiscal management much more difficult. A regular cash-flow statement is also needed.

Policy and Development Issues

The main development issue is the devolution of administrative responsibilities to communities on the outer islands, and the improvement of infrastructure and services there. In 2000, the Government continued to devolve administrative responsibilities, including some expenditure management, to outer island councils (*Falekaupule*). This was in line with the medium-term development strategy's focus on ensuring greater equality of income distribution between the capital island of Funafuti and the outer islands. The Falekaupule Trust Fund was invested with professional fund managers in Australia in February 2000 with initial capital of A$11.2 million. The island communities themselves, the Government, and the first tranche of a loan from the Asian Development Bank funded it.

As part of a program to improve facilities for outer island communities, in 2000 the Government purchased three water

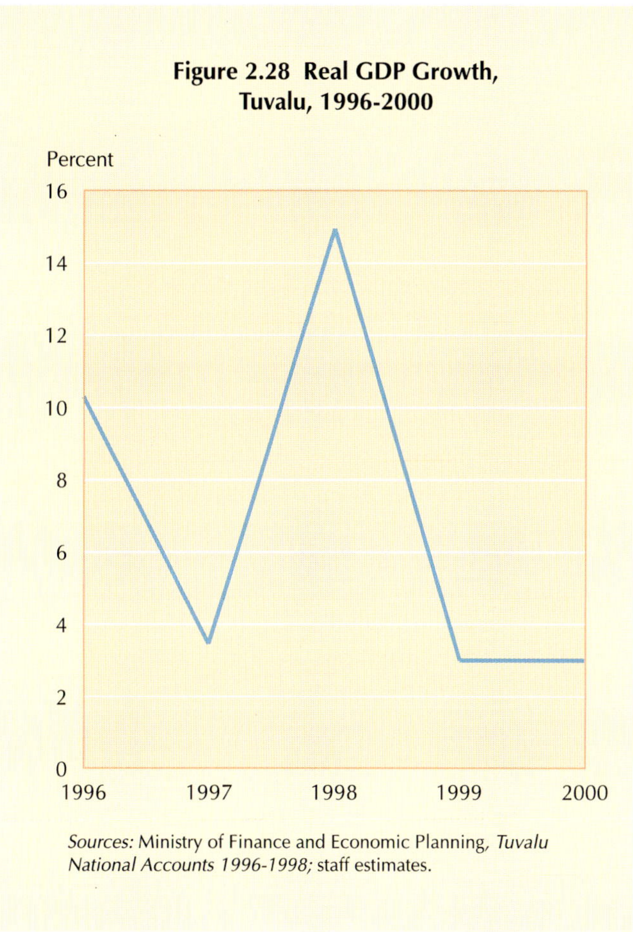

Sources: Ministry of Finance and Economic Planning, *Tuvalu National Accounts 1996-1998;* staff estimates.

desalinating systems and five solar water pumps. In addition, it is renovating and expanding the water supply system and embarking on an electrification program for the outer islands. A range of issues needs to be resolved, such as the structure of electricity tariffs and the identity of the organization to manage the electricity supply. Another pressing issue for outer island communities is the availability of a regular and reliable freight service to the capital, and improved cargo handling facilities. Telecommunications is another essential service that needs improvement on the outer islands, as some of them have only a few lines.

Health and education on the outer islands are areas of concern. Island communities receive only infrequent visits from doctors, while some islands have no permanently posted doctors. Some health clinics also need to be upgraded.

Vanuatu

The economy recovered in 2000 with 2.8 percent growth in real GDP, led by tourism and construction. Growth is likely to continue at about this level in the medium term. However, fiscal discipline and implementation of reforms remain critical for the economy's future prospects.

Recent Trends and Prospects

Following a contraction of 3.0 percent in 1999, the economy recovered in 2000 with estimated growth of 2.8 percent, led by tourism and construction. Sustained marketing campaigns in Australia by the National Tourism Office and political instability in neighboring countries boosted the number of visitors to Vanuatu. Major construction projects included the Efate ring road, the expansion of the main airports on Efate and Santo, rehabilitation works from cyclone Dani, and an urban infrastructure project. The agriculture sector continued to experience weakness.

Copra and beef exports weakened but kava exports strengthened significantly in 2000; imports stayed at around the previous year's level. Despite a trade deficit, a small surplus on the current account is estimated in 2000, compared with a deficit in 1999. However, a sizable deficit of at least 4 percent of GDP is estimated on the capital account in 2000, largely due to outflows from commercial banks. At the end of 2000, foreign reserves were estimated at 5.4 months of import cover, compared with 5.9 months at the end of 1999.

The budgeted deficit in 2000 was 3 percent of GDP, but as a result of the rollover of development projects from 1999's budget, it reached around 8 percent. Controls on recurrent expenditure were very tight during the year and helped contain further expenditure growth. Total tax revenue for 2000 was only slightly below the levels forecast in the budget, though value-added tax collection was in line with forecasts.

External debt service amounted to only 1.3 percent of exports of goods and services and 5.7 percent of domestic revenue in 2000. At the end of the third quarter of 2000, domestic credit and net foreign assets were at similar levels to those at the end of 1999. The most noticeable monetary development in 2000 was a decline in private sector credit of 8 percent by the end of the third quarter and a substantial rise in net credit to the Government. At the end of the third quarter, domestic borrowing to finance the deficit was much larger than expected, mainly reflecting delays in concessionary financing and a buildup of government commitments to aid projects.

The main monetary initiative in 2000 was the reintroduction of foreign exchange guidelines on 23 February 2000, when foreign reserves fell to less than five months of import cover. In anticipation both of modest growth and stable inflation, and an acceptable level of official reserves, the Reserve Bank indicated in its October 2000 monetary policy statement that there was no immediate requirement to adjust the monetary policy stance.

The vatu is pegged to a basket of major trading partner currencies. During the first nine months of 2000, it appreciated by 7.4 percent against the Australian dollar and by 4.6 percent against the euro, but depreciated by about 10 percent against the US dollar and by about 4 percent against the yen. This may have impacted adversely on the competitiveness of exports, especially to Europe. Inflation has remained moderate in recent years; interest rate spreads widened to an average of 9.7 percent for the first three quarters of 2000. Given the dependence of Vanuatu on imports from Australia and the exchange rate arrangements between the vatu and the Australian dollar, price movements in Vanuatu are closely aligned to those in Australia.

The economy is projected to grow at modest rates of 3–3.5 percent a year in 2001 and 2002, helped mainly by a recovery in agriculture and continued success of tourism. Over this period, the trade account is forecast to improve as exports recover. The current account is projected to record a modest deficit in 2001 followed by a small surplus in 2002. Private capital outflows are expected to be considerably lower in these two years, and anticipated aid transfers should help rebuild reserves. The overall budget deficit is targeted to be no more than 2 percent of GDP over the next two or three years, with annual surpluses in the recurrent budget and external concessionary funds financing the overall deficit.

For the 2001 budget, the Government proposes several new revenue initiatives, along with a higher revenue projection. In 2001, expenditure is projected to decline as a proportion of GDP, and a modest budget deficit of 1 percent of GDP is forecast. Debt-service costs are projected to rise to 6.5 percent by 2002 as repayments of recently acquired external debt begin. Provided the vatu remains stable, inflation is expected to be around 2 percent in 2001 and 2002.

Issues in Economic Management

Policy initiatives in the 2001 budget focused on three objectives: stable government, private sector development, and social equity and sustainability. Relevant measures include balancing the recurrent budget; implementing the next phase of the Government's Comprehensive Reform Program (CRP), which emphasizes outer island development; and establishing impact monitoring systems for these reforms. Effective implementation of reforms remains critical to maintaining the forecast rate of growth.

The interest rate structure in Vanuatu is characterized by very wide spreads between average lending and deposit rates (see Figure 2.29). Interest rate spreads widened from an average of 8.3 percent in 1996 to 10.4 percent in the third quarter of 2000, to give an average of 9.7 percent in the first three quarters of 2000. Furthermore, certain lending practices greatly widen the effective spread. For example, borrowers are commonly required to borrow twice as much as they need and put half their loan on deposit. The high margins and practices like these reflect weak competition in the banking sector and lack of access to overseas funds (because of recent capital controls).

Policy and Development Issues

The CRP was first formulated and implemented in 1998, and is subject to a process of continual reformulation. It is supported by a loan from the Asian Development Bank and focuses on promoting economic growth through a strategy oriented on the private sector. This strategy entails comprehensive governance reforms, various nondistortionary measures to improve the economic environment for private sector activity, and a range of social and other reforms to improve economic and social conditions at the village level. Both public expenditure management and the utilization of external assistance are expected to improve as a result of the CRP. The Government now needs to integrate it into the budget process and the macroeconomic framework.

Regional and outer island development has been a longstanding and challenging objective for governments in Vanuatu. Outside the major towns of Port Vila and Luganville, infrastructure is poor and government services rarely available. The pro-

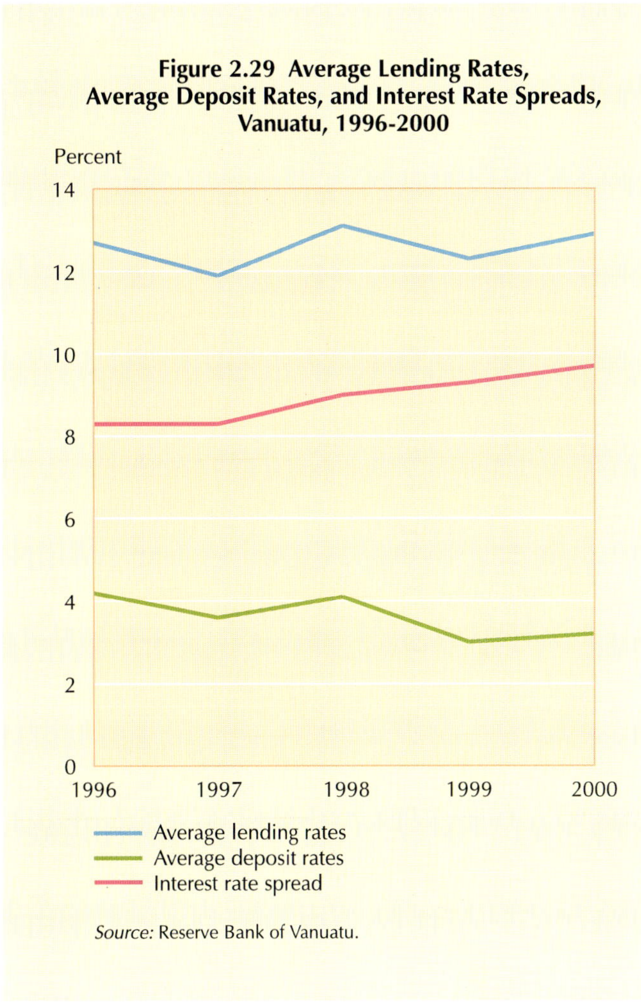

Source: Reserve Bank of Vanuatu.

posed Outer Island Infrastructure Development Program, an important component of the CRP, is designed to tackle these weaknesses. The Program is near the implementation stage and 14 projects have been identified on road, marine, storage, and airstrip infrastructure. Four of these projects are already being funded. Important features of the Program are (i) the emphasis on components to ensure sustainability and (ii) the integration with planning initiatives in the regions and outer islands to ensure support there.

PART III

Asia's Globalization Challenge

Asia's Globalization Challenge

The inhabitant of London could order by telephone, sipping his morning tea in bed, the various products of the whole earth, in such quantity as he might see fit, and reasonably expect their early delivery upon his doorstep; he could at the same moment and by the same means adventure his wealth in the natural resources and new enterprises of any quarter of the world, and share, without exertion or even trouble, in their prospective fruits and advantages; or he could decide to couple the security of his fortunes with the good faith of the townspeople of any substantial municipality in any continent that fancy or information might recommend. .... The internationalisation [of the ordinary course of social and economic life] was nearly complete in practice.

J.M. Keynes, The Economic Consequences of the Peace, 1919

INTRODUCTION

As we enter a new millennium, the effects of internationalization—now known as globalization—are everywhere apparent. It is an opportune time to take stock of this process, which has played a major role in sustaining the economic expansion of the global economy in the second half of the 20th century. As the quote from Keynes indicates, it is not a new phenomenon. Yet in the post-Second World War era, globalization is seemingly shrinking the planet as barriers to trade are dismantled, transport and communications costs fall, and global production systems are formed and managed by giant multinational corporations.

Globalization can be defined as the ongoing economic, technological, social, and political integration of the world that began after the Second World War. There are several dimensions to this dynamic process, including the increased internationalization of economic markets as reflected, for example, in trade and financial capital flows. However, there are also institutional and social changes that are taking place within the geographic borders of nation states, though these are much more difficult to quantify. Institutional changes include modifications in policy, in industrial organization, and in the administration of laws and regulations that govern the behavior of economic agents. Globalization is impacting the institutional framework in both developing and industrial countries; it is changing the way in which governments view their developmental role in society.

A brief review of data indicates the extent of globalization since the end of the Second World War. Total world merchandise trade (exports plus imports, by value) surged from about 23 percent of nominal world gross domestic product (GDP) in 1960 to about 39 percent in 1999 (see Table 3.1). Three factors have been behind this explosive growth. First, the effective rates of protection of artificial barriers to international trade (built up as a consequence of two world wars and a depression) such as tariffs and quotas, have fallen by as much as 80–90 percent after the end of the Second World War (Mussa 2000). Second, the costs of transportation and communications have dropped substantially. Ocean shipping costs have fallen in the last 50 years by as much as 75–80 percent. Communications costs have also been reduced significantly, stimulating greater trade in nonfactor services. Outsourcing has increased, particularly in automobiles and electronics, and the vertical integration of production has given way to multiple production platforms in distant locations coordinated from a central hub. Third, as globalization has expanded market size, international competition among firms has intensified. In the industrial countries, this accelerated research and development (R&D) expenditures and innovation as firms competed increasingly on product quality. In developing countries, particularly in Asia, technology-embodying capital goods imports increased as firms competed in global markets by using borrowed technology to produce goods at lower cost.

Parallel to the rising trend of trade in goods and services, private financial capital inflows to developing countries have increased rapidly in the past two decades. Developing countries in Asia and Latin America have received the bulk of these flows (see Figure 3.1). In Asia, such inflows are mainly to a few of the developing member countries (DMCs) of the Asian Development Bank (ADB) such as the People's Republic of China (PRC), Indonesia, and Malaysia. In the years immediately following the Second World War, most of the foreign direct investment (FDI) was made by US firms investing in Europe. Later, FDI among industrial and developing countries began to grow rapidly (see

Table 3.1 Total Merchandise Trade
(percent of world GDP)

	1960	1970	1980	1991	1992	1993	1994	1995	1996	1997	1998	1999
World	23.1	25.2	41.9	32.5	32.5	31.8	33.7	36.4	37.2	38.9	38.8	38.8
Industrial countries	15.7	18.7	28.5	23.2	22.9	21.7	22.8	24.5	24.7	25.5	26.2	26.2
Developing countries	7.5	6.5	13.4	9.3	9.6	10.1	10.9	11.9	12.5	13.4	12.6	12.6

Note: Data are based on customs trade statistics.
Sources: International Monetary Fund, *International Financial Statistics* (CD-ROM, March 2001); World Bank, *World Development Indicators* (CD-ROM, 2000); World Bank website (www.worldbank.org).

Table 3.2). At its peak, before the Asian financial crisis of 1997/98, about 40 percent of FDI went to developing countries.

The international flow of portfolio (stocks and bonds) and other investment funds (including bank lending) also rose as markets were deregulated and as investors became aware of profit-making opportunities in other countries. There were two main surges involving developing countries in this volatile component of the capital account. The first, in the late 1970s and early 1980s, was a surge in short-term bank lending, largely to Latin America that ended with the second oil shock in 1978. The second, in the late 1980s and the early 1990s, was larger and more broad based, involving substantial flows of portfolio investment and short-term credit to many developing countries in Asia. Strongly influenced by capital account liberalization, exchange control dismantling, rapid growth in equity markets, and low interest rates in industrial countries, this boom began to fade after the 1995 Mexican peso crisis and collapsed following the Asian financial crisis of 1997/98. By the end of 1998, total capital flows to developing countries were down by about 87 percent from the peak in 1996.

The increased flows of goods, services, and investment funds across national boundaries appear to be associated with rising world economic growth. As argued in *Asian Development Outlook 1999* (Part 3), economic development theory suggests that openness allows an economy to make better use of its resources through greater specialization in production of the goods and services that it produces relatively cheaply, which it can trade for goods and services produced more efficiently abroad. In particular, trade enables developing countries to import capital and other intermediate inputs that are critical to long-run growth. These critical inputs bring with them new technology. A more open trade regime also encourages competition between local and foreign firms, thereby raising the level of efficiency of domestic firms. There is adequate empirical evidence to support this view of the positive impact of globalization on national economic growth and per capita income—see, for example, Frankel and Romer (1999). Moreover, as more countries have been drawn into the global economy, world economic growth has accelerated.

Table 3.2 Foreign Direct Investment Inflows
($ billion)

	1980	1991	1992	1993	1994	1995	1996	1997	1998	1999
World	52.2	154.7	167.2	215.5	238.6	317.3	363.4	448.3	759.1	1,090.1
Industrial countries	46.4	114.1	117.6	144.7	141.6	204.1	224.0	271.2	565.0	878.0
Developing countries	5.8	40.6	49.6	70.8	97.0	113.2	139.5	177.1	194.1	212.1
Asia	2.5	19.3	24.6	44.4	54.6	60.9	71.1	75.7	84.6	86.9

Note: Data across countries are not consistent, i.e., the years for which data are available may vary from those shown.
Source: International Monetary Fund, *International Financial Statistics* (CD-ROM, March 2001).

Figure 3.1 Capital Inflows to Developing Countries

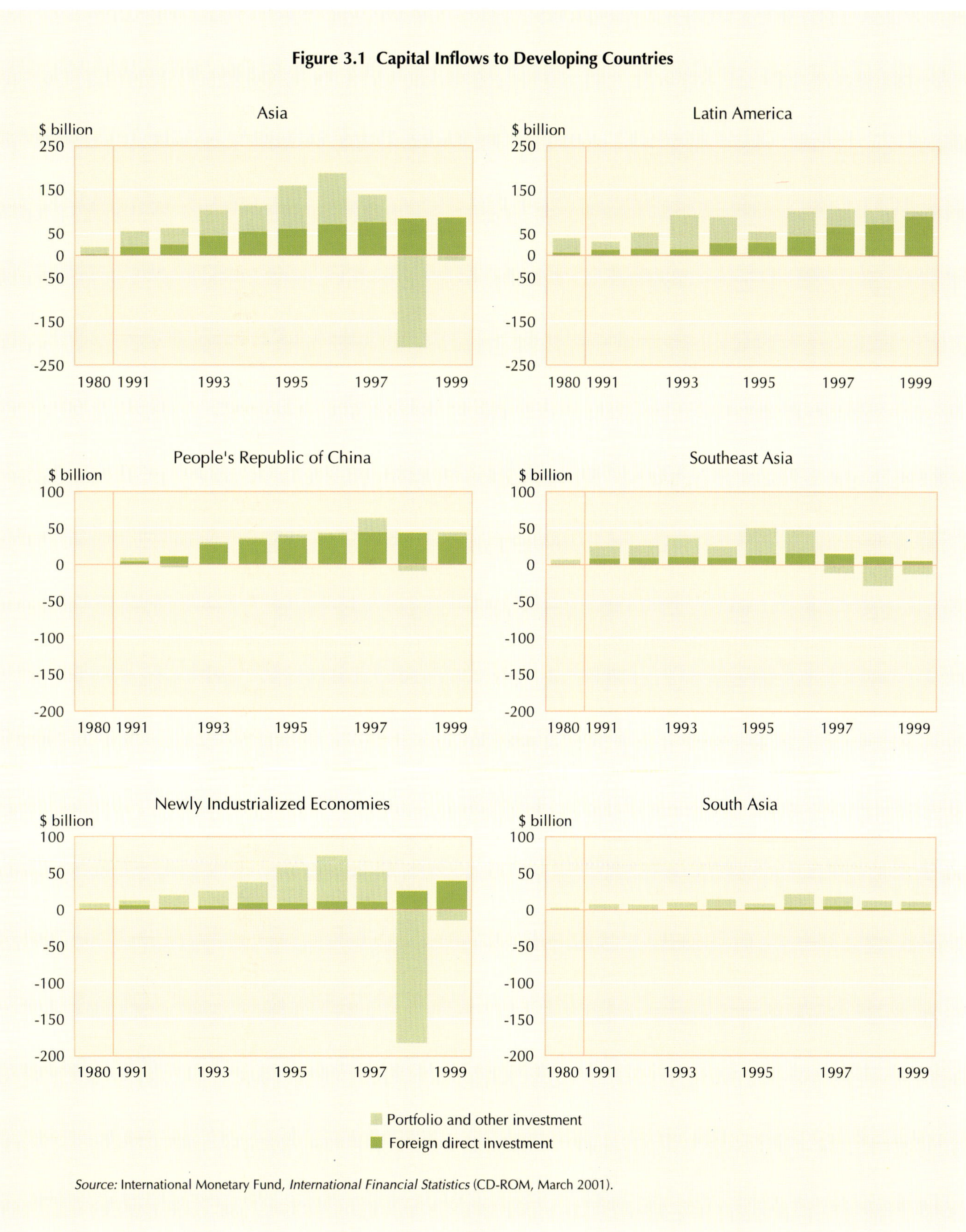

Source: International Monetary Fund, *International Financial Statistics* (CD-ROM, March 2001).

Yet accelerated economic growth is only one dimension of a complex and pervasive phenomenon that invokes debates on a wide range of issues such as human development, labor, and environmental standards. In particular, fears have been expressed that openness may accelerate the degradation of the environment and may also contribute to the exploitation of labor. Discussion of these issues is not attempted here but Lukas (2000) provides a review of the evidence on these points.

The following section, *The Asian Growth Experience and Globalization*, analyzes Asian growth performance in the context of globalization. Two major themes are developed. The first is that an increasing number of DMCs have capitalized on globalization to achieve rapid growth and poverty reduction. Participation in the global economy strengthened through growth in international trade and movement of capital and labor. The second theme is that policies and institutions were tailored to facilitate growth based on factor accumulation, particularly in the early stages of the growth process.

The policies and institutional options that must be developed and put in place to maximize the benefits of globalization as well as to minimize its risks are discussed in the subsequent section, *Policies for Adapting to Globalization*. Policymakers must continue to be alert and responsive to both the opportunities and the challenges of globalization if DMCs are to continue to capitalize on the process. This section has two major themes. The first is that development strategies should be modified both to adapt to a changing global economic environment and to take advantage of the opportunities that come with globalization. The Asian development approach, emphasizing rapid technology transfer to create export industries was, and is, quite successful. Yet, as DMCs move closer to the global technology frontier, certain modalities, such as innovation based on FDI and R&D, will become more important. Moreover, the revolution in information and communications technology (ICT) will continue to create opportunities in goods and services export markets, but those countries with the appropriate ICT infrastructure and personnel will best be able to exploit these opportunities. The second theme is that there are also risks to a globalization strategy and policies must be formulated to minimize them. Greater volatility is probably the biggest risk that accompanies globalization. The section discusses ways to reduce the volatility in economic performance that has been associated with globalization. These include policies to monitor and regulate capital flows, develop an appropriate exchange rate regime, and minimize fluctuations in productivity and investment. The section ends with a review of social programs that can minimize the impact of volatility on the poorest groups in society.

The third section, *Institutional Options in a Globalizing Environment*, deals with mechanisms for bringing about institutional change in a globalizing world. Institutional changes are slow to take root because they are often subject to strong forces of inertia. However, a crisis can trigger institutional change. In this section emphasis is placed on reforming institutions at different levels of government. Economies must choose a proper mix of institutions to effect policy change. These may be national, regional, or global. It is argued that many policy issues relating to globalization can still be addressed at the national level even though regional and global institutions have greater importance as the world's economies become more integrated.

In the final section, *Conclusions—Toward a Framework for Globalization*, the policies suggested in the previous sections are synthesized against a background of the potential for globalization and the remaining impediments to further globalization.

THE ASIAN GROWTH EXPERIENCE AND GLOBALIZATION

The rapid growth of Asia in the last three decades, particularly of the newly industrialized economies (NIEs) of Hong Kong, China; Republic of Korea (Korea); Singapore; and Taipei,China, as well as the economies of Southeast Asia, has been widely documented. This rapid progress in economic development occurred through export-led growth accompanied by high savings and investment rates, competitive pricing, a supportive macroeconomic framework, inflows of new technology, and a dynamic response to the changing pattern of overseas demand. This was a strategy that was eminently successful in much of Asia and one that other developing countries began to emulate (as discussed in *Emerging Asia*, ADB 1997).

Since that book was published, a regional financial crisis has changed the course of Asia's emergence. Nevertheless, the region remains dynamic and still features many of the policies that were responsible for this high growth in the past. Not unexpectedly, Asia's strong growth performance unleashed a major debate about the factor inputs that were responsible for this growth. The general point was that factor inputs of labor and capital (as opposed to new technology) accounted for much of the growth in DMCs over the past three decades (see further discussion on this in Box 3.1).

To the extent that Asian growth was unprecedented in the history of developing economies, its uniqueness lies in the arrangements developed to participate in globalization and to close the technological gap. It has been argued that the success that it has had in catching up reflects its reliance on market forces in combination with government guidance for achieving the requisite allocation of resources (World Bank 1993). Governments pursued policies and nurtured institutions to promote savings. Financial systems were organized around a relatively small number of large banks, which could be influenced and directed by the authorities. They funneled these savings into investment. Subsidies were provided for firms in strategic sectors. Barriers to entry ensured that these investments were profitable (Rodrik 1995, Cho 1996).

Box 3.1 Sources of Economic Growth in Developing Member Countries

One way to understand the rapid economic development of Asia during the past three decades is to review the results of some of the numerous cross-country studies that use the growth accounting method to identify sources of economic growth. These studies estimate the relative contributions to growth in per capita GDP of increases in physical capital, increases in labor or human capital, and increases in total factor productivity (TFP) arising, for example, from changes in technology.

A general consensus on the relative importance of factor accumulation and increases in TFP in the growth of the NIEs and Southeast Asia (East Asia) is beginning to emerge, although the database remains weak and there are numerous methodological problems. Over the last 40 years, growth in East Asia has relied disproportionately on inputs of capital and labor and less on increases in the efficiency with which those inputs are used. Young (1992) and Krugman (1994) conclude that there was essentially no TFP growth in East Asia from the late 1960s to the late 1980s. Kim and Lau (1994), using a different methodology, find that TFP accounted for about a third of the growth of real GDP from the 1960s to 1990 in the NIEs. This contrasts strikingly with the US, where TFP accounted for fully 80 percent of the growth of real GDP between 1948 and 1990.

Apparently, East Asia achieved its high-growth "miracle" primarily by boosting and sustaining investment rates while absorbing excess agricultural labor into industry. Increases in TFP, while not negligible, made a relatively small contribution to overall output growth. This is particularly true for the period until the late 1980s. This conclusion, however, should be interpreted in the context of the speed of development. While the share of TFP in output growth was somewhat lower in DMCs than in the Organisation for Economic Co-operation and Development (OECD) member countries, TFP growth was not necessarily low. Sarel (1996), for example, calculates that, in the NIEs, TFP growth as a percent of output per capita growth was comparable to that of the US during 1975–1990. Thus, TFP growth was not unusually low in DMCs but it did not explain high rates of economic growth; factor accumulation did.

There is less agreement on the meaning of this overall pattern of growth, stressing capital accumulation in achieving very high rates of growth. Is it evidence of East Asia's singular success at promoting savings and investment? Is this pattern normal for economies at East Asia's stage of economic development? Or does it reflect a distinctive Asian growth model and the region's pursuit of a unique development strategy?

To address these questions, one can place the East Asian experience in an international context. Hayami (1998) concludes that the relative contribution of increases in TFP growth to GDP growth is higher, while the relative contribution of factor accumulation is lower, in all the advanced industrial countries. The closer an economy is to the technological frontier (measured by relative per capita output in the nonprimary sector and epitomized by the US in the 20th century), the larger the relative contribution of productivity growth appears to be. Thus, for the postwar period as a whole, France, Germany, and UK were closer to the US than to Japan, and so depended more heavily on TFP growth than Japan. Japan, in turn, was closer to France, Germany, and UK than to the NIEs, and so was relatively more reliant on TFP growth than the NIEs.

Thus, growth depends disproportionately on factor accumulation—capital accumulation in particular—in its initial stages is emphasized in the 19th century context by Gerschenkron (1962). When the late-developing economy becomes able to utilize modern industrial technologies, the equilibrium capital/labor ratio shifts up. During this transition, the economy exhibits a relatively high level of investment and a correspondingly high rate of growth, subject to the availability of savings. The foreign technologies developed by previous industrialists are embodied in this capital equipment. Absolute, as well as relative, rates of TFP growth may be low at this early stage of economic development either because the capacity to innovate is particularly late to develop or because the processes of importing technology and of innovating at home compete for the same limited domestic resources.

If this interpretation is correct, then similar patterns should emerge in the history of the industrial economies. There are suggestions of such patterns in Japan and Europe in the postwar period, since these economies were then far behind the US in terms of technical efficiency, and productive capital stocks were significantly below equilibrium levels due to wartime destruction. They could grow quickly and close much of the gap with the technological leader simply by sustaining high levels of investment in capital that embodied the backlog of technologies available in the US. Indeed, the US itself looked remarkably like the high-growth Asian economies of today when it began catching up with the technological leader (in that case, the UK) in the 19th century.[1] The share of output growth accounted for by the growth of TFP was little more than a third. As the US closed the gap and assumed technological leadership after 1890 (Nelson and Wright 1992), the relative contribution of TFP growth to the growth of GDP rose.

To conclude, there is a hint of a distinctive Asian model, one that results in higher growth in GDP and higher rates of capital accumulation.[2] But, in broad terms, Asian growth is not unique, however different it looks from that of many high-income countries in the 1990s. Factor accumulation has mattered more, the growth of TFP less, because the region was relatively late developing. And as DMCs approach the technological frontier, they will find it harder to sustain rapid growth with high investment, since they will already have in place many of the technologies embodied in new capital equipment.

Interest-rate controls made it more difficult for firms not favored by the authorities to bid for scarce finance. Land reform, public spending on rural infrastructure, deliberative councils, and tripartism—coordinated negotiations over wages and other determinants of industrial development involving labor, management, and government—provided the necessary reassurance that the returns to these high levels of savings and investment would be widely shared (Campos and Root 1996).

These policies and institutions were tailored to facilitate growth that was based on factor accumulation rather than on increases in total factor productivity (TFP), and they were successful. (TFP—or changes therein—attempts to measure output growth that can be accounted for by the growth of labor and capital inputs.)

As DMCs continue to close the gap with the technological leaders, however, they will have to "graduate" from a growth model based on accumulation to one based on innovation.[3] They will have to adapt their institutions accordingly. And they will have to do so in a manner consistent with the opportunities and constraints of globalization.

This need for knowledge, learning, and policy adjustment in the context of globalization is explored in the next section, *Policies for Adapting to Globalization*. Now we turn briefly to a discussion of Asian patterns of globalization.

Globalization Trends

After the Second World War, on gaining independence, many Asian countries began exporting primary products to the industrial countries. In the 1960s, the NIEs began to export labor-intensive manufactured products to Europe, Japan, and the US. Subsequently, Southeast Asian countries (Indonesia, Malaysia, Philippines, and Thailand—the ASEAN 4) and the PRC joined them as exporters of labor-intensive manufactured goods. With time, these economies gradually moved into higher value-added, and skill- and capital-intensive exports. As a result of these trends, the share of manufactured exports increased dramatically in many DMCs (Table 3.3).

Asian exporters increased their market share in traditional manufactured exports through improved quality and competitive prices. They also moved into those markets where the income elasticity of demand for imports in the industrial countries was high, thereby guaranteeing rapid export growth. These included a range of skill- and technology-intensive industries such as electronics, computers, and pharmaceuticals.

Much of the impetus for strengthening international economic ties came from Japan and the US following the Korean War. The US made substantial infrastructure investments in both Taipei,China and Korea and supported land reform. Both these Asian economies enjoyed technology transfers from joint

Table 3.3 Share of Manufactured Exports to Total Exports of Selected DMCs, Selected Years
(percent)

Economy	1975	1980	1985	1990	1995	1999
Hong Kong, China	97.9	97.8	98.1	98.6	99.3	99.6
Korea	81.9	90.5	91.8	94.1	94.3	92.9
Singapore	50.2	51.9	53.9	73.6	86.4	88.5
Taipei,China	81.4	88.2	90.7	93.6	94.1	96.6
People's Republic of China	—	49.7	49.4	74.4	85.6	89.8
Indonesia	—	4.0	13.9	38.4	52.2	58.3
Malaysia	31.4	28.4	32.1	55.8	77.0	82.2
Philippines	22.1	39.7	62.2	72.6	82.7	93.8
Thailand	23.8	39.8	42.7	64.8	74.2	78.0
India	50.9	59.0	58.3	74.7	76.4	—
Pakistan	52.1	50.3	67.4	77.3	84.7	83.8
Sri Lanka	11.1	18.6	33.8	62.0	—	76.1

— Not available.
Source: Staff estimates.

ventures with Japanese companies, adopting aspects of Japanese industrial policy, methods of production, inventory control, and distribution. In the mid-1980s, FDI began to flow into labor-intensive industries. These "sunset" industries were no longer viable in Japan because of high wages and a strong yen. This flow of FDI from Japan helped develop further manufacturing industries across the region, accelerating growth and technology transfer. The above description does not, however, capture the economic development style of some other Asian countries that adopted globalization after experimenting with other approaches for quite some time.

The cases of the two economic giants of Asia—the PRC and India—are thus worth a more detailed look. These economies did not begin the transition to globalization until much later. Until 1978, the PRC remained virtually isolated from market economies, trading almost exclusively with other centrally planned economies. In the 1980s, however, it undertook a series of liberalization measures that began to open up the economy. In India, self-imposed near isolation lasted until the early 1990s. The trade-to-GDP ratio actually declined between 1950 and 1990. However, in the 1990s, several parts of the economy were liberalized and international trade increased.

People's Republic of China. Having observed the initial success of the NIEs, the PRC embarked on a wide-ranging series of socioeconomic reforms in the late 1970s that eventually propelled it from an inwardly focused, highly centralized economy to one of the most important manufacturing and trading nations in the world. The first reforms were in the rural economy. In the household responsibility system, which replaced the commune system, communes leased plots to individual households for 15 years (later 30 years). The household delivered a fixed quota of production to the village and kept the balance to consume or to sell in private markets that quickly developed. The results were remarkable. From 1978 to 1986, the value of farm output at current prices nearly tripled. Rising rural incomes created a demand for consumer goods, which were increasingly supplied by town and village enterprises (TVEs)—collectively owned firms formed by local governments that took advantage of increased rural savings and the pool of available labor created by increased farming efficiency. Industrial production in the countryside accelerated, growing at an average of 30 percent per annum during the 1980s (Kennedy and Vietor 2001). The TVEs' share of industrial output rose quickly from almost nothing to more than a third of total industrial output.

As industrial output rose, trade and investment reforms were quickly transforming an isolated country that had no FDI inflows and a ratio of total trade to GDP of only 10 percent in the mid-1970s, compared with more than 30 percent in many NIEs and Southeast Asian economies. Three related sets of reforms facilitated this transformation. The first was trade reform undertaken on a piecemeal basis from the late 1970s through the 1980s. Local governments licensed new foreign trade corporations (FTCs) to bypass the 12 FTCs authorized by the central Government. By the end of the 1980s, the number of FTCs had mushroomed to over 5,000 and the number of domestic firms with trading rights had increased to over 10,000. This liberalization of the trading environment at the firm level was accompanied by a gradual liberalization of the tariff regime.

The second policy initiative was liberalization of FDI. This was much more radical because it overturned a policy of careful monitoring of foreign activities in the country, even though the initial reforms were confined to a few coastal areas in the southern part of the country. The PRC was able to attract enormous inflows of FDI, so that by the mid-1990s it was the largest recipient of FDI among developing countries. Three coastal cities (Shenzen, Shantou, and Xiamen) and a province (Hainan) were designated as "special economic zones" in 1980, and this was expanded to 14 coastal cities in 1984. These regions have grown at double-digit rates ever since.

The third set of reforms involved the exchange rate. The currency was devalued in real terms over the 1980s and early 1990s and foreign currency transactions were gradually deregulated. The current account (though not the capital account) was made fully convertible in the late 1990s. The special economic zones generally enjoyed a greater level of external sector liberalization.

These reforms led to a dramatic transformation of the PRC's links with the outside world. Exports grew very fast for two decades, in absolute terms, from $10 billion in 1978 to $195 billion in 1999 and as a percent of GDP from less than 7 percent to about 20 percent over the same period. The response of FDI was slower at first, but increased rapidly by the end of the 1990s. From $57 million in 1980, it grew to over $40 billion by the mid-1990s, an increase of 700 percent in less than 20 years. The special economic zones were the focal point for both exports and FDI, particularly in the 1990s: by the end of that decade, enterprises with foreign investments accounted for over 40 percent of total exports.

To take advantage of the spread of the "new economy," the PRC has recently made rapid strides in the development and spread of fiber optic technology to increase telecommunications capacity. Both fixed and mobile line capacity has ballooned in the past decade from virtually nothing to about 15 lines per 100 inhabitants, higher than in any DMC apart from the NIEs and Malaysia.

India. The country followed a strategy of growth controlled and directed by the Government for most of the period from independence in 1947 until the beginning of the 1990s. This strategy focused on control of the economy through four complementary policies: extensive regulation of international trade and investment, control of key sectors of production, central control of domestic investment, and an elaborate system of licensing and regulation.

In pursuit of an import-substitution strategy, the Government introduced regulations to control foreign exchange transactions and imports, with the former allocated according to a priority list. Debt repayments received the highest priority, followed by capital goods, raw materials, and lastly, consumer goods, which were rarely approved. Policies toward foreign investment depended upon the ability to earn foreign exchange and the Government's attitude to the role that the foreign investment could play. Between 1957 and 1970, joint ventures were encouraged but the first oil shock and a balance-of-payments crisis resulted in a reversal of policy. After the second oil price shock of the late 1970s, the policy was reversed again.

To control key sectors of the economy, the Government nationalized several industries including commercial banks, life insurance companies, and large firms in processing and manufacturing fertilizer, mining, chemicals, steel, and oil. By the 1980s, the Government owned nearly half the country's industrial assets. The returns were low and efficiency poor. Because the financial sector was owned by the state and foreign capital investment was controlled, the Government had a virtual lock on how investment was allocated in the economy.

The Government controlled virtually all business activity (both entry and exit) through licenses as well as many prices. This regulatory control extended to all private firms as well as the public sector. The control of production capacity was introduced to prevent duplication and reduce "unnecessary competition," but tended to protect inefficient firms.

Industrial policy throughout this period pushed development toward more capital-intensive industries and away from the economy's comparative advantage in labor-intensive products, even though many incentives for small businesses were on the books. The end result of this bureaucratic network of subsidies, taxes, prohibitions, and controls was a highly inefficient and cumbersome economic system that grew slowly at 3 percent per annum, without much competition or new technology. Isolated from the global economy, India produced the same products year after year at high costs. By the beginning of the 1990s, India had been left far behind in nearly every respect by the NIEs and the countries of Southeast Asia.

In the 1990s, the worsening balance-of-payments crisis forced the Indian Government to reconsider its policy stance. Considerable progress was made in overhauling foreign trade and investment regulations, in reducing state control of industry, in liberalizing the financial sector, in freeing up investment decisions, and in eliminating many regulations on capacity creation and import licensing. The rupee was devalued and made fully convertible on the current account in 1991. Most import licenses were eliminated and tariffs were lowered and simplified. The rules for approving FDI were revamped and the ceiling on foreign ownership removed. The Government also made a concerted effort to reduce the role of the public sector in the economy, including opening up some sectors to the private sector, selling government assets, and closing loss-incurring businesses. Capacity licensing was significantly reduced and the banking system

was opened up to foreign ownership and entry. Interest rates were partially deregulated.

There was, and continues to be, debate about the nature of reforms and, in some political quarters, there is opposition to them. Despite these difficulties, the ongoing reforms have had a significant effect on those sectors of the economy where openness and competition have been most apparent. Economic growth accelerated, particularly since 1996, to 7 percent by the end of the 1990s. FDI has flowed in, total trade as a proportion of GDP has increased to nearly 20 percent, the economy is more open, and portfolio investment has increased. Finally, the ICT sector, especially software exports, has become a showpiece for the reform effort as many new companies have been listed on stock exchanges both at home and abroad.

Many areas remain where the reforms have been less effective or have not been implemented at all. Disputes have arisen regarding FDI, including the validity of contracts and property rights. Approval procedures have kept FDI from flowing into smaller and potentially more dynamic enterprises. Nevertheless, India has made significant strides toward opening up the economy.

International Trade Trends

As more DMCs adopted an export-oriented growth strategy, world trade accelerated as did trade among DMCs. Figure 3.2 compares the shares of exports to DMCs from selected countries in 1985 and 1999. In both Hong Kong, China and Taipei,China, trade with the PRC increased while the PRC's trade with the region fell as OECD markets became more important. Korea began to export more manufactured goods such as automobiles to the rest of Asia. For Singapore, trade with Indonesia and Malaysia, particularly in electrical products became increasingly important. In India, the opening up of the economy in the 1990s helped the country integrate more with its Asian neighbors. In Indonesia, the increased trade within the region has been in exports of primary materials—particularly oil—and of labor-intensive manufactures.

Interestingly, at the same time that trade among DMCs was increasing, with few exceptions the share of exports to Japan decreased, sometimes quite substantially (see Figure 3.3). For Indonesia and Malaysia, this represents a decline in primary exports such as oil, rubber, and palm oil. For the PRC, Korea, and Philippines, it probably reflects the fact that during the 1990s the Japanese economy, and hence its demand for imports, grew more slowly than the US economy, which became a more important export market for many DMCs during the long US expansion of the 1990s.

Capital Movements

As they adopted more liberal trade policies, many DMCs opened their economies to financial capital flows. Referring to

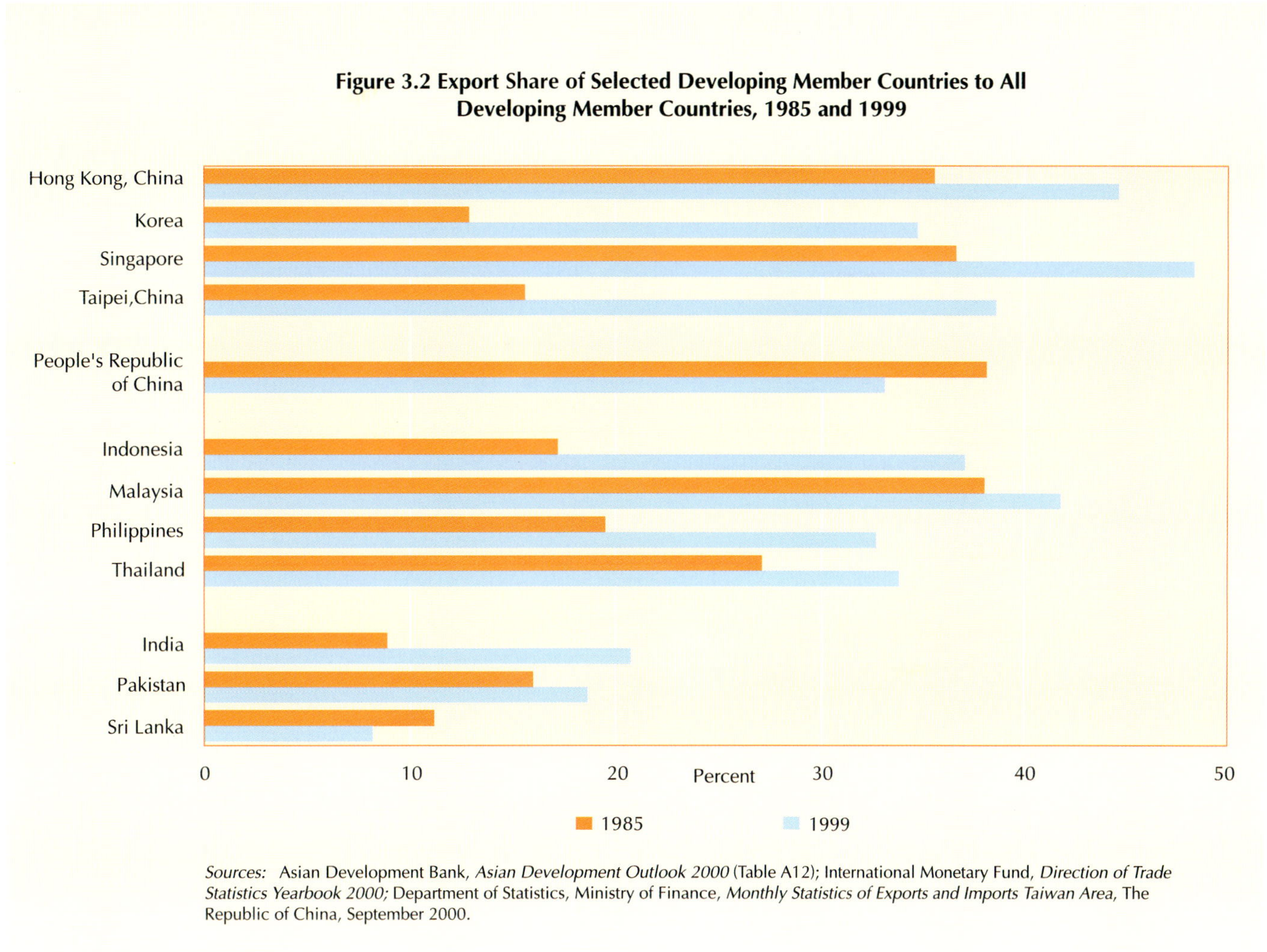

Figure 3.2 Export Share of Selected Developing Member Countries to All Developing Member Countries, 1985 and 1999

Sources: Asian Development Bank, *Asian Development Outlook 2000* (Table A12); International Monetary Fund, *Direction of Trade Statistics Yearbook 2000;* Department of Statistics, Ministry of Finance, *Monthly Statistics of Exports and Imports Taiwan Area*, The Republic of China, September 2000.

Figure 3.1, inflows accelerated throughout the first part of the 1990s, nearly tripling between 1990 and 1997. Between 1997 and 1999, however, there was a sharp reversal in capital inflows to Asia as a result of the financial crisis—from inflows of $188 billion in 1996 to outflows of $125 billion in 1998 as portfolio and other investment inflows turned sharply negative. Only FDI inflows remained positive in 1998, continuing to grow, particularly to the NIEs.

Until the financial crisis, the PRC managed to attract the bulk of FDI to the Asian region. Total FDI inflows to the PRC surged more than 10-fold between 1990 and 1998 and its share of total regional FDI inflows rose from 20 percent to over 50 percent. However, other countries were also able to build up FDI quite rapidly. FDI inflows nearly doubled in the NIEs and more than doubled in Southeast Asia between 1990 and 1997. FDI inflows increased quite rapidly in South Asia, albeit from a low base. Portfolio and other investment was much more volatile than FDI, reacting more dramatically to the financial crisis.

Other investment, mostly bank loans, reversed from an inflow of $37 billion in 1996 in Southeast Asia to an outflow of $19 billion in 1997 and further to an outflow of $28 billion in 1998. In the NIEs, the reversal came a year later, from inflows of $40 billion in 1997 to outflows of nearly $30 billion in 1998. In the PRC, the reversal was more modest—from an inflow of about $20 billion to an outflow of $9 billion between 1997 and 1998.

Overall, within Asia there has been greater financial integration over time while the pattern of financial integration has followed the pattern of trade. Generally, dollar-denominated asset markets have shown significant growth, particularly in Hong Kong, China; and Singapore, while financial integration has grown among PRC; Hong Kong, China; and Taipei,China. Furthermore, with greater financial liberalization, many more international and regional banks and financial institutions are competing for business throughout Asia.

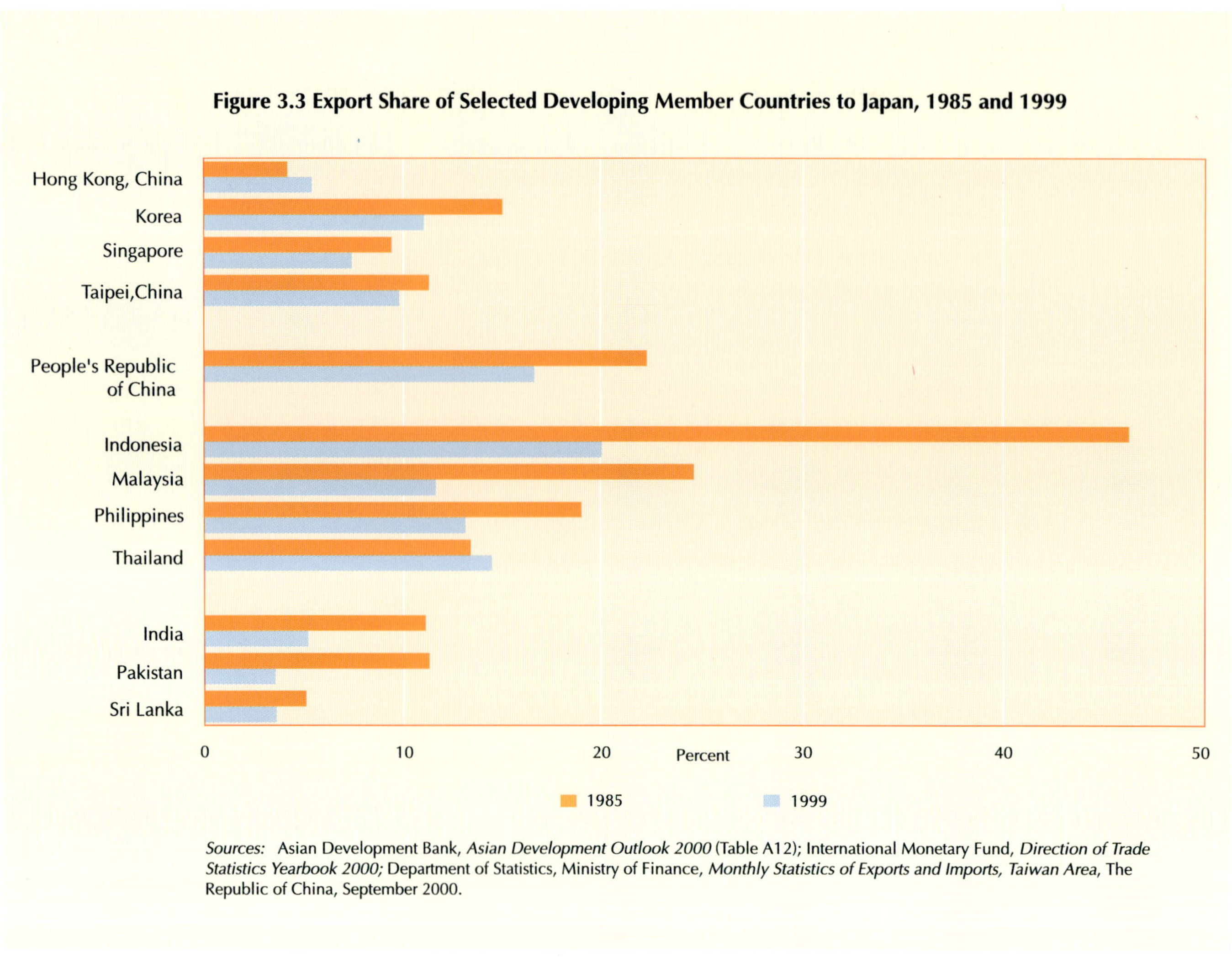

Sources: Asian Development Bank, *Asian Development Outlook 2000* (Table A12); International Monetary Fund, *Direction of Trade Statistics Yearbook 2000;* Department of Statistics, Ministry of Finance, *Monthly Statistics of Exports and Imports, Taiwan Area,* The Republic of China, September 2000.

Labor Movements

DMCs have experienced a trend toward integration on many levels, including labor markets. Although migration trends are harder to gauge, since labor movements are often unrecorded, the broad pattern is clear.

Richer Asian countries that grew rapidly in the 1980s and 1990s now have low levels of unemployment and are experiencing a growing need for a variety of skills that are in short supply among the domestic labor force. While the movement of unskilled labor has received wide publicity, there is also a strong flow of immigrants in some skilled and professional occupations. The main recipients of this new wave of migration have been Japan; Singapore; and Taipei,China; and more recently, Malaysia and Thailand. Japan and Taipei,China have attracted labor from all over Asia while Singapore has experienced a large volume of migration from Malaysia.

Some countries have been both significant importers and exporters of labor. For a few years before the Asian financial crisis, Thailand was importing labor from Myanmar, Viet Nam, and to a lesser extent Cambodia and the Lao PDR. Yet it also sent many migrants to the Middle East. Malaysia has been importing labor from Indonesia and sending migrants to Singapore.

Cambodia, Indonesia, Lao PDR, Philippines, and Viet Nam have higher levels of unemployment and somewhat lower standards of living than the NIEs and the rest of Southeast Asia. Thus, these countries have been the major suppliers of migrants to the rest of the region. In the case of the Philippines, facility with the English language has allowed migrants to move to many different countries.

Recently, with the advent and spread of the Internet and the new economy, it is jobs that are beginning to move in search of labor rather than the reverse. Using advanced telecommunica-

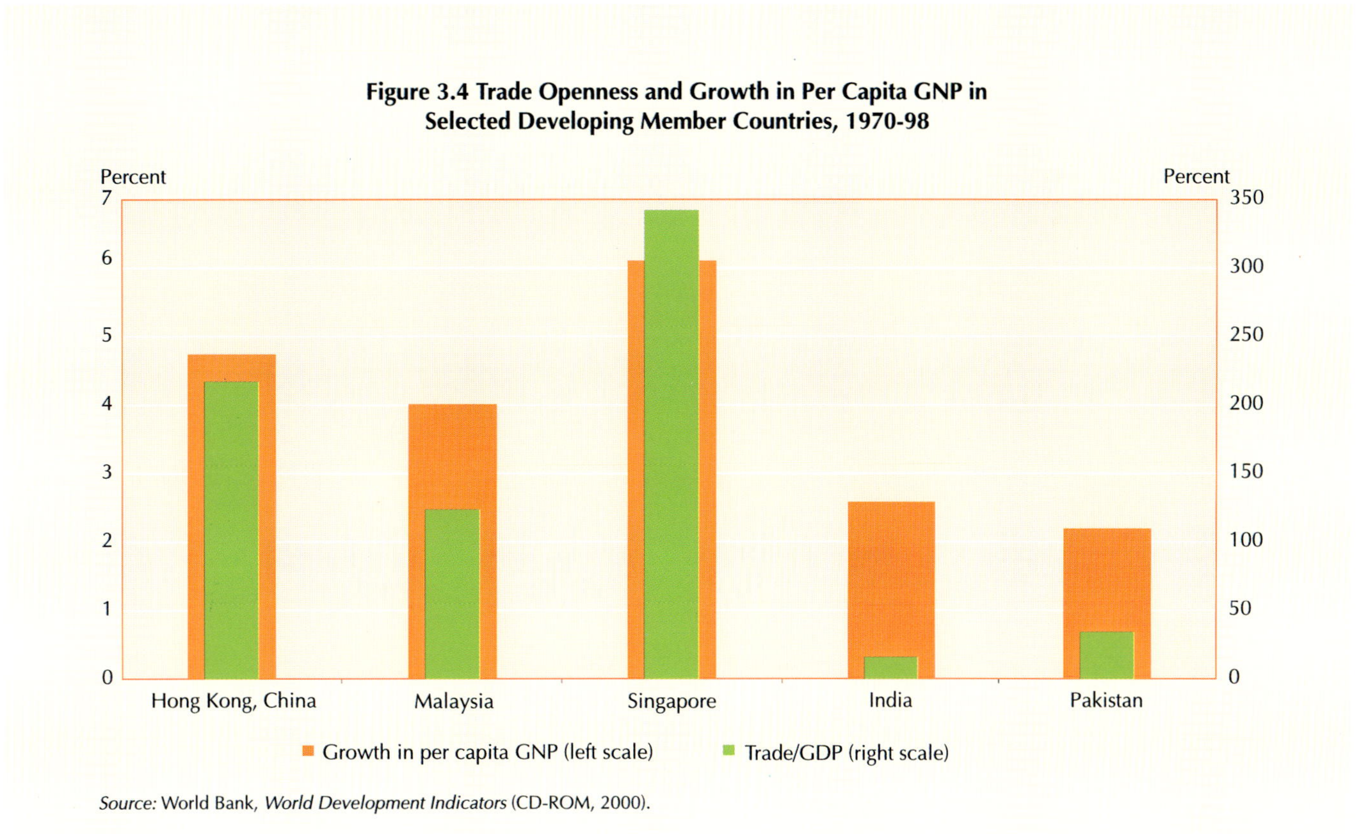

Figure 3.4 Trade Openness and Growth in Per Capita GNP in Selected Developing Member Countries, 1970-98

Source: World Bank, *World Development Indicators* (CD-ROM, 2000).

tions technology, many tasks can be easily and efficiently outsourced to developing countries. Some examples include data entry, software programming and development, Internet website development, computer help lines, and some accounting functions. This has resulted in an increase in services income to Asia.

The Pacific DMCs have witnessed substantial migration to New Zealand and Australia from some of the closer islands including the Cook Islands and Tonga, and to the US from Samoa, Marshall Islands, and Federated States of Micronesia. This migration is general in nature and is the result of slow growth in job opportunities in the domestic market and of pressure from rapid population growth.

Globalization and Poverty

In this section, we have discussed Asia's growth experience and globalization. Economic theory and evidence support the proposition that a strategy of openness leads to high rates of economic growth and poverty reduction. It is posited that a reduction of barriers to trade tends to increase the demand for relatively abundant factors of production. In the case of Asia, these have been initially unskilled and semiskilled laborers, i.e., those most likely to be poor. Evidence to support this proposition—that openness generally reduces poverty—is presented in two stages. As Figure 3.4 demonstrates for selected DMCs, countries that are more open to trade tend to enjoy higher rates of growth. Numerous studies support this result, including Sachs and Warner (1995), OECD (1998), and Gwartney and Lawson (2000). Next, as Figure 3.5 shows, there is a strong negative relationship between growth in the incidence of poverty and the rate of long-run economic growth. This relationship is exemplified by the NIEs and Southeast Asian countries, where the development of outward-looking, export-oriented industries resulted in rapid income growth and a reduction in poverty during the 1980s and 1990s. In these two groups of economies, incomes grew at an average rate of over 6 percent between 1987 and 1998 while the poverty rate (the percent of the population with an income below $1 per day) declined from 23 percent to 9.6 percent over the same period (World Bank 2001, IMF 2000). The implication is that globalization, when accompanied by appropriate domestic policies, can promote poverty reduction. However, as will be discussed in the section *Policies for Adapting to Globalization*, globalization can increase economic volatility, to which the poor are more vulnerable.

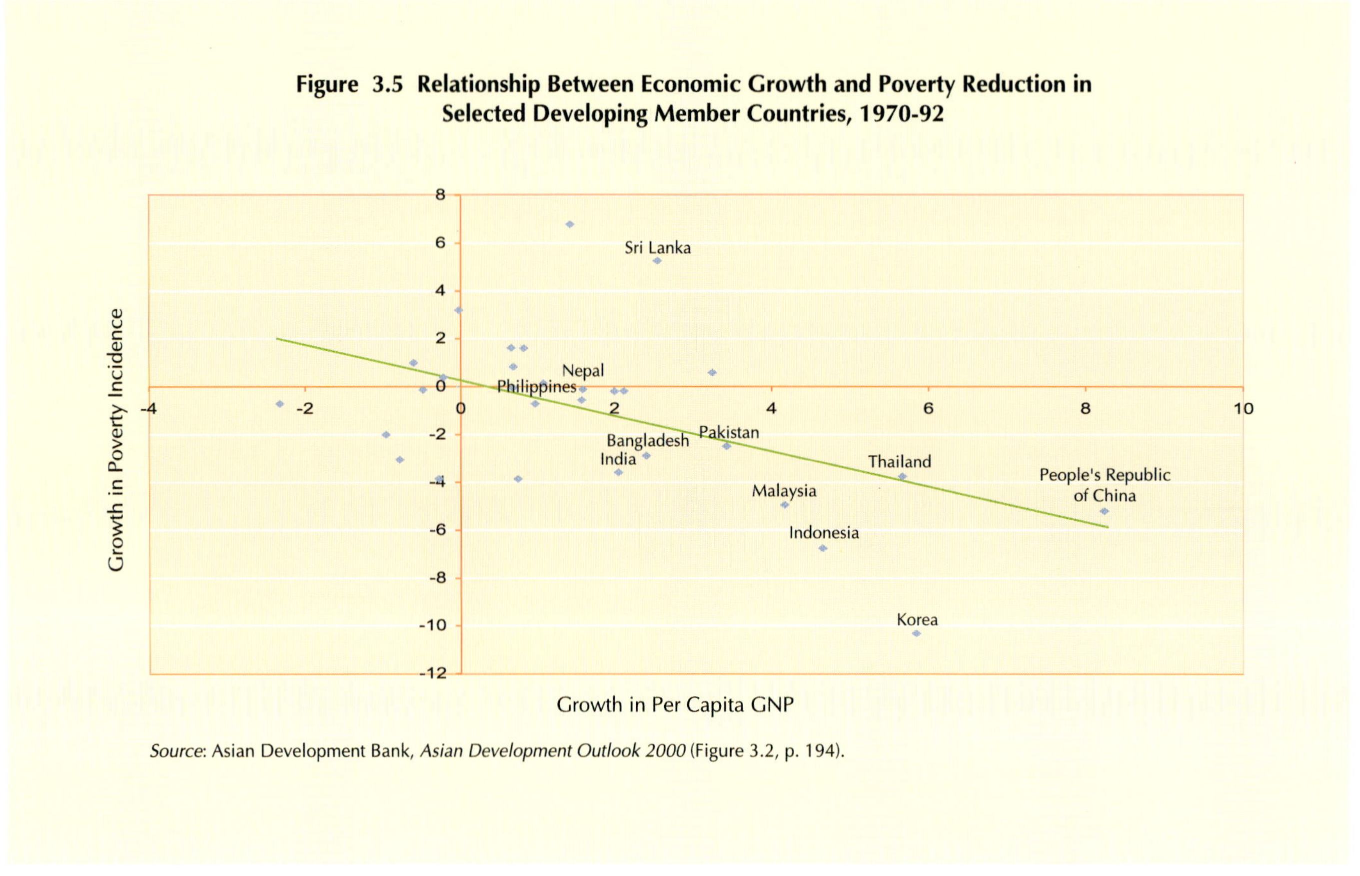

Figure 3.5 Relationship Between Economic Growth and Poverty Reduction in Selected Developing Member Countries, 1970-92

Source: Asian Development Bank, *Asian Development Outlook 2000* (Figure 3.2, p. 194).

POLICIES FOR ADAPTING TO GLOBALIZATION

The preceding section showed how some Asian countries achieved substantial progress in economic development and poverty reduction with variants of the basic strategy of external sector liberalization, high savings and investment rates, and technology transfer from industrial countries. However, even as some Asian countries approach the world technological frontier, a new economy is emerging. Moreover, national policymakers are increasingly concerned about the possible risks of globalization. Indeed, they must continue to improve their understanding and appreciation of the potential benefits as well as the challenges that globalization presents.

This section first looks at how policymakers can maximize the benefits of globalization through dynamic management of the national system of economic learning and by adapting to the economic realities of the new economy. Next, it considers how to minimize risks by managing the volatility that results from a more integrated global economy, and by protecting the most vulnerable groups of society from them.

Maximizing Benefits

Managing Economic Learning

Each country, either implicitly or explicitly, has a network of policies and institutions in place to manage innovation or economic learning.[4] This network is the public and private institutional framework used to support R&D-led and market-mediated efforts to create, absorb, and adapt new technology for commercial use. International comparisons emphasize the diversity of such networks even within Asia (see e.g., Mowery and Oxley 1995). There are, however, sufficient similarities among the systems within the region to justify considering an "Asian approach" to development, innovation, and economic learning.

This Asian approach, in its early stages of development, was designed to bring in technologies from outside the region (emulation or imitation) rather than develop new technologies (innovation). This made sense for Asian economies that were relatively late to develop and could take rapid strides simply by importing and assimilating foreign technologies. Thus many countries emulated the 1950s Japanese Ministry of Economy, Trade and Industry "METI-model" of industry creation. Governments sought to promote—through techniques such as initial subsidies and cooperative industrial policies—industries thought to have export potential based on production cost advantages and the adaptability of foreign technology. There was no need to create technologies from scratch when technologies used abroad could be acquired and profitably exploited more quickly. Box 3.2 describes the stages of the development process through which these latecomers to particular industries that were already established in industrial countries overcame the technological barriers to entry.

But the longer the Asian rates of growth have continued to outstrip those in the US, Europe, and Japan, the closer DMCs have drawn to the technological frontier. This has important implications. As the frontier is approached, the opportunities for rapid progress through emulation diminish and the ability to innovate becomes increasingly important (Krugman 1985). Put another way, as convergence proceeds, growth responds less to

capital formation and more to R&D and other sources of productivity advance. Yet the ability to adapt distant technologies to produce goods for distant markets on its own will not necessarily facilitate the transformation to innovative systems. The production of new technologies tends to take place close to a firm's home base (Freeman 1995, Patel 1995) and technological spillovers, particularly from new ideas, weaken with distance (Keller 2000), perhaps because this new knowledge is not yet standardized or widely understood. Thus there is an apparent need to redesign the Asian approach to encourage innovation rather than emulation as countries close in on the technological frontier. Indeed, the Asian approach is already evolving in this direction. Yet because institutions inevitably exhibit inertia, Asian economic systems remain less well suited to nurturing the radical innovations needed if they are to remain near the frontier in a dynamic, global economy. This will become more apparent through a brief review of traditional channels for technology acquisition and government policies used to support the Asian modality of economic learning and export promotion.

Box 3.2 Stages of Innovation

In the industrial countries, a new industry is usually born through a major technological innovation, and passes through a turbulent period of standardization and growth before it matures, perhaps even dying out as it is supplanted by a new technology. The process by which Japan, the NIEs, and some of the Southeast Asian countries such as Malaysia and Thailand initiated industrial development is a variation of this life cycle. Several authors have stylized this process. Matthews and Cho (2000) describe four stages:

Preparation. The first stage is preparation, when a skill base of engineers and scientists is developed. This can be achieved through domestic or overseas education, and may involve specialized training. Foreign experts can temporarily augment the domestic skill base while the Government initiates training programs. This stage also involves the establishment of a local R&D base (perhaps regional) including local institute and overseas research links, to create technical absorptive capacity. For example, in Korea, the Advanced Institute of Science and Technology and other government-funded institutes recruited scientists and engineers trained overseas to facilitate technology transfer and to promote local R&D.

Seeding. Seeding involves the initial acquisition of technology through a variety of channels, including technological licensing and associated training, joint ventures, technological consortia, subcontracting, collaborative R&D, and mergers with technology-based smaller firms. Most Asian economies adopted several of these methods. For example, in Taipei,China, licensing was more prevalent while in Singapore joint ventures with multinationals were more popular.

Propagation. In this stage, a group of successful exporters arises. Appropriate infrastructure has to be developed to support these firms so that they can compete internationally. This includes physical infrastructure to transport raw materials and finished products and telecommunications hardware and software. It often also involves public sector research agencies, trade associations, and regulatory authorities. In the electronics industry these include the Taiwan Semiconductor Industry Association in Taipei,China and the Institute of Microelectronics Centre for Wireless Communications in Singapore. Thus, a dynamic industrial complex is created that can survive and prosper in an ever-changing and challenging international competitive environment.

Sustainability. To achieve sustainability in international markets, firms have had the support of the Government and of each other through trade associations and the development of linkages with overseas firms for marketing and distribution. This includes possible assistance in product development, underwriting of R&D, helping to develop domestic subcontracting, guidance on moves into own-brand production based on foreign technology, and assisting in product development. In the case of Korea, the Government prodded the semiconductor industry after it had become well established in conventional semiconductor technology. In the case of Taipei,China, the authorities helped develop new products and processes and then improved and adapted these technologies and diffused them to the private sector, in some cases by even creating their own company.

Source: Matthews and Cho (2000, pp. 91-92).

Channels. Channels for the acquisition of technology include capital goods imports, licensing arrangements, joint ventures, FDI, and outsourcing. Of these, capital goods imports, licensing, and joint ventures have long been the staples of the Asian approach. New technologies are usually embodied in new capital goods, and importing such equipment allows a country to immediately benefit from foreign technological advances and also opens up opportunities for learning through reverse engineering. The use of this mode of technology acquisition is evident from the fact that the NIEs have historically had a higher propensity to import capital goods in comparison to other developing economies.

The scattered data available on licensing arrangements suggest substantial reliance on this channel in some countries as a complement to the import of capital goods. OECD (1992) reports that Korean spending on licenses for technology grew 10-fold between 1982 and 1991. In developing national industries, Asian governments, with the notable exception of Singapore, historically preferred licensing or joint ventures that involve local management over standalone foreign operations, based on the belief that the former options offer greater scope for technology transfer while the latter allows the multinational corporation too much control.[5] However, relative to capital goods imports and licensing, FDI has the advantage that it is a channel for transferring managerial and technical expertise, which comes bundled with foreign plant and equipment as well as marketing and distribution networks. Such expertise is particularly valuable when the importing country is attempting to implement relatively sophisticated foreign technologies with a high knowledge component. The technologies transferred through wholly owned foreign projects tend to be newer and closer to the technological frontier than those associated with joint ventures and licensing agreements.

Finally, in sectors where economies of scale are smaller and foreign managerial and technical expertise is less essential, multinational corporations frequently outsource elements of the production process and local firms can thus acquire foreign technologies via contract manufacturing and assembly operations. Such operations are a source of "learning by doing". They become increasingly attractive relative to inviting in multinational corporations in a world where ICT allows domestic production to be networked with foreign production.[6] Most of the economies in Southeast Asia, as well as PRC; Hong Kong, China; and Taipei,China have become part of such production networks in the past decade.

Table 3.4 shows the evolution of these different sources in the Korean case. The special importance of capital goods imports as a source of technology transfer to Korea is apparent throughout the period. Also evident, however, is the economy's reliance on FDI in the early to mid-1970s. Thereafter, however, the importance of FDI declines relative to total flows, as policy sought to emphasize different channels for technology transfer and to protect indigenous producers from multilateral compe-

tition. In its place, licensing as a source of technology transfer was promoted. Comparable figures for Taipei,China would highlight that economy's greater reliance on licensing, while those for Malaysia and Singapore would show the importance of FDI by multinationals.

Policies. Policies have been used to foster each of these channels of technology transfer. In addition to the application of uniform tariff rates that do not discriminate against capital goods, Asian governments have pursued policies designed to maximize the knowledge spillovers associated with licensing, FDI, capital goods imports, and outsourcing, and have often required licensing agreements as a condition for foreign multinationals to establish operations locally. This encouraged domestic firms to bundle imports of heavy electronic machinery with licenses to produce copies of the equipment, and supported entry by domestic producers into the production of this equipment (Ozawa 1985). Thus, Korea both protected domestic producers and placed pressure on foreign joint venture partners in the 1970s to withdraw and leave the field to indigenous firms (Matthews and Cho 2000).

Macroeconomic, financial, and trade policies can also be regarded as an important part of the Asian approach. Stable monetary and fiscal policies, complemented by favorable demographics, supported high and rising savings rates. Much of these savings were channeled through government-controlled banking (and postal savings) systems that provided concessionary credit to firms in technologically progressive sectors. More controversially, controls on financial capital exports were used by Japan; Korea; and Taipei,China early on to ensure that domestic savings, once mobilized, supported domestic capital formation, while the PRC continues to do so.[7] Where economies of scale were important, and where multidivisional structure was seen as necessary to capture technological spillovers, the Korean Government provided preferential credit for the growth of *chaebol*. Large economies of scale (falling unit costs as the scale of production increases) or dynamic economies of scale (falling unit costs as the firm gains experience through learning by doing) characterize leading-edge technologies (e.g., integrated steel production in the 1970s and 1980s, semiconductor manufacture in the 1990s). Export promotion thus provided the dual benefits of allowing firms to overcome the constraints imposed by limited domestic markets, while exposing them to the discipline of foreign competition. The significance of all these policies is that they helped the small economies turn globalization to their advantage.

Asian countries are not the only ones to pursue policies to encourage the transfer of advanced technologies from abroad and to facilitate their dissemination, though some (particularly the PRC, the NIEs, and Southeast Asia) have arguably had more success in globalizing their economies than countries in other late-developing regions. Nelson (1992) and Matthews and Cho (2000) attribute the superior

Table 3.4 Channels of Technology Leverage in All Industries in Korea, 1962-91
($ million)

	1962–66	1967–71	1972–76	1977–81	1982–86	1987–91
Foreign direct investment	47	219	879	721	1,768	5,636
Licensing	1	16	97	451	1,185	4,359
Technology consultants	0	17	18	55	332	1,348
Capital goods imports	316	2,541	8,841	27,928	44,705	52,188
Total	364	2,793	9,835	29,205	47,990	63,498

Source: Based on Hong (1994), Table 7.

performance of the Asian model of economic learning to three factors.

First, the more successful Asian economies emphasized the importance of having the skilled labor force needed to understand the principles underlying foreign technologies, which facilitates the adoption of foreign techniques by domestic producers and allows substitutes for foreign capital goods to be produced at home with a relatively short lag.[8] Hong Kong, China; Singapore; and Taipei,China have larger shares of postsecondary students enrolled in scientific and engineering fields than most other developing economies and encourage their best students to acquire advanced training abroad. One of Singapore's first initiatives to support its efforts to attract foreign high-technology firms was to train a cadre of "knowledge workers" (Matthews and Cho 2000). Korea and Taipei,China established publicly funded advanced research institutes staffed by scientists and engineers trained in foreign universities, encouraging them to establish links with commercial firms. Such initiatives have likely enhanced domestic absorptive capacity for adopting and adapting foreign technology.

Second, Nelson, as well as Matthews and Cho, argue that the Asian model was successful because it was combined with an emphasis on export promotion. This meant that domestic firms were subject to relatively intense competition and this applied pressure on them to emulate best practice, specifically the best-practice techniques of their competitors—namely, foreign-owned and operated firms.

The third argument is that the Asian approach was successful because restraints on entry and other policy interventions were guided by well-defined rules and because technocrats enjoyed the bureaucratic autonomy necessary to avoid "capture" by domestic industry (World Bank 1993). Bureaucrats are protected by civil service systems that ensure adequate compensation, recruitment, and promotion based on merit (i.e., exams), and strictly enforced dismissal policies. Japan, Korea, and Singapore are the paradigmatic cases. In some cases, early land reform and support for small and medium-scale industries were similarly important for preventing the emergence of large interest groups positioned to capture the policy-making process.

The second and third points are widely debated. The intensity of domestic competition to which producers in Asia's rapidly industrializing economies were exposed is debatable. Incumbent firms that enjoyed protection from both foreign competitors and potential domestic entrants may have, in some instances, devoted more energy to lobbying the Government against granting licenses to new entrants than to raising productivity. Moreover, domestic firms producing nontraded goods were not subject to as much competition as firms producing for export. The third argument became controversial as a result of the Asian financial crisis. Commentators, who once wrote approvingly of "bureaucratic autonomy," now decry "crony capitalism." Possibly, problems of capture have intensified with time. The longer industrial targeting policies are pursued, the more intimate the connections between the policymakers and the policy beneficiaries. In addition, as the economy becomes more technically sophisticated, monitoring the performance of the enterprises receiving preferential treatment becomes more difficult for the bureaucrats.

Adapting to Globalization. Adapting to globalization is an ongoing process. The argument that the policies of bureaucratic direction that worked well at an earlier stage of Asia's technological development will work less well today is a specific illustration of a more general point: economic learning is dynamic—its structure and operation vary over time. In their early stages of industrial development, Asian economies, particularly the NIEs, relied heavily on arm's-length transactions—technology licensing and purchase of foreign capital goods—and less on FDI, joint ventures, and outsourcing.

Adopting licensed technologies arguably requires more limited adaptations of domestic economic structure than FDI and joint ventures, which will be attractive to foreign firms only if the economy is comprehensively restructured. Licensing also tends to be a source of less sophisticated technologies.[9] Thus, as economies approach the technological frontier, they increasingly rely on FDI as a source of foreign technology. It is notable that Southeast Asia has rejected the arm's-length approach and welcomed FDI in the 1990s. Because joint ventures also tend to transfer older and less sophisticated technologies than other forms of FDI (Smarzynska 1999), there is a similar tendency to move away from them as a country approaches the technological frontier. Economic evolution is also reflected in the growing R&D intensity of domestic firms and thus the gradual shift from emulation to innovation.

Although economic systems tend to evolve as economies mature, the policies and institutions developed for and appropriate to earlier stages of economic development tend to get locked in, posing obstacles to further development. Thus, if small firms are disproportionately responsible for the development of new technologies as numerous studies suggest (Acs and Audretsch 1987, 1990), industrial policies conducive to the growth of large conglomerates, such as those of Korea, will eventually become obstacles to innovation. If the development of new technologies requires venture capital allocated through securities markets, then the earlier forms of capital allocation—through intimate banking relationships that extend funding in large chunks to preferred customers with established technologies—will inhibit innovation.

Moreover, as globalization proceeds, economic learning and evolution as described may no longer be available to latecomers. The multinational corporations that are the sources of advanced technologies are inclined to license latecomers only when prevented from setting up their own operations in foreign markets. As more developing-country markets are thrown open to FDI, it becomes harder for individual governments to insist on licensing as an alternative. This is evident in the greater tendency for Singapore and Hong Kong, China and the countries of Southeast Asia to rely on FDI and to fit into modularized production networks involving a variety of outsourcing arrangements. Insofar as firms can outsource the production of components internationally, governments will find it more difficult to promote the transfer of advanced technologies by requiring the entire production process to be undertaken in their country.

Globalization makes it more difficult for Asian economies to approach the technological frontier by importing capital goods, luring FDI, and licensing foreign technologies. If it is correct that these economies, as they reach more advanced stages of technical development, must in any case rely more heavily on indigenous technical change, then the priority system of incentives will have to be reordered. More flexible, smaller firms and outsourcing arrangements will have to be further developed. Securities markets will have to grow. Governments' command over resources and technocrats' efforts to control their allocation will have to be reduced.

This is not to say that the Asian approach will become indistinguishable from that of its counterparts elsewhere. On the contrary, certain features of the Asian approach such as sound macroeconomic management, fiscal discipline, and maintenance of a low-inflation environment, are eminently well suited to a globalized, technically fluid world. These are strengths on which the Asian approach in the 21st century can build. Export orientation and the emphasis on export competitiveness remain admirable characteristics of economic systems faced with rapidly changing technologies and the globalization of production. Governments should still encourage and actively support collaboration between universities, technical institutes, and private-sector firms, as well as promote the commercialization of new technologies.

That said, the Asian approach has to be reoriented and those who do this quickly will be the first to reap the benefits. This will require the same concerted efforts that Asian economies employed to initiate industrialization and technology transfer from the West after the Second World War. The role of government in this process also needs to be reconsidered, given the desirability of a flexible and responsive private sector: this role will likely be to support the development of human resources, including engineers, scientists, and ICT and financial sector professionals.

Exploiting the New Economy

In the past 20 years, as the Asian approach allowed economic convergence of DMCs toward the economic structures prevailing in industrial countries, these industrial economies—and, indeed, the world economy—underwent a rapid transformation. The previous section *Asian Growth and Globalization Experience* reviewed evidence of the strong trend toward globalization: increased international trade in final products, intermediate and capital goods, and services; larger flows of financial capital, including commercial loans, FDI, and portfolio investment; and, to a lesser extent because substantial barriers to migration still exist, greater labor mobility.

An indication of the scope of this transformation is that economists estimate that more than half the world's total output of goods and services is now contestable (meaning that producers must keep prices competitive to avoid losing market share to potential entrants). This process of globalization, itself unleashed by policies of economic liberalization and technological breakthroughs in ICT, is reinforcing the huge impact of those ICT forces reshaping the economic landscape into the new economy, (which is also known as the "information economy," or the "knowledge-based economy"). This section reviews in more detail the characteristics of the ICT revolution, its impact on economic performance, and the implications for DMCs.

ICT Revolution. The ICT revolution is multifaceted. One aspect is the rapid development of computing hardware and software, including much greater power, smaller size, and lower prices. This triggered the rapid spread of powerful computers to offices and to nonpoor households around the world (although not to the poor, giving rise to the term "digital divide"). A second aspect is the development of high-speed transmission of information by relay stations, satellite, and fiber optic cables. This spurred massive public and private investment to upgrade information systems. A third aspect is the digitization of information—not only words and data but sound and video as well, generating new business applications such as computer-aided design (CAD) or practices such as teleworking. These technological advances resulted in an explosion in the use of fax machines, cellular phones, and the Internet, creating a services sector specializing in the provision and analysis of information that is growing much faster than the rest of the economy.

The US is the leading exponent of these trends, as can be seen in labor-force and value-added statistics. The high-technology share of industrial value added in manufacturing in the US rose to over 25 percent in the late 1990s from 18 percent in 1970, while its share in GDP also increased. The services sector has grown at the expense of manufacturing as computer programmers, managers, and office workers have replaced, for example, riveters, forklift operators, and other manufacturing workers. Managerial and professional jobs have risen as a share of total employment (22 percent of the workforce in 1979 compared with nearly 30 percent in 2000), while the number of people employed in occupations requiring lower skills has fallen. In 1960, there were fewer than 5,000 computer programmers, 0.1 percent of the workforce; by 2000, their number had grown to over 1.3 million, almost 1.0 percent of the workforce.

The growth of ICT, computers, and the Internet has transformed the face of the US economy and its relationship to other economies. Housing and automobiles were the driving force behind economic growth for many years. Slowly they are being supplanted by ICT, which now accounts for about one third of total US GDP growth each year. Because of enormous gains in productivity in computers, the costs of ICT (adjusted for quality) have fallen significantly. This contributed to price stability, despite the fact that until recently the US economy has been in the longest peacetime expansion in its history. Some economic historians equate this trend with the technological breakthroughs that fueled the development of the railroads in the 19th century or of the automobile in the 20th century.

In that sense, ICT is a technology that transcends its own particular industry, spilling over into the entire economy, increasing productivity, and changing the way businesses operate. The new economy has brought with it a dramatic acceleration in innovation, an explosion of new products, shorter product cycles, greater competition, and improved business efficiency. There are more new firms being set up and more old firms going out of business. As part of the revolution in ICT, the world computer microchip market has grown at double digits

for many years and its share in GDP has also increased, even though chip prices have fallen substantially. This is particularly true in several DMCs for which semiconductors are an important export.

Combined with the growth of the Internet, ICT has the potential to reduce costs and increase efficiency (through Internet-based transactions) to such an extent that levels of sustainable growth may increase substantially. Retailing over the Internet, known as business to consumer (B2C) selling is slowly taking hold. Such firms as amazon.com, a large Internet book retailer, pioneered this retailing method, but many large traditional retailers now have websites.

B2C transactions are expected eventually to be dwarfed by business to business (B2B) Internet transactions, which should reduce the search costs for firms seeking least-cost and high-quality suppliers. However, despite such examples of earlier adoption, such as the agreement between General Motors and Ford to develop a joint parts network, firms have been slow to switch to reliance on the Internet for B2B transactions because of uncertainty over reliability. Relations with suppliers are often nurtured over long periods. Currently, only a small fraction of all B2B transactions takes place over the Internet. Nevertheless, the potential cost savings are tremendous even if only a few percent of B2B transactions shift to the Internet in the next few years.

ICT and Economic Performance. The impact of the ICT revolution on economic performance is difficult to quantify. Measuring the impact of ICT, computers, and the Internet is complicated because these three components are interrelated and because long time series to analyze the data are lacking. Since 1996, a sharp acceleration in the rate of growth in labor productivity has been seen in the US. In manufacturing, for example, the annual growth rate of labor productivity, as measured by output per hour, has steadily increased, ranging from 2.81 percent in 1996 to 6.14 percent in 1999. This is unusual. Historically, labor productivity tends to fall in recession and accelerate in the initial stages of recovery. The current surge in productivity is the first time in the postwar period that the surge has come when the economy has been in a sustained upswing in output growth. Some experts have suggested that the ICT revolution is responsible for this.

There is some controversy about these results. The International Monetary Fund (IMF), for example, suggests that the productivity surge is the result of a rebound from lower productivity earlier in the 1990s and that estimates of TFP do not show a significant increase in recent years. IMF also argues that the improved trade-off between inflation and unemployment may be the result of demographic shifts that have moved more of the workforce into middle age where unemployment is low, while the proportion of teenagers in the labor force, where unemployment is high, has shrunk (IMF 1999a). Other economists have confined their study to the direct impact of computers on output in sectors where they have been heavily utilized, such as ICT, banking, and some parts of manufacturing. While the impact of computers on productivity in these industries is estimated to be large, the contribution to total productivity is relatively small, both because these sectors are still quite small (though growing rapidly), and because productivity enhancement is less apparent in other sectors of the economy. Nevertheless, it is clear that the ICT revolution is having a significant impact on the pace and character of world development, creating a new economic development paradigm for DMCs.

DMCs and the New Economy. The extent to which DMCs are integrated into the new economy varies across countries. In the US, electronic data processing and interchange (the first stage of the information revolution) have penetrated all levels of the economy and the use of ICT in banking and finance as well as industry is widespread. More recently, the use of the Internet has blossomed and is being used for retail sales (B2C), purchases by businesses (B2B), and inventory and management purposes. The success of auction sites demonstrates the possibility of consumer to consumer (C2C) transactions. In Europe, the use of the Internet is not as widespread as in the US, but Europe is similarly well developed in the use of ICT for banking and finance and for certain accounting and management functions. Some DMCs are at par with the US and Europe in certain areas, such as Singapore and Hong Kong, China; and perhaps Taipei,China; and Korea.

In varying degrees, the NIEs, PRC, India, and the ASEAN-4 countries have experience in production of electronics exports in which the new economy best business practices of outsourcing and flexible production systems are already highly developed. These economies might be relatively well placed to take advantage of unfolding opportunities in the new economy, provided they can adapt their economic systems (as discussed in the previous section). Several possible trends can be identified.

First, growth of trade will create additional opportunities to develop export markets. The volume of world trade has grown faster than GDP for several decades as barriers to trade have fallen. More openness in trade and the flow of capital should facilitate the spread of the new economy to DMCs, particularly those where international trade has played a significant role in economic development.

Second, the ICT revolution could create opportunities for DMCs to export skill-intensive services. India, Philippines, and Singapore have already developed substantial software and data entry platforms in the past decade. In the future, this expertise could be extended to help bring these economies into a position where they can enter the knowledge and information aspects of the new economy more fully.

Third, growth of the Internet may create a more level playing field. The capacity of poorer countries to market retail products and to bid for subcontracting jobs in industrial countries may be enhanced by the spread of the Internet. However, the extent of this penetration will depend to a large extent on whether these countries can compete in this market by supplying quality products or inputs in a timely manner. The Internet has the capacity to cut search costs and improve economic efficiency, but only if it is embraced throughout the economy. If this occurs, successful new Internet-based companies will be able to take advantage of economies of scale in a globalized market.

Fourth, DMCs will receive greater payoffs from improving education and skills. The returns to education are generally thought to be quite high. The emphasis in the past has been on returns to women's education and the synergies that these investments have with health, fertility, population growth, and infant mortality. In the future there will also be high returns to investment in vocational and tertiary education in the fields of computer science (from data entry to advanced programming), software development, and the Internet. Already, private sector training in these occupations has expanded rapidly in India, Malaysia, Philippines, Singapore, and Thailand. This should be preferred to public education to minimize the waste of public resources since foreign companies often recruit ICT specialists, contributing further to an economy's brain drain. Yet it should be noted that the ICT revolution might reduce the tendency for highly skilled labor to emigrate. Since many ICT applications are not bound geographically, labor services can be provided from separate locations. Moreover, numerous ICT professionals have emigrated and then returned to their home countries to start up new companies, particularly in India.

Fifth, more opportunities to develop niche markets through foreign partnerships, outsourcing, and strategic alliances will appear as the ICT revolution allows increased modularization of product delivery. Internet B2B transactions should improve the efficiency of existing supply chains, lead to more outsourcing opportunities, and increase the importance of strategic alliances such as those developed in small and medium-sized enterprises in Taipei,China that allowed them to compete internationally. These enterprises have been able to take advantage of their marketing and distribution networks worldwide even while they have offloaded production lines in which they have lost comparative advantage to other economies, particularly the PRC where labor costs are cheaper. Hong Kong, China; and Singapore, in which the traditional entrepôt businesses are booming because of the increase in world trade, have been aggressively expanding their ICT infrastructure to improve their ability to take advantage of the Internet and globalization.

ICT Infrastructure. ICT infrastructure will be increasingly critical, in all the DMCs, to an economy's ability to capitalize on globalization. A case can be made for looking at the ICT (and related) sectors of the economy as an important special case for developing national policies with a sectoral focus. The sector is growing rapidly, provides an important linkage to the global economy and, from the experience of the US, has the potential to be a source of rapid productivity gains.

For the ICT sector in DMCs to flourish, several prerequisites must be met. First, ICT has to be supported by a vibrant telecommunications sector. This will require large expenditures in Southeast Asia and South Asia, to bring these subregions to par with the NIEs. It will also need a partnership between the public and private sectors as well as appropriate technological transfer from industrial countries and perhaps the NIEs. Education is also essential and it too involves a marriage between the public and private sectors. The public sector should be responsible for basic education and for the acquisition of computer literacy on a widespread basis, as well as upgrading science and mathematics training. The growth of the private sector is necessary to provide easy and economical access for students and others to ICT as well as to computer education. Policy support for private sector ICT development, including standards for assuring the compatibility of systems (hardware and software) is justified by the positive spillovers of ICT to the rest of the economy. Finally, intellectual property rights have to be safeguarded by strengthened laws on copyright and patent rights.

Minimizing the Risks

Volatility in a Globalizing World

Recent Asian experience suggests that globalization can be a source of macroeconomic volatility, which generally reduces economic welfare. The view holds that, as DMCs integrate into the global economy, they are increasingly exposed to external disturbances. For example, the slump in global semiconductor prices, an instance of an adverse terms-of-trade shock, is blamed for undermining the Korean economy and other countries in Southeast Asia in the run-up to the 1997/98 crisis (Goldstein 1998). And as markets become more globalized, economies become increasingly susceptible to contagious spillovers from national, regional, and global financial shocks. As an example of the size of these shocks, in the six quarters prior to the onset of the Asian financial crisis in July 1997, capital inflows into Indonesia, Korea, Philippines, and Thailand totaled $86.8 billion while in the subsequent six quarters there was an outflow of $77.9 billion.

That the PRC did not succumb to the financial crisis has been ascribed to the fact that it retained capital controls and consequently was not deeply integrated into global financial markets. More generally, Eichengreen et al. (1995) have shown that countries are more likely to be able to contain speculative pressure when they are not yet integrated into these markets. This is not to suggest that the costs of globalization swamp the benefits, but to emphasize the importance of developing institutions and pursuing policies aimed at limiting volatility and minimizing its adverse social consequences.

General Effects of Volatility. There is now ample evidence of the costs of macroeconomic volatility. Ramey and Ramey (1995) estimate that a unit increase in the standard deviation of the "innovation" in GDP reduces the rate of per capita GDP growth by one fifth of 1 percent per annum.[10] Easterly and Kraay (1999) produce similar results. Upon controlling for other determinants of the rate of GDP growth, the Inter-American Development Bank (IDB) (1995) finds that growth is negatively influenced by volatility in the terms of trade, the real exchange rate, monetary policy, and fiscal policy. Using data ending in 1992, IDB estimates that real GDP (measured in growth rates) was half again as volatile in the NIEs, Southeast Asia, and South Asia as in the advanced industrial countries, primarily because of volatility in domestic macroeconomic policies. However, IDB's estimates imply that this volatility reduced growth in the NIEs and Southeast Asia over the period 1960-1985 by only about a tenth of 1 percent a year, suggesting that the volatility was not particularly damaging to overall economic growth. There is also evidence that the variability of international capital flows played a prominent role in increasing volatility in Asian economies during the 1990s.

Effects of Volatility on Productivity and Investment. The negative association of volatility with growth reflects adverse impacts on productivity and investment. Productivity will suffer if unpredictable changes in relative prices lead firms to choose sub-optimal technologies. Countries where volatility is high also display relatively low investment rates, reflecting the reluctance of entrepreneurs to commit to projects when prices and macroeconomic conditions change unpredictably. While investment rates in the NIEs and Southeast Asia are quite high by international standards, recent empirical work suggests that they would have been still higher (by an additional two to three percentage points of GDP) if volatility had been as low as in the US, Europe, and Japan (see IDB 1995, Goldberg 1993, Kenen and Rodrik 1986).

The most damaging forms of volatility are financial crises. These crises are incompatible with growth: they lead to stop-go policies, interfere with the operation of the domestic financial system, cause distress to the corporate sector, and force governments to curtail public investment. According to Bordo and Eichengreen (2000), the typical post-1972 crisis cost the country in which it occurred a cumulative 9 percent of GDP—that is, more than one year's growth for several Asian countries that were growing at between 7 and 10 percent during the late 1980s and early 1990s. Different types of crises have different output effects: the estimates of these authors suggest output costs ranging from 3 percent for banking crises, to 7 percent for currency crises, to 15 percent for "twin" crises (i.e., those with both banking and currency components).

Crises have multiple causes, but one unquestionably important cause is financial fragility, which becomes increasingly important as capital flows increase. Because creditors will rationally hesitate to tie up their funds in a volatile macroeconomic environment, volatility encourages reliance on short-term debt, which heightens the fragility of financial systems. Creditors will similarly hesitate to invest in assets denominated in domestic currency when exchange rates are volatile. This is a "double mismatch problem". The balance sheets of domestic financial and nonfinancial firms display either a maturity mismatch (a combination of long-term assets and short-term liabilities) or a currency mismatch (a combination of assets denominated in domestic currency and liabilities denominated in foreign currency). This leaves domestic markets vulnerable to destabilization by sudden changes in financial conditions, such as the loss of investor confidence (as seen in the Asian financial crisis).

Effects of Volatility on Poverty and Social Indicators. Ample evidence now shows that volatility has undesirable consequences for the distribution of income, poverty, and educational attainment. The poor, unskilled, and uneducated are least able to protect themselves by hedging their incomes and diversifying their investments; it is not surprising that they should suffer disproportionately from volatility. Gavin and Hausmann (1995) find, in a cross-sectional study of countries, that the volatility of real GDP has a strong negative effect on the equality of income distribution. Other studies (e.g., Guitan 1995) have similarly found that countries with more volatile rates of inflation display higher levels of income inequality. Moreover, some evidence suggests that crises and the policy adjustments they entail are particularly bad for income distribution and that their unequalizing effects are especially pronounced in middle-income countries (the category into which many Asian economies fall—see Bourguignon et al. 1991).

Similar results are found for poverty rates. The poor and near poor tend to be employed in sectors and activities that suffer from volatility; and cuts in social spending in times of crisis fall disproportionately on their shoulders (Morley 1994). As noted above, households near the poverty line have the least savings, the worst collateral, and the most tenuous access to credit and insurance. Moreover, volatility aggravates poverty through its negative impact on growth. Ravallion (1997) estimates that the elasticity of poverty, as measured by the proportion of the population falling below the poverty line with respect to the growth of per capita income, lies between -1.5 and -3.5. Dollar (2000) obtains similar results for a larger sample of countries. Crises are an extreme case in point, in that the elasticity of poverty with respect to income rises sharply in crisis periods. In Indonesia in 1997/98, the rate of increase of poverty is estimated to have been 10 times the rate of decline in income and consumption. Poverty increased by 47.8 percent in Indonesia and by 13 percent in Thailand. In Korea, where most people live in cities, poverty rates doubled in urban areas. A simulation in Malaysia suggested a 36 percent rise in poverty.

The sharp increase in poverty in Korea is consistent with the surge in unemployment in that country. Korean labor markets are more formalized than those in the other crisis-affected Asian countries and wages are consequently less flexible. Whereas sharp falls in wages and the ability of the informal sector to absorb the unemployed softened the blow to employment in some of the other countries, in Korea more of the labor market adjustment occurred on the employment side. As a result, unemployment rose from 2.0 percent to 6.8 percent. Another contributing factor was the much smaller share of smallholder agriculture in Korea. Korean agriculture was consequently less capable of absorbing many of those who were displaced in the urban sector. This should be compared with Indonesia where real wages fell by 34 percent (against 12.5 percent in Korea) and where unemployment increased from 4.9 percent to only 5.5 percent. However, both the Korean and Indonesian figures hide considerable rises in underemployment. The increase in unemployment in Malaysia was also relatively moderate (2.5 percent to 3.2 percent), but primarily because Malaysia relies quite heavily on foreign workers who bore the brunt of the crisis. Many were retrenched and left the country.

There were further differences in changes in labor force participation rates across countries. People were discouraged from seeking work in Korea and Malaysia and participation rates fell. In Thailand, participation rates remained constant. In sharp contrast, participation rates in Indonesia increased substantially. Indonesia is the poorest of these countries, and the very poor have little option but to generate work for themselves and to search for work if traditional markets dry up or if they are made redundant. The increase in participation was much greater among women than men. In 1996, 55 percent of women over 25 years of age were in the labor force. This share had increased to 72 percent by 1998. Indonesian women are working longer hours for lower rates of pay than they were before the crisis.

Cutler et al. (2000), in a study of several successive Mexican crises, find that crisis-related volatility worsens health outcomes. In the 1995/96 crisis, mortality rates were 5–7 percent higher than in the immediate precrisis years. The greatest percentage increase was among the elderly. This effect seems to operate mainly by reducing incomes and placing a heavier burden on the medical sector, rather than by forcing less healthy members of the population into the labor force or by compelling primary caregivers to go to work.

Finally, volatility is associated with low levels of educational attainment. It affects education partly through its impact on inequality. In economies that are volatile, the poor, who are already on the margin of subsistence, may be forced periodically to withdraw their children from school so that they can contribute to household income, and this interruption of attendance hinders educational attainment. Governments, forced by crises to cut social services, may be unable to sustain adequate levels of spending on schooling and retain capable teachers.

Where volatility hinders the development of financial markets, families find it particularly difficult to insure against all these risks, forcing them to rely on their children for relatively inefficient insurance. These effects are likely to be most pronounced in poorer countries suffering larger shocks: thus school enrollment rates fell in Indonesia but not in Korea or Thailand in 1998 (Frankenberg et al. 1999).

Managing Volatility in a Globalizing World

If globalization can increase volatility and volatility—particularly in the case of crises—can slow growth and exacerbate poverty, then it is important to adopt policies and develop institutions to limit such volatility and minimize its impact on society's most vulnerable groups. Although there is less than universal agreement on how to limit volatility and safeguard against crises, there appears to be a broad consensus in favor of the following.

First, although the positive impact on the growth of merchandise trade and FDI is now widely recognized, the benefits of portfolio capital flows continue to be questioned. In principle, the portfolio investment permitted by capital account liberalization should relax financial constraints on growth, deepen domestic financial markets, and make direct investment more attractive by facilitating the hedging of exposures and the repatriation of profits. Yet, some commentators are concerned that the interaction of portfolio capital flows with preexisting distortions can heighten volatility and create crisis risk. The results of Klein and Olivei (1999) can be interpreted in this light. The authors find that portfolio capital flows stimulate financial deepening and, by inference, growth in relatively high-income countries, where policy and market distortions are least; but if anything, such flows have a perverse effect on financial development in low-income non-OECD countries.

Second, however, as globalization proceeds, statutory restrictions on transactions on the capital account will become increasingly difficult to operate without disrupting other forms of economic activity. FDI and multinational production will lead to a growing volume of cross-border transactions by financially sophisticated agents attempting to circumvent controls. As small firms penetrate export markets, they will gain the ability to evade controls through leads and lags and over- and underinvoicing. The spread of information and communications technology will open up avenues for evasion by households—by facilitating international financial transactions via the Internet, for example. Thus, the effective operation of capital controls will require increasingly comprehensive and invasive restrictions on economic behavior, extending to domains well beyond the financial. This is something that individuals are unlikely to welcome and something that they can effectively oppose in an age of democratization.

In the final analysis, capital account liberalization is likely to become increasingly difficult to resist as economic and financial globalization proceeds. This heightens the importance of coordinating international financial liberalization with the elimination of distortions that would otherwise cause such liberalization to heighten volatility and crisis risk. In concrete terms, this means that the following actions should be taken.[11]

Strengthening the Financial Sector. Capital account liberalization should follow rather than precede recapitalization of the banking sector, the reinforcement of prudential supervision and regulation, and the removal of blanket guarantees. If bank capitalization is inadequate, managers will be inclined to excessive risk taking, and the offshore funding available through the capital account will permit them to leverage these risks. If bank liabilities are guaranteed on the grounds that widespread bank failures would be devastating to a financial system dominated by banks, foreign investors will not hesitate to provide the requisite funding. A simple explanation of why the resolution costs of banking crises have been larger in the 1980s and 1990s than earlier decades, and larger in emerging than advanced economies, is the coincidence of these domestic financial weaknesses with premature capital account opening.

The removal of interest rate controls is necessary to avoid potential disintermediation when capital accounts are liberalized and depositors have overseas alternatives. Yet Hellman et al. (2000) have questioned whether deposit rate decontrol is desirable on the grounds that forcing banks to compete for deposits erodes franchise value and thereby encourages excessive risk taking when a financial safety net exists. However, reviewing evidence from the 1980s when deposit rate controls were prevalent, McKinnon and Mathieson (1981) and Edwards (1984) emphasize the risk of disintermediation if interest rate controls are maintained. Once the capital account is opened, the retention of deposit rate controls will no longer be feasible. Thus, it is essential to intensify prudential supervision and eliminate implicit guarantees to prevent financial institutions protected by the official safety net from taking on excessive risk.

The corollary is that capital account restrictions should remain in place until prudential supervision is strengthened and implicit guarantees are removed. Unfortunately, maintaining barriers to capital flows and foreign financial competition may diminish the pressure for restructuring; developing countries may never achieve the state where their domestic financial system has been strengthened enough to allow the capital account to be liberalized. This suggests using capital account liberalization to force the issue. But recent experience in Asia and elsewhere casts doubt on the notion that external liberalization that increases the urgency of complementary financial reforms will necessarily deliver the needed reforms before crisis strikes. The lesson from the Asian financial crisis is that the process of financial sector reform should proceed quickly, yet prudently.

Liberalizing FDI. FDI is the form of foreign investment that is most likely to come packaged with managerial and technological expertise. It is also the form least likely to aggravate weaknesses in the domestic banking system, or be associated with capital flight and creditor panic. This suggests liberalizing inward foreign investment as the first stage of financial-side opening. This advice would seem obvious but for the many governments that have failed to heed it. As of 1996, 144 of 184 countries surveyed by IMF still maintained some controls on FDI. One element of the Korean crisis was the Government's reluctance to allow inward FDI and its readiness, in the face of foreign pressure, instead to open other components of the capital account.[12]

Some authors such as Dooley (1997) and Kraay (1998) question whether FDI is more stable than other capital flows. In fact, data on the volatility of flows do not generally suggest a strong contrast between direct investment and portfolio capital. But, as noted above, FDI was much more stable than portfolio flows during the Asian financial crisis. Moreover, there is an obvious sense in which a foreign direct investor cannot easily unbolt machines from the factory floor to take part in a creditor panic.[13]

Internationalizing the Banking System. The case for liberalizing FDI early in the process of external financial opening extends to the banking system. Entry by foreign banks is a low-cost way of upgrading the banking sector's risk-management capacity. The knowledge spillovers that figure prominently in discussions of other forms of FDI also apply to the financial sector. Moreover, insofar as their home-country regulators oversee foreign banks, opening the banking sector to foreign investment should raise the average quality of prudential supervision. And insofar as foreign banks are better capitalized, they are less likely to engage in excessive risk taking. For all these reasons, entry by foreign banks can accelerate the upgrading of domestic financial arrangements that is a prerequisite for further capital account liberalization (Demirgüç-Kunt et al. 1998).

Two caveats should be noted here. First, foreign entry tends to squeeze margins, reduce franchise values, and intensify pressure on weak intermediaries. Hence, the stabilizing impact of opening the banking system may take some time to work. The first-best solution is to strengthen the domestic financial system early in the process of capital account opening (as emphasized above). Failing that, it may be desirable to phase in competition from foreign banks (rather than throwing the domestic market open to foreign entry all at once). This is the method that several Asian economies have chosen.

Second, entry by foreign banks will undermine the effectiveness of measures designed to limit portfolio flows. International banks with local branches and ongoing relationships with domestic broker-dealers will find it easier than other international investors to purchase the domestic securities needed to short the currency, whether controls are in place or not. It follows that banks should be permitted to fund themselves offshore only late in the process. This is a lesson of the financial crisis, particularly in Korea, and is seen in the literature on sequencing capital account liberalization. Equally, it is important to avoid creating artificial incentives for bank-to-bank lending. Thailand opened other components of the capital account before giving banks access to offshore funds. But it then created the Bangkok International Banking Facility, under which Thai banks borrowing offshore (and loaning the proceeds in domestic currency) received favorable tax and licensing treatment. In part this policy can be understood as an attempt to develop Bangkok as an international financial center; in part it reflects the Government's tendency to use banks as an instrument of industrial policy. Either way, it is indicative of policies that are incompatible with the goal of limiting volatility.

Regulating Foreign Exposure. The preceding discussion might be taken as encouragement for governments to micromanage the process of liberalization. But efforts to fine-tune the capital account carry their own dangers. They threaten to create a heavy administrative bureaucracy prone to rent seeking and capture. Financial development makes it progressively easier for participants to evade the authorities' efforts by relabeling positions and repackaging obligations. Interventions that rely on markets rather than on bureaucrats minimize these risks. This is the attraction of the Chilean approach to capital-import taxes. The Chileans required a noninterest-bearing deposit of one year's duration from investors seeking to import capital from abroad. The tax was initially set at 20 percent in 1991, raised to 30 percent in 1992, reduced to 10 percent in June 1998, and set to zero in October that year, while the scope of capital flows to which it was applied was progressively widened. Investors could opt to pay the central bank a sum equivalent to the forgone interest without actually placing the deposit with the bank, and some investors chose to do this.

Since the deposit had to be maintained for a year, the implicit tax fell more heavily on investors with short horizons than on those prepared to stay for the long term. It was transparent and insulated from administrative discretion. It also offered less scope for evasion than other taxes designed to fall on some foreign investments but not others. However, the effectiveness of these measures has been highly debated (Ulan 2000).

Developing Stock and Bond Markets. The sudden withdrawal of foreign deposits can jeopardize the stability of the banking system. In contrast, when investors liquidate their positions in stock and bond markets, securities' prices adjust, which is less destabilizing to the financial system. Certainly, a stock or bond market crash can damage the balance sheet position of banks that hold stocks and bonds. It can make life difficult for entities, including the government, with funding needs and for which the prices of their liabilities are an important signal of creditworthiness.

When banks and firms can fund themselves by floating bonds as well as by issuing short-term debt, the destabilizing impact on their balance sheets of sharp changes in market interest rates will be reduced. And when they can fund themselves by issuing bonds denominated in domestic and foreign currency, the destabilizing financial impact of sharp changes in exchange rates will be reduced. This suggests developing bond markets as a way of diversifying the sources of corporate debt, and stock markets as a way of avoiding excessive reliance on debt in general. It also suggests liberalizing foreign access to domestic stock and bond markets before freeing banks to fund themselves offshore.

Stock and bond markets tend to develop only after bank finance is well established. In part, this is due to the additional information requirements of these markets. Moreover, bond markets tend to develop only once a reliable market has arisen in a benchmark asset, typically treasury bonds, involving transactions that provide liquidity and minimum efficient scale and whose prices provide a reference point for other issues. And the development of a deep and liquid treasury bond market in turn requires a government with a record of sound and stable macroeconomic and financial policies. Otherwise, banks become the captive customers for government bond placements (which is not good for their balance sheets) in return for which they receive other favors (such as guarantees) that give rise to financial sector problems.

Firms in countries where equity finance is available are likely to enjoy additional advantages in a globalized world. In terms of managing volatility, firms in countries with well-developed equity markets will be less dependent on short-term finance and less susceptible to liquidity crises. Such firms will also be less highly leveraged than those in countries (such as in Asia) where debt finance is the norm, which makes their balance sheets less sensitive to the changes in interest rates that exposure to globalized financial markets can bring. Compared with countries where debt is denominated in foreign currency, they will suffer less damage from exchange rate changes. And in a technologically dynamic world, where firms are forced to choose between as yet unproven competing technologies, equity finance has advantages in terms of competitiveness and innovation.

In the absence of financial disclosure following recognized auditing and accounting practices, firms will find outsiders reluctant to purchase their securities for fear of market manipulation by insiders; hence, stock market capitalization and turnover will be low. With inadequate contract enforcement and equitable bankruptcy procedures, investors will be reluctant to invest for fear that issuers will walk away from their obligations. And when adequate mechanisms for corporate control are lacking, investors will be reluctant to purchase minority stakes in publicly traded enterprises for fear of being expropriated by majority stakeholders. This is why significant stock market capitalization and turnover tend to be observed relatively late in the process of financial development. It is why many countries, and developing countries in particular, rely on banks for intermediation services—banks having a comparative advantage through long-term relationships with their clients in assembling information and enforcing contracts.

Creating active stock and bond markets thus requires putting in place a regulatory framework mandating the disclosure of accurate and up-to-date financial information, the use of recognized auditing and accounting standards, penalties for insider trading and market manipulation, and statutes protecting the rights of minority shareholders. In the US, putting these prerequisites in place took several decades (Bordo et al. 1999). Late-developing economies in Asia and elsewhere can expedite this process by importing proven regulatory processes.[14] Still, developing deep and active stock and bond markets is a long and challenging process. Success will not be achieved overnight and it is a relatively expensive undertaking.

Accumulating Reserves. The response of many Asian countries to the volatility of 1997/98 has been to accumulate a cushion of international reserves. The strategy has met with support from academics and officials. Feldstein (1999) has encouraged emerging markets to accumulate reserves as insurance against the disruptive domestic financial effects of abrupt capital outflows. Guidotti (1999) and Greenspan (1999) have similarly suggested that countries hold foreign exchange reserves equal to all the short-term debt scheduled to fall due over the next 12 months. They point to the success of economies with substantial reserves (Taipei,China for example) in withstanding the financial crisis. An IMF study (Bussière and Mulder 1999) suggests that countries may want to hold even larger reserves, perhaps as much as twice that suggested by Messrs. Guidotti and Greenspan. Countries that run chronic current account deficits should hold still larger reserves, as should those seeking to limit exchange rate variability.

This advice can be questioned. First, even large foreign exchange reserves such as Taipei,China's are small relative to the liquidity of the markets. A confidence crisis can cause investors to try to transfer abroad not only short-term foreign liabilities but also domestic assets. Converting these claims into foreign currency is likely to be impossibly expensive for a government or central bank seeking to support a currency peg. Moreover, large reserves can create greater volatility in bank-to-bank lending. Normally, interest rates are lower in the major money centers than in an emerging market that has recently stabilized and opened its capital account, encouraging foreign investors to funnel money into the country. The larger the reserves are, the more confident investors will be that they will be able to take out their investment without suffering losses when sentiment turns and the banking system comes under pressure. Hence, bank-to-bank lending will be greater, and the costs of a banking crisis will be higher.

Moreover, holding reserves against short-term external liabilities is expensive, since US treasury bonds bear lower interest rates than Thai or Korean bank deposits. The implication is straightforward: if short-term foreign borrowing comes with risks that are expensive to insure against, is it not better to avoid it in the first place? Clearly, countries seeking protection from volatility should accumulate a cushion of reserves. But this must be balanced against the costs.

Arranging Commercial Credits. The other approach to ensuring the availability of adequate liquidity in an emergency is to negotiate commercial credit lines in advance. From the standpoint of the borrowing countries, these lines would provide additional resources to insure against shocks to investor confidence. If foreign investors refuse to renew their maturing loans, the authorities can draw on their credit lines to finance the lender of last resort operations appropriate for dealing with a liquidity crisis.

Argentina, Mexico, and Indonesia negotiated facilities with international banks that, in return for a commitment fee, allowed them to draw on hard currency credits. These facilities typically omit the clause on no adverse material change that permits banks to back out of an agreement in the event of a crisis. Indonesia made two drawings on its standby facilities, totaling $1.5 billion.

That these credits are a form of insurance again raises the issue of how adverse selection is overcome. The success of Argentina, Mexico, and Indonesia in purchasing this insurance suggests that the problem of asymmetric information that might otherwise cause the market to break down can be overcome at least partially by posting collateral. These countries' success in negotiating these arrangements suggests that at least some other countries, which can show evidence of institutional reform and a record of strong policies, could do likewise. However, commercial credit lines are likely to be available only to countries with relatively strong policies.

Insurance unavoidably creates the danger of moral hazard. Moreover, these arrangements are essentially unconditional; in contrast to IMF loans, access is not contingent on the country agreeing to specific adjustment measures. Consequently, access to additional funds may encourage some governments to engage in additional risk taking and put off adjustment. The "penalty rate" they pay to draw on these lines may be some deterrent, but the question remains whether it is enough.

A further weakness of these arrangements is that the international banks will be able to hedge their exposures. At the same time that they provide additional credits, they can draw down on their other exposure to the country or sell short government bills and bonds. The sell-off in the Mexican bond market that occurred when the Government drew on its lines in the Fall of 1998 may have been an instance of this effect. Thus, countries relying on this technique may have less insurance than they think.

Strengthening Monetary and Fiscal Institutions. Limiting volatility in a financially globalized world requires building credible policy-making institutions. The greater the credibility of the individuals and institutions responsible for monetary policy, the less the danger that a shock will incite an investor panic and a self-fulfilling crisis. As a matter of fact, if policymakers have accumulated sufficient credibility, the markets will do much of the stabilizing work for them. If inflation accelerates, for example, pushing up interest rates and depressing the prices of short-term interest-bearing assets, investors anticipating that the acceleration of inflation is only temporary will buy into temporarily depressed fixed-income markets, thereby stabilizing asset prices and interest rates. If the currency depreciates, investors will similarly purchase assets denominated in domestic currency at their temporarily depressed prices, providing capital inflows that work to strengthen the exchange rate.

Similarly, the more credible fiscal policy is, the greater will be the fiscal authorities' capacity to pursue countercyclically stabilizing budgetary policies. If they are committed to running budgets that are balanced over the cycle, they will be able to borrow and run deficits in recessions. If, on the other hand, their intentions are suspect, they will have to cut spending and/or raise taxes in recessions, rendering fiscal policy pro-cyclical and aggravating rather than limiting volatility. One possible option that enhances credibility and provides a degree of flexibility for dealing with volatility is to give the authorities a mandate and the independence to pursue it. For monetary policy this is the well-known formula of independence for the central bank and a mandate to pursue price stability. For fiscal policy there is an analogous argument for creating an independent fiscal authority responsible for setting a ceiling for the budget deficit and a set of rules for cutting expenditure in the event that the fiscal authorities overrun it (Eichengreen et al. 1999).

This is only one of a variety of possible formulas for enhancing the credibility of policy-making institutions. An increasingly popular approach in many parts of the world is inflation targeting. Here a regime in which the central bank is given a mandate to pursue an explicit target for inflation may share with the public its forecasts and its model of the links from monetary policy to inflation, and it is held accountable for missing that target. Its advantages are greater flexibility than a rigid monetary rule but it has the same stabilizing impact on market expectations. Its principal limitation is that it can make policy credible only when the central bank has the independence required to pursue it. Not only must the central bank enjoy statutory independence, but it must also have political support for its independent status to limit the prospect that its autonomy will be compromised if it pursues policies that are not congenial to the government. Moreover, its mandate to pursue low inflation must be supported by a broadly compatible government economic policy stance. In particular, if the fiscal authorities are prone to chronic deficits, monetary policy may have to be used to fill the fiscal gap (the "fiscal dominance" problem), in which case the stated objective of pursuing policies of low inflation will lack credibility.

In the case of fiscal policy, alternatives to rigid rules include delegating more agenda-setting and vetoing power to a single agent—typically, the finance minister or the prime minister. They may have more of an incentive to internalize the externalities associated with excessive deficits, and to adopt more centralized and hierarchical budgetary procedures (von Hagen and Harden 1994, Alesina and Perotti 1994). Still other means of building credibility are conceivable. But, whatever the solution, policy credibility is essential to sustain the confidence of investors in a globalized world.

Managing Exchange Rates. One of the most difficult challenges posed by globalization, recent experience suggests, is how to manage the national currency in a financially interlinked world. Since the fixed rate system established at Bretton Woods was abandoned in 1972, countries have been free to establish their own exchange rate system. There are three possibilities. First is the hard peg where a currency is fixed using a currency board or where the currency of another country has been adopted. Second is a series of arrangements often referred to as a "soft peg" where the currency is tied to another currency or a basket of currencies either through a peg, a crawling peg, or bands around a reference rate. Finally is the free float, where the value of the currency is either allowed to fluctuate freely or where there is a managed float. In the managed float no central rate is specified but the central bank may intervene to influence the exchange rate.

In the past decade there has been a movement toward the first and last solutions (see Figure 3.6). There are several reasons for this. Each of the major financial crises in the past few years has involved countries with a soft peg.[15] Large and liquid international capital markets make it more difficult for national authorities to support a shaky currency peg, since the resources of the markets far outstrip the reserves of even the best-armed central banks and governments. Effective defense of the exchange rate requires raising interest rates and restricting domestic credit, something that will have significant costs unless the economy is strong.[16] If the markets detect a chink in the country's armor—high unemployment, a heavy load of short-term debt, or a weak banking system—that could render the authorities reluctant to raise interest rates to defend the currency, then they will pounce, exposing the authorities' weakness.

Maintaining an exchange rate peg or band in open capital markets can be especially difficult for emerging market economies. Many of these depend on exports of a few primary commodities, rendering them vulnerable to terms-of-trade

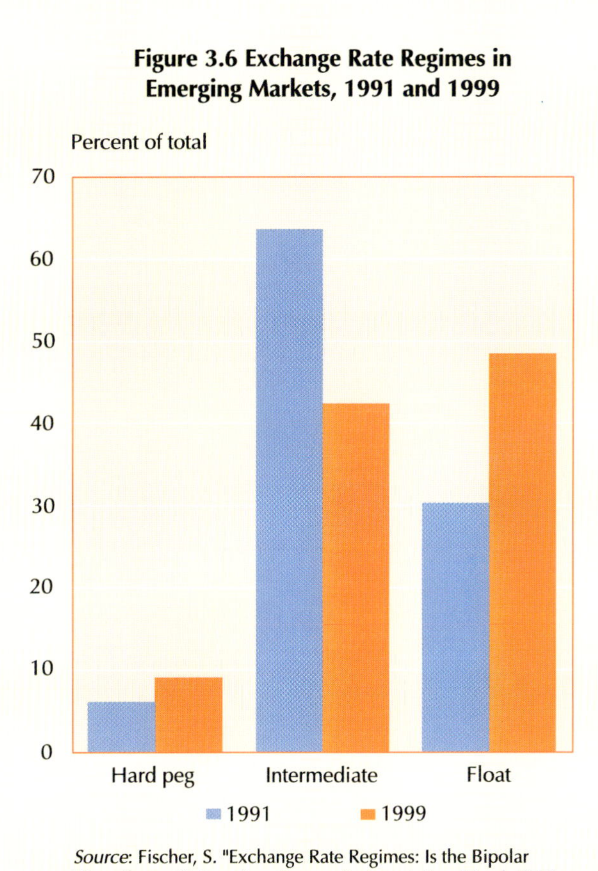

Figure 3.6 Exchange Rate Regimes in Emerging Markets, 1991 and 1999

Source: Fischer, S. "Exchange Rate Regimes: Is the Bipolar View Correct?" *American Economic Association*, March 2001.

shocks. Their financial systems are small in comparison with world markets, even with the assets of a handful of hedge funds and investment banks. Their fragile banking systems are incapable of withstanding sharp hikes in interest rates, while their political systems cannot deliver a broad-based consensus in favor of exchange rate stabilization over and above all other economic and social goals.

Moreover, while the devaluation of a previously pegged currency can enhance international competitiveness and even stimulate growth, the Mexican and Asian crises suggest that currency devaluations in developing countries can be strongly contractionary. When developing countries borrow in foreign currency, depreciation increases the burden of debt service and worsens the financial condition of domestic banks and firms. Because those banks and firms do not hedge their foreign exposures, they are hard hit when the currency band collapses.

Indonesia illustrates the consequences. For some time prior to the outbreak of the Asian financial crisis, the country had been operating a crawling band, allowing for fluctuations of plus or minus 4 percent against a basket of currencies. Typical of many emerging economies, it had relatively high interest rates, which made it attractive to international investors. These large capital inflows worked to push the rupiah toward the strong end of its band. Because the authorities were committed to limiting exchange rate fluctuations (and because the strength of the currency lent credibility to that commitment), domestic banks, and more particularly corporations, accumulated unhedged foreign exposures.

When the Thai baht depreciated, capital flows in Indonesia reversed direction. In one day, 13 August 1997, the rupiah went from the strong edge of the band (which had been widened to 6 percent) to the weak edge. This 12 percent depreciation was a sharp shock to Indonesian corporations with unhedged exposures, whose solvency was now cast into doubt. Now openly questioning the stability of the economy, investors scrambled out of the rupiah. Further interest rate increases to defend the currency were out of the question, given the financial distress in the corporate sector and the banking system. Instead, the authorities abandoned the band, allowing the exchange rate to drop further. With the damage already done to the economy, it dropped precipitously, falling by as much as 10 percent a day.

This synopsis makes an essential point about the fragility of currency bands and the high costs of their collapse. With hindsight, it did not really matter whether Indonesia had a currency band or not. All the Asian currencies were tied in one way or other to the US dollar and many of them collapsed because of the size of the unhedged short-term capital that had flowed in during the 1993 to 1996 boom and that then flowed out in 1997 and 1998.

For which extreme should Asian economies opt—a hard peg along Hong Kong, China lines or a free float in the Korean style? The choice is typically framed in terms of the trade-off between credibility and flexibility. With the adoption of a hard peg, domestic monetary policy is dictated by the central bank of the country whose currency provides the external anchor, and the peg automatically acquires all the credibility accumulated by the issuer of the anchor currency. The commitment to the currency peg is enshrined in the adoption of a constitutional amendment or requires a super-majority vote in the parliament or congress mandating the central bank or government to defend the rate. By ensuring greater exchange rate stability, the economy's access to foreign capital is enhanced.

Floating rates, in contrast, maximize the flexibility with which the authorities can use monetary policy for economic stabilization. They leave the central bank free to intervene as a lender of last resort to financial markets. However, some commentators dispute the stabilizing value of exchange rate changes when shocks are real rather than monetary and a country's external obligations are denominated in foreign currency. They similarly question the capacity of the central bank to act as an effective lender of last resort when

domestic banks and firms incur debts denominated in foreign currency.[17]

Which approach will be more attractive to most DMCs? Again, the diversity of economic structures and different stages of economic and financial development in the region hinders any attempt to generalize. But insofar as most DMCs are quite open, standard arguments on optimum currency areas favor hard pegs. At the same time, the diversification of DMC exports across markets—and the tendency of exporters in the region to sell to the Japanese and US markets simultaneously—makes a hard peg to any single currency less attractive. Because DMCs have relatively underdeveloped domestic bond markets, they borrow long term mainly in foreign currency, and sharp exchange rate changes can then wreak havoc with the domestic currency cost of external debt servicing. In other words, a flexible exchange rate will make obtaining foreign funding difficult. But because savings rates in Asia are so high, foreign funding is less essential: banks and firms seeking external finance can obtain it at home via the banking system and supplier credits. To the extent that the real side of many DMCs is relatively flexible, the value of monetary autonomy is less. But insofar as policies and policy-making institutions are relatively credible by international standards, the capacity to exploit the advantages of such credibility is greater.

The existence of so many cross-cutting considerations suggests that not all DMCs will prefer the same exchange rate arrangement. Currently only PRC; Hong Kong, China; and Malaysia have adopted pegs and the rest are floating. The float is generally free but some DMCs seem to be returning to soft pegs. Along these lines, a recent study by Calvo and Reinhart (2000) shows that many countries that are categorized as having floating currencies are, in effect, holding loose pegs. They found a high correlation between exchange rates and central bank reserves that suggest significant central bank intervention. This interventionist tendency has accelerated in recent months—in the immediate aftermath of the financial crisis, exchange rates were much more flexible (see Table 3.5)—and one possible reason for this is the expectation that loose pegging will have the same effect as a free float but with less volatility.

Policies to Minimize Risks to the Poor

Globalization will be accepted most readily if its benefits are widely shared. The fact that economies that are more deeply integrated into global markets tend to have larger public sectors can be understood as providing social protection for those who cannot protect themselves from the volatility and pressures of globalization (Rodrik 1998). Such protection helps support the broad-based political coalition needed to sustain a commitment to openness. In addition, it facilitates the quick policy adjustments needed to absorb globalization-related shocks, since people will see that the immediate costs of adjustment, like the benefits, are being equitably shared.[18]

For countries seeking to capitalize on globalization, two policies may help in minimizing the risks to the poor of globalization. For the short term, insurance against shocks is needed. For the long term, measures are required to foster the accumulation of forms of human capital that are useful in an economically globalized world, specifically among socioeconomic groups that have not traditionally possessed them.

In the context of globalization, risks can range from sharp changes in relative prices on world markets to full-blown economic and financial crises. Building an effective social safety net and ramping up programs in response to a crisis can be inefficient and time-consuming, and is therefore difficult. This makes it important to put in place lasting social infrastructure protection. Whereas general principles underlying social safety nets are well documented, specific programs need to be designed in light of particular financial and country-specific conditions.[19]

The short-term safety net should provide employment for those able to work. Public works programs providing jobs for the poor, often referred to as workfare, have been shown to be a relatively efficient way of providing immediate relief, especially where local input is used in selecting projects and where the workers are the beneficiaries of the public works (see Ravallion 1999). Workers can be offered public employment at a wage equal to, say, 90 percent of the wage for unskilled agricultural labor. Workfare designed in this way will protect the poorest workers against the loss of income without drawing other workers away from private employment or encouraging welfare dependency.

South Asia has been a pioneer among developing countries in the development of workfare programs. The Indian state of Maharashtra is known for its Employment Guarantee Scheme, which targets the poor.[20] Bangladesh has experimented with similar programs, though these have been limited by the availability of donor resources to finance them. Sri Lanka's Janasaviya Program makes entitlement to food coupons conditional on a household supplying 24 days of labor monthly to rural public works projects; it enjoys dedicated budgetary funding. These programs are not free of shortcomings: women receive only a small proportion of the benefits that a man receives, many of the assets created are of poor quality, maintenance of the assets is inadequate, and wages are often too high to provide efficient self-targeting (Subbarao et al. 1995). Still, they are an obvious element of the social safety net that societies need to build to protect their poorest members (see Box 3.3).

Aside from crisis management what difference, if any, does globalization make to the poverty agenda? The standard agenda for poor countries like those of South Asia is land reform, education, the abolition of pricing policies that discriminate against agriculture, and the creation of stable macroeconomic and legal frameworks. A relatively equal distribution of land encourages family farmers to adopt economically and organizationally efficient modes of cultivation. Education is associated with the adoption of relatively innovative agricultural technologies, which—perhaps more importantly from the point of view of income distribution and poverty reduction—facilitates the movement of labor to jobs that are often higher paid. Market liberalization and stable macroeconomic and legal frameworks stimulate growth, which benefits the poor. These points are well known. So what differ-

Table 3.5 Exchange Rate Flexibility

Currency	Precrisis January 1995 to July 1997	Crisis August 1997 to December 1998	Healing/Normalization January 1999 to October 2000
Baht (Thailand)	0.07	0.18	0.17
Won (Korea)	0.12	0.24	0.13
Singapore dollar (Singapore)	0.09	0.70	0.20
Rupiah (Indonesia)	0.01	0.41	0.32
Ringgit (Malaysia)	0.22	0.21	0.00
Peso (Philippines)	0.02	0.21	0.12
New Taiwan dollar (Taipei,China)	0.07	0.38	0.16

Note: Estimates of index of exchange rate flexibility where 0 = completely inflexible, 1 = completely flexible. The index is computed as SDFX(SDFX+SDRES) where SDFX is the standard deviation of log changes of dollar exchange rates and SDRES the standard deviation of change in central bank reserves divided by the lagged stock of the monetary base (i.e., the portion of potential FX volatility that has been neutralized by central bank intervention). The underlying notion is that for a currency to be deemed flexible, its variability must increase relative to underlying market pressures.
Source: Merrill Lynch, *Global Economic Trends*, December 2000, p. 11.

Box 3.3 Social Safety Nets

A safety net should have three major characteristics. First, it should provide targeted transfers for those unable to work. Workfare should be supplemented with cash transfers targeted at subgroups, such as the elderly and pregnant women. Effective targeting maximizes budgetary efficiency. Yet, making targeting effective is a perennial problem in such programs, since politically powerful groups seem to be able to insist on a share of the spoils. India's public distribution system has long been criticized for failing to target its benefits to the poor.[21] Bangladesh's public food distribution scheme is said to cost six times the value of the transfers received by the targeted households. The Philippines' generalized food subsidy system costs the government three pesos for every peso transferred to households; in addition, the households in question are not generally the poorest.[22]

Second, the safety net should provide microcredit for those affected by the fallout from financial crises. Crisis conditions can force poor households into distress sales of productive assets, which depress their postcrisis income and productivity. Disruptions in financial markets can interrupt access to trade and producer credit needed to obtain essential inputs and products. Limited amounts of microcredit extended in response to these disruptions should therefore minimize the adverse consequences for poor households.

Here, too, Asia has considerable experience with such programs, providing a foundation on which to build. India's Integrated Rural Development Program provides credit to means-tested households for purchase of nonland assets. Bangladesh's Grameen Bank has developed a scheme to provide microcredit to the poor. Under this scheme, loans are extended to groups of five to eight self-selected persons who agree to form a group in order to monitor one another. Rates of repayment and economic impacts have been impressive. Credit has been effectively channeled to the ultrapoor, including women. Studies suggest that participants' incomes rose by more than 50 percent relative to those of the control groups (Khandker et al. 1994).

Third, in the event of a crisis, the existing safety net programs should be used as the basis for poverty reduction measures. Scaling up existing workfare, microcredit, and targeted transfer programs in response to a crisis is easier than creating new programs from scratch. Additional support can be built on the existing administrative infrastructure and distributed through existing channels. While South Asia has much experience in the administration of such programs, the limited success of the poverty reduction efforts in the NIEs and Southeast Asia in 1997/98 can be understood in terms of the absence of preexisting safety net programs that could have been quickly strengthened.

The proportionate increase in spending on such programs was largest in Korea, where it rose from negligible levels prior to the financial crisis to nearly 5 percent of the budget, and in Indonesia, where the budgetary share rose from extremely low levels to 3.6 percent. However, in both cases only a fraction of the poor were covered. In Korea, safety net programs covered only a third of the poor prior to the crisis, and this share fell to 17 percent in 1998 despite rapid increases in spending. As of June 1998, only 7 percent of the 1.5 million unemployed had received unemployment benefits. The number of those participating in the Korean Government's newly created workfare scheme reached 200,000 at the beginning of 1999, but there were more than 700,000 applicants for these positions (despite the fact that they paid submarket wages), again indicating the partial nature of coverage. Indonesia, for its part, introduced a public works scheme and a rice distribution program. Estimates suggest that no more than a third of poor Indonesian households have participated in some form or other (see World Bank 2000). Birdsall and Haggard (2000) argue that well-organized rural lobbies prevented these programs from being extended to the urban poor. While the rice distribution scheme made available to targeted households 10 kilograms of medium-grade rice each month at subsidized prices, this was equivalent to only a small fraction of the income of a household living at the poverty line.

---

ence, if at all, does globalization make to the antipoverty agenda?

Because globalization exposes national economies to external shocks, it requires workers as well as firms to act quickly. The implication is that educational spending should impart general knowledge rather than technical training and sector-specific skills. The literature on this subject (e.g., Heckman 2000) shows that such general knowledge is imparted most efficiently in the early stages of the education process. This suggests targeting educational subsidies at primary education and ensuring that the poorest (especially females) are included. The first point feeds into an obvious Asian strength: the high-performing Asian economies have long allocated a substantial share of edu-

cational spending to basic as opposed to higher education.[23] In contrast, the second observation points to the need to reorient the approach to educational planning in Asia, which has traditionally focused on vocational training of sorts that are likely to be less easily transferred in a rapidly changing high-tech world.

Recent contributions to the development literature (e.g., Lopez et al. 1998) suggest that more equal access to education has a positive impact on average per capita income. The obstacle to more equal distribution of education, according to much of the development literature, is the poverty trap—the fact that the extra income from child labor, which is indispensable to poor families, comes at the expense of the child's longer-term prospects of escaping poverty through education.[24]

Insofar as openness leads poor countries to specialize in the production and export of labor-intensive goods, there is the danger that globalization may draw poor children out of school. Targeted subsidies for school attendance are the obvious policy response. Bangladesh's Food-for-Education Program, which offers a stipend to selected participants (somewhat more than the equivalent of 13 percent of monthly earnings for boys and 20 percent for girls) has demonstrated an ability to ensure nearly full school attendance by those who participate.

Early evidence similarly suggests that Indonesia's Stay-in-School Program, which provides grants to the poorest schools and transfers to the poorest students, has been similarly effective (see Birdsall and Haggard 2000). Such programs have the additional advantage that local schools are important stakeholders, leading them to become actively involved in monitoring and administering their operations.

INSTITUTIONAL OPTIONS IN A GLOBALIZING ENVIRONMENT

As Asian economies integrate further into the global economic system they face a number of challenges and opportunities. In many cases these can be addressed by the private sector. However, in some instances governments will have to be involved. Because of the nature of the globalization process, they will have to adopt new approaches and be willing to develop new institutions and policies to address the issues presented by continued globalization. Governments will no longer be able to rely solely on national initiatives, although these will still be important. They must go further in developing relationships and participate with other countries in institution building to deal with global issues at both the regional and global levels. In this section, the focus is on the macroeconomic landscape, eschewing more detailed microeconomic and sector policy issues. Particular attention is paid to the dynamics of institution building as it relates to globalization.

Establishing an Institutional Framework

Economists tend to assume the existence of appropriate institutions. Put another way, if a certain set of institutions were to be efficient, economists assume that they will develop in response to latent demand (Davis and North 1971). Thus, if new technologies generated by start-up firms are the motor for growth, and if supporting their development requires financial markets capable of providing venture capital, then a market-based financial system will spring up in response to the profit incentives perceived by aspiring venture capitalists. And if, to attract FDI, countries must adopt demanding corporate disclosure standards and legal systems affording strong protection for creditor rights, then they will do so in order to prevent FDI from being

diverted to jurisdictions that are quicker to respond. It is important to understand why this may not occur in an orderly fashion.

Institutions can be understood as coordinating mechanisms—as coordinating the actions of different economic and social agents.[25] They do so by providing standards for socially constructive behavior. Because they function as standards, they are a source of network externalities.[26] And like any technology that throws off network externalities, once established they tend to become locked in. As David (1993) has put it, institutions, by virtue of their inertial character, become the "carriers of history."

Because institutions have an inertial character, radical institutional change is the exception, not the rule. Wholesale change requires the political and economic system to be displaced from its equilibrium. It follows that radical change often occurs in response to major shocks—crises, for example. (A model of the linkage is provided by Drazen and Grilli 1993.) By definition, crises disrupt the operation of existing institutions. That disruption creates a vacuum in which new arrangements can develop. This is the story told in Olson (1982) of institutional change in the wake of war and crisis. More generally, the suboptimal performance of existing institutions that has been made clear by a crisis can foster the consensus needed for agreement on changes in prevailing arrangements. Thus, the political and economic crises of the 1940s and 1950s are commonly credited with creating a hothouse environment conducive to the growth of the institutions that served Asia so well in its period of rapid economic growth. Economies like Korea and Taipei,China emerged from the Second World War and the Asian conflicts that erupted in its wake in a parlous economic state. In Korea, for example, years of foreign occupation and civil war had left the population on the margin of subsistence. The political disputes and the fact that the NIEs and Southeast Asia were a principal battleground of the Cold War created a crisis of national survival in countries across the region. This crisis in turn cultivated the political support for the institutional changes needed to strengthen the state and the economy. Land reform was carried out in Korea and Taipei,China which allowed the benefits of rising agricultural productivity to be widely shared and created a rural middle class. Korea; Singapore; and Taipei,China developed effective tripartism. Powerful urban interests were induced to acquiesce to government programs that were designed to develop the rural infrastructure necessary for balanced growth. Regime leaders had the political autonomy to develop independent technocracies and performance-based civil service systems. These institutional ingredients of Asia's "miracle" are by now well understood. The point here is that their development should be seen as a social response to this crisis of national survival.

In the wake of the Asian financial crisis of 1997/98, it is again clear that a crisis can catalyze reform.[27] This is particularly evident in the steps taken by DMCs to update and strengthen their financial institutions, with the aim of restoring investor confidence, and the long-run goal of equipping themselves with the institutional prerequisites for navigating a world of global finance. Prudential supervision and regulation have been strengthened, and new rules have been adopted to encourage arm's-length dealing between financial institutions and their customers. Governments have encouraged the development of bond markets that were long suppressed in favor of bank-based intermediation. Foreign investment has been liberalized in nearly all countries in the region. Thailand replaced its Alien Business Law with new provisions allowing foreign firms to hold up to 100 percent equity in Thai banks, and 39 sectors have been opened to increased foreign participation. Korea, meanwhile, opened real estate, securities dealing, and other financing business to foreign investors and granted foreigners the right to purchase 100 percent of the equity of domestic firms. The NIEs and Southeast Asia have taken comprehensive action to facilitate mergers and acquisitions, both domestic and international. However, Indonesia and Malaysia appear to be exceptions: the Indonesian system does not favor mergers and acquisitions, while Malaysia appears to favor domestic but not international mergers and acquisitions.

Indonesia and Thailand have adopted significant legislative changes to their bankruptcy systems. In the second half of 1998, Indonesia created a specialized commercial court with jurisdiction over bankruptcy-related matters and adopted an automatic stay provision similar to that provided for under the US bankruptcy code. In Thailand, new bankruptcy legislation pushed through over political opposition had a positive impact on the equity valuation of financial and nonfinancial companies (Foley 1999). Such reforms can be seen as prerequisites for growth and stability in a financially globalized world. While financial reform has long been on Asia's agenda, it is hard to imagine such rapid progress in the absence of the crisis. However, while crisis can breed reform, reform without crisis is to be preferred. The question is how this is best achieved.

Global Initiatives

The process of achieving reform without crisis can be organized at the global level. Thus IMF, the World Bank, and the Financial Stability Forum, with impetus from the governments of the Group of Seven leading industrial nations, have launched a multi-pronged effort to encourage industrial and developing countries to upgrade their financial practices and institutions. The focus of this effort is on institutional arrangements in areas like data dissemination; fiscal, monetary, and financial policy transparency; banking regulation and supervision; securities and insurance regulation; accounting, auditing, and bankruptcy; and corporate governance. The mechanism is the promulgation of international standards for acceptable practice in these areas that all countries, including Asian countries, must

meet, and efforts to encourage compliance through a combination of IMF surveillance, peer pressure, and market discipline.[28] In other areas such as product and process standards and classification mechanisms such as International Organization for Standardization classifications, the important role of global agencies is clear.

The case for these global initiatives is straightforward. If markets are global, so must be their regulation and the institutions through which that regulation takes place. In a world of systemic risk, economic and financial institutions take on the character of a global public good. Institutional arrangements affecting, among other things, prudential supervision and the conduct of monetary-cum-exchange-rate policies are of critical interest not just to the initiating country but also to the rest of the world. Global initiatives to influence national practices are justified as a way of internalizing these externalities.

The danger is that these global initiatives will subject countries to blueprint formulas, denying them the opportunity to design regulatory institutions responsive to their distinctive traditions. This is where standards come in. Standards, which define criteria that all countries should meet but allow them to meet them in different ways, offer a way of reconciling the common imperatives created by participation in international markets with the diversity of economic systems. The complaint that IMF's structural interventions are arbitrary and capricious at least partly explains the backlash that they have provoked; with the promulgation of standards, objective criteria will exist to which IMF can refer when it demands structural reforms.

At the same time, such an approach raises compelling objections. The official donor community as a whole does not possess the resources to design and monitor compliance with detailed international standards in all the relevant areas. In its early country reports on the observance of standards and codes, IMF has been forced to rely on self-evaluations by the subject countries, a practice that threatens the objectivity of the process. For IMF to carry out this function in a satisfactory way would require a very significant increase in its staff and a radical change in expertise, both of which are unlikely for the foreseeable future (see IMF 1999b).

Moreover, reservations have been voiced about how much can be accomplished through the promulgation of international standards. The definition of acceptable standards causes disagreement—as seen in the dispute between the US and the European Union over accounting standards or the wide variation among advanced industrial countries in the provisions of bankruptcy and insolvency codes. The danger is that an international standard broad enough to encompass these variations will tend toward a lowest common denominator. Moreover, standards, by defining the minimum acceptable threshold, may weaken the incentive for countries to do better. What will prevent governments from taking steps to meet the letter of the requirement without in fact satisfying its spirit?

Such qualms are reinforced by experience with the most important experiment in standards setting to date, the International Convergence of Capital Measurement and Capital Standards, or the 1988 Basle Capital Accord (the Basle Accord). The Basle Accord established an 8 percent minimum (weighted) capital adequacy standard for international banks. It deserves some credit for steps taken subsequently, by countries represented on the Basle Committee on Banking Supervision and others, to bring capital adequacy up to this minimum. Reassuringly, the existence of the Basle Accord has not prevented countries like Argentina from doing better. But, at the same time, the Basle Accord has been subject to evasion. The gap between the reported and actual capital of countries with banking crises is a case in point. The Basle Accord did nothing to head off these crises or resolve them.

Banks have discovered ways of shifting assets subject to high capital charges off their balance sheets through securitization and the use of derivative securities without modifying the underlying risks. This should serve as a warning of the danger that the standards setters will always be one step behind the markets. Finally, experience with the Basle Accord demonstrates that poorly designed standards, or standards that lag behind circumstances, can create perverse incentives. One need only recall the incentive in the Basle Accord to engage in short-term lending to non-OECD countries. While lending to OECD banks was given a risk weight of 20 percent irrespective of the term of the loan, lending to non-OECD banks carried this reduced weight only for loans of less than a year, whereas loans of longer maturity carried the full 100 percent risk weight. This led to a shift toward short-term portfolio asset holdings that were easily liquidated during the Asian financial crisis.

In hindsight, the perverse incentives conferred by the Basle Accord on international banks are clear. But there is a more fundamental point. If institutional arrangements at the global level are to be appropriate for a wide variety of experiences, they must be carefully developed and drafted only after intensive policy discussions with all the relevant parties. Economists disagree among themselves over the design of an efficient bankruptcy law, over the stabilizing or destabilizing effects of additional data disclosure, and over the merits of fixed versus flexible exchange rates. In addition, the high-income countries themselves continue to show a diversity of institutional arrangements. Therefore, global initiatives to change national institutions and practices in a particular way must be considered very carefully to ensure that they will indeed reduce risk and increase financial stability.

The Regional Option

To some extent, the external shocks associated with the forces of globalization can be moderated by regional initiatives. The coordination of policies and institutions between countries can be addressed at the regional level, while the need for continued diversity of policies and institutions can be satisfied by differences in these practices between regions. Insofar as the cross-border externalities associated with national policies are felt mainly by countries within a region, this creates an argument for coordination at the regional level. In addition, arguments can be made for coordinating exchange rate and R&D policies at the regional rather than the global level. Some evidence suggests that the spread of currency crises was mainly a regional phenomenon (Glick and Rose 1999) and perhaps a better coordinated regional response, such as the Chiang Mai initiative to expand swap lines among Asian currencies, could have been less disruptive. Eaton et al. (1998) similarly show that R&D spillovers are primarily concentrated in the region in which R&D takes place and that their magnitude diminishes with physical distance.

Frameworks for addressing such problems at the regional level have developed in other parts of the world, providing precedents that DMCs could follow. The European Monetary System, the precursor to European Economic and Monetary Union, illustrates the scope for regional cooperation in the monetary-cum-exchange rate domain. The Consultative Group on International Agricultural Research, which encourages its participating centers to share the fruits of their agricultural research and which is primarily funded by multilateral institutions, is an example of similar arrangements for R&D.

While regional associations like ASEAN and the South Asian Association for Regional Cooperation (SAARC) already exist, they have mainly been concerned with trade issues (see also Box 3.4). There is a growing belief that Asia needs a broad-based regional free trade zone to interact more effectively with countries of the North American Free Trade Agreement and the European Union.

Interest in the regional option has attracted new attention in Asia in the wake of the 1997/98 financial crisis. This was a reflection of the perception that the advice and conditionality of the international financial institutions were inadequately tailored to the particulars of the crisis and that these institutions failed to capture the distinctive features of the Asian approach to growth and economic learning. This experience has given rise to discussions for the establishment of an Asian Monetary Fund. Similarly, the Chiang Mai initiative can be seen as a way of addressing regional financial pressures. Discussions of the case for a common basket peg for Asian countries (Williamson 1999) are seen as responding to the dilemma of having to choose between a hard peg and a floating exchange rate. Asian countries can avoid this difficult choice by agreeing to a collective peg and supporting one another in its maintenance. In Europe—where it has promoted cooperation—this style of institution building encouraged the harmonization of policies and institutions, created a zone of monetary and financial stability, and led to a measure of political integration. In Asia,

---

Box 3.4 Regional Cooperation in the Asian and Pacific Region

Globally, there has been a growing trend toward greater political, economic, and social integration among countries, both interregionally and intraregionally. Among DMCs, economic integration has increased significantly over the past decades as evidenced by the significant rise of regional cooperation schemes. This may be attributed to various factors including (i) growing trade interdependence, (ii) rapid expansion of investment flows, (iii) fundamental shifts toward market-based open policy, (iv) economic liberalization, and (v) internationalization of capital and production networks.

Recognizing the potential for greater regional cooperation for development, there has been an array of regional cooperation initiatives. The more popular and larger regional cooperation initiatives include the Asia-Pacific Economic Cooperation (APEC) forum, the Association of Southeast Asian Nations (ASEAN), the ASEAN Free Trade Area (AFTA), and the South Asian Association for Regional Cooperation (SAARC).

Regional cooperation has provided a mechanism for participating countries to enter into a process of dialogue that has contributed to maintaining peace, goodwill and mutual trust. It has also provided an opportunity for cooperation in areas that transcend trade and investment, such as social sectors, capacity building, and governance.

Initial discussions have been held on the establishment of an Asian regional institution equivalent to the Bank for International Settlements that would develop guidelines for banks and provide supervisory advice. In the wake of the Asian financial crisis, proposals were made for currency swapping arrangements between central banks outside the framework of IMF and the World Bank. Ideas about an Asian Economic Community have also been brought forward. However, none of these arrangements has yet been implemented.

From a social perspective, the key challenges for DMC governments joining regional cooperation groupings are to ensure that the benefits of cooperation are evenly distributed, especially to the poor and disadvantaged, and to try to compensate for the negative impacts of globalization in the cultural, social, and environmental dimensions of development.

---

however, the motivations for regional cooperation are different from Europe's and are in their infancy. DMCs have less interest in a regional trade arrangement since much of their trade is with the US, and regional preferences could antagonize powerful political bodies and jeopardize extra-Asian market access.

Moreover, Asia has shown virtually no desire for political integration, given the various political tensions since the Second World War, often exacerbated by outside influences. Rather, the impetus for monetary cooperation reflects the desire to create a zone of financial stability. The fear created by the financial crisis is that small currencies and large financial markets are incompatible. Asian central banks, on their own, lack the resources to cope with global financial flows, even with the position-taking ability of a few highly leveraged institutions. Confronted with the vast liquidity of global capital markets, unilateral floats and unilateral pegs are subject, in this view, to speculative manipulation, and both are therefore equally uncomfortable for the government attempting to operate them. The solution is the pooling of reserves designed to marshal sufficient resources for the authorities to counter speculative pressures and, ideally, maintain the stability of intra-Asian rates. Whether desire for such financial cooperation proves strong enough to support wider regional cooperation will only be known in time.

Multilateral liberalization is another area where a regional focus may be an appropriate catalyzing force. DMCs need to concentrate on their own priorities during the next round of World Trade Organization (WTO) multilateral trade negotiations, the so-called Millennium Round. Coordination among DMCs could be effective in putting forward an agenda of proposals that would benefit the entire region. General tariff reduction, reduction of agricultural subsidies in industrial countries, elimination of preferential tariffs in regional arrangements, and antidumping safeguards are some of the areas where DMCs could develop a set of their own proposals.

National Initiatives

If one accepts the argument for diversity of national practices, a uniform mode of governance across countries cannot be optimal. Nonetheless, scholars seeking to go further distinguish three forms of governance: the strong state, the decentralized state, and the participatory state. The strong state model vests responsibility for designing and implementing institutional arrangements with an authoritarian government and its bureaucratic arm. Korea and Singapore prior to the 1990s are representative of this model. The decentralized state encourages experimentalism and competition among local jurisdictions, on the same grounds that the national approach encourages experimentation and competition among countries. Thus, federal systems generally encourage competition among their states and this has led to some successes. Policies of devolution in the PRC, which led to the emergence of town and village enterprises, can be seen in a similar light.

The participatory approach, in a world of globalized markets, may have advantages, according to Rodrik (1999). He argues that democratic governance facilitates the development of institutions that produce greater short-term stability, ease adjustment to adverse shocks, and deliver superior distributional outcomes. The implication is that these characteristics will be particularly advantageous in a globalized world where volatility is pervasive, small states are susceptible to adverse shocks emanating from international markets, and income distribution is under strain.

Sah (1991) observes that democracies empower a wider range of decision makers and argues that this diversification implies less risk in an environment of imperfect information; hence, democracy should be positively associated with short-term stability. Rodrik (1997) provides cross-sectional evidence for the period 1960–1989 supportive of this hypothesis. He also reports evidence that democracies adjusted more successfully to external (terms-of-trade) disturbances over this period. A stronger point follows: more open democracies with less executive autonomy handle shocks better. Rodrik (1997) observes that the recent experience of the NIEs and Southeast Asia is consistent with these conclusions. Korea and Thailand, with their more open, participatory political regimes, handled the crisis better than Indonesia, by providing an alternative to riots, protests, and demonstrations and by facilitating the smooth transfer of power to new leaders.

Finally, there is evidence that participatory systems pay higher wages and are characterized by less income inequality, since participation leads to the development of more elaborate social insurance and transfer mechanisms.

CONCLUSIONS—TOWARD A FRAMEWORK FOR GLOBALIZATION

What is the Future of Globalization?

This third part of *Asian Development Outlook 2001* has reviewed the opportunities and risks that globalization presents for DMCs. Its premise is that powerful technological, economic, and political forces are at work that are likely to render the world economy even more globalized in the future than it is today. Since the Second World War, the decline in the cost of international transportation and communications, the spread of global production networks, and the progress in drawing countries and regions—once only marginally integrated into the world economy—more deeply into the global system, have been quite substantial. Yet, globalization has considerably further to go. The extent of participation in international trade and capital flows varies enormously across countries.

This is in part due to the existence of a number of barriers to further integration of countries with global markets. Foremost among these are barriers to trade. Despite significant reductions in them brought about by eight rounds of multilateral trade negotiations since 1949, widespread restrictions on trade, especially nontariff barriers, exist in most developing countries. These serve to artificially raise the cost of imported goods and services, harming domestic consumers and foreign producers while inhibiting the efficient allocation of resources in each country, and impeding economic growth and structural reforms in many countries. If differences between nations on

the appropriate emphasis at a new round of WTO negotiations can be resolved (see Box 3.5), further reductions in trade barriers may further stimulate globalization.

For DMCs, late 20th and early 21st century globalization is also coinciding with an important change in the sources of economic growth. For the last four decades, DMCs have recorded rapid rates of growth by maintaining high rates of factor accumulation—capital accumulation in traded-goods sectors in particular—and by selling their products in world markets. Policies and the institutions through which these policies are made have been adapted to this growth model: they have promoted savings and investment, favored investment in traded goods sectors, and rewarded export performance. But as Asia's high-growth economies mature, the source of their growth will progressively shift from factor accumulation to TFP growth. This will require changes in policies and institutions. In addition, low-income DMCs that wish to follow their high-income predecessors down the path of labor-intensive, export-oriented manufacturing using technologies imported via licensing will find their task complicated by globalization. Countries like the PRC and India are attempting to implement this strategy. Competition is intense. Selling the products of low-wage manufacturing industries in global markets will become increasingly cutthroat. And as more countries compete for foreign investment, their ability to acquire technology via licensing will be correspondingly curtailed. Sustaining growth in this setting will require telescoping the transition from accumulation- to innovation-based growth. In turn, this will require accelerating the evolution of policies and the renovation of policy-making institutions.

That the need for stable macroeconomic policies, sound regulatory arrangements, and good governance is obvious does not make them unimportant. Appropriate policies are easier to prescribe than to implement and their specifics are likely to vary over time as an economy evolves. A brief set of policy recommendations that arise from this review of Asia's globalization challenge is presented below:

Trade Policies

Trade liberalization played a major role in stimulating development in many DMCs. Further progress in this area will reinforce the trend toward globalization that has been so beneficial:

- In order to minimize the efficiency losses and economic distortions brought about by trade barriers, trade policy instruments need to be modified. The first step of a liberalization strategy is replacing nontariff barriers by tariffs. The move from quantitative restrictions to tariffs is a healthy one because the latter are relatively less protective than the former. More importantly, a tariff is a price instrument and thus changes in international prices feed through more readily into the domestic economy. The knowledge

Box 3.5 Developing Countries and the World Trade Organization

In January 1995, WTO, which superseded the General Agreement on Tariffs and Trade, was mandated to expand world trade and in the process further generate integration of the global economy. However, the attempt to launch a new round of multilateral trade negotiations in December 1999 failed because there were substantial differences among countries over its content and structure. On the one hand, industrial countries were pressing for a broad-based agenda and for negotiations to be concluded within three years so as to maintain momentum in bringing down trade barriers. On the other hand, several developing countries believed that negotiations should concentrate on problems of implementing the agreements reached in the last round of negotiations (the Uruguay Round) and on its "built-in agenda," which provided for new negotiations only in agriculture and services.

The position of the developing countries reflected three immediate concerns. First, the Uruguay Round and its implementation process did little to improve market access for their exports of goods and services. Second, they felt that WTO rules were unbalanced in several important development-related areas such as the protection of intellectual property rights and the use of industrial subsidies, while the special and differential treatment, which the Uruguay Round accorded them, was inadequate. Third, insufficient human and financial resources and weak institutional capacities restricted the ability of many developing countries to exploit the opportunities open to them under the WTO system, particularly in respect of its dispute settlement mechanism, as well as the inability to comply fully with their multilateral obligations. Developing countries need to grapple with these issues and, once a consensus for the new round is built up, they need to proactively participate in it with the objective of further integrating themselves into the global economy.

of and link with global prices is essential for domestic producers. Not knowing the relative costs of imports, domestic producers cannot commit themselves to production for exports.

- A second set of policies toward openness and greater neutrality of trade regimes consists of (i) lowering the average level of protection and (ii) reducing the average dispersion, or variance of protection. If the dispersion is not reduced, as the average tariff declines, the tariff structure may become less neutral and more discriminatory, and therefore, highly distorting. A reform strategy that reduces tariffs on intermediate capital goods but leaves those on finished

products intact—which was a common phenomenon in developing economies—ends up increasing effective protection, even though it reduces the average level of tariffs.

Human Resources Development, Technology, and Infrastructure Issues

While it is recommended that the role of government in coordinating resource allocation be generally diminished, public investment in human and physical capital can still play a critical role in stimulating economic development. Specifically, in the current context:

- It must be recognized that education plays a key role in successfully adapting to a globalizing world. The emphasis within the education system will depend on the level of educational skills already attained. On the one hand, more emphasis on basic education, rather than vocational training, will provide semi-skilled workers with the solid but flexible foundation necessary to adapt to a rapidly changing environment. On the other hand, DMCs need a core of highly trained engineers, scientists, financial sector personnel and technicians that can facilitate the absorption of new technology and innovation and transfer it to domestic firms. Which of these concerns is more critical will depend on local conditions, but significant investments in education are clearly warranted.

- Among the economies at the lower end of the technological ladder, it is still possible to achieve effective and productive integration into the global system by importing capital goods, attracting FDI, and licensing foreign technology. It will also be important to maintain competitiveness in the new economy environment through selected investments in telecommunications infrastructure and computer literacy programs. These investments should take advantage of public-private partnerships where possible, depending on local circumstances.

Institutional Factors

The optimal role of government is increasingly a dynamic concept. To remain successful, institutions must adapt. Specifically:

- As DMCs approach the technological frontier, they will have to rely more on innovation than capital accumulation. This may necessitate radical changes to the policies and institutions supporting preexisting systems of innovation as they can pose a barrier to technical change. Thus existing policies that favor large firms and conglomerates may have to change to policies that favor more flexible and innovative smaller firms. Moreover, the current emphasis on centralized bank-based finance might also need to evolve toward greater reliance on securities markets, which may prove more efficient in providing venture capital for new technology start-ups. Generally, an environment conducive to innovation will involve less government command over resources.

- The process of adapting institutions to the imperatives of globalization takes place at the global, regional, and national levels. Actions at these levels should be seen as complementary to each other. At the global level, institutional arrangements that define standards to be met by all countries but that permit individual countries to meet them in different ways offer the best chance of success. This is because they reconcile the common imperatives created by participation in international markets with the diversity of national economic systems and structures. Insofar as cross-border externalities associated with national policies are felt mainly by countries within a region, coordination at the regional level is considered to offer better outcomes than global initiatives. This is considered to be especially relevant in the context of coordinating exchange rate and R&D policies.

Macroeconomic Stabilization

Stable, credible macroeconomic policies are critical to efforts to limit volatility in capital markets. Specifically:

- Monetary and financial institutions have to be strengthened if volatility is to be reduced. The hallmark of these policies should be credibility and prudence. Inflation targeting has much to recommend although it may be too constraining in some instances. On the fiscal side, rigid rules are probably not as acceptable. Nevertheless, large deficits should be avoided to minimize the buildup of public sector debt and the crowding out of private sector activity.

- Exchange rate regimes that featured a soft peg to the US dollar were one of the primary causes of the Asian financial crisis and the volatility in output, exchange rates, and financial markets that ensued. In the aftermath of the crisis, most countries have adopted floating rate regimes. This has been the preferred solution, except in PRC; Hong Kong, China; and Malaysia, where policies and financial resources are sufficient to hold a peg to the US dollar. However, in the case of a hard peg, countries must be willing to adopt a strong anti-inflation policy and be ready to accept deflation if necessary, particularly as a way to meet competition in international markets when competitors have depreciated

their currencies. It is not generally recommended that countries return to a soft peg as that would require frequent interventions by the central bank to maintain the peg.

Strengthening the Financial System and Capital Account Liberalization

Capital account liberalization is likely to become increasingly difficult to resist as economic and financial globalization proceeds. This point heightens the importance of coordinating domestic financial liberalization with the elimination of distortions that would otherwise cause such liberalization to heighten volatility. These measures must include increasing bank capitalization where appropriate, strengthening prudential supervision and regulation, and eliminating implicit guarantees to prevent financial institutions from taking excessive risks:

- FDI is the form of foreign investment that comes packaged with managerial and technological expertise. It is also least likely to aggravate weaknesses in the domestic banking system or to be associated with panic. For these reasons liberalization of FDI should be the first step in liberalizing the capital account.

- Greater competition should be selectively introduced to strengthen the banking system, increase efficiency, and enhance the quality of banking services. Foreign competition should perhaps be phased in so that the domestic banks have time to adjust. It must also be recognized that opening the financial market to foreign banks might increase the flow of portfolio investment. Thus, banks should be allowed to fund themselves offshore only after other policies to strengthen the financial system have been put in place.

- Using market-based initiatives to regulate capital flows (thus mitigating the volatility of portfolio and other investment flows) is preferable to administrative measures. An example is the Chilean system of requiring a year-length deposit of all investors seeking to import capital. This implicitly places a disproportionate tax on short-term investors.

- Bond and stock markets should be developed to provide greater stability to the financial system. The development of bond markets helps diversify sources of corporate debt, while that of stock markets avoids excessive reliance on debt in general. However, developing deep and liquid bond and stock markets is likely to take time given the need to put in place regulatory requirements mandating the disclosure of up-to-date financial information, the use of recognized auditing and accounting standards, penalties for insider trading, and statutes protecting minority shareholders.

Poverty Measures

Globalization will be accepted most readily if its benefits are widely shared. Two sets of policies can help achieve this:

- For the short term, insurance against shocks is needed. These include short-term safety nets for those unable to work, and public works programs for those who are. These social safety net programs should be targeted to maximize efficiency, although experience in India, Bangladesh, and Philippines demonstrates that this is difficult. Microcredit programs are an important element of these programs to avoid distress asset sales. Moreover, these social safety nets need to be in place prior to a crisis if they are to be effective.

- In the long term, policies are required to foster the accumulation of forms of human capital that are useful in a globalized world. The ability to respond quickly to global changes will be more important. This means less focus on vocational training and more on basic education, particularly for women, who because of their familial obligations, are least able to reeducate themselves as adults.

In closing, it may be put forward that DMCs experienced the economic and financial crisis of 1997/98 because they failed to recognize the risks that came with large portfolio inflows that were ultimately linked with liberalization of financial markets and globalization. The challenge for DMCs now is how to capitalize on the opportunities for growth and development afforded by globalization while at the same time minimizing the risks of volatility, dealing with possible crises, and managing other issues that may arise as the process continues.

Endnotes

[1] Per capita incomes were already high in the US prior to the initiation of industrialization and the emergence there of the modern multidivisional corporation, which might be taken to indicate that the country was the technological leader. So too might the country's singular success at machine building, as reflected in the Crystal Palace Exhibition in 1851 in the UK. But this reflected an unusual abundance of productive land and natural resources, which put a floor under real wages, and the country's singular success at producing labor-saving machinery for a relatively small number of industries. See Temin (1966) and James and Skinner (1985).

[2] Two caveats are worth noting. First, the data for the US display a decline in the relative contribution of TFP growth in the period after 1965, reflecting the productivity slowdown of the 1970s and 1980s. Extending these estimates into the 1990s—the period of the new economy—would of course strengthen the interpretation in the text. In contrast, extending the data for Japan into the 1990s would cast further doubt on the interpretation emphasizing a growing role for TFP growth. The 1990s was a decade when output growth in Japan was depressed but domestic investment was sustained at high levels. As a matter of simple arithmetic, productivity growth was slow. But this, plausibly, was a cyclical aberration, reflecting the country's economic and financial crisis, rather than a change in the secular pattern of growth.

[3] Many have already closed the gap. Hong Kong, China and Singapore are already richer per capita than the average OECD economy, while Korea and Taipei,China are within the OECD range of income per capita.

[4] Freeman (1987) and Nelson (1992) call them "national innovation systems" while Kim (1997) and Matthews and Cho (2000) call them "national systems of economic learning".

[5] There is mixed evidence on this point. Belderbos et al. (2000) find that local content and related spillovers tend to be lower in Japanese electronics firms' greenfield subsidiaries (plants for products with no local competition) than in their joint ventures with the ASEAN-4 economies and the PRC. Saggi (1999), however, argues that evidence that licensing and joint ventures lead to more learning by local firms is scant to nonexistent.

[6] Such as computer-aided design production technology that can be easily split among different producers without loss of quality and/or precision.

[7] At the same time, Hong Kong, China; and Singapore promoted savings, investment, and technology transfer while permitting—indeed, encouraging—the free international flow of portfolio capital.

[8] Thus, Urata and Kawai (2000) measure technology transfer by comparing the level of TFP between parent firms and overseas affiliates, and find that transfer is highest for Asian economies with relatively ample supplies of scientists and engineers.

[9] Mansfield et al. (1982) estimate that technologies transferred by US multinationals have historically been 10 years old on average, while the comparable figure for licensing and joint ventures is 13 years.

[10] Innovation is the component not easily explained by an econometric relationship, i.e., the random fluctuation.

[11] More details on the points that follow can be found in Eichengreen (2000), from which this discussion draws.

[12] Admittedly, Thailand's lifting of most restrictions on inward FDI in import-competing industries in the 1970s and on export industries

in the 1980s did not prevent a serious crisis. But the problem there was that the country also opened the capital account to portfolio flows without strengthening its financial system and rationalizing prudential supervision.

[13] A study by Sarno and Taylor (1999), using time-series data for Asian and Latin American countries and Kalman filtering methods, in fact finds that FDI flows have a larger permanent component than bank credit, equity flows, bond flows, or official credit.

[14] They can also follow the example of US companies prior to the emergence of deep and liquid domestic securities markets. US railways, the large corporations of their time, issued bonds and debentures in London as a way of circumventing the underdevelopment of American financial markets. However, this will not create an investor base with an appetite for issues denominated in domestic currency.

[15] Mexico in 1994, Asia in 1997, Russia and Brazil in 1998, and Argentina and Turkey in 2000.

[16] In technical terms, the availability of reserves allows the authorities to engage in sterilized intervention, in which they attempt to support the exchange rate by selling foreign exchange without at the same time altering the domestic money supply. But when speculative sales of the currency are large relative to reserves, this strategy will not remain feasible. A credible defense will then require the authorities to buy the domestic currency that market participants sell, reducing the supply of domestic credit, raising interest rates, dampening investment, and making it more difficult for weak banks and corporations to borrow.

[17] See Hausmann et al. (1999) and Buiter (1999) for two discussions that question the value of monetary autonomy.

[18] The advantages of shared growth are a theme of much of the recent literature on the Asian approach: see, for example, World Bank (1993) and Campos and Root (1996). Rodrik (1997) links the concept to ease of adjustment to external shocks.

[19] See, for example, Ferreira et al. (1999).

[20] The relatively low wage, which is only a fraction of the formal sector minimum wage, encourages self-selection by the poor.

[21] An exception is the state of Kerala, where the poorest 60 percent of the population have historically received 80—90 percent of the benefits. Other Indian states are now using various forms of means testing to more effectively target public distribution system benefits. Sri Lanka's food stamp program also appears to be relatively well targeted.

[22] In the first half of the 1990s, the National Capital Region and Cagayan Valley (close to the capital), which account for less than 3 percent of the poor (measured in terms of nutrition), received 35 percent of the subsidized rice (Subbarao et al. 1995).

[23] World Bank (1993) takes the contrast between Venezuela and Korea as illustrative: whereas Venezuela allocated 43 percent of its education budget to higher education in 1985, in the same year Korea allocated only 10 percent to higher education. While government finance in Korea accounts for nearly 100 percent of the direct costs of primary schooling, it provides less than 50 percent of such costs for tertiary education.

[24] The ancillary assumption is that parents cannot borrow to finance schooling.

[25] As Campos and Root (1996, p. 1) put the point, "Regime leaders in the high-performing Asian economies understood that the challenge of economic growth required the coordination of expectations of different sectors of the population."

[26] A network externality arises when the value of a product to a consumer changes as the number of users changes. For example, as the number of homes and offices connected to the Internet increases, the value of having Internet access increases for each subscriber because there are more potential uses for the Internet connection.

[27] A similar argument has been made about the debt crisis and the "lost decade" of the 1980s catalyzing reform in Latin America by, among others, Edwards (1995).

[28] See www.imf.org/external/standards.

REFERENCES

Acs, Z.J. and D.B. Audretsch. 1987. "Innovation, Market Structure, and Firm Size." *Review of Economics and Statistics* 69, pp. 567-575.

Acs, Z.J. and D.B. Audretsch. 1990. *Innovation and Small Firms,* Cambridge: MIT Press.

Alesina, Alberto and Roberto Perotti. 1994. "Budget Deficits and Budget Institutions." Unpublished manuscript. Harvard University and Columbia University.

Asian Development Bank. 1997. *Emerging Asia: Changes and Challenges.* Manila: Asian Development Bank.

————. 1999. *Asian Development Outlook 1999.* Manila: Asian Development Bank.

————. 2000. *Asian Development Outlook 2000 Update.* Manila: Asian Development Bank.

Belderbos, Rene, Rioganni Capannelli, and Kyoji Fukao. 2000. "The Local Content of Japanese Electronics Manufacturing Operations in Asia." In Takatoshi Ito and Anne Krueger (eds.), *The Role of Foreign Direct Investment in East Asian Economic Development.* Chicago: University of Chicago Press, pp. 9-48.

Birdsall, Nancy and Stephan Haggard. 2000. *After the Crisis: The Social Contract and the Middle Class in East Asia.* Washington, DC: Carnegie Endowment for International Peace.

Bordo, Michael and Barry Eichengreen. 2000. "Is the Crisis Problem Growing More Severe?" Unpublished manuscript. Rutgers University and University of California, Berkeley.

Bordo, Michael, Barry Eichengreen, and Douglas Irwin. 1999. "Is Globalization Today Really Different Than Globalization A Hundred Years Ago?" NBER Working Paper No. 7195. Cambridge, Massachusetts: National Bureau of Economic Research. June, 1999.

Bourguignon, François, Jaime de Melo, and Akiko Suwa. 1991. "Distributional Effects of Adjustment Policies: Simulations for Archetype Economies in Africa and Latin America." *World Bank Economic Review* 5, pp. 339-366.

Buiter, Willem. 1999. "Optimum Currency Areas: Why Does the Exchange Rate Regime Matter? With an Application to UK Membership in EMU." Unpublished manuscript. Bank of England and Cambridge University.

Bussière, Matthieu and Christian Mulder. 1999. "External Vulnerability in Emerging Market Economies: How High Liquidity Can Offset Weak Fundamentals and the Effects of Contagion." IMF Working Paper WP/99/98. July.

Calvo, Guillermo A. and Carmen M. Reinhart "Fear of Floating." NBER Working Paper No. 7993. Cambridge, Massachusetts: National Bureau of Economic Research. November 2000.

Campos, Jose Edgardo and Hilton Root. 1996. *The Key to the Asian Miracle: Making Shared Growth Credible.* Washington, DC: The Brookings Institution.

Cho, Yoon Je. 1996. "Government Intervention, Rent Distribution, and Economic Development in Korea." In Masahiko Aoki, Hyung-Ki Kim, and Masahiro Okuno-Fujiwara (eds.), *The Role of Government in East Asian Economic Development.* Oxford: Clarendon Press, pp. 208-232.

Cutler, David, Felicia Knaul, Rafael Lozano, Oscar Mendez, and Beatriz Zurita. 2000. "Financial Crisis, Health Outcomes and Aging: Mexico in the 1980s and 1990s." NBER Working Paper No. 7746. Cambridge, Massachusetts: National Bureau of Economic Research. June.

David, Paul. 1993. "Why Are Institutions the 'Carriers of History'?" Unpublished manuscript. Stanford University.

Davis, Lance and Douglas North. 1971. *Institutional Change and American Economic Growth.* Cambridge: Cambridge University Press.

Demirgüç-Kunt, Asli, Ross Levine, and Hong-Ghi Min. 1998. "Opening to Foreign Banks: Issues of Stability, Efficiency, and Growth." In Seongtae Lee (ed.), *The Implications of Globalization of World Financial Markets.* Seoul: Bank of Korea, pp. 83-115.

Dollar, David. 2000. "Growth is Good." Unpublished manuscript. World Bank.

Dooley, Michael P. 1997. "A Model of Crises in Emerging Markets." NBER Working Paper No. 6300. Cambridge, Massachusetts: National Bureau of Economic Research. December, 1997.

Drazen, Allan and Vittorio Grilli. 1993. "The Benefits of Crises for Economic Reforms." *American Economic Review* 83, pp. 598-607.

Easterly, William and Aart Kraay. 1999. "Small States, Small Problems." Policy Working Paper No. 2139. Washington, DC: World Bank.

Eaton, Jonathan, Eva Gutierrez, and Samuel Kortum. 1998. "European Technology Policy." NBER Working Paper No. 6827. Cambridge, Massachusetts: National Bureau of Economic Research. December.

Edwards, Sebastian. 1984. "The Order of Liberalization of the External Sector in Developing Countries." *Essays in International Finance* 156. International Finance Section, Department of Economics, Princeton University.

Eichengreen, Barry. 2000. "Taming Capital Flows." *World Development* (May), pp. 1105-1116.

Eichengreen, Barry, Ricardo Hausmann, and Juergen von Hagen. 1999. "Reforming Budgetary Institutions in Latin America: The Case for a National Fiscal Council." *Open Economies Review* 10, pp. 415-442.

Eichengreen, Barry, Andrew Rose, and Charles Wyplosz. 1995. "Exchange Market Mayhem: The Antecedents and Aftermath of Speculative Attacks." *Economic Policy* 21, pp. 249-312.

Feldstein, Martin. 1999. "Self-Protection for Emerging Market Economies." NBER Working Paper No. 6907. Cambridge, Massachusetts: National Bureau of Economic Research. January.

Ferreira, Francisco, Giovanna Prennushi, and Martin Ravallion. 1999. "Protecting the Poor from Macroeconomic Shocks: An Agenda for Action in a Crisis and Beyond." Unpublished manuscript. World Bank.

Fischer, Stanley. "Exchange Rate Regimes: Is the Bipolar View Correct?" *American Economic Association*, March 2001.

Foley, C.F. 1999. "Going Bust in Bangkok: Lessons from Bankruptcy Law Reform in Thailand." Unpublished manuscript. Harvard University.

Frankel, Jeffrey and David Romer. 1999. "Does Trade Cause Growth?" *American Economic Review*, 89, No. 3, pp. 379-399. June 1999.

Frankenberg, Elizabeth, Duncan Thomas, and Kathleen Beegle. 1999. "The Real Costs of Indonesia's Economic Crisis." Labor and Population Program Working Paper No. 99-04. Santa Monica: The Rand Corporation (March).

Freeman, Chris. 1987. *Technology Policy and Economic Performance: Lessons from Japan.* London: Frances Pinter.

———. 1995. "The 'National System of Innovation' in Historical Perspective." *Cambridge Journal of Economics* 19, pp. 5-24.

Gavin, Michael and Ricardo Hausmann. 1995. "Overcoming Volatility in Latin America." IMF Seminar Paper No. 95/34 (August).

Gerschenkron, Alexander. 1962. *Economic Backwardness in Historical Perspective.* Cambridge: Harvard University Press.

Glick, Reuven and Andrew K. Rose. 1999. "Contagion and Trade: Why are Currency Crises Regional?" *Journal of International Money and Finance* 18, pp. 603-617.

Goldberg, Linda. 1993. "Exchange Rates and Investment in United States Industry." *Review of Economics and Statistics* 75, pp. 575-588.

Goldstein, Morris. 1998. *The Asian Financial Crisis.* Washington, DC: Institute for International Economics.

Greenspan, Alan. 1999. "Remarks by Chairman of the Board of Governors of the Federal Reserve Before The World Bank Conference on Recent Trends in Reserves Management." Washington, DC, 29 April.

Guidotti, Pablo. 1999. "Currency Reserves and Debt." Speech to the World Bank Conference on Recent Trends in Reserves Management. Washington, DC, 29 April.

Guitan, Manuel. 1995. "Monetary Policy: Equity Issues in IMF Policy Advice." Unpublished manuscript. IMF.

Gwartney, James, and Robert Lawson. 2000. Economic Freedom of the World: 2000 Annual Report. Vancouver, B.C.: Fraser Institute.

Hausmann, Ricardo, M. Gavin, C. Pages-Serra, and E. Stein. 1999. "Financial Turmoil and the Choice of Exchange Rate Regime." Unpublished manuscript. Inter-American Development Bank.

Hayami, Yujiro. 1998. "Toward an East Asian Model of Economic Development." In Yujiro Hayami and Masahiko Aoki (eds.), *The Institutional Foundations of East Asian Economic Development.* London: Macmillan, pp. 3-36.

Heckman, James J. 2000. "Policies to Foster Human Capital." *Research in Economics* 54, pp. 3-56.

Hellman, Thomas, Kevin Murdock, and Joseph Stiglitz. 2000. "Liberalization, Moral Hazard in Banking, and Prudential Regulation: Are Capital Requirements Enough?" *American Economic Review* 90, pp. 147-165.

Inter-American Development Bank (IDB). 1995. *Overcoming Volatility: Economic and Social Progress in Latin America.* Washington, DC: IDB.

International Monetary Fund (IMF). 1999a. *World Economic Outlook.* October. Washington, DC.

———. 1999b. "International Standards and Fund Surveillance: Progress and Issues." Washington, DC. (16 August). Available: www.imf.org/external/np/rosc/stand.htm.

———. 2000. World Economic Outlook Database. September. Available: www.imf.org/external/pubs/ft/weo/2000/02/data/index.htm.

James, John and Jonathan Skinner. 1985. "The Resolution of the Labor Scarcity Paradox." *Journal of Economic History* 45, pp. 513-540.

Keller, Wolfgang. 2000. "Geographic Localization of International Technology Diffusion." NBER Working Paper No. 7509. Cambridge, Massachusetts: National Bureau of Economic Research. January.

Kenen, Peter B. and Dani Rodrik. 1986. "Measuring and Analyzing the Effects of Short-Term Volatility of Real Exchange Rates." *Review of Economics and Statistics* 68, pp. 311-315.

Kennedy, Robert E. and Richard H.K. Vietor. "Globalization and Growth." Harcourt College Publishers, 2001, p. 4.

Khandker, S., B. Khalily, and Z. Khan. 1994. *Sustainability of Grameen Bank: What Do We Know?* Washington, DC: World Bank.

Kim, J. and L.J. Lau. 1994. "The Sources of Economic Growth of the East Asian Newly Industrialized Countries." *Journal of the Japanese and International Economy* 8, pp. 235-271.

Kim, Linsu. 1997. *From Imitation to Innovation: The Dynamics of Korea's Technological Learning,* Boston: Harvard Business School Press.

Klein, Michael and Giovanni Olivei. 1999. "Capital Account Liberalization, Financial Depth and Economic Growth." NBER Working Paper No. 7384. Cambridge, Massachusetts: National Bureau of Economic Research. October.

Kraay, Aart. 1998. "In Search of the Macroeconomic Effects of Capital Account Liberalization." Unpublished paper. World Bank.

Krugman, Paul. 1985. "A Technology-Gap Model of International Trade." In Douglas Hague (ed.), *Structural Adjustment in Developed Open Economies*. New York: St. Martin's Press, pp. 35-49.

————. 1994. "The Myth of Asia's Miracle." *Foreign Affairs* 73, pp. 62-78.

Lopez, Ramon, Vinod Thomas, and Yan Wang. 1998. "Addressing the Education Puzzle: The Distribution of Education and Economic Reform." Policy Research Working Paper No. 2031. Washington, DC: World Bank.

Lukas, Aaron. 2000. "WTO Report Card III: Globalization and Developing Countries." Briefing Paper No. 10, Cato Institute.

Mansfield, E., A. Romeo, M. Schwartz, D. Teece, S. Wagner, and P. Brach. 1982. *Technology Transfer, Productivity and Economic Policy*. New York: W. W. Norton.

Matthews, John A. and Dong-Sung Cho. 2000. *Tiger Technology: The Creation of a Semiconductor Industry in East Asia*. Cambridge: Cambridge University Press.

McKinnon, Ronald and Donald Mathieson. 1981. "How to Manage a Repressed Economy," *Essays in International Finance* No. 145. International Finance Section, Department of Economics, Princeton University.

Morley, Samuel. 1994. *Poverty and Inequality in Latin America*. Washington: Inter-American Development Bank.

Mowery, David and Joanne Oxley. 1995. "Inward Technology Transfer and Competitiveness: The Role of National Innovation Systems." *Cambridge Journal of Economics* 19, pp. 67-93.

Mussa, Michael. 2000. "Factors Driving Global Economic Integration." Paper presented in Jackson Hole, Wyoming at a symposium sponsored by the Federal Reserve Bank of Kansas City on Global Opportunities and Challenges, 25 August 2000.

Nelson, Richard. 1992. "National Innovation Systems: A Retrospective on a Study." *Industrial and Corporate Change* 1, pp. 347-374.

Nelson, Richard and Gavin Wright. 1992. "The Rise and Fall of American Technological Leadership: The Postwar Era in Historical Perspective." *Journal of Economic Literature* 30, pp. 1931-1964.

Olson, Mancur. 1982. *The Rise and Decline of Nations*. New Haven: Yale University Press.

Organisation for Economic Co-operation and Development. 1992. *Industrial Policy in OECD Economies*. Paris: OECD.

————. 1998. *Open Markets Matter*. Paris: OECD. p. 40.

Ozawa, T. 1985. "Macroeconomic Factors Affecting Japan's Technology Inflows and Outflows: the Postwar Experience." In N. Rosenberg and C. Frischtak (eds.), *International Technology Transfer*. New York: Praeger.

Patel, Pari. 1995. "Localised Production of Technology for Global Markets." *Cambridge Journal of Economics* 19, pp. 141-153.

Radelet, S. and Jeffrey Sachs. 1998. "The Onset of the Asian Financial Crisis." NBER Working Paper No. 6680. Cambridge, Massachusetts: National Bureau of Economic Research. August.

Ramey, Garey and Valerie Ramey. 1995. "Cross-Country Evidence on the Link Between Volatility and Growth." *American Economic Review* 85, pp. 1138-1151.

Ravallion, Martin. 1997. "Can High-Inequality Developing Countries Escape Absolute Poverty?" *Economics Letters* 56, pp. 51-57.

————. 1999. "Appraising Workfare." *Work Bank Research Observer* 14, pp. 31-48.

Rodrik, Dani. 1995. "Getting Interventions Right: How South Korea and Taiwan Grew Rich." *Economic Policy* 20, pp. 53-97.

————. 1997. "Globalization, Social Conflict and Economic Growth." Unpublished manuscript. Harvard University.

————. 1998. "Why Do More Open Economies Have Bigger Governments?" *Journal of Political Economy* 106, pp. 997-1032.

————. 1999. "Institutions for High-Quality Growth: What They are and How to Acquire Them." Unpublished manuscript. Harvard University (October).

Rodrik, Dani and Andres Velasco. 1999. "Short-Term Capital Flows." Unpublished manuscript. Harvard University and New York University (April).

Sachs, Jeffrey and Andrew M. Warner. 1995. "Economic Reform and the Process of Global Integration." Brookings Papers on Economic Activity No.1.

Saggi, Kamal. 1999. "Trade, Foreign Direct Investment, and International Technology Transfer: A Survey." Unpublished manuscript. Southern Methodist University.

Sah, Raaj K. 1991. "Fallibility in Human Organizations and Political Systems." *Journal of Economic Perspectives* 5, pp. 67-88.

Sarel, Michael. 1996. "Growth in East Asia What We Can and What We Cannot Infer." International Monetary Fund, Economic Issues. International Monetary Fund. Washington, DC.

Sarno, Lucio and Mark P. Taylor. 1999. "Hot Money, Accounting Labels, and the Permanence of Capital Flows to Developing Countries: An Empirical Investigation." *Journal of Development Economics* 59, pp. 337-364.

Smarzynska, Beata K. 1999. "Technological Leadership and Foreign Investors' Choice of Entry Mode." Unpublished manuscript. World Bank.

Subbarao, K., Jeanine Braithwaite, and Jyotsna Jalan. 1995. "Protecting the Poor During Adjustment and Transitions." Human Capital Development and Operations Policy Working Paper No. 58. Washington, DC: World Bank (July).

Temin, Peter. 1966. "Labor Scarcity and the Problem of American Industrial Efficiency in the 1850s." *Journal of Economic History* 26, pp. 361-379.

Ulan, Michael K. 2000. "Is a Chilean-Style Tax on Short-Term Capital Inflows Stabilizing?" *Open Economies Review* 11, pp. 149-177.

Urata, Shujiro and Hiroki Kawai. 2000. "Intrafirm Technology Transfer by Japanese Manufacturing Firms in Asia." In Takatoshi Ito and Anne Krueger (eds.), *The Role of Foreign Direct Investment in East Asian Economic Development.* Chicago: University of Chicago Press, pp. 49-78.

von Hagen, Jürgen and Ian J. Harden. 1994. "National Budget Processes and Fiscal Performance." *European Economy Reports and Studies* 3, 311-408

Williamson, Jeffrey. 1993. "Human Capital Deepening, Inequality, and Demographic Events Along the Asia-Pacific Rim." In Naohiro Ogawa, Gavin Jones, and Jeffrey Williamson (eds.), *Human Resources in Development Along the Asia-Pacific Rim.* Singapore: Oxford University Press, pp. 129-158.

Williamson, John. 1999. "The Case for a Common Basket Peg for East Asian Currencies." In Stefan Collignon, Jean Pisani-Ferry and Yung Chul Park (eds.), *Exchange Rate Policies in Emerging Asian Countries.* London: Routledge, pp. 327-343.

World Bank. 1993. *The East Asian Miracle: Economic Growth and Public Policy.* Washington, DC: World Bank.

————. 2000. *Global Economic Prospects and the Developing Countries.* Washington, DC: World Bank.

World Bank. 2001. Global Poverty Monitoring. Available: www.worldbank.org/research/povmonitor/index.htm.

Young, Alwyn. 1992. "A Tale of Two Cities: Factor Accumulation and Technical Change in Hong Kong and Singapore." In Olivier Blanchard and Stanley Fischer, *NBER Macroeconomics Annual 1992.* Cambridge: MIT Press, pp. 13-64.

Statistical Appendix

Statistical Notes

The Statistical Appendix presents selected economic indicators for 39 developing member countries (DMCs) of the Asian Development Bank (ADB) in a total of 23 tables. These are presented by account, namely: (i) production and demand sectors of the national income accounts, (ii) consumer price index, (iii) money supply, (iv) components of the balance of payments, (v) external debt and debt service, (vi) exchange rate, and (vii) the budget of the central government. These tables contain time series information from 1995 to 2000. Except for fiscal and external variables, such as the budget of the central government, exchange rate, external debt and debt service, the tables give projections for 2001 and 2002. The table on foreign direct investment shows data from 1994 to 1999 (the latest year for which data are available). The following sections describe the source, scope, and conceptual definition of the data in each table.

Historical data are derived mostly from ADB's Statistical Database System; official sources; statistical publications; secondary publications; and working papers and other internal documents of ADB, International Monetary Fund (IMF), World Bank, and the United Nations. Some of the preliminary data for 2000 are official estimates or staff estimates calculated from quarterly or monthly data available for the year. Projections for 2001 and 2002 are staff estimates.

Despite limitations arising from differences in statistical methodology, definition, coverage, and practice, efforts were made to standardize the data. The aim is to allow comparability of data over time and across DMCs, and to ensure consistency across accounts. Data-splicing and data-rebasing techniques were also used to merge data sets and to fill in data gaps.

Data in the tables refer to either calendar year or fiscal year. All data for Bangladesh, India, Federated States of Micronesia, Marshall Islands, Myanmar, Nepal, Pakistan, and Tonga are on a fiscal year basis. For Bhutan, Cook Islands, Lao PDR, Maldives, and Sri Lanka, some data refer to calendar year while others refer to the fiscal year. For the rest of the DMCs, data on national accounts, consumer or wholesale price index, monetary accounts, and balance of payments are reported for the calendar year. Government finances for all DMCs are reported on a fiscal year basis.

Regional averages or totals for the DMCs and for each of the five country groupings are incorporated in 10 of the 23 tables. These tables include growth rate of gross domestic product (GDP), growth rate of per capita GDP, changes in consumer or wholesale price index, growth rate of merchandise exports and imports, trade balance, current account balance in absolute levels, current account balance as a percentage of GDP, foreign direct investment, and external debt outstanding.

For 1997–2000, the share in total output of the five countries most affected by the crisis has fallen. In contrast, the combined share of the People's Republic of China and India increased to nearly 50 percent in 2000. The rapid change in output share is a result of converting GDP in local currency to GDP in US dollars, which gives larger weights to countries with stable currencies, such as the Indian rupee and the yuan. Given the strong growth of the People's Republic of China and India and their larger than normal weights in the region, the net effect is to suggest an artificially higher growth for Asia. To address this distortion, the *ADO 2001* averages are computed as simple, weighted arithmetic means using the average of GDP values in 1995–1996, in current US dollars. The computation of averages for country groupings for Tables A1, A2, A9, and A16 is based on these weights.

Because of data problems, data for Azerbaijan, the Central Asian republics, Mongolia, and Myanmar are excluded from the computation of averages.

Tables A1, A2, A3, A4, A5, and A6: Growth and Structure of Production. The definitions used in these tables relating to output growth and production are generally based on the United Nations System of National Accounts. Table A1 shows annual growth rates of GDP valued either at constant market prices or at constant factor costs. Most DMCs use constant market price valuations. The exceptions are Bhutan, Fiji Islands, India, Lao PDR, Nepal, Pakistan, Solomon Islands, Sri Lanka, and Tuvalu, which use GDP at constant factor cost.

Table A2 presents the growth rate figures for real per capita GDP. Real per capita GDP is obtained by dividing GDP valued at either constant market prices or factor cost, by population.

Tables A3, A4, and A5 present the annual growth rates of real gross value added in agriculture, industry, and services, respectively. The agriculture sector includes agricultural crops, livestock, poultry, fisheries, and forestry. Mining and quarrying, manufacturing, construction, and utilities fall under the industry sector. The services sector comprises transportation and communications, trade, banking and finance, real estate, public administration, and other services. For Korea, Malaysia, and Nepal, other items comprising imputed bank service charges, other services, and government services are included in the computation. The sectoral growth rates are consistent with the reported GDP values in Table A1. Adding-up restrictions are imposed where numerical discrepancies are noted or where reclassifications of the sectors are implemented.

Table A6 shows the sectoral shares of GDP based on constant market prices. For Bhutan, Cambodia, India, Kiribati, Lao PDR, Pakistan, Solomon Islands, Sri Lanka, and Tuvalu, the sectoral shares of GDP are based on constant factor costs. For Marshall Islands, the shares are based on current market prices.

Tables A7 and A8: Savings and Investment. Gross national savings (GNS) or gross domestic savings (GDS) are computed as the difference between gross national product (GNP) or GDP, and total consumption expenditure. They are expressed as a proportion of GNP or GDP. For some DMCs, gross savings data are obtained from official sources. Gross savings may differ from either GNS or GDS by being derived from the consolidated income and outlay account, and include private transfers recorded in the balance of payments. Gross domestic investment (GDI) is calculated as the sum of gross fixed capital formation and changes in stocks. For Korea and Viet Nam, GDS is computed as the sum of GDI and current account balance. For Thailand, gross savings is equal to net savings plus provision of consumption of fixed capital. For Lao PDR, gross national savings is obtained from official sources.

Table A7 gives the ratio of GDS to GDP, calculated from official sources. For Bangladesh, Lao PDR, and Viet Nam, the ratio of GNS to GDP is used. Table A8 presents the ratio of GDI to GDP. All figures used in computing the ratios in Tables A7 and A8 are in current market prices. The data are obtained from official sources.

Table A9: Consumer Prices. This table presents the annual inflation rate based on the consumer price index (except for India) as obtained from official local sources. For DMCs for which data are not available locally, data were obtained from IMF. For most DMCs, the reported inflation rates are period averages. For Kazakhstan, Kyrgyz Republic, Tajikistan, and Viet Nam, the end-of-period consumer price index is used. For India, the inflation rate is based on the wholesale price index.

Table A10: Growth of Money Supply. This table tracks the annual percentage change in broad money as represented by M2. M2 is defined as the sum of M1 and quasi-money, where M1 denotes currency in circulation plus demand deposits, and quasi-money consists of time and savings deposits, plus foreign currency deposits. For India, M3 is used as the measure of liquidity. M3 is M2 deposits with reserve bank of India. All data for M2 are obtained from country sources, except for Cambodia and Sri Lanka, which are taken from ADB's Statistical Database System.

Tables A11 and A13: Growth Rates of Merchandise Exports and Imports. Historical data for 1995–1999 and some preliminary estimates for 2000 on merchandise exports and imports are taken from the balance-of-payments accounts, except for Hong Kong, China data, which are taken from the external trade account. These figures are on a free-on-board basis. Export and import statistics are reported on a calendar year basis except for Bangladesh, Bhutan, India, Marshall Islands, Federated States of Micronesia, Nepal, and Tonga, which use fiscal year figures. For Cambodia, export data refer to domestic exports only, while import data refer to retained imports only. Retained imports are total imports net of reexports, but include project aid imports and an estimate of unrecorded imports. Data for Kyrgyz Republic, Marshall Islands, Solomon Islands, Tajikistan, Tonga, and Uzbekistan are derived from IMF documents.

Table A12: Direction of Exports. For each DMC, the table indicates the percentage share of that economy's exports going to each of its major trading partners (other DMCs, Japan, United States, European Union, and Australia and New Zealand). With the exception of Taipei,China, for which data are obtained directly from local sources, data are from IMF's *Direction of Trade Statistics*.

Tables A14, A15, and A16: Balance of Payments. The balance of trade is the difference between merchandise exports and merchandise imports. The current account balance is the sum of the balance of trade, net trade in services and factor income, and net transfers. In the case of Lao PDR, Pakistan, Thailand, and Viet Nam, official transfers are excluded from the current account balance. The balance-of-payments data for the DMCs are obtained from local sources except for Kyrgyz Republic, Marshall Islands, Solomon Islands, Tajikistan, Tonga, and Uzbekistan, where data are obtained from IMF documents.

Table A17: Foreign Direct Investment. Data on net inflows for 1994–1999 are obtained from the World Bank's selected indicators on aggregate net resource flows and external debt. Direct investment capital refers to equity capital, reinvested earnings, and other capital associated with the transactions of enterprises.

Tables A18 and A19: External Debt. For most DMCs, external debt outstanding includes long-term debt, short-term debt, and IMF credit. Principal repayments and interest payments on long-term debt and IMF credit, and interest payments on short-term debt, are lumped together in the debt-service payment. For most DMCs, data are collected from official country sources, except for Kyrgyz Republic, Tajikistan, and Uzbekistan where the data come from IMF documents, and for Indonesia where the data are obtained from the World Bank. The debt-service ratio is computed as a proportion of total exports of goods and services. For Cambodia, debt excludes debt to the Russian Federation. For Pakistan, total external public debt is reported. For Tajikistan, imports of alumina and electricity are deducted from exports of goods and services.

Table A20: Foreign Exchange Rates. The annual average exchange rates of the DMCs are quoted in local currencies per unit of US dollar. IMF's *International Financial Statistics* is the source of basic data for Fiji Islands, Indonesia, Nauru, Papua New Guinea, Samoa, Solomon Islands, and Tonga. For all other DMCs, the sources are official country publications.

Tables A21, A22, and A23: Government Finance. These tables account for only central government finance on a fiscal year basis. Government expenditure includes both current and capital expenditures. Likewise, total revenue includes current revenue and capital receipts. For Lao PDR, Sri Lanka, and Viet Nam, expenditure includes net lending. For Kazakhstan, Kyrgyz Republic, Tajikistan, and Uzbekistan, revenue excludes proceeds from privatization. In most DMCs, the overall budget surplus or deficit is the balance between government revenue and expenditure, including grants. For India, the overall balance excludes small savings. For Cambodia, it excludes adjustments but includes grants, for Thailand it includes non-budgetary expenditures from loans. For Pakistan, Sri Lanka and Viet Nam, it excludes grants. All ratios are reported as a percentage of GDP at current market prices. Data are from official country sources.

Table A1 Growth Rate of GDP
(percent per year)

	1995	1996	1997	1998	1999	2000	2001	2002
Newly industrialized economies	7.4	6.3	5.8	-2.9	7.9	8.4	4.3	5.6
Hong Kong, China	3.9	4.5	5.0	-5.3	3.1	10.5	4.0	5.5
Korea, Republic of	8.9	6.8	5.0	-6.7	10.9	8.8	3.9	5.5
Singapore	8.0	7.5	8.5	0.1	5.9	9.9	5.0	6.0
Taipei,China	6.4	6.1	6.7	4.6	5.4	6.0	5.1	5.8
Central Asian republics, Azerbaijan, and Mongolia	-5.4	0.6	1.8	1.5	4.7	7.8	3.3	4.8
Azerbaijan	11.4	1.3	5.8	10.0	7.4	11.0	—	—
Kazakhstan	-8.2	0.4	1.7	-1.9	2.7	9.6	4.0	7.0
Kyrgyz Republic	-5.4	7.1	9.9	2.1	3.7	5.0	5.0	5.2
Mongolia	6.3	2.4	4.0	3.5	3.2	0.5	3.0	4.0
Tajikistan	-12.5	-4.4	1.7	5.3	3.7	5.0	5.0	6.0
Turkmenistan	-7.2	-6.7	-11.4	7.0	16.0	17.0	—	—
Uzbekistan	-0.9	1.6	5.2	4.4	4.4	3.0	3.0	3.0
People's Republic of China	10.5	9.6	8.8	7.8	7.1	8.0	7.3	7.5
Southeast Asia	8.4	7.4	3.5	-9.0	3.1	5.1	4.0	4.8
Cambodia	6.7	5.5	3.7	1.8	5.0	4.5	5.0	6.0
Indonesia	8.2	7.8	4.7	-13.1	0.8	4.8	4.2	4.5
Lao People's Democratic Republic	7.0	6.9	6.9	4.0	5.2	5.5	6.0	6.5
Malaysia	9.8	10.0	7.3	-7.4	5.8	8.5	4.9	6.0
Myanmar	6.9	6.4	5.7	5.8	10.9	—	—	—
Philippines	4.7	5.8	5.2	-0.6	3.3	3.9	3.1	4.2
Thailand	9.3	5.9	-1.4	-10.8	4.2	4.2	3.5	4.5
Viet Nam	9.5	9.3	8.2	4.4	4.7	6.1	6.4	6.9
South Asia	6.8	7.0	4.7	6.1	5.8	5.8	5.8	6.5
Bangladesh	4.9	4.6	5.4	5.2	4.9	5.5	5.7	6.0
Bhutan	7.4	6.0	7.3	5.5	5.9	6.1	5.5	6.0
India	7.3	7.5	5.0	6.6	6.4	6.0	6.2	7.0
Maldives	7.2	8.3	7.8	8.9	8.8	4.2	5.7	—
Nepal	2.9	2.9	4.9	3.3	4.4	6.4	5.5	—
Pakistan	5.2	6.8	1.9	4.3	3.1	4.8	3.8	4.7
Sri Lanka	5.5	3.8	6.3	4.7	4.3	6.0	4.5	5.0
Pacific DMCs	-0.6	5.7	-2.9	-2.0	4.1	-1.8	3.4	5.0
Cook Islands	-4.4	-0.2	-2.8	-2.3	2.7	3.2	3.2	3.3
Fiji Islands	2.5	3.1	-0.9	1.4	9.6	-9.3	4.8	4.8
Kiribati	3.5	4.3	1.0	7.3	2.3	-4.0	2.0	2.0
Marshall Islands	2.7	-15.9	-9.4	-16.0	0.8	-2.3	—	—
Micronesia, Federated States of	3.4	-1.6	-4.8	-1.7*	1.3	2.5	1.4	2.8
Nauru	—	—	—	—	—	—	—	—
Papua New Guinea	-3.3	7.7	-3.9	-3.8	3.2	0.8	3.1	5.7
Samoa	6.4	7.3	1.0	3.4	5.3	7.0	4.0	4.0
Solomon Islands	10.5	3.5	-2.3	1.1	-1.3	-14.0	3.4	3.0
Tonga	2.9	-0.2	0.6	2.5	3.5	5.3	2.0	2.0
Tuvalu	-5.0	10.3	3.5	14.9	3.0	3.0	5.0	5.0
Vanuatu	-2.9	4.8	0.2	-0.1	-3.0	2.8	3.5	3.0
Average	8.3	7.6	5.9	0.2	6.3	7.1	5.3	6.1

— Not available.

Table A2 Growth Rate of Per Capita GDP
(percent per year)

	1995	1996	1997	1998	1999	2000	2001	2002	Per Capita GNP ($) 1999
Newly industrialized economies	6.1	4.5	4.5	-4.1	6.7	7.4	3.2	3.9	
Hong Kong, China	1.9	—	3.7	-6.5	1.9	9.2	2.8	—	24,280
Korea, Republic of	7.8	5.7	4.0	-7.6	9.7	8.3	3.0	4.7	8,490
Singapore	4.6	3.3	4.7	-3.3	5.3	6.3	2.5	3.5	29,610
Taipei,China	5.5	5.3	5.8	3.5	4.3	5.2	4.2	4.9	13,310
Central Asian republics, Azerbaijan, and Mongolia	-4.1	1.0	3.1	0.9	2.4	7.8	0.8	2.7	
Azerbaijan	—	—	—	—	—	—	—	—	550
Kazakhstan	-6.3	2.0	3.3	-0.2	2.6	13.5	1.5	5.3	1,230
Kyrgyz Republic	-8.5	5.5	8.3	0.6	2.2	3.6	—	—	300
Mongolia	4.8	0.8	2.5	2.1	1.9	-0.8	1.7	2.7	350
Tajikistan	-14.0	-6.0	0.1	3.7	2.3	6.6	—	—	290
Turkmenistan	—	—	—	—	—	—	—	—	660
Uzbekistan	-2.7	-0.3	3.3	2.8	2.9	3.0	—	—	720
People's Republic of China	9.3	8.4	7.7	6.7	6.1	7.0	6.3	6.5	780
Southeast Asia	6.5	5.5	1.9	-10.5	1.6	3.6	2.4	3.0	
Cambodia	2.4	0.2	1.7	-2.9	2.3	1.3	1.5	2.8	260
Indonesia	6.8	5.9	3.1	-14.4	-0.6	3.2	2.6	2.9	580
Lao People's Democratic Republic	6.8	4.4	4.3	1.4	2.7	0.9	2.1	2.8	280
Malaysia	6.8	7.5	4.9	-9.5	3.3	6.0	2.5	3.6	3,400
Myanmar	5.0	4.5	3.9	3.8	8.9	—	—	—	—
Philippines	2.2	3.4	2.9	-2.7	1.1	1.8	0.9	—	1,020
Thailand	8.0	4.8	-2.2	-11.8	3.2	3.3	2.6	3.7	1,960
Viet Nam	6.8	7.6	6.6	4.2	3.4	5.2	2.7	5.3	370
South Asia	4.7	5.1	2.6	4.3	4.0	3.9	4.1	4.7	
Bangladesh	3.0	3.5	3.5	3.6	3.3	3.8	4.0	4.3	370
Bhutan	4.1	2.9	4.2	2.4	2.5	2.9	2.3	2.7	510
India	5.2	5.5	2.9	5.2	4.6	4.4	4.5	5.2	450
Maldives	7.2	6.3	5.8	6.9	6.7	2.3	3.7	—	1,160
Nepal	2.7	0.9	2.4	0.9	2.1	3.5	5.7	—	220
Pakistan	2.7	4.2	-0.5	-0.4	0.8	1.4	1.5	2.4	470
Sri Lanka	4.4	2.7	5.1	3.5	2.9	4.5	3.1	3.8	820
Pacific DMCs	-2.4	3.8	-4.4	-3.8	2.9	-3.2	2.1	3.6	
Cook Islands	-3.9	-3.2	6.2	2.8	10.9	-7.2	3.2	3.3	—
Fiji Islands	1.3	2.2	-1.7	-0.7	7.7	-10.9	2.9	2.9	2,210
Kiribati	1.2	2.0	-1.3	4.9	0.1	-6.1	—	—	910
Marshall Islands	1.3	-17.0	-10.6	-17.2	-0.5	-3.7	0.5	—	1,560
Micronesia, Federated States of	1.4	-3.5	-6.5	-3.6	-0.7	0.6	-0.6	0.9	1,810
Nauru	—	—	—	—	—	—	—	—	—
Papua New Guinea	-5.2	5.7	-5.7	-5.6	2.2	-0.1	2.2	4.7	800
Samoa	5.9	6.8	0.5	2.8	4.8	6.5	3.5	3.5	1,060
Solomon Islands	6.5	-0.2	-5.9	-2.5	-4.9	-17.2	-0.4	—	750
Tonga	4.1	-2.1	-0.2	1.8	2.9	4.6	—	—	1,720
Tuvalu	-6.2	8.9	-2.6	12.2	1.8	—	—	—	—
Vanuatu	-5.4	2.1	-2.3	-2.7	-5.5	0.2	1.0	0.5	1,170
Average	6.7	5.9	4.5	-1.1	5.0	5.9	4.0	4.6	

— Not available.
GNP Gross national product.

Table A3 Growth Rate of Value Added in Agriculture
(percent per year)

	1995	1996	1997	1998	1999	2000	2001	2002
Newly industrialized economies								
Hong Kong, China	—	—	—	—	—	—	—	—
Korea, Republic of	—	—	—	—	—	—	—	—
Singapore	-3.1	3.5	0.1	-6.9	-1.1	-1.5	0.2	0.2
Taipei,China	2.8	-0.3	-1.5	-6.6	2.7	-1.3	3.0	3.0
Central Asian republics, Azerbaijan, and Mongolia								
Azerbaijan	—	—	—	—	—	—	—	—
Kazakhstan	-24.4	-5.0	-0.8	-18.9	28.0	-3.3	1.0	0.6
Kyrgyz Republic	-2.0	15.2	12.3	2.9	8.2	3.9	—	—
Mongolia	4.2	4.4	4.3	6.4	—	—	—	—
Tajikistan	—	—	0.2	6.5	3.8	—	—	—
Turkmenistan	—	—	—	—	—	—	—	—
Uzbekistan	2.0	-7.3	5.8	4.1	5.9	3.2	—	—
People's Republic of China	5.0	5.1	3.5	3.5	2.8	2.4	2.8	2.8
Southeast Asia								
Cambodia	7.5	2.2	5.8	2.5	1.5	-0.6	3.7	3.6
Indonesia	4.4	3.1	1.0	-1.3	2.7	1.7	2.4	2.5
Lao People's Democratic Republic	3.1	2.8	7.0	3.7	5.0	4.4	4.8	5.1
Malaysia	-2.5	4.5	0.7	-3.3	3.8	0.4	1.2	1.3
Myanmar	4.8	5.0	3.7	4.5	11.5	—	—	—
Philippines	0.9	3.8	3.1	-6.4	6.0	3.4	1.6	—
Thailand	4.1	4.0	-0.4	-3.2	2.7	1.2	1.0	2.0
Viet Nam	4.8	4.4	4.3	2.8	5.2	3.6	4.2	4.7
South Asia								
Bangladesh	-0.3	3.1	6.0	3.2	4.8	6.4	—	—
Bhutan	4.0	6.4	3.1	1.3	3.0	2.4	4.0	4.0
India	-0.9	9.6	-1.9	6.5	0.7	0.9	1.9	3.5
Maldives	1.6	1.9	1.3	7.3	4.0	1.0	3.8	—
Nepal	-0.3	4.4	4.1	1.0	2.7	5.0	4.0	—
Pakistan	6.6	11.7	0.1	3.8	1.9	7.2	2.9	4.5
Sri Lanka	3.3	-4.6	3.0	2.5	4.5	2.5	0.9	1.8
Pacific DMCs								
Cook Islands	-2.5	4.3	12.2	2.8	2.5	—	—	—
Fiji Islands	-3.3	1.9	-13.0	-7.2	16.6	-0.6	4.2	1.6
Kiribati	-7.9	5.3	-14.5	8.1	1.0	-1.8	—	—
Marshall Islands	-3.9	-13.3	-4.6	-12.0 ·	3.5	—	—	—
Micronesia, Federated States of	—	—	—	—	—	—	—	—
Nauru	—	—	—	—	—	—	—	—
Papua New Guinea	-0.1	11.0	2.0	-14.0	3.7	0.9	6.5	3.5
Samoa	15.0	2.6	-6.8	6.7	1.1	2.9	—	—
Solomon Islands	7.7	-4.3	1.2	-8.3	-4.1	-26.6	6.3	—
Tonga	—	-8.2	2.4	0.3	-3.0	4.8	—	—
Tuvalu	0.6	-16.2	5.8	0.7	—	—	—	—
Vanuatu	1.3	10.5	1.5	7.3	7.4	-2.4	3.9	3.5

— Not available.

Table A4 Growth Rate of Value Added in Industry
(percent per year)

	1995	1996	1997	1998	1999	2000	2001	2002
Newly industrialized economies								
Hong Kong, China	—	—	—	—	—	—	—	—
Korea, Republic of	—	—	—	—	—	—	—	—
Singapore	9.6	7.2	7.4	1.0	6.5	10.3	8.5	9.0
Taipei,China	2.6	4.2	6.1	2.7	4.7	6.0	5.4	5.9
Central Asian republics, Azerbaijan, and Mongolia								
Azerbaijan	—	—	—	—	—	—	—	—
Kazakhstan	-8.6	0.3	4.1	-2.4	2.8	14.6	8.0	10.0
Kyrgyz Republic	-12.3	2.6	19.8	-1.8	-3.8	6.0	—	—
Mongolia	14.6	-3.2	-3.3	3.8	—	—	—	—
Tajikistan	—	—	-2.0	8.1	5.0	10.3	—	—
Turkmenistan	—	—	—	—	—	—	—	—
Uzbekistan	0.1	6.0	6.5	5.8	6.1	5.8	—	—
People's Republic of China	13.9	12.1	10.5	8.9	8.1	9.6	8.1	8.3
Southeast Asia								
Cambodia	20.3	11.7	20.4	8.6	11.4	16.0	11.0	14.1
Indonesia	10.4	10.7	5.2	-14.0	1.9	5.5	4.9	5.3
Lao People's Democratic Republic	13.1	17.3	8.1	8.5	7.5	7.3	7.5	8.0
Malaysia	14.9	14.4	7.5	-10.9	8.0	14.7	7.5	9.2
Myanmar	12.7	10.7	8.9	6.1	13.7	—	—	—
Philippines	6.7	6.4	6.1	-2.1	0.9	3.6	2.9	—
Thailand	10.9	6.9	-1.9	-13.3	9.5	5.2	5.0	6.0
Viet Nam	13.6	14.5	12.6	7.3	7.6	9.7	9.6	9.9
South Asia								
Bangladesh	9.9	7.0	5.8	8.3	4.9	5.6	—	—
Bhutan	17.0	8.4	3.8	7.7	12.4	10.3	7.0	9.1
India	11.4	6.0	5.9	3.6	6.4	6.6	6.5	6.9
Maldives	8.6	3.9	11.6	21.1	17.5	5.8	6.9	—
Nepal	4.0	8.3	6.4	2.3	6.0	8.7	7.5	—
Pakistan	4.9	5.4	1.0	6.8	2.5	3.0	3.1	5.5
Sri Lanka	7.8	5.6	7.7	5.9	4.8	6.4	5.6	6.1
Pacific DMCs								
Cook Islands	-15.9	-5.0	6.4	-6.2	4.6	—	—	—
Fiji Islands	1.8	5.3	1.4	3.1	7.4	-14.9	1.8	8.0
Kiribati	-23.0	-4.4	19.6	35.3	41.9	-34.5	—	—
Marshall Islands	18.7	-30.5	0.0	31.2	3.0	—	—	—
Micronesia, Federated States of	—	—	—	—	—	—	—	—
Nauru	—	—	—	—	—	—	—	—
Papua New Guinea	-8.6	10.1	-17.0	9.7	4.3	-3.3	-1.3	9.8
Samoa	0.6	6.6	-4.0	-8.9	4.0	10.1	—	—
Solomon Islands	34.1	32.0	-14.1	5.5	22.3	-30.7	2.2	—
Tonga	—	11.3	-4.1	4.2	12.3	4.9	—	—
Tuvalu	-13.1	85.6	4.0	21.5	—	—	—	—
Vanuatu	-2.2	-5.7	-3.1	6.6	-6.0	6.6	2.8	2.3

— Not available.

Table A5 Growth Rate of Value Added in Services
(percent per year)

	1995	1996	1997	1998	1999	2000	2001	2002
Newly industrialized economies								
Hong Kong, China	—	—	—	—	—	—	—	—
Korea, Republic of	—	—	—	—	—	—	—	—
Singapore	7.4	7.9	9.5	-0.6	4.7	8.7	3.0	3.5
Taipei,China	8.9	7.8	7.4	6.2	6.0	6.3	5.0	5.8
Central Asian republics, Azerbaijan, and Mongolia								
Azerbaijan	—	—	—	—	—	—	—	—
Kazakhstan	—	—	—	-0.1	-0.7	7.9	2.1	4.5
Kyrgyz Republic	-4.4	-0.2	0.6	3.9	3.4	5.5	—	—
Mongolia	0.2	4.6	9.0	0.3	—	—	—	—
Tajikistan	—	—	—	—	—	—	—	—
Turkmenistan	—	—	—	—	—	—	—	—
Uzbekistan	-25.8	9.9	21.3	9.5	12.6	13.0	—	—
People's Republic of China	8.4	7.9	9.2	8.3	7.5	7.8	7.5	7.6
Southeast Asia								
Cambodia	4.2	4.8	-3.7	-1.3	5.8	4.0	3.0	3.5
Indonesia	7.6	6.8	5.6	-16.5	-1.0	5.2	4.1	4.4
Lao People's Democratic Republic	10.2	8.5	7.5	4.8	5.7	6.4	6.6	7.0
Malaysia	8.4	7.1	8.6	-4.7	4.2	4.3	3.0	3.5
Myanmar	7.3	6.5	6.7	7.0	9.2	—	—	—
Philippines	5.0	6.4	5.4	3.5	4.1	4.4	4.2	—
Thailand	9.0	5.3	-1.2	-10.0	-0.1	3.8	2.5	3.6
Viet Nam	9.8	8.8	7.1	3.0	2.1	4.4	4.9	5.3
South Asia								
Bangladesh	5.5	4.3	4.9	4.8	4.9	5.0	0.0	0.0
Bhutan	7.0	5.1	13.4	6.3	4.5	5.6	7.0	7.0
India	10.3	7.1	9.0	9.2	9.6	8.3	8.1	8.5
Maldives	8.7	10.8	9.6	9.5	8.7	3.5	5.8	—
Nepal	6.0	5.8	4.6	6.5	5.5	6.6	6.0	—
Pakistan	4.8	5.0	3.6	3.2	4.1	4.5	4.6	4.4
Sri Lanka	4.9	6.0	7.1	5.1	4.0	7.2	5.3	5.6
Pacific DMCs								
Cook Islands	-3.4	-0.6	-6.9	-3.5	2.5	—	—	—
Fiji Islands	5.0	2.5	2.4	3.3	7.8	-9.4	6.5	4.4
Kiribati	4.0	5.1	2.4	7.3	-1.0	-1.6	—	—
Marshall Islands	2.6	-4.4	-5.5	2.8	1.6	—	—	—
Micronesia, Federated States of	—	—	—	—	—	—	—	—
Nauru	—	—	—	—	—	—	—	—
Papua New Guinea	0.0	3.4	5.9	-7.6	4.7	4.6	3.9	3.9
Samoa	6.6	10.9	5.7	8.3	7.3	7.1	—	—
Solomon Islands	-0.2	-2.2	-2.8	3.7	-8.0	-13.0	1.7	—
Tonga	—	1.8	0.9	3.4	4.4	5.3	—	—
Tuvalu	-4.8	2.6	2.7	16.0	—	—	—	—
Vanuatu	-4.1	5.0	0.4	-3.1	-5.7	3.9	3.5	3.0

— Not available.

Table A6 Sectoral Share of GDP
(percent)

	Agriculture			Industry			Services		
	1970	**1980**	**2000**	**1970**	**1980**	**2000**	**1970**	**1980**	**2000**
Newly industrialized economies									
Hong Kong, China	—	—	—	—	—	—	—	—	—
Korea, Republic of	29.8	14.2	—	23.8	37.8	—	46.4	48.1	—
Singapore	2.2	1.1	0.1	36.4	38.8	33.2	61.4	60.0	66.6
Taipei,China	17.3	8.4	2.4	32.3	42.8	34.6	50.4	48.8	63.0
Central Asian republics, Azerbaijan, and Mongolia									
Azerbaijan	—	—	—	—	—	—	—	—	—
Kazakhstan	—	—	8.6	—	—	31.9	—	—	59.5
Kyrgyz Republic	—	—	34.5	—	—	24.9	—	—	40.6
Mongolia	33.1	17.4	39.9	26.3	33.3	24.0	40.6	49.3	36.1
Tajikistan	—	—	—	—	—	—	—	—	—
Turkmenistan	—	—	—	—	—	—	—	—	—
Uzbekistan	—	—	28.8	—	—	20.6	—	—	50.6
People's Republic of China	42.2	25.6	11.9	44.6	51.7	64.0	13.2	22.7	24.1
Southeast Asia									
Cambodia	—	—	38.1	—	—	21.7	—	—	40.2
Indonesia	35.0	24.4	16.7	28.0	41.3	43.5	37.0	34.3	39.8
Lao People's Democratic Republic	—	—	51.7	—	—	22.7	—	—	25.6
Malaysia	—	22.9	8.7	—	35.8	46.8	—	41.3	44.6
Myanmar	49.5	47.9	—	12.0	12.3	—	38.5	39.8	—
Philippines	28.2	23.5	19.9	33.7	40.5	34.4	38.1	36.0	45.7
Thailand	30.2	20.2	9.9	25.7	30.1	44.5	44.1	49.7	45.7
Viet Nam	—	42.7	23.4	—	26.3	35.7	—	31.0	41.0
South Asia									
Bangladesh	—	49.4	24.3	—	14.8	24.7	—	35.8	51.0
Bhutan	—	56.7	32.5	—	12.2	32.4	—	31.1	35.1
India	44.5	38.1	24.0	23.9	25.9	27.1	31.6	36.0	48.9
Maldives	—	—	9.5	—	—	15.5	—	—	75.0
Nepal	—	61.8	38.8	—	11.9	20.7	—	26.3	40.5
Pakistan	40.1	30.6	26.2	19.6	25.6	24.9	40.3	43.8	48.9
Sri Lanka	30.7	26.6	20.6	27.1	27.2	27.3	42.2	46.2	52.1
Pacific DMCs									
Cook Islands	—	—	22.6	—	—	7.2	—	—	70.2
Fiji Islands	30.2	22.5	18.4	23.1	21.7	25.0	46.7	55.8	56.6
Kiribati	—	—	—	—	—	—	—	—	—
Marshall Islands	—	—	—	—	—	—	—	—	—
Micronesia, Federated States of	—	—	—	—	—	—	—	—	—
Nauru	—	—	—	—	—	—	—	—	—
Papua New Guinea	—	—	29.9	—	—	35.7	—	—	34.4
Samoa	—	—	17.9	—	—	24.0	—	—	58.1
Solomon Islands	—	52.5	22.1	—	10.0	15.4	—	37.4	62.5
Tonga	—	47.6	28.6	—	11.0	15.8	—	41.4	55.6
Tuvalu	—	—	—	—	—	—	—	—	—
Vanuatu	—	—	21.9	—	—	10.7	—	—	67.4

— Not available.

Table A7 Gross Domestic Savings
(percent of GDP)

	1995	1996	1997	1998	1999	2000	2001	2002
Newly industrialized economies								
Hong Kong, China	30.5	30.7	31.1	30.1	30.5	32.2	32.7	30.0
Korea, Republic of	35.4	33.5	32.5	33.9	32.7	30.9	31.0	30.0
Singapore	50.2	50.1	52.1	52.4	51.8	49.8	51.0	52.0
Taipei,China	27.0	26.6	26.4	26.0	26.1	24.8	26.1	26.6
Central Asian republics, Azerbaijan, and Mongolia								
Azerbaijan	—	—	—	—	—	—	—	—
Kazakhstan	15.3	19.8	17.1	14.9	16.9	20.8	20.3	20.4
Kyrgyz Republic	5.5	-0.6	13.8	-6.1	3.2	—	—	—
Mongolia	—	—	—	18.5	20.0	19.0	21.0	22.0
Tajikistan	—	—	—	—	—	—	—	—
Turkmenistan	—	—	—	—	—	—	—	—
Uzbekistan	27.1	22.7	18.7	16.5	17.3	16.5	—	—
People's Republic of China	42.5	41.1	41.5	39.8	38.0	38.0	38.2	38.5
Southeast Asia								
Cambodia	4.4	5.3	6.1	5.4	7.3	6.6	6.8	6.9
Indonesia	30.6	30.1	31.5	26.5	20.2	22.0	20.9	21.3
Lao People's Democratic Republic	11.5	12.4	9.4	14.8	16.4	14.6	15.0	15.5
Malaysia	39.7	42.9	43.9	48.5	47.3	46.9	44.9	46.1
Myanmar	13.5	11.6	11.9	12.0	13.0	—	—	—
Philippines	14.5	14.6	14.2	12.8	14.9	17.0	15.0	15.5
Thailand	33.8	33.5	32.5	33.2	30.1	30.0	31.8	33.1
Viet Nam	13.6	17.6	21.1	19.2	24.1	25.0	24.0	24.1
South Asia								
Bangladesh	16.7	16.0	18.6	20.6	20.8	21.4	21.8	22.3
Bhutan	43.9	34.2	25.5	24.1	22.4	20.7	19.0	17.3
India	25.1	23.2	23.5	22.0	22.3	22.7	22.8	23.1
Maldives	—	—	—	—	—	—	—	—
Nepal	16.3	13.8	14.0	13.8	13.6	15.5	—	—
Pakistan	14.2	17.4	12.8	15.4	12.3	14.0	11.6	13.5
Sri Lanka	15.3	15.3	17.3	19.1	19.8	19.0	18.9	19.3
Pacific DMCs								
Cook Islands	—	—	—	—	—	—	—	—
Fiji Islands	12.2	13.9	12.6	10.0	—	—	—	—
Kiribati	—	—	—	—	—	—	—	—
Marshall Islands	—	—	—	—	—	—	—	—
Micronesia, Federated States of	—	—	—	—	—	—	—	—
Nauru	—	—	—	—	—	—	—	—
Papua New Guinea	41.2	31.0	22.4	22.4	—	—	—	—
Samoa	—	—	—	—	—	—	—	—
Solomon Islands	—	—	—	—	—	—	—	—
Tonga	—	—	—	—	—	—	—	—
Tuvalu	—	—	—	—	—	—	—	—
Vanuatu	26.1	—	—	—	—	—	—	—

— Not available.

Table A8 Gross Domestic Investment
(percent of GDP)

	1995	1996	1997	1998	1999	2000	2001	2002
Newly industrialized economies								
Hong Kong, China	34.8	32.1	34.5	29.0	25.1	27.5	26.2	29.0
Korea, Republic of	37.2	37.9	34.2	21.2	26.7	28.7	29.0	29.5
Singapore	34.6	36.8	39.2	32.6	32.4	31.3	32.0	32.5
Taipei,China	25.3	23.2	24.2	24.9	23.4	22.8	23.4	23.5
Central Asian republics, Azerbaijan, and Mongolia								
Azerbaijan	—	—	—	—	—	—	—	—
Kazakhstan	23.3	16.1	15.6	14.3	17.9	17.1	17.3	16.9
Kyrgyz Republic	18.3	25.2	21.7	15.4	18.0	—	—	—
Mongolia	—	—	—	25.0	27.0	26.0	25.0	25.0
Tajikistan	—	—	—	—	—	—	—	—
Turkmenistan	—	—	—	—	—	—	—	—
Uzbekistan	24.2	23.0	18.9	20.9	17.1	15.9	—	—
People's Republic of China	40.8	39.6	38.2	37.4	37.0	37.1	37.0	37.2
Southeast Asia								
Cambodia	12.9	15.2	14.4	12.0	18.4	18.8	20.0	22.0
Indonesia	31.9	30.7	31.8	16.8	12.2	17.9	15.0	17.0
Lao People's Democratic Republic	24.5	29.0	26.2	24.9	22.7	20.4	21.6	22.2
Malaysia	43.6	41.5	43.0	26.6	22.3	27.0	25.0	26.2
Myanmar	14.2	12.3	12.5	12.4	13.2	—	—	—
Philippines	22.5	24.0	24.8	20.2	18.6	17.6	16.0	19.0
Thailand	41.8	41.6	33.3	20.3	19.9	22.0	25.3	27.5
Viet Nam	27.1	28.1	28.3	23.8	20.1	23.0	24.5	26.0
South Asia								
Bangladesh	19.1	20.0	20.7	21.6	22.2	22.4	23.3	24.1
Bhutan	48.7	43.9	34.8	40.5	41.2	42.4	44.1	45.8
India	26.8	24.5	25.0	23.0	23.3	23.5	23.8	24.3
Maldives	—	—	—	—	—	—	—	—
Nepal	25.2	27.3	25.3	24.8	20.5	23.7	—	—
Pakistan	18.3	18.9	17.9	17.3	15.0	15.0	15.5	16.2
Sri Lanka	25.7	24.2	24.4	25.1	27.1	29.0	27.0	27.5
Pacific DMCs								
Cook Islands	—	—	—	—	—	—	—	—
Fiji Islands	12.5	10.0	10.1	15.4	11.0	—	—	—
Kiribati	—	—	—	—	—	—	—	—
Marshall Islands	—	—	—	—	—	—	—	—
Micronesia, Federated States of	—	—	—	—	—	—	—	—
Nauru	—	—	—	—	—	—	—	—
Papua New Guinea	22.1	22.7	21.1	17.7	—	—	—	—
Samoa	—	—	—	—	—	—	—	—
Solomon Islands	—	—	—	—	—	—	—	—
Tonga	13.7	—	—	—	—	—	—	—
Tuvalu	68.0	69.0	58.2	24.9	—	—	—	—
Vanuatu	32.7	—	—	—	—	—	—	—

— Not available.

Table A9 Change in Consumer Prices
(percent per year)

	1995	1996	1997	1998	1999	2000	2001	2002
Newly industrialized economies	4.7	4.3	3.5	4.6	-0.1	1.1	2.2	2.5
Hong Kong, China	9.1	6.3	5.9	2.8	-4.0	-3.7	1.0	4.0
Korea, Republic of	4.5	4.9	4.5	7.5	0.8	2.3	3.0	2.5
Singapore	1.7	1.3	2.0	-0.3	0.0	1.3	1.5	2.0
Taipei,China	3.7	3.1	0.9	1.7	0.2	1.3	1.7	1.8
Central Asian republics, Azerbaijan, and Mongolia	315.7	41.5	31.2	9.7	20.2	15.2	10.6	10.0
Azerbaijan	411.7	19.8	3.6	-0.8	-8.5	2.2	—	—
Kazakhstan	60.3	28.7	11.2	1.9	17.8	9.8	5.5	4.9
Kyrgyz Republic	43.5	32.0	23.4	10.5	35.9	18.7	9.1	7.2
Mongolia	56.8	53.2	36.6	9.4	7.6	11.6	8.0	6.0
Tajikistan	2,131.9	40.6	164.0	2.7	31.0	24.0	12.4	11.0
Turkmenistan	1,005.3	992.4	83.7	16.7	23.5	—	—	—
Uzbekistan	304.6	54.0	58.8	17.7	29.1	28.2	22.5	22.0
People's Republic of China	17.1	8.3	2.8	-0.8	-1.4	0.4	2.0	2.5
Southeast Asia	7.4	6.6	5.3	26.5	9.4	2.7	5.4	4.4
Cambodia	8.1	7.1	8.0	14.8	4.0	-0.8	5.0	5.0
Indonesia	9.5	7.9	6.2	58.5	20.7	3.8	9.0	6.0
Lao People's Democratic Republic	19.6	13.0	15.5	90.0	128.4	23.2	9.0	7.5
Malaysia	3.4	3.5	2.7	5.3	2.8	1.6	2.6	2.8
Myanmar	21.8	20.0	33.9	49.1	11.4	—	—	—
Philippines	8.0	9.0	5.9	9.8	6.7	4.4	7.0	6.0
Thailand	5.8	5.9	5.5	8.1	0.3	1.6	2.0	2.6
Viet Nam	12.9	4.4	3.6	9.2	0.1	-0.6	3.0	5.0
South Asia	8.7	5.9	5.4	6.3	4.2	6.2	5.4	4.8
Bangladesh	8.9	6.7	2.5	7.0	8.9	3.4	3.0	5.0
Bhutan	8.2	9.3	7.4	9.0	9.2	3.6	7.3	5.4
India	8.0	4.6	4.4	5.9	3.3	7.0	5.5	4.8
Maldives	5.5	6.2	7.6	-1.4	3.0	-1.1	—	—
Nepal	7.6	8.1	7.8	4.0	11.4	3.5	5.5	—
Pakistan	13.0	10.8	11.8	7.8	5.7	3.6	6.0	4.5
Sri Lanka	7.7	15.9	9.6	9.4	4.7	6.2	8.0	6.0
Pacific DMCs	11.3	8.9	3.9	10.1	10.0	11.5	8.3	5.0
Cook Islands	0.9	-0.6	-0.4	0.7	1.4	2.0	1.0	1.0
Fiji Islands	2.2	3.1	3.4	5.7	2.0	1.1	3.5	3.5
Kiribati	4.1	-1.5	2.2	4.7	0.4	2.0	1.5	—
Marshall Islands	6.8	10.5	5.8	2.9	2.0	-1.9	2.0	2.3
Micronesia, Federated States of	4.0	4.0	3.0	-2.6	1.9	2.8	—	—
Nauru	1.7	4.0	6.1	4.0	6.7	7.5	4.0	—
Papua New Guinea	17.2	11.9	3.9	13.5	14.9	17.9	11.6	6.2
Samoa	-2.9	5.4	6.8	2.2	0.6	0.5	3.0	3.0
Solomon Islands	9.6	11.8	8.1	12.4	8.0	6.6	5.8	5.0
Tonga	0.3	2.7	2.0	3.0	3.9	5.3	5.0	3.5
Tuvalu	5.0	0.0	1.4	0.8	1.0	5.0	1.5	1.5
Vanuatu	2.2	0.9	2.8	3.3	2.0	2.7	2.0	2.0
Average	9.2	6.2	4.0	8.0	2.3	2.1	3.4	3.3

— Not available.

Table A10 Change in Money Supply (M2)
(percent per year)

	1995	1996	1997	1998	1999	2000	2001	2002
Newly industrialized economies								
Hong Kong, China	14.6	10.9	8.3	11.8	8.1	8.8	10.0	12.0
Korea, Republic of	15.6	15.8	14.1	27.0	27.4	25.7	27.0	24.0
Singapore	8.5	9.8	10.3	30.2	8.5	-2.1	4.0	6.0
Taipei,China	9.4	9.1	8.3	8.8	8.3	6.5	7.0	6.7
Central Asian republics, Azerbaijan, and Mongolia								
Azerbaijan	—	—	—	—	—	—	—	—
Kazakhstan	109.0	16.6	28.2	-14.1	84.3	45.9	21.3	21.6
Kyrgyz Republic	78.2	21.3	25.4	17.2	33.9	12.3	—	—
Mongolia	32.9	25.8	32.5	-1.7	31.6	17.6	14.0	12.0
Tajikistan	—	93.2	110.7	30.7	29.2	30.0	25.2	24.0
Turkmenistan	—	—	—	—	—	—	—	—
Uzbekistan	151.9	119.0	45.6	28.1	32.1	27.1	25.2	25.2
People's Republic of China	29.5	25.3	20.7	14.9	14.7	12.3	13.0	14.0
Southeast Asia								
Cambodia	44.3	40.4	16.6	15.7	17.3	28.5	24.0	20.0
Indonesia	27.6	29.6	23.2	62.3	11.9	15.6	11.8	12.4
Lao People's Democratic Republic	16.4	26.7	65.8	120.7	72.4	45.7	20.0	20.0
Malaysia	24.0	19.8	22.7	1.5	13.7	5.3	7.9	11.5
Myanmar	38.4	38.9	30.2	27.6	30.1	—	—	—
Philippines	25.2	15.8	20.5	8.2	19.3	5.2	10.0	10.0
Thailand	17.0	12.6	16.4	9.5	2.1	3.6	4.0	6.5
Viet Nam	22.6	22.5	26.1	25.6	39.3	40.6	30.0	25.0
South Asia								
Bangladesh	21.1	10.7	9.9	11.4	15.4	18.6	16.0	16.0
Bhutan	29.9	30.4	30.9	41.7	21.4	21.4	20.0	20.0
India	13.7	15.2	18.0	19.4	13.9	16.0	15.0	15.0
Maldives	15.6	26.0	23.1	22.8	3.6	9.1	5.7	—
Nepal	16.1	14.4	11.9	21.9	20.9	21.8	13.0	—
Pakistan	17.2	13.8	12.2	14.5	6.2	9.4	11.3	15.0
Sri Lanka	19.2	10.8	13.8	9.7	13.3	13.0	13.5	11.0
Pacific DMCs								
Cook Islands	—	6.9	15.6	12.1	16.7	-2.3	—	—
Fiji Islands	4.3	0.9	-8.7	-0.3	14.2	-5.7	—	—
Kiribati	-0.9	11.7	-3.1	11.1	0.3	5.0	—	—
Marshall Islands	—	—	—	—	—	—	—	—
Micronesia, Federated States of	—	—	—	—	—	—	—	—
Nauru	—	—	—	—	—	—	—	—
Papua New Guinea	10.7	32.0	6.9	1.8	8.9	-0.7	—	—
Samoa	21.8	5.1	13.2	5.0	12.5	11.4	—	—
Solomon Islands	9.5	15.0	6.7	4.8	4.9	9.5	7.4	—
Tonga	17.1	2.8	14.1	2.4	15.0	8.5	—	—
Tuvalu	—	—	—	—	—	—	—	—
Vanuatu	13.3	10.1	-0.3	12.6	-9.2	-1.4	5.0	5.0

— Not available.

Table A11 Growth Rate of Merchandise Exports
(percent per year)

	1995	1996	1997	1998	1999	2000	2001	2002
Newly industrialized economies	20.8	4.6	4.0	-8.2	5.5	19.6	7.5	9.5
Hong Kong, China	14.8	4.0	4.0	-7.5	-0.1	16.1	5.3	8.5
Korea, Republic of	31.2	4.3	6.7	-4.7	9.9	21.1	9.0	10.5
Singapore	21.0	6.4	-0.2	-12.1	4.5	20.3	5.0	10.0
Taipei,China	19.9	3.8	5.4	-9.5	9.9	22.3	11.8	9.8
Central Asian republics, Azerbaijan, and Mongolia	48.6	9.1	7.9	-16.1	0.4	25.4	-0.3	10.7
Azerbaijan	—	—	—	—	—	—	—	—
Kazakhstan	65.6	15.7	9.6	-14.9	2.0	52.6	1.3	12.9
Kyrgyz Republic	20.3	29.9	18.8	-15.2	-13.5	9.1	—	—
Mongolia	31.5	-12.2	16.6	-12.1	4.7	15.0	15.0	13.0
Tajikistan	39.4	-1.2	-3.1	-21.4	13.6	11.4	10.8	8.3
Turkmenistan	—	—	—	—	—	—	—	—
Uzbekistan	18.2	1.7	4.5	-18.0	-2.7	-5.9	9.4	4.7
People's Republic of China	24.9	17.9	20.9	0.5	6.1	27.8	10.0	15.0
Southeast Asia	23.8	6.1	7.3	-4.7	11.5	17.8	8.6	12.1
Cambodia	-45.2	10.1	81.0	13.0	17.9	31.3	15.0	12.0
Indonesia	18.0	5.8	12.2	-10.5	1.7	28.2	8.1	11.2
Lao People's Democratic Republic	4.3	2.6	-1.4	7.6	-10.3	8.3	7.5	9.0
Malaysia	26.6	7.2	0.7	-7.3	16.9	14.5	11.8	14.8
Myanmar	1.9	-0.5	8.7	10.1	1.7	—	—	—
Philippines	29.4	17.7	22.8	16.9	18.8	8.7	3.0	8.0
Thailand	24.8	-1.9	3.8	-6.8	7.4	19.6	7.0	11.0
Viet Nam	28.2	41.2	24.6	2.4	23.2	24.3	12.0	13.0
South Asia	20.2	6.5	4.8	-0.1	5.8	15.5	10.6	12.4
Bangladesh	37.1	11.8	14.0	16.8	2.9	8.2	15.0	15.0
Bhutan	10.2	39.6	1.7	12.0	-5.9	6.6	5.0	5.0
India	20.3	5.6	4.5	-3.9	11.6	17.0	12.0	13.0
Maldives	12.7	-6.0	15.8	3.4	-4.3	13.2	12.7	—
Nepal	-9.7	1.9	10.2	11.9	18.2	42.3	13.5	—
Pakistan	16.1	7.1	-2.6	4.2	-10.7	8.4	14.6	14.1
Sri Lanka	18.6	7.6	13.3	3.4	-3.9	19.8	3.2	4.2
Pacific DMCs	13.0	1.6	-13.1	-17.7	13.4	0.2	-3.4	1.3
Cook Islands	10.4	-31.0	-10.1	13.8	10.7	—	—	—
Fiji Islands	6.1	23.6	-14.5	-24.1	26.4	-20.1	-4.4	9.4
Kiribati	42.0	-27.9	16.2	-4.9	31.8	-10.1	—	—
Marshall Islands	23.1	-12.2	-29.0	-47.2	-4.0	9.7	5.1	—
Micronesia, Federated States of	152.3	22.1	-7.0	-46.8	-16.4	106.3	—	—
Nauru	—	—	—	—	—	—	—	—
Papua New Guinea	13.4	-2.4	-14.8	-16.1	12.2	7.9	-2.3	-0.4
Samoa	149.6	15.9	42.3	30.0	-3.6	—	—	—
Solomon Islands	18.2	-3.4	7.1	-19.0	6.2	-29.2	12.0	10.0
Tonga	3.1	-26.4	3.9	-9.8	1.7	-9.9	—	—
Tuvalu	4.3	9.8	-2.0	-84.8	—	—	—	—
Vanuatu	13.2	7.5	16.8	-3.9	-26.3	30.6	0.8	8.6
Average	22.2	6.9	7.3	-5.7	6.9	20.5	8.3	11.2

— Not available.

Table A12 Direction of Exports
(percent share)

From \ To	DMCs 1985	DMCs 1999	Japan 1985	Japan 1999	US 1985	US 1999	EU 1985	EU 1999	Australia/New Zealand 1985	Australia/New Zealand 1999	Others 1985	Others 1999
Newly industrialized economies												
Hong Kong, China	35.6	42.1	4.2	5.4	30.8	23.9	11.8	—	2.3	1.5	15.3	27.1
Korea, Republic of	12.9	30.3	15.0	11.0	35.6	20.6	10.4	—	1.3	1.9	24.7	40.9
Singapore	36.8	43.4	9.4	7.4	21.2	19.2	10.1	—	4.4	3.1	18.0	28.8
Taipei,China	13.4	30.7	11.3	9.8	48.1	25.4	5.5	—	2.7	—	19.0	—
Central Asian republics, Azerbaijan, and Mongolia												
Azerbaijan	—	—	—	—	—	—	—	—	—	—	—	—
Kazakhstan	—	18.9	—	1.4	—	4.0	—	—	—	0.1	—	75.7
Kyrgyz Republic	—	29.0	—	0.1	—	1.5	—	—	—	—	—	69.4
Mongolia	3.1	58.9	1.1	3.2	5.5	13.8	20.5	—	—	—	69.8	—
Tajikistan	—	29.3	—	—	—	5.2	—	—	—	—	—	70.6
Turkmenistan	—	—	—	—	—	—	—	—	—	—	—	—
Uzbekistan	—	32.3	—	1.4	—	1.2	—	—	—	—	—	65.1
People's Republic of China	38.2	31.3	22.3	16.6	8.5	21.5	7.8	—	0.8	1.6	22.5	29.0
Southeast Asia												
Cambodia	67.9	—	7.0	—	—	—	13.2	—	0.0	—	11.9	—
Indonesia	17.2	33.5	46.2	20.0	21.7	16.1	6.0	—	1.2	3.2	7.6	27.2
Lao People's Democratic Republic	71.9	21.4	6.6	3.8	2.7	4.0	0.5	—	5.5	0.1	12.7	70.7
Malaysia	38.1	37.2	24.6	11.6	12.8	21.9	13.6	—	1.9	2.8	9.1	26.5
Myanmar	47.1	40.3	8.4	6.8	0.8	16.3	8.4	—	0.0	0.8	35.4	35.8
Philippines	19.5	24.3	19.0	13.1	35.9	29.6	13.8	—	2.1	0.7	9.7	32.3
Thailand	27.1	30.1	13.4	14.5	19.7	21.5	17.8	—	1.9	2.5	20.1	31.4
Viet Nam	15.9	23.3	4.7	17.2	—	5.7	6.2	—	0.3	8.5	72.9	45.3
South Asia												
Bangladesh	14.5	4.9	7.2	1.6	18.1	31.2	13.0	—	1.8	0.4	45.5	61.9
Bhutan	—	—	—	—	—	—	—	—	—	—	—	—
India	8.9	19.8	11.1	5.2	18.9	22.2	16.7	—	1.4	1.3	43.0	51.5
Maldives	50.8	9.5	10.1	1.2	24.3	17.1	4.0	—	—	—	10.9	72.2
Nepal	41.4	31.4	0.7	0.8	35.3	30.7	20.3	—	0.1	0.2	2.3	36.9
Pakistan	16.0	18.6	11.3	3.6	10.0	22.9	20.9	—	1.1	1.6	40.6	53.3
Sri Lanka	11.2	8.0	5.1	3.6	22.3	39.9	17.9	—	1.7	1.3	41.9	47.2
Pacific DMCs												
Cook Islands	—	—	—	—	—	—	—	—	—	—	—	—
Fiji Islands	22.5	10.9	3.0	4.5	4.9	14.8	31.0	—	18.2	37.5	20.4	32.3
Kiribati	7.1	13.4	4.3	40.0	—	15.0	—	—	0.4	2.3	88.2	29.3
Marshall Islands	—	—	—	—	—	—	—	—	—	—	—	—
Micronesia, Federated States of	—	—	—	—	—	—	—	—	—	—	—	—
Nauru	—	—	—	—	—	—	—	—	—	—	—	—
Papua New Guinea	9.9	15.0	22.1	11.7	4.0	4.6	46.5	—	12.0	26.5	5.6	42.2
Samoa	0.3	2.2	0.9	0.9	59.4	12.0	5.8	—	29.7	69.4	3.9	15.5
Solomon Islands	11.1	43.4	52.1	35.4	2.4	0.8	26.3	—	3.2	2.0	5.0	18.4
Tonga	5.9	2.0	0.2	59.0	3.2	19.0	0.5	—	83.1	11.5	7.1	8.5
Tuvalu	63.7	5.9	—	—	—	—	—	—	8.1	2.0	28.2	92.1
Vanuatu	1.4	5.5	6.7	11.2	0.0	25.3	25.4	—	1.6	1.2	65.0	56.8
DMCs	25.3	33.3	16.4	11.2	26.3	21.7	10.7	—	2.1	2.1	19.2	31.7

— Not available.

Table A13 Growth Rate of Merchandise Imports
(percent per year)

	1995	1996	1997	1998	1999	2000	2001	2002
Newly industrialized economies	22.9	5.2	3.1	-19.3	7.6	25.2	7.3	10.7
Hong Kong, China	19.1	3.0	5.1	-11.6	-2.7	18.5	4.7	9.0
Korea, Republic of	31.9	12.3	-2.2	-36.2	29.1	36.3	8.0	13.0
Singapore	21.7	5.4	0.7	-23.1	9.0	22.2	8.0	13.0
Taipei,China	21.2	-0.1	10.1	-7.4	6.2	27.3	10.8	9.5
Central Asian republics, Azerbaijan, and Mongolia	29.7	24.1	-0.3	-9.7	-14.6	-11.7	24.4	11.8
Azerbaijan	—	—	—	—	—	—	—	—
Kazakhstan	26.7	24.4	8.3	-7.0	-15.4	-10.5	50.2	15.0
Kyrgyz Republic	24.6	47.5	-17.5	17.0	-27.6	1.4	—	—
Mongolia	50.2	2.0	-1.5	9.5	2.9	17.1	12.0	10.0
Tajikistan	22.2	-6.2	3.0	-9.7	-4.5	13.6	9.2	6.8
Turkmenistan	—	—	—	—	—	—	—	—
Uzbekistan	18.8	31.0	-11.2	-22.0	-11.9	-8.0	3.5	3.8
People's Republic of China	15.5	19.5	3.7	0.3	15.8	36.8	20.0	15.0
Southeast Asia	34.1	5.7	-0.6	-26.4	8.1	22.9	16.1	19.1
Cambodia	-19.3	20.4	5.8	1.6	21.4	33.1	14.5	13.0
Indonesia	26.6	8.1	4.5	-30.9	-4.2	33.3	15.4	17.3
Lao People's Democratic Republic	4.4	17.1	-6.0	-14.7	0.3	6.6	10.6	10.0
Malaysia	30.5	1.1	1.8	-26.6	13.0	25.2	23.7	27.5
Myanmar	23.1	6.3	17.8	15.6	-7.8	—	—	—
Philippines	23.7	20.8	14.0	-18.8	4.1	2.1	5.0	10.0
Thailand	46.5	0.6	-13.4	-33.8	16.9	31.3	13.0	14.0
Viet Nam	59.3	25.5	-0.2	-1.1	1.1	31.0	16.0	17.0
South Asia	21.6	12.5	2.3	-5.7	10.5	11.4	6.8	8.3
Bangladesh	39.2	19.1	-7.5	5.4	6.6	4.4	8.0	9.0
Bhutan	4.6	14.1	18.4	3.7	20.5	12.8	10.0	10.0
India	21.6	12.1	4.6	-7.1	16.5	13.0	10.0	9.5
Maldives	20.9	12.6	15.6	1.5	13.6	-1.0	10.7	—
Nepal	21.7	5.8	21.6	-12.4	-10.3	20.1	—	—
Pakistan	18.5	16.7	-6.4	-8.4	-6.7	-0.2	9.3	8.8
Sri Lanka	11.4	2.4	7.8	0.4	1.5	22.4	2.6	1.0
Pacific DMCs	10.2	13.1	0.0	-22.2	2.0	-16.3	8.7	-3.1
Cook Islands	-0.4	-10.8	10.8	-20.9	9.8	—	—	—
Fiji Islands	5.8	10.4	-2.6	-25.0	6.3	-26.8	6.4	7.0
Kiribati	32.5	8.4	1.6	-13.8	21.2	0.8	—	—
Marshall Islands	8.5	-0.9	-10.0	2.9	4.2	-1.3	2.9	—
Micronesia, Federated States of	-10.0	-1.5	6.7	1.7	5.6	12.6	—	—
Nauru	—	—	—	—	—	—	—	—
Papua New Guinea	7.8	23.3	-1.6	-27.0	-0.1	-5.5	36.6	-3.9
Samoa	15.2	8.1	-0.9	-2.2	19.2	—	—	—
Solomon Islands	8.4	-2.0	38.5	-29.8	-4.6	-14.8	12.5	—
Tonga	31.5	-10.8	-9.5	29.7	-28.2	11.6	—	—
Tuvalu	6.4	9.8	28.8	18.6	—	—	—	—
Vanuatu	6.4	2.5	-3.6	-5.5	-0.1	-0.7	1.1	6.5
Average	24.3	7.7	2.2	-17.2	9.0	25.0	11.4	13.1

— Not available.

Table A14 Balance of Trade
($ million)

	1995	1996	1997	1998	1999	2000	2001	2002
Newly industrialized economies	-9,826	-13,549	-9,300	55,776	48,574	29,673	33,103	27,569
Hong Kong, China	-19,594	-18,352	-21,121	-10,946	-5,997	-11,387	-10,601	-12,618
Korea, Republic of	-4,444	-14,965	-3,179	41,627	28,371	16,601	19,687	17,456
Singapore	977	2,224	1,118	14,779	11,158	11,400	8,030	4,659
Taipei,China	13,235	17,543	13,882	10,316	15,042	13,058	15,986	18,071
Central Asian republics, Azerbaijan, and Mongolia	153	-1,396	-438	-1,193	546	4,378	2,195	2,308
Azerbaijan	—	—	—	—	—	—	—	—
Kazakhstan	114	-335	-277	-801	344	4,087	1,670	1,725
Kyrgyz Republic	-122	-252	-15	-221	-84	-50	—	—
Mongolia	-18	-87	-10	-117	-40	—	—	—
Tajikistan	-59	-16	-64	-145	-32	-51	-44	-35
Turkmenistan	—	—	—	—	—	—	—	—
Uzbekistan	238	-706	-73	91	359	392	569	618
People's Republic of China	18,050	19,535	46,222	46,613	36,206	32,095	13,620	15,663
Southeast Asia	-21,694	-22,089	-5,182	45,372	56,271	56,737	44,667	31,618
Cambodia	-333	-428	-231	-173	-232	-321	-348	-351
Indonesia	6,533	5,948	10,074	18,428	20,643	24,900	23,950	23,725
Lao People's Democratic Republic	-276	-368	-331	-212	-249	-260	-298	-331
Malaysia	39	4,407	3,652	17,637	22,772	19,560	12,759	2,621
Myanmar	-896	-1,016	-1,280	-1,536	-1,311	—	—	—
Philippines	-8,944	-11,342	-11,127	-28	4,295	6,690	6,263	6,105
Thailand	-14,662	-16,148	-4,624	12,235	9,271	5,527	2,170	293
Viet Nam	-3,155	-3,142	-1,315	-980	1,080	641	170	-443
South Asia	-18,861	-24,115	-23,366	-19,039	-23,537	-23,925	-23,116	-22,052
Bangladesh	-2,361	-3,063	-1,998	-1,600	-1,897	-1,780	-1,519	-1,258
Bhutan	-27	-13	-32	-25	-59	-73	-86	-101
India	-11,359	-14,815	-15,507	-13,246	-17,098	17,789	18,672	-18,690
Maldives	-151	-186	-215	-216	-262	-247	-271	—
Nepal	-922	-990	-1,245	-995	-765	-803	—	—
Pakistan	-2,537	-3,704	-3,145	-1,867	-2,085	-1,435	-1,136	-740
Sri Lanka	-1,504	-1,344	-1,225	-1,091	-1,370	-1,798	-1,431	-1,263
Pacific DMCs	724	416	-32	104	394	716	487	591
Cook Islands	-44	-40	-45	-35	-38	-31	-31	-32
Fiji Islands	-235	-189	-262	-192	-119	-52	-101	-98
Kiribati	-28	-33	-33	-27	-33	-34	—	—
Marshall Islands	-51	-53	-41	-50	-52	-51	-52	—
Micronesia, Federated States of	-92	-86	-95	-109	-118	-122	—	—
Nauru	—	—	—	—	—	—	—	—
Papua New Guinea	1,358	1,011	662	717	937	1,155	731	776
Samoa	-83	-90	-84	-78	-97	-40	—	—
Solomon Islands	14	11	-36	-6	10	-13	-16	-10
Tonga	-57	-54	-47	-66	-44	-52	—	—
Tuvalu	-7	-8	-6	-7	—	—	—	—
Vanuatu	-51	-54	-46	-43	-51	-43	-44	-46
Total	-31,455	-41,198	7,902	127,633	118,453	99,675	70,955	55,697

— Not available.

Table A15 Balance of Payments on Current Account
($ million)

	1995	1996	1997	1998	1999	2000	2001	2002
Newly industrialized economies	11,403	817	16,811	64,136	54,612	40,434	40,036	42,960
Hong Kong, China	—	—	—	—	—	—	—	—
Korea, Republic of	-8,507	-23,006	-8,167	40,365	24,477	11,044	8,697	5,806
Singapore	14,436	12,821	17,927	20,334	21,751	21,797	23,600	26,850
Taipei,China	5,474	11,002	7,051	3,437	8,384	7,593	7,739	10,304
Central Asian republics, Azerbaijan, and Mongolia	-549	-2,268	-1,550	-1,914	-464	765	812	673
Azerbaijan	—	—	—	—	—	—	—	—
Kazakhstan	-213	-750	-794	-1,236	-233	676	568	673
Kyrgyz Republic	-235	-425	-138	-371	-185	—	—	—
Mongolia	8	-37	27	-77	9	—	—	—
Tajikistan	-89	-77	-60	-113	-38	—	—	—
Turkmenistan	—	—	—	—	—	—	—	—
Uzbekistan	-20	-979	-585	-117	-16	89	244	—
People's Republic of China	1,618	7,243	29,718	29,325	15,649	14,000	12,000	10,000
Southeast Asia	-42,259	-33,467	-21,267	27,436	38,458	34,577	24,822	19,176
Cambodia	-109	-109	21	-7	-52	-141	-165	-183
Indonesia	-6,431	-7,660	-5,095	4,097	5,783	7,800	4,550	2,550
Lao People's Democratic Republic	-251	-306	-282	-129	-160	-92	-121	-140
Malaysia	-8,644	-4,064	-5,935	9,503	12,606	7,830	5,162	3,274
Myanmar	-446	-414	-656	-600	-494	—	—	—
Philippines	-3,297	-3,953	-4,351	1,546	7,239	8,649	7,726	7,571
Thailand	-20,281	-14,380	-3,130	14,263	12,416	9,952	7,690	6,819
Viet Nam	-2,801	-2,580	-1,839	-1,238	1,121	580	-20	-716
South Asia	-10,495	-11,943	-11,028	-6,972	-7,924	-9,155	-7,757	-6,740
Bangladesh	-920	-1,637	-909	-470	-653	-442	—	—
Bhutan	-34	-37	-56	-47	-100	-127	-118	-124
India	-5,910	-4,619	-5,500	-4,038	-4,163	-6,509	-5,972	-5,590
Maldives	-18	-7	-34	-24	-65	-29	-40	—
Nepal	-343	-390	-289	-245	4	-82	—	—
Pakistan	-2,484	-4,575	-3,846	-1,921	-2,381	-977	-1,025	-613
Sri Lanka	-786	-677	-393	-227	-566	-989	-601	-413
Pacific DMCs	675	446	-69	112	222	464	-80	-96
Cook Islands	—	5	1	2	—	4	5	5
Fiji Islands	-19	62	34	-6	28	22	6	25
Kiribati	-3	-16	2	16	9	-1	—	—
Marshall Islands	2	20	20	-1	-5	7	14	—
Micronesia, Federated States of	49	56	18	13	10	7	—	—
Nauru	—	—	—	—	—	—	—	—
Papua New Guinea	648	310	-116	60	144	425	-125	-130
Samoa	10	11	17	15	5	—	—	—
Solomon Islands	13	12	-38	17	35	7	22	—
Tonga	-22	-11	-2	-18	0	-10	—	—
Tuvalu	1	0	—	—	—	—	—	—
Vanuatu	-5	-4	-6	16	-3	3	-1	4
Total	-39,607	-39,171	12,615	112,124	100,554	81,084	69,833	65,973

— Not available.

Table A16 Balance of Payments on Current Account
(percent of GDP)

	1995	1996	1997	1998	1999	2000	2001	2002
Newly industrialized economies	1.4	0.1	1.9	7.4	6.3	4.7	4.6	5.0
Hong Kong, China	—	—	—	—	—	—	—	—
Korea, Republic of	-1.7	-4.4	-1.7	12.7	6.0	2.4	1.9	1.1
Singapore	17.3	14.0	19.0	24.8	25.9	23.6	24.0	25.0
Taipei,China	2.1	3.9	2.4	1.3	2.9	2.4	2.5	3.0
Central Asian republics, Azerbaijan, and Mongolia	-1.8	-5.8	-4.5	-5.5	-1.3	2.5	2.6	3.6
Azerbaijan	—	—	—	—	—	—	—	—
Kazakhstan	-1.3	-3.6	-3.6	-5.4	-1.1	3.8	3.3	2.4
Kyrgyz Republic	-15.7	-23.2	-7.8	-22.6	-14.8	-9.4	-9.3	-7.8
Mongolia	0.7	-3.1	2.6	-13.2	-14.1	-14.8	-11.0	-10.0
Tajikistan	-14.6	-7.4	-5.4	-9.3	-3.5	-5.7	-6.5	-5.6
Turkmenistan	—	—	—	—	—	—	—	—
Uzbekistan	-0.2	-7.0	-4.0	-0.8	-0.1	0.7	2.1	3.3
People's Republic of China	0.2	0.9	4.1	3.1	1.6	1.5	1.2	1.0
Southeast Asia	-7.5	-5.3	-3.5	4.7	6.6	5.2	3.6	3.0
Cambodia	-3.6	-3.5	0.7	-0.3	-1.7	-4.6	-5.0	-5.1
Indonesia	-3.2	-3.4	-2.4	4.3	4.1	5.1	2.9	1.3
Lao People's Democratic Republic	-14.5	-16.4	-16.1	-10.0	-11.2	-5.8	-6.6	-6.7
Malaysia	-9.7	-4.0	-5.9	13.1	15.9	8.8	5.5	3.2
Myanmar	-0.4	-0.3	-0.4	-0.2	-0.1	—	—	—
Philippines	-4.4	-4.8	-5.3	2.4	9.4	11.5	8.0	5.0
Thailand	-12.1	-7.9	-2.1	12.7	10.2	8.2	6.5	5.6
Viet Nam	-13.5	-10.5	-6.9	-4.6	4.0	2.0	-0.1	-1.9
South Asia	-2.2	-2.4	-2.3	-1.4	-1.6	-1.9	-1.7	-1.5
Bangladesh	-2.4	-4.0	-2.1	-1.1	-1.4	-1.0	-1.5	-1.8
Bhutan	-12.1	-12.1	-15.9	-12.0	-24.9	-28.5	-25.0	-25.0
India	-1.7	-1.2	1.3	1.0	-0.9	-1.3	-1.2	-1.0
Maldives	-4.5	-1.7	-6.8	-4.2	-11.1	-4.6	-5.9	—
Nepal	-8.1	-8.9	-6.0	-5.4	0.1	-1.5	—	—
Pakistan	-4.1	-7.2	-6.1	-3.0	-3.9	-1.6	-1.7	-1.0
Sri Lanka	-6.0	-4.9	-2.6	-1.4	-3.6	-6.0	-3.8	-2.5
Pacific DMCs	9.0	5.2	-0.9	1.2	3.0	6.4	—	—
Cook Islands	—	—	—	—	-7.0	5.9	6.3	6.6
Fiji Islands	-1.1	3.4	1.9	-0.4	1.8	1.6	0.4	1.6
Kiribati	-5.8	-32.0	5.2	34.0	18.8	-5.0	—	—
Marshall Islands	1.5	20.6	21.7	-1.5	-5.5	7.6	14.5	—
Micronesia, Federated States of	22.8	25.4	8.5	5.8	4.2	2.7	—	—
Nauru	—	—	—	—	—	—	—	—
Papua New Guinea	14.6	6.0	-2.4	1.6	4.0	11.7	-3.5	-3.4
Samoa	5.0	5.2	7.5	6.7	2.0	—	—	—
Solomon Islands	4.1	3.4	-8.8	4.5	9.9	2.5	7.4	—
Tonga	-13.3	-6.3	-1.0	-12.2	-0.1	-6.7	—	—
Tuvalu	4.7	2.7	—	—	—	—	—	—
Vanuatu	-2.1	-1.8	-2.5	7.0	-1.4	1.2	-0.3	1.5
Average	-1.5	-1.3	0.5	4.1	3.7	2.8	2.6	2.5

— Not available.

Table A17 Foreign Direct Investment
($ million)

	1994	1995	1996	1997	1998	1999
Newly Industrialized Economies	9,360	8,982	11,310	10,929	10,908	16,317
Hong Kong, China	—	—	—	—	—	—
Korea, Republic of	810	1,776	2,326	2,844	5,415	9,333
Singapore	8,550	7,206	8,984	8,085	5,493	6,984
Taipei,China	—	—	—	—	—	—
Central Asian republics, Azerbaijan, and Mongolia	45	1,070	1,200	1,430	1,280	1,667
Azerbaijan	—	—	—	1,115	1,023	510
Kazakhstan	—	964	1,137	1,321	1,151	1,587
Kyrgyz Republic	38	96	47	84	109	50
Mongolia	7	10	16	25	19	30
Tajikistan	—	—	—	—	—	—
Turkmenistan	—	—	—	—	—	—
Uzbekistan	—	—	—	—	—	—
People's Republic of China	33787	35,849	40,180	44,237	43,751	38,753
Southeast Asia	9,662	12,593	15,889	17,264	12,717	6,986
Cambodia	69	151	294	204	121	126
Indonesia	2,109	4,346	6,194	4,677	-356	-2,745
Lao People's Democratic Republic	59	95	160	91	46	—
Malaysia	4,342	4,178	5,078	5,137	2,163	1,553
Myanmar	126	277	310	387	315	216
Philippines	1,591	1,478	1,517	1,222	2,287	573
Thailand	1,366	2,068	2,336	3,746	6,941	6,213
Viet Nam	—	—	—	1,800	1,200	1,050
South Asia	1,581	2,931	3,510	4,899	3,541	2,911
Bangladesh	11	2	14	141	190	179
Bhutan	—	—	—	—	—	—
India	973	2,144	2,426	3,577	2,635	2,169
Maldives	9	7	9	11	12	12
Nepal	—	—	19	23	12	4
Pakistan	421	723	922	716	500	370
Sri Lanka	166	56	120	430	193	177
PacificDMCs	156	557	152	108	220	294
Cook Islands	—	—	—	—	—	—
Fiji Islands	68	70	2	16	75	-33
Kiribati	—	—	—	—	—	—
Marshall Islands	—	—	—	—	—	—
Micronesia, Federated States of	—	—	—	—	—	—
Nauru	—	—	—	—	—	—
Papua New Guinea	57	455	111	29	110	297
Samoa	—	—	—	—	—	—
Solomon Islands	2	2	6	34	9	10
Tonga	—	—	—	—	—	—
Tuvalu	—	—	—	—	—	—
Vanuatu	30	31	33	30	27	20
Total	54,599	61,993	72,258	78,893	72,436	66,928

— Not available.

Table A18 External Debt Outstanding
($ million)

	1995	1996	1997	1998	1999	2000
Newly industrialized economies	—	—	—	—	—	—
Hong Kong, China	—	—	—	—	—	—
Korea, Republic of	—	—	—	—	—	—
Singapore	—	—	—	—	—	—
Taipei,China	—	—	—	—	—	—
Central Asian republics, Azerbaijan, and Mongolia	7,037	8,910	10,634	10,524	11,578	9,363
Azerbaijan	—	—	—	—	—	—
Kazakhstan	2,054	2,606	3,290	4,007	4,056	3,979
Kyrgyz Republic	594	742	966	1,133	1,374	—
Mongolia	524	532	609	739	850	935
Tajikistan	817	867	1,104	1,178	1,062	—
Turkmenistan	—	—	—	—	—	—
Uzbekistan	3,047	4,163	4,665	3,467	4,237	4,449
People's Republic of China	106,600	116,300	131,000	146,000	151,800	156,000
Southeast Asia	314,234	335,297	371,677	365,900	361,592	316,932
Cambodia	2,035	2,101	2,129	2,210	2,045	2,033
Indonesia	124,398	128,940	136,173	150,884	150,096	130,791
Lao People's Democratic Republic	2,165	2,263	2,320	2,437	2,490	—
Malaysia	33,946	38,892	60,699	41,541	42,528	41,303
Myanmar	5,770	5,184	5,063	5,609	5,999	—
Philippines	37,829	40,145	45,682	47,817	52,210	51,846
Thailand	100,832	108,742	109,276	105,084	95,648	80,248
Viet Nam	7,258	9,029	10,336	10,319	10,576	10,710
South Asia	122,548	147,073	148,535	153,467	156,155	162,263
Bangladesh	16,800	14,500	14,400	14,800	15,300	15,800
Bhutan	137	117	120	133	157	176
India	94,387	93,470	94,320	98,232	98,435	103,009
Maldives	152	164	156	172	213	228
Nepal	2,378	2,215	2,633	2,382	2,521	2,544
Pakistan	—	28,121	28,709	29,000	30,480	31,010
Sri Lanka	8,694	8,486	8,197	8,748	9,049	9,496
Pacific DMCs	2,298	2,315	2,422	2,204	2,412	2,083
Cook Islands	—	—	—	—	—	—
Fiji Islands	274	252	244	225	261	—
Kiribati	7	10	10	9	9	9
Marshall Islands	149	133	126	115	88	69
Micronesia, Federated States of	127	118	114	110	98	86
Nauru	—	—	—	—	—	—
Papua New Guinea	1,297	1,368	1,510	1,313	1,495	1,445
Samoa	178	168	168	161	155	159
Solomon Islands	166	163	148	158	175	183
Tonga	58	62	61	60	67	62
Tuvalu	—	—	—	—	—	—
Vanuatu	43	42	42	53	64	71
Total	55,277	609,895	664,268	678,095	683,537	664,641

— Not available.

Table A19 Debt-Service Ratio
(percent of exports of goods and services)

	1995	1996	1997	1998	1999	2000
Newly industrialized economies						
Hong Kong, China	—	—	—	—	—	—
Korea, Republic of	—	—	—	—	—	—
Singapore	—	—	—	—	—	—
Taipei,China	—	—	—	—	—	—
Central Asian republics, Azerbaijan, and Mongolia						
Azerbaijan	—	—	—	—	—	—
Kazakhstan	8.6	16.2	25.3	22.4	27.3	24.6
Kyrgyz Republic	17.8	8.5	5.7	7.0	8.3	—
Mongolia	12.1	11.8	6.3	7.3	9.7	5.3
Tajikistan	30.4	34.4	12.4	11.4	7.6	13.0
Turkmenistan	—	—	—	—	—	—
Uzbekistan	4.8	8.9	10.0	12.5	16.7	28.7
People's Republic of China	10.6	10.5	6.1	7.5	9.6	8.0
Southeast Asia						
Cambodia	—	—	1.2	2.1	1.8	2.4
Indonesia	36.1	43.2	30.0	31.7	30.3	30.1
Lao People's Democratic Republic	5.7	5.9	9.0	9.9	9.6	11.2
Malaysia	6.6	6.6	5.5	6.7	6.0	5.0
Myanmar	22.8	14.1	6.5	5.9	9.4	—
Philippines	15.3	12.3	11.3	11.5	12.4	14.2
Thailand	11.4	12.3	15.7	21.4	19.4	15.4
Viet Nam	12.1	9.8	11.1	13.2	10.7	9.2
South Asia						
Bangladesh	10.3	12.1	11.4	8.6	9.0	9.5
Bhutan	18.3	25.7	10.4	9.0	14.7	5.0
India	24.3	21.2	19.0	18.0	16.0	15.1
Maldives	3.3	3.1	5.6	3.1	3.7	3.8
Nepal	5.6	6.0	4.5	6.1	6.1	5.3
Pakistan	34.9	33.9	39.3	35.5	29.4	30.4
Sri Lanka	16.5	15.3	13.3	13.3	15.2	13.8
Pacific DMCs						
Cook Islands	—	—	—	—	—	—
Fiji Islands	6.0	4.1	2.9	4.1	3.4	2.6
Kiribati	0.8	1.3	1.4	1.4	1.2	1.2
Marshall Islands	37.9	41.2	46.7	47.5	—	—
Micronesia, Federated States of	43.0	50.0	49.0	61.0	58.0	49.0
Nauru	—	—	—	—	—	—
Papua New Guinea	20.8	17.7	17.0	22.5	27.3	16.9
Samoa	6.5	6.1	6.9	7.0	7.1	7.0
Solomon Islands	5.2	7.3	4.6	17.9	10.1	10.4
Tonga	8.3	12.8	10.8	8.1	3.8	12.0
Tuvalu	—	—	—	—	—	—
Vanuatu	1.5	1.5	1.7	1.1	1.0	1.3

— Not available.

Table A20 Exchange Rates to the Dollar
(annual average)

	Currency		1995	1996	1997	1998	1999	2000
Newly industrialized economies								
Hong Kong, China	Hong Kong dollar	HK$	7.7	7.7	7.7	7.7	7.8	7.8
Korea, Republic of	Won	W	771.3	804.5	951.3	1401.4	1188.8	1131.0
Singapore	Singapore dollar	S$	1.4	1.4	1.5	1.7	1.7	1.7
Taipei,China	New Taiwan dollar	NT$	26.5	27.5	28.7	33.5	32.3	31.2
People's Republic of China	Yuan	Y	8.4	8.3	8.3	8.3	8.3	8.3
Central Asia Republics, Azerbaijan and Mongolia								
Kazakhstan	Tenge	T	61.0	67.3	75.4	78.3	119.5	142.3
Kyrgyz Republic	Som	Som	10.8	12.8	17.4	20.8	39.0	47.7
Mongolia	Tugrik	Tug	448.6	548.4	790.0	840.8	1,021.9	1,076.4
Tajikistan	Tajik ruble	TJR	135.0	298.0	564.0	783.0	1235.0	—
Uzbekistan	Sum	SUM	29.8	40.1	66.3	94.5	124.9	236.9
Southeast Asia								
Cambodia	Riel	KR	2,467.3	2,644.7	2,991.3	3,769.6	3,814.4	3,861.3
Indonesia	Rupiah	Rp	2,248.6	2,342.3	2,909.4	10,013.6	7,855.2	8,422.0
Lao People's Democratic Republic	Kip	KN	819.0	926.2	1,260.0	3,296.2	7,108.2	8,218.0
Malaysia	Ringgit	RM	2.5	2.5	2.8	3.9	3.8	3.8
Myanmar	Kyat	MK	5.6	5.9	6.2	6.3	6.2	—
Philippines	Peso	P	25.7	26.2	29.5	40.9	39.1	44.2
Thailand	Baht	B	24.9	25.3	31.4	41.3	37.8	40.2
Viet Nam	Dong	D	11,038.0	11,033.0	12,292.0	13,893.0	14,029.0	14,514.0
South Asia								
Bangladesh	Taka	Tk	40.2	40.9	42.7	45.4	47.8	50.3
Bhutan	Ngultrum	Nu	31.4	34.3	35.8	38.4	42.6	43.6
India	India Rupee	Re/Rs	33.4	35.5	37.1	42.5	43.3	45.8
Maldives	Rufiyaa	Rf	11.8	11.8	11.8	11.8	11.8	11.8
Nepal	Nepalese rupee	NRe/NRs	51.9	56.7	58.0	66.0	68.2	68.8
Pakistan	Pakistan rupee	PRe/PRs	31.5	35.9	40.9	44.9	49.1	50.1
Sri Lanka	Sri Lanka rupee	SLRe/SLRs	51.3	55.3	59.0	64.6	70.4	75.9
Pacific DMCs								
Cook Islands	New Zealand dollar	NZ$	1.5	1.5	1.5	1.9	1.9	2.2
Fiji Islands	Fiji dollar	F$	1.4	1.4	1.4	2.0	2.0	2.1
Kiribati	Australian dollar	A$	1.4	1.3	1.4	1.6	1.6	1.7
Marshall Islands	US dollar	US$	1.0	1.0	1.0	1.0	1.0	1.0
Micronesia, Federated States of	US dollar	US$	1.0	1.0	1.0	1.0	1.0	1.0
Nauru	Australian dollar	A$	1.3	1.3	1.3	1.6	1.5	1.6
Papua New Guinea	Kina	K	1.3	1.3	1.4	2.1	2.5	2.7
Samoa	Tala	ST	2.5	2.4	2.6	3.0	3.0	3.2
Solomon Islands	Solomon Islands dollar	SI$	3.4	3.6	3.7	4.8	5.1	5.1
Tonga	Pa'anga	T$	1.3	1.2	1.3	1.5	1.6	1.7
Tuvalu	Australian dollar	A$	1.4	1.3	1.4	1.6	1.6	1.7
Vanuatu	Vatu	Vt	113.0	111.6	115.9	127.5	129.1	133.9

— Not available.

Table A21 Central Government Expenditure
(percent of GDP)

	1995	1996	1997	1998	1999	2000
Newly industrialized economies						
Hong Kong, China	17.0	15.3	14.7	19.0	18.1	—
Korea, Republic of	19.9	21.2	18.0	20.5	20.9	20.7
Singapore	13.2	14.9	18.4	18.0	17.6	17.6
Taipei,China	27.4	26.2	25.9	26.1	26.0	23.6
Central Asian republics, Azerbaijan, and Mongolia						
Azerbaijan	—	—	—	—	—	—
Kazakhstan	25.7	19.8	20.4	21.8	24.6	23.0
Kyrgyz Republic	33.2	25.3	25.1	29.8	30.6	—
Mongolia	23.3	23.8	27.8	—	—	—
Tajikistan	—	17.9	17.0	15.8	16.6	14.4
Turkmenistan	—	—	—	—	—	—
Uzbekistan	38.1	39.9	32.3	34.5	33.2	31.8
People's Republic of China	11.7	11.7	12.4	13.8	16.1	17.8
Southeast Asia						
Cambodia	16.5	15.9	13.7	14.9	16.1	17.4
Indonesia	14.9	15.6	15.7	18.8	17.4	21.6
Lao People's Democratic Republic	21.9	22.1	21.3	26.9	20.6	21.0
Malaysia	22.1	22.3	21.0	21.7	22.7	—
Myanmar	9.9	9.3	8.0	6.9	5.8	4.2
Philippines	18.2	18.6	19.3	19.1	21.8	19.3
Thailand	—	—	—	—	—	—
Viet Nam	24.1	23.7	24.8	22.5	21.2	22.0
South Asia						
Bangladesh	14.6	13.4	13.5	13.3	13.8	15.0
Bhutan	41.0	40.6	39.1	32.1	42.3	44.4
India	14.2	14.0	14.3	14.6	15.5	15.5
Maldives	36.3	32.4	32.3	31.5	36.6	37.4
Nepal	17.8	17.1	16.5	16.9	15.5	16.1
Pakistan	22.8	24.2	22.0	23.7	22.4	23.4
Sri Lanka	30.5	28.5	26.4	26.3	25.1	26.6
Pacific DMCs						
Cook Islands	44.3	44.8	31.1	39.0	31.4	32.3
Fiji Islands	33.7	37.1	41.3	44.4	30.9	32.4
Kiribati	107.4	115.5	120.1	126.3	120.7	117.5
Marshall Islands	104.3	61.9	65.5	59.2	56.8	59.5
Micronesia, Federated States of	81.0	75.0	66.0	79.0	76.0	66.0
Nauru	—	—	—	—	—	—
Papua New Guinea	29.3	27.0	28.4	27.1	30.8	32.7
Samoa	52.7	46.1	38.9	34.0	38.6	34.6
Solomon Islands	40.4	38.6	33.2	37.1	41.3	34.0
Tonga	33.5	30.7	36.3	32.5	26.6	28.4
Tuvalu	—	—	121.9	95.9	82.0	94.8
Vanuatu	30.1	27.1	25.7	32.2	27.0	33.0

— Not available.

Table A22 Central Government Revenue
(percent of GDP)

	1995	1996	1997	1998	1999	2000
Newly industrialized economies						
Hong Kong, China	16.7	17.5	21.2	17.2	18.9	—
Korea, Republic of	20.4	21.2	20.6	21.8	22.3	25.5
Singapore	21.0	21.8	21.8	20.5	20.1	21.1
Taipei,China	22.5	21.7	22.7	22.7	20.0	18.3
Central Asian republics, Azerbaijan, and Mongolia						
Azerbaijan	—	—	—	—	—	—
Kazakhstan	21.6	17.2	16.7	17.9	21.1	23.1
Kyrgyz Republic	16.7	15.9	16.2	18.0	17.8	—
Mongolia	23.9	23.9	26.6	—	—	—
Tajikistan	—	12.1	13.7	12.1	13.5	13.7
Turkmenistan	—	—	—	—	—	—
Uzbekistan	34.6	34.3	30.1	31.1	30.5	30.6
People's Republic of China	10.7	10.9	11.6	12.6	14.0	15.0
Southeast Asia						
Cambodia	8.5	9.0	9.6	8.9	11.7	12.0
Indonesia	15.5	15.8	15.7	15.1	15.1	16.8
Lao People's Democratic Republic	17.7	16.5	14.8	17.3	16.6	15.9
Malaysia	22.9	23.0	23.3	19.9	19.5	—
Myanmar	6.5	6.9	7.8	7.2	4.9	4.5
Philippines	17.7	18.7	19.0	17.2	16.0	15.2
Thailand	—	—	—	—	—	—
Viet Nam	23.3	22.9	20.9	20.5	18.8	18.7
South Asia						
Bangladesh	9.7	9.0	9.2	9.3	9.0	8.9
Bhutan	41.1	42.8	36.8	33.1	40.5	40.4
India	14.2	13.8	15.4	15.9	15.3	15.8
Maldives	29.9	29.9	30.9	29.6	32.5	33.4
Nepal	11.2	10.8	10.5	10.5	10.3	10.7
Pakistan	17.2	17.8	15.6	16.0	16.3	17.2
Sri Lanka	20.4	19.0	18.5	17.2	17.6	16.7
Pacific DMCs						
Cook Islands	41.7	37.7	31.7	31.4	30.5	33.7
Fiji Islands	29.9	29.1	30.7	40.6	30.1	28.9
Kiribati	93.5	75.0	119.8	134.6	119.9	111.8
Marshall Islands	73.8	80.5	74.6	74.7	67.3	64.7
Micronesia, Federated States of	80.0	75.0	66.0	72.0	68.0	66.4
Nauru	—	—	—	—	—	—
Papua New Guinea	28.8	27.6	28.7	25.3	28.2	30.9
Samoa	45.5	47.6	39.1	36.0	38.9	33.9
Solomon Islands	35.6	34.7	29.0	35.5	38.6	29.5
Tonga	29.6	31.6	31.4	30.0	26.4	29.2
Tuvalu	—	—	89.0	131.7	103.0	193.1
Vanuatu	27.4	25.4	25.1	24.7	25.7	25.0

— Not available.

Table A23 Overall Budget Surplus/Deficit of Central Government
(percent of GDP)

	1995	1996	1997	1998	1999	2000
Newly industrialized economies						
Hong Kong, China	-0.3	2.2	6.6	-1.8	0.8	-0.9
Korea, Republic of	0.5	0.0	-1.5	-4.2	-2.7	1.1
Singapore	7.8	6.9	3.4	2.5	2.6	3.5
Taipei,China	-5.3	-4.2	-3.8	-3.4	-6.0	-4.8
Central Asian republics, Azerbaijan, and Mongolia						
Azerbaijan	—	—	—	—	—	—
Kazakhstan	-4.0	-2.6	-3.7	-4.2	-3.5	0.1
Kyrgyz Republic	-17.3	-9.5	-9.0	-9.5	-12.0	-9.4
Mongolia	-3.0	-3.0	-9.2	-14.3	-11.9	-10.8
Tajikistan	—	-5.8	-3.3	-3.8	-3.1	-0.7
Turkmenistan	—	—	—	—	—	—
Uzbekistan	-4.1	-7.4	-2.1	-3.4	-2.7	-1.2
People's Republic of China	-1.0	-0.8	-0.8	-1.2	-2.1	-2.8
Southeast Asia						
Cambodia	-3.5	-2.8	-0.4	-2.7	-1.5	-1.7
Indonesia	0.6	0.2	0.0	-3.7	-2.3	-4.8
Lao People's Democratic Republic	-4.2	-5.6	-6.5	-9.6	-4.0	-5.1
Malaysia	0.8	0.7	2.4	-1.8	-3.2	-5.5
Myanmar	-3.5	-2.5	-0.2	0.3	-0.9	0.3
Philippines	0.6	0.3	0.1	-1.8	-3.7	-4.1
Thailand	—	—	—	-2.4	-2.8	-2.2
Viet Nam	-1.4	-1.3	-4.8	-2.6	-2.8	-3.0
South Asia						
Bangladesh	-5.3	-4.4	-4.3	-4.1	-4.8	-6.1
Bhutan	0.1	2.3	-2.4	1.0	-1.8	-3.9
India	-4.3	-4.1	-4.8	-5.1	-5.5	-5.1
Maldives	-6.4	-2.5	-1.4	-1.9	-4.1	-4.0
Nepal	-4.8	-4.4	-3.9	-4.6	-3.9	-3.9
Pakistan	-5.6	-6.4	-6.4	-7.7	-6.1	-6.5
Sri Lanka	-10.1	-9.4	-7.9	-9.2	-7.5	-9.8
Pacific DMCs						
Cook Islands	-2.6	-7.2	0.6	-7.6	-0.9	1.5
Fiji Islands	-3.8	-8.0	-10.6	-3.7	-0.8	-3.5
Kiribati	-13.8	-40.4	-0.3	8.3	-0.8	-5.7
Marshall Islands	-30.5	18.5	9.1	15.6	10.5	5.2
Micronesia, Federated States of	-1.0	0.0	0.0	-7.0	-8.0	0.4
Nauru	—	—	—	—	—	—
Papua New Guinea	-0.5	0.5	0.2	-1.7	-2.6	-1.8
Samoa	-7.3	1.4	0.3	2.0	0.3	-0.7
Solomon Islands	-4.8	-3.9	-4.1	-1.6	-2.7	-4.5
Tonga	-3.8	0.9	-4.8	-2.5	-0.2	0.8
Tuvalu	—	—	-32.9	35.8	21.0	98.2
Vanuatu	-2.7	-1.7	-0.6	-7.5	-1.3	-8.0

— Not available.